Contents

2 Religion and ethics

Photo credits

1 Philosophy of religion

Chapter 1

The nature or attributes of God

1 Introduction

Chapter checklist

The chapter begins by considering some of the theological and religious issues of defining the qualities of God. It then looks specifically at the issues entailed in ideas of omnipotence, omniscience, benevolence and eternity. Discussion of how these issues and ideas interconnect, and their implications for free will, is the subject of the next chapter, although some preliminary points are made here. Throughout the chapter, there is reference to the historical development of ideas, with reference to key figures such as Aquinas. Issues about the language used in defining terms are also discussed, providing a link to later chapters on religious language. Revision pointers, study advice and guidance on possible essay questions may be found at the end of the chapter.

Key term

Attribute A quality or characteristic. God is believed to have attributes such as omnipotence, mercy and justice.

It is natural for someone who believes in God to think about the nature of that God. Believers ask themselves, 'what is God like?' or 'what **attributes** does God have?' But any connection with God is a connection with a reality that is not a 'being among beings' and is utterly unlike anything in our experience. In his inmost nature, God is, as Jewish, Muslim and Christian scriptures all attest, a reality that passes all understanding. These scriptures would also consider it blasphemous to say we know the mind of God.

The Book of Job makes direct reference to the gap between God and humankind:

> *How then can a mortal be righteous before God?*
> *How can one born of woman be pure?*
> *If even the moon is not bright*
> *and the stars are not pure in his sight,*
> *how much less a mortal, who is a maggot,*
> *and a human being who is a worm!*
>
> Job 25:4–6

It also refers to the way the heavens and the earth are in awe of God.

> *These are indeed but the outskirts of his ways;*
> *and how small a whisper do we hear of him!*
> *But the thunder of his power who can understand?*
>
> Job 26:14

Such poetic references – to God's infinite might coupled with his unknowability – recur throughout scripture.

And yet there is a human curiosity about what God is. In the centuries before Christ, Jewish writers emphasised the universality and singularity of their God compared with the many local deities of other faiths. To them, the idea of one God (monotheism) was superior, in that God had a greatness to which nothing else could compare. However, while these writers asserted God's greatness, they didn't consider what that greatness entailed. It was in subsequent discussions that ideas about omnipotence and omniscience arose. Neither term occurs in scripture. In the earliest formulations of faith, such as the creeds, God is described as 'Almighty' and the 'creator of all', but there was no clear formulation of what precisely the terms meant. Even the Council of Trent (1545–63), which is known for its careful definitions, drew back from exactness, reminding priests in its catechism that in the Creed:

> ... *great mysteries lie concealed under almost every word...*

Catechism of the Council of Trent for Parish Priests, Part I, Article 1

None of this has prevented earnest philosophical debate about what the term 'almighty' means when speaking of God.

The particular problem – as we shall see – is that we are attempting to understand the terms used about God with our own very limited intellectual apparatus. None of us has seen the 'fullness of God', and most people have only glimpses of things in the world that they interpret as giving them an insight into the nature of God, and even then they might have misinterpreted the phenomenon incorrectly.

2 Divine attributes

Over the centuries of monotheistic belief, philosophers and theologians, in their conversations about God, have thought about the divine nature and its qualities, even though the same theologians have always recognised the limitations of human language in attempting to define those attributes. At different times in history, believers have seen God in different ways. For example, many, perhaps most, modern Christian believers talk of having a personal relationship with God, yet, in 1645, John Biddle was imprisoned for the alleged blasphemy of treating God in such personal terms. At different times, different aspects of God have been treated as most prominent, and different thinkers have drawn attention to various qualities. Many disputes between religious thinkers have been about what aspects of God should be considered most important, and people accuse each other of overlooking key features, perhaps emphasising God's justice and law at the expense of his mercy, or his greatness at the expense of his love and concern for each individual.

The Catholic Encyclopedia, published in 1907, listed God's attributes as follows:

- Simplicity
- Infinity
- Immutability
- Unity
- Truth
- Goodness
- Beauty
- Omnipotence
- Omnipresence
- Intellect
- Will
- Personality
- All-wise
- Self-existent
- Justice
- Love.

But even in this listing, as the *Encyclopedia* points out, there is argument, and no effort is made to claim that this list is complete. Even if it were a complete list, there would still be problems in determining what exactly these mean in relation to God.

Any attempt to consider each of these characteristics, and to consider whether they are appropriate or comprehensive, would be a task to fill a library of books, and even then, to spend many of those pages explaining why our understandings, when applied to God, would be incomplete. The very idea of attributes is two-edged. When I see something or someone as beautiful, for example, I do not merely say that she has beauty, but that I perceive that person *as* beautiful. I attribute to her the quality of beauty.

Attributing qualities is fraught with difficulties. For example, I may, for example, be wholly wrong in my attribution. I may say somebody is honest only to discover that he is an accomplished conman and serial liar. In this case, I have *misattributed* the quality.

It's also very difficult to agree criteria for attributes. A person can find beauty in a painting which another person strongly dislikes, and it is difficult, perhaps impossible, to settle the argument conclusively. That is to say, there are no objective criteria which set out what beauty is and isn't. There is also a linguistic question here, whether the language we use is sufficient to capture the essence of beauty, or whether it falls short. What does it mean to say something is beautiful?

Three qualities will be discussed in this chapter in turn – omnipotence, omniscience and benevolence. As we shall see, none is without its problems, even when considered singly, as we do here. Questions about what each attribute means are as important as whether it is correct to make the attribution in the first place.

(a) Omnipotence

The literal meaning of **omnipotence** is 'all-powerful' – the idea that God can do anything. The difficulty lies in determining what that 'anything' might be.

Descartes argued that omnipotence meant that God could do absolutely anything. This was different from the view of St Thomas Aquinas, who thought that it meant that God could do anything that was logically possible.

Consider the question of whether God could create a square circle. For St Thomas, this would be an absurd question, because the concept of a square circle makes no sense. According to the rules of logic, it is a contradiction in terms – the phrase 'square circle' is meaningless nonsense words. For Aquinas, it makes no sense to accuse God of being less than omnipotent because he cannot do the logically impossible. He argues:

> *As the principles of sciences such as logic, geometry or arithmetic are taken from the formal principles of things which are essential to their natures, it follows that God could not make things that go against these principles. For example ... it would be impossible to have a circle in which the lines drawn from the centre to the circumference were not equal or for a triangle not to have three angles equal to two right angles.*

Thomas Aquinas, *Summa Contra Gentiles*, Book II, Section 25

Key question

How can we know whether we are correct in attributing a quality to God?

Key term

Omnipotence The ability to perform any act. In relation to God, Aquinas argues that omnipotence is the ability to perform any act which is logically possible.

Key persons

St Thomas Aquinas (1224/5–74): Dominican friar, and perhaps the greatest medieval philosopher. Aquinas was at the forefront of attempts to rethink existing philosophical and theological thought in the light of the Aristotelian revival. Best known for his *Summa Theologica, Summa Contra Gentiles* and dozens of other works.

René Descartes (1596–1650): French philosopher and mathematician, best known for his *Meditations on First Philosophy* and *Meditations*. A rationalist, he used systematic doubt of sense experience as the basis of his system, seeking a basis for knowledge on his *cogito, ergo sum*. He is often referred to as the father of modern philosophy.

Descartes' view was different: he argued that God's existence is prior to the laws of logic, so God is not bound by those laws. It is difficult to see how this can be, as we can have no conception of logical impossibilities and can give no coherent definition of the qualities of a square circle.

It seems that Aquinas has given us a more rational definition of omnipotence than that of Descartes, but there are further issues, even with this narrower definition. Is God able to ride a bicycle? A human can ride a bicycle because she has a sense of balance and has two working legs, eyes to see, hands to hold the handlebar and so on. If she lacked any of these, then her ability to ride a bicycle would be impaired, even if she knew in theory how bicycles are ridden. If God is not conceived as being flesh and blood or even in the same plane of existence as human beings, then we struggle to see how God has the ability to ride anything like a bicycle. To say this is not to say he would lack the power if he chose to move the bicycle, but moving a bicycle is not the same as riding one. It is rather to question whether as a non-material – and hence legless – reality, he would be able to cycle, any more than a fish could ride a bicycle. To ride a bicycle is *logically* possible – there is no logical contradiction in being able to ride a bicycle, and it is demonstrably

Key question

Is it possible to find any coherent definition of omnipotence that can be applied to God?

See Year 1, pages 116–17.

Key term

Paradox of omnipotence Some things seem impossible to do for an omnipotent being. If God used his omnipotence to make a stone so heavy that no one could lift it, including himself, then he would not be omnipotent. But if he could not make such a stone, then it would seem he would not be omnipotent.

possible for people to do so – but to someone or something without certain attributes it would be *physically* impossible. There are other forms of impossibility than merely the logical.

All this suggests that the definition of omnipotence should be narrower than Aquinas imagines. Many modern philosophers have chosen to take the view that the meaning of omnipotence is that God can do anything it is logically possible for God to do. If we consider this in a little more depth, we recognise that certain uses of power would seem inconsistent with the nature of God.

If you think back to when you studied the problem of evil earlier in your studies, you will recall St Augustine of Hippo arguing that God cannot be the one who created evil as it would be contrary to his nature.

Augustine understands omnipotence to mean not that God can do anything at all, but that he can do anything he wills or chooses to do. He says:

> ... He [God] is called omnipotent because He does what He wills, not because He suffers what He does not will. If that were to happen to Him, He would not be omnipotent. It follows that He cannot do some things precisely because He is omnipotent.

St Augustine of Hippo, *The City of God*, Chapter 10

Augustine's approach is rich and interesting, and perhaps more coherent than some views we have previously looked at. He argues, in essence, that God's omnipotence needs to be understood as meaning that he can do whatever he chooses to do. The power to do evil acts in God's case would be at best theoretical, as his will is always to do good. In other words, his divine power means that he 'self-imposes' certain limitations that are contrary to his nature – it is precisely because God is omnipotent that he does not commit evil or unjust actions.

Augustine appeals to something in human experience. I am not omnipotent because I know from my experience that I do not have the power to do everything I want. I cannot be rich, just because I want to be rich. I cannot by the power of thought be everywhere I want to be nor do everything I want to do. I may describe myself as frustrated in my wishes, and I shall almost certainly be very conscious of my powerlessness. I am very aware of my limitations and the boundaries of choices open to me. For Augustine, God is omnipotent because he knows no such frustration: what he wills he is able to do.

Think about our own experience. We feel restricted and impotent when we cannot do what we want to do, but we feel no lack of power about being unable to do something we have no interest in doing. I cannot walk a tightrope, but it doesn't restrict me in any significant way: I have no wish to do so.

If Augustine is right, that omnipotence means being able to do everything God wishes, without hindrance or limitation, then various problems raised by the so-called **paradox of omnipotence** seem to disappear. This paradox is the same one that caused Aquinas and Descartes to consider whether God could create a square circle. It also raises questions such as whether God could make a table that he had not made, or make a stone so heavy that no one, including himself, could lift it. At a deeper level it raises questions about whether an omnipotent God could alter the past.

If the limited approach suggested by Augustine is adopted, it is possible to argue that, for questions like the unliftable stone, or altering the past, we might ask why God would want to do any of these things. What would be the point of a square circle? Is God's omnipotence open to challenge because he could not do something that he had no wish to do?

Modern philosophers have, in general, opted for limited interpretations of omnipotence. Anthony Kenny argues:

> Divine omnipotence ... if it is to be a coherent notion, must be something less than the complete omnipotence which is the possession of all logically possible powers which it is logically possible for a being with the attributes of God to possess. (If the definition is not to be empty, 'attributes' must here be taken to mean these properties of Godhead which are not themselves powers: properties such as immutability and goodness.) This conception of divine omnipotence is close to traditional accounts while avoiding some of the incoherences ...

Anthony Kenny, 'The Definition of Omnipotence', *The Concept of God*, 1987, pages 131–2

Different philosophers have, then, sought to understand God's attribute of omnipotence in terms of whether it should be subject to the limits of logical possibility or divine self-limitation. An alternative would be to return to what some have described as a semantic approach, understanding the word 'omnipotence' in a scriptural way – given the difficulties in attempting to comprehend a concept which surpasses human understanding – so that there is a religious aspect to it. When a believer describes God, she does not provide a scientific definition; but neither does she seek to do so. When she describes God as omnipotent, she does so in awe and prayer and worship, aware of her own limitation when she speaks to and about God. In calling God 'omnipotent' she is describing her own finitude and dependence as much as she wants to express his greatness.

(b) Omniscience

Just as there are difficulties with the definition of omnipotence, so too with **omniscience**, the idea that God is all-knowing. What does this mean?

Philosophers debate precisely what it means *to know*. If God knows everything, then we need to ask both what it means for someone to *know* something, and in God's case, what is the *everything* that God is supposed to know?

(i) Divine knowledge and its interaction with temporal existence

The philosopher Sir Michael Dummett, in his Gifford Lectures of 1996, gave an interesting definition of omniscience. He reminds us firstly of the differences between God's sense of knowledge and ours, which is much more subjective:

God has no particular point of view, no location in the world, no perspective contrasted with other perspectives. He knows, not by the effect of objects or events upon His perceptual equipment, but by His comprehension of all truth. How God apprehends things as being must be how they are in themselves.

Michael Dummett, *Thought and Reality*, 2006, page 96

This point is very important. Whatever God's knowledge would be like, it is not like human knowledge. We are creatures with perspective and human faculties. I am always *here* and not *there*. As I learn more, and change more, my understanding and knowledge change. Only I can live my life and have my knowledge. Dummett reminds us that God's knowledge is beyond perspective, as it includes everything. One consequence of this, presumably, is that by knowing everything, God has complete understanding of everything. As humans, we often get things out of proportion, misunderstanding their true significance in relation to everything else. This would not happen if we knew, as God does, the true facts of everything.

Dummett goes on to characterise the nature of God's knowledge:

… for every true proposition, He knows that it is true. But we have no right to assume that, for every intelligible question, God knows an answer to it; if there is no answer, there is nothing for him to know…. [W]hen we speak of God's knowledge, we are using the tense of timelessness.

Ibid., page 108

This point of Dummett is interesting in several ways.

The first is whether every true proposition can be known timelessly – Dummett speaks of God knowing things 'in a tense of timelessness'. It is certainly true for certain realities. For example, the sentence 'The *Titanic* struck an iceberg on 14 April 1912 and sank in the early hours of 15 April', if it is true, is a proposition referring to a fixed historical fact. If it is true, it will always be true; and if God knows everything, then presumably he would always have known that the sentence described a true event even if the event was future to us. We can see how this could be timelessly true.

The problem is that the truth of some sentences depends on time and place. For example, if I said to someone 'I am right behind you', this could be a true sentence for me at a particular time, but not at another. A sentence like this is true only at a particular time and place, and true only for the speaker at that moment. Philosophers refer to these kinds of sentences as *indexical sentences*. The question we may ask is whether a sentence of this sort can be known *as true* in a timeless way. If not, we might have to suggest that God's knowledge is not timeless or that he has a different understanding about indexical sentences – one that is not timeless.

This thought raises further issues. Dummett's account of God's omniscience is quite limited. If God's knowledge consists in knowing for every true proposition that it is true, does that exhaust the concept of knowledge? Would someone know everything if he knew every possible fact, past, present and future? He would surely only have full knowledge if there were no knowledge other than knowledge of facts.

(ii) Types of knowledge

But there seem to be other kinds of knowledge. For example, there is *knowing what it is like to be something.* The American philosopher, Thomas Nagel, in 1974, wrote a very famous article, 'What Is It Like To Be a Bat?'. He argues that we have no idea of what it is like to be a bat – we do not have bat sense, minds or vocabulary.

If we apply this thought to God, then it is difficult to see how God's knowledge can include knowing what a non-God experience is like. To take a simple example, I do not know what will happen between now and my next birthday, or whether I shall be alive to see it. I can guess what the next months might hold, but I do not know. Now, suppose that God knows everything that will happen to me. Unlike me, he knows what presents I will receive for my next birthday, whether I shall fall under a bus or win the lottery. But if he knows everything, and is never ignorant, can he know what it is like to be ignorant?

Another type of knowledge is *knowing how to do something.* Certain types of knowledge can only be achieved through practice. Consider, for example, knowing how to ride a bicycle. I can only know how to ride a bicycle through practice. There is an important difference between knowing how a bicycle is ridden and how to ride a bicycle. So does God know how to ride a bicycle? If God has never ridden a bicycle can he be said in any significant way to know how to do so? If I had never ridden a bicycle, no one would say I knew how to ride a bicycle, however many books about cycling I had read.

So, just as omnipotence needs to be conditioned in some way, the same appears to be true for omniscience. We might suggest that God's omnipotence means that he knows everything it is logically possible for God to know. In order to be truly omniscient, God would simultaneously need to know everything, including what it is like to be ignorant. This could be held to be contradictory in some way, and therefore not logically possible, and for some philosophers this is problematic. One way of responding to this might be to argue that God knows everything he would need or wish to know. God is not prevented from the fullness of being God in any relevant way.

This does not exhaust the philosophical issues of omniscience. If we think about God's knowledge, or his other qualities, questions arise in relation to whether he is timeless or not. If God knows everything it is logically possible for God to know, what is logically possible will be different for a God who is constrained by time than it is for one who is outside and beyond time. Some of these issues will be discussed in the next chapter.

(c) Benevolence

We have seen that any attempt to define divine omnipotence or omniscience is very difficult as these are ideas that stretch language and which need qualification in some way if we are to make sense of them. Definitions are even more challenging when we come to consider God as benevolent.

Key question

Is it possible for the idea of omniscience to cover every type of knowledge? Does knowing every truth rule out certain kinds of experiential knowledge?

Key question

Can a truly benevolent and omnipotent God permit the existence of evil and suffering?

The strict meaning of '**benevolence**' is well-wishing. We use the term sometimes of amiable characters who seem to wish everyone well, look on people's foibles with kindness and seem – together with a sunny disposition – to see good in everyone and everything.

But is a God who wishes everyone well truly good? Or, indeed, truly omnipotent? We may ask whether a good person simply *wishes* the good for people or rather *does* good for people. I might wish life to be pleasant for everyone, but if I do nothing to bring goodness into people's lives, that benevolence seems worthless. Aristotle remarked that a just person could only be truly just if he performed just acts – simply having a nice feeling was not enough. It seems not enough to *be* good. One cannot truly *be* good without *doing* good (though, of course, one might do good things for bad reasons. Just doing good is not enough to make one a good person). It seems reasonable, therefore, to say of God that if he is truly good, then that goodness is not simply a matter of well-wishing, benevolence, but also well-doing, **beneficence**.

If God were merely well-wishing, he could be a very sweet, perhaps even jolly, God – and there would be no problem of evil. He might, like a cheery old gentleman, wish people would be nice to each other, and shake his head sadly when they are not. But that is not the Jewish, Christian or Muslim understanding of God. God cannot only wish good things, but also do them. That is why he is described as omnipotent and why the problem of evil is so significant. God is not understood as a helpless though well-wishing bystander. Being omnipotent, he could do something about the evil and suffering that afflict the universe, but apparently he does nothing, or, at least, very little. He might perform the occasional miracle, alleviating some pain here or there, but daily people starve to death, are massacred, raped, killed in accidents, fall ill, to say nothing of the pain of non-human animals. The problem of evil rests on the question of how a good God could stand back in the face of such evil.

Some argue that God's goodness lies in being good in himself. He has the goodness of not being subject to decay, rupture, disintegration or being threatened by an equal or overwhelming power. We would describe something as very good if it never broke, never went wrong and could not be destroyed (what a perfect car that would be!). The difficulty here is that this is a different use of the term 'good' from a moral one. A good meal or a good car is not *morally* good. Even if the meal or the car is good for someone, they have no intention of helping anyone. A Porsche may be a good car, but it does not *choose* to be good. It has no intention to please: it just does. But to describe someone as morally good is to say that she has good intentions – she chooses for herself to do good for people. She is good because she wants to be good, not because she happens to be useful. Most people have an understanding of God which includes his choosing good as an act of divine will. God not only *is* good, but consciously *wills* good.

(i) Just judgement of human actions

The Dominican philosopher, Brian Davies, argues that God's goodness must not be a case of simply being well behaved as a good child might be. He takes issue with Richard Swinburne's claim in *The Coherence of Theism* (1993, page 184) that 'God is so constituted that he always does the morally best action ... and no morally bad action'. For Davies, this claim is overly simplistic (reductionist):

> *The idea seems to be that God is good because he manages, in spite of alternatives open to him, to be **well behaved**.*
>
> Brian Davies, 'Is God a Moral Agent?' *Whose God? Which Tradition?*, 2008, page 103

Davies argues that Aquinas does not conceive of God as a moral *person*. The Bible sees God as righteous in the sense that he never breaks a covenant with his people and is always true to his own nature. A bad person is one who goes against his own – and human – nature in a destructive way. God is perfectly good because he never contradicts his own nature. For Davies:

Key quote

... Aquinas would say that God could never command us to torture children because, in effect, that would involve him in contradicting himself, or going against his nature as the source of creaturely goodness... And this, of course, is not to suggest that God's goodness consists in him acting in accordance with moral norms to which he responds in any sense.

Brian Davies, 'Is God a Moral Agent?' *Whose God? Which Tradition?*, 2008, page 122

In a recent article, the British philosopher, M. B. Wilkinson, argues that God's goodness should be understood as part of his creative action. He is not a 'person among persons', as a moral agent would be. According to Wilkinson, living a moral life should not be seen as simply following moral rules laid down by God. Instead:

> *God makes humankind creative of good. When he commands the right because it is right, this should, I think, be understood as commanding what our intelligence and imagination choose as the good for humans. It is an injunction to be human in the fullest sense, which includes values such as autonomy.*
>
> M. B. Wilkinson, 'God, Goodness, Fact and Value'. *Síntese – Rev. de Filosofia*, v.42, n.134, 2015, page 416

There are other problems too. How can God be perfectly benevolent and perfectly just? To be just is to be understood as giving each person what he deserves (rewarding the good and punishing the evil). For many people, the idea is that God sends good people to heaven and bad ones to hell. But, as we mentioned when considering the problem of evil in Year 1, hell is part of the totality of evil.

See Year 1, page 124.

If I commit an evil act on earth, most societies believe that there should be an end to that punishment (even if, in some legal systems, that end is death), a moment when that person's punishment is over. Could it ever be just to sentence someone to suffering without end, with no hope of any kind of release – even the relief of death – and no hope of reform or redemption? As John Hick pointed out, if this kind of hell were to exist it would itself be part of the problem of evil.

But there is an equal problem if God does not reward good deeds and punish sinners. The sense of justice in people goes very deep. Perhaps the earliest complaint of even a tiny child is: 'That's not fair'. It seems incompatible with the idea of a just and good God to pay no attention to the merit of people's actions.

St Thomas Aquinas draws attention to the special nature of justice in God. He distinguishes between different types of justice:

> *There are two kinds of justice. One is about mutual giving and receiving, as in buying and selling, and other types of commerce and exchange. The Philosopher (Ethic. v, 4) [Aristotle] calls this 'commutative justice', which directs exchange and business. This does not belong to God because, as the Apostle [St Paul] says: 'Who has given a gift to him, to receive a gift in return?' (Romans: 11:35). The other type of justice is about distribution, and is called distributive justice. In this a ruler or a steward gives to each person what his rank deserves. Just as the right order shown in ruling a family or any kind of large group displays the ruler's justice of this type, the order of the universe, seen both in the effects of nature and in effects of will, demonstrates the justice of God. This is why Dionysius says (Div. Nom. viii, 4): 'We are bound to see that God is truly just, when we realise that he gives to all existing things what is proper to the condition of each; and he preserves the nature of everything in the order and gives the powers that properly belong to it.'*

Summa Theologica (S.T.) I, 21, a.1, c

Aquinas' argument is that God's justice is not and cannot be like ours on earth. For God, certain types of justice do not apply. God needs nothing from us. We do not trade with God in the way a shopkeeper and customer might trade honestly with each other. For Aquinas, God's justice is about giving everyone what they need. God's goodness works with his justice. Aquinas says:

Key quote

God's justice is about what is appropriate to him, as he gives to himself what is due to himself. It is also right for a created thing to possess what is appropriate to it; so it is due to man to have hands, and that other animals should serve him. In this God exercises justice, giving to each thing ... what is due to it. This comes from the former [God's justice towards himself]. What is due to each thing is what it needs according to the divine wisdom. Although God gives each thing its due, he himself owes no debt. He is not responsible to other things but everything else is responsible to him. This is why justice, therefore, in God is sometimes as the appropriate accompaniment of his goodness; sometimes as the reward of what people deserve. Anselm refers to both views when he says (*Prosolog.* 10): 'When you punish the wicked, it is just, since it is what they deserve; and when you spare the wicked, it is also just; since it shows your goodness.'

S.T. I, 21, a.1, ad 3

For Aquinas, then, God's justice lies in doing the right thing as a good God who wills a good universe. God is not answerable to anyone: he is the standard of justice:

> As good as understood by intellect is the object of the will, it is impossible for God to will anything but what his own wisdom understands as good. His wisdom is, as it were, his law of justice, by which his will is right and just. Therefore, what he does according to his will is done justly. In the same way, we act justly when we do what we should according to law. But while law comes to us from something superior to us, God is a law unto himself.

S.T. I, 21, a.1, ad 2

Aquinas reminds us that God cannot be answerable to some higher abstract standard: if God is a perfect being and is perfectly wise, then his standard of justice is the only possible one. Justice is demonstrated in the goodness of his creation and, according to Aquinas, by giving all creatures what they need to flourish ('What is due to each thing is what it needs according to the divine wisdom'). Of course, we are still troubled by the problem of evil. Some people seem not to have what they need. Some are born without normal limbs or the mental capacities needed for a full human life as lived by others. It is difficult to reconcile this with the justice described by Aquinas. If we say that God's justice is mysterious to us, as we are not God and cannot properly or rightly judge him, that is not an explanation, but neither are we able – if God is supreme – to find another standard by which to accuse God of injustice.

Perhaps an answer lies not in a simple question of whether God gives equally to everyone, but whether God *is just*. The American philosopher William Frankena and others have pointed out that the moral principle of justice does not mean treating everyone in the same way, but rather making the same relative contribution to the good of people's lives. It would not be justice to send everyone, without exception, to university. Many would be unhappy there, and many would be unable to cope. A state may not give the same level of welfare support to everyone. Just treatment means treating the needs of each person as seriously as those of everyone, which means giving more welfare aid to those who need it more, perhaps because of illness, poverty or disability. This might mean giving some people more in terms in resources and money to allow the same relative level of fulfilment.

(ii) Responses to God's just judgement of human actions

To be just might not mean the same as treating everyone in exactly the same way. If this is true, then God's justice would mean that everyone is equally valued even if not treated identically. But this raises other issues when we consider God's mercy, especially towards those not of his church or who have had no opportunity to encounter or believe in him.

There are many descriptions of the nature of mercy. John Calvin in his theology emphasised the unworthiness of any human compared with God. Throughout his works, there is emphasis on the greatness of God and the 'littleness' of human existence in comparison. In Part II, Chapter 3 of the *Institutes of the Christian Religion,* he argues that humankind has a

Key question

How is it possible for God to be perfectly just yet merciful?

corrupt nature and, as such, is damnable. He denies the existence of free will but argues that God demonstrates his mercy through the election of certain godly people. By granting his salvation to these, God reveals his goodness. They are small in number and their election is demonstrated by their membership of the Church and by the goodness of their lives. Outside the Church, there is no salvation, but even within the Church those saved are few:

Key quote

...regard must be had both to the secret election and to the internal calling of God, because he alone 'knoweth them that are his' (2. Tim. 2:19); and as Paul expresses it, holds them as it were enclosed under his seal, although, at the same time, they wear his insignia, and are thus distinguished from the reprobate. But as they are a small and despised number, concealed in an immense crowd, like a few grains of wheat buried among a heap of chaff, to God alone must be left the knowledge of his Church, of which his secret election forms the foundation. Nor is it enough to embrace the number of the elect in thought and intention merely. By the unity of the Church we must understand a unity into which we feel persuaded that we are truly ingrafted. For unless we are united with all the other members under Christ our head, no hope of the future inheritance awaits us.

John Calvin, *Institutes of the Christian Religion*, trans. Henry Beveridge, Part IV, 1.2

Critics of Calvinism argue whether this is truly merciful. Many have no opportunity ever to be members of the Christian Church. Those who are not part of God's 'secret elect' might ask whether it is the sign of the true goodness of God to choose a small number and to offer neither redemption nor hope of it to others. Calvin's response is to argue that there is no injustice and no reason for the damned to complain as no one deserves to be saved. God exercises his mercy in selecting a small number for salvation.

Nevertheless, it could be argued that Calvin's vision of hell creates problems for the goodness of God. For Aquinas, hell was separation from God, chosen by those who rejected him. For Aquinas, hell is not a place of fire and torture — it is the separation from God which is the anguish. Calvin's view is more literal and more traditional:

Unhappy consciences find no rest, but are vexed and driven about by a dire whirlwind, feeling as if torn by an angry God, pierced through with deadly darts, terrified by his thunderbolts and crushed by the weight of his hand; so that it were easier to plunge into abysses and whirlpools than endure these terrors for a moment. How fearful, then, must it be to be thus beset throughout eternity!

John Calvin, *Institutes of the Christian Religion*, trans. Henry Beveridge, Part III, 25.12

Calvin also touches on a wider issue. Most Christians accept the idea of *extra ecclesiam nulla salus* (outside the Church, there is no salvation). Yet, we know good people who are not Christian, and there remain the enormous numbers who never have the opportunity to become members of the Church. Would a good and merciful God condemn these? The Roman Catholic Church for centuries insisted on the requirement of baptism for salvation, but accepted a notion of 'Baptism of Desire' whereby those who had faith in God and lived their lives according to his values might be saved. The Second Vatican Council seemed to go further:

> All this holds true not only for Christians, but for all men of good will in whose hearts grace works in an unseen way. For, since Christ died for all men, and since the ultimate vocation of man is in fact one, and divine, we ought to believe that the Holy Spirit in a manner known only to God offers to every man the possibility of being associated with this paschal mystery.

> Pastoral Constitution on the Church in the Modern World, *Gaudium et Spes*, 22

The argument here was that all deserving people can receive the mercy of God. The subsequent Catechism would assert:

> Those who, through no fault of their own, do not know the Gospel of Christ or his Church, but who nevertheless seek God with a sincere heart, and, moved by grace, try in their actions to do his will as they know it through the dictates of their conscience – those too may achieve eternal salvation.

> Catechism of the Catholic Church, 847

Some ultra-traditionalist Catholics have argued against this view, which at first sight seems more consistent with a good and merciful God. Leonard Feeney (1897–1978), an American Jesuit, was excommunicated in 1953 for his insistence on a narrow interpretation of the doctrine, but he still has followers. But it seems difficult to make sense of terms such as 'God is good' and 'God is merciful' on this apparently narrow view. It contrasts strongly with comments of Pope Francis in a General Audience:

> We are all sinners but we are all forgiven: we all have the possibility of receiving his pardon, which is the mercy of God; we need not fear, therefore to recognise ourselves sinners, to confess ourselves sinners, because every sin was carried by the Son to the Cross.

> Pope Francis, General Audience, 6 April 2016

The contrast with the God envisaged by Calvin is considerable. It is important to recognise, of course, that Pope Francis does not argue that everyone is saved, but that God's mercy lies in an offer to everyone.

The contemporary philosopher Vincent Brümmer, a member of the (Calvinist) Dutch Reformed Church, has argued that we can make sense of justice and mercy only if we think of God as personal. For Brümmer, forgiveness does not consist in *condoning* an action, or suggesting somehow that it doesn't matter very much. The one who forgives must be prepared to absorb the pain out of love for the sinner. The sinner must also accept the wrongdoing:

If I repudiate the damage I have done to our fellowship by confessing myself in the wrong, and express my change of heart and my desire for the restoration of our fellowship by asking your forgiveness; and if you, by forgiving me, show your willingness with me again, then our fellowship will not only be restored, but might also be deepened and strengthened.

Vincent Brümmer, *What Are We Doing When We Pray?*, 2008, page 99

Here we encounter a common issue with thoughts about the attributes of God. Some issues of God's goodness seem soluble only by thinking of God as not a personal being, not a super*human* being – but then other questions seem to require that God is personal, if we are to make sense of forgiveness and mercy.

3 Conclusions

We seem to be in a place without easy answers. We began by looking at terms that sound fairly straightforward but – even when looking at each attribute individually – there are difficulties. These are questions usually of *meaning* of words but also about possibility. Is there a definition of omnipotence or benevolence that could work in practice?

The difficulty is compounded when we ask ourselves how the attributes of God work in relation to each other, the theme of our next chapter, where we consider these four qualities in relation to issues of free will. In your studies of the problem of evil, you will have encountered already the issues of reconciling God's goodness, with his omnipotence and knowledge.

See Year 1, Chapter 8.

If God is benevolent, then why does he permit evil and suffering as he could – presumably – do something about it and, being omniscient, has full knowledge of it? Other problems arise. If God is perfectly just, how then can he be perfectly merciful? This raises the question of what it means to be merciful. Does it mean condoning something if we say God forgives? Is being merciful giving people more than they deserve? But can it be just for God to act this way? The concept of justice seems to mean rewarding or punishing people to exactly the right extent that their conduct deserves, yet mercy seems to be giving more than people deserve.

Each of these problems raises the issue known by philosophers as that of the *compossibility of the divine attributes*. 'Compossibility' is about certain things being able to happen at the same time in the same way. The states of drunkenness and absolute sobriety are not possible in the same way at the same time for the same person. In the same way, in the next chapter, we shall consider how these different attributes of God could co-exist.

Study advice

With God's attributes there is no agreement – as we have seen – about what is meant by descriptions such as 'omnipotent' or even whether such terms have significant meaning. This can make the topic feel very nebulous to study, with discussions of all sorts of issues along the way.

A fruitful way around this, for study and revision, is to take for each attribute you must study, a provisional definition, such as Dummett's on omniscience, and then to list in your notes three or four potential problems. Realistically, most of us cannot remember more than three or four issues in a topic, so, as you work through your notes, pick out two or three which seem to you to be most important – and which you feel confident you understand and can write about – then make notes on these, relating them back to your provisional definition, to see where it might need to be modified.

In addition, whatever arguments you pick out as most relevant and interesting, think of material always in relation to the issues of language. All our philosophising about God is done in human language. What you consider in later chapters is relevant for you here too. Philosophy should never be thought of as learning a series of discrete topics. Each new topic provides an opportunity for revisiting and reconsidering other parts of your thought, considering whether ideas need further refinement and questioning.

Summary diagram: The nature or attributes of God

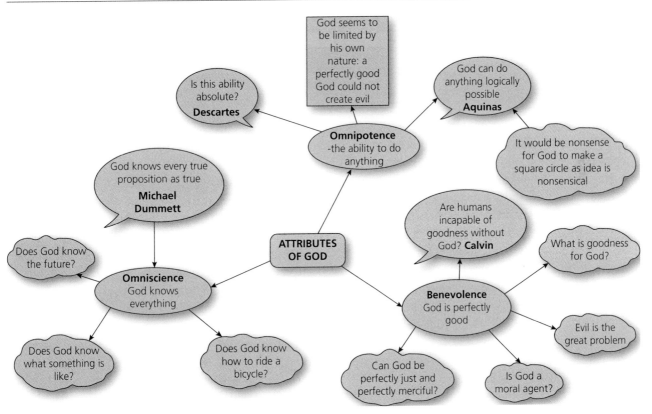

By the end of this chapter you should be able to explain thoughtfully the issues involved in finding reasonable definitions of God's attributes, especially omnipotence, omniscience and benevolence. You should be able to reflect on whether these attributes can ever be usefully expressed in human language and the limits of that language.

Can you give brief definitions of:

- omnipotence
- omniscience
- benevolence
- benificence
- mercy?

Can you explain:

- how Descartes argues that God's omnipotence is unlimited
- the idea that omnipotence and omniscience might apply only to the logically possible
- the issues of different types of knowledge
- the problems of reconciling perfect love with perfect justice?

Can you give arguments for and against:

- the idea that God's omnipotence means that he can do anything
- the idea that God's knowledge is knowledge of absolutely everything
- the claim that God can be perfectly good and perfectly just
- the claim that we can grasp the meaning of God in human terms?

Sample question and guidance

Assess the belief that God is omnipotent.

This question is one which looks simple but could be a trap for the unwary. It asks for more than a simple description of the idea of omnipotence. Asking you to assess the concept means that you need to consider very carefully whether the concept is coherent – that is, makes some sense – and what it might mean. Think about what it would mean to be omnipotent. Does it mean, as Descartes thought, that God could do anything at all, or, as Aquinas thought, anything logically possible? Is even the latter too wide?

Is omnipotence simply the ability of God to do anything he wants to do? Are objections such as the unliftable stone irrelevant to the religious concept of 'omnipotence'?

It is worth discussing the issues of human language and whether asking about omnipotence should be understood in terms of precise definition or as a poetic/religious usage. Certainly you need to demonstrate awareness that the ability of language to capture the essence of God is very limited. You might even conclude, as Kenny does, that perhaps we can say nothing significant at all.

Further essay questions

'An omnipotent God cannot escape responsibility for the evils of the world.' Discuss.

To what extent is it true to say God knows everything?

'A just God cannot be a merciful one.' Discuss.

Going further

There is a considerable literature on God's attributes.

A useful collection of material may be found in *The Concept of God* in the *Oxford Readings in Philosophy*, ed. Thomas V. Morris (Oxford University Press, 1997). Individual chapters are clearly signposted by topic.

A little more difficult, overall, is Keith Ward, *Concepts of God* (Oneworld, 1998).

Interesting material on human understanding of God can be found in Roger Scruton, *The Face of God* (Continuum, 2014) as well as in *Whose God? Which Tradition?* ed. D. Z. Phillips (Ashgate, 2008).

The collection *God, Mind and Knowledge*, ed. Andrew Moore (Ashgate, 2014) has a series of very interesting essays by philosophers including Anthony Kenny and John Cottingham. In the same series, *God, Goodness and Philosophy,* ed. Harriet A. Harris (Ashgate, 2013) has a wealth of material.

Especially rewarding in this area is Richard Swinburne, *The Coherence of Theism* (second edition, Oxford University Press, 2016). The largely rewritten work deals with all the issues discussed in this chapter. Swinburne in this book attempts to answer many of the criticisms made by those who argue that the very idea of God and his attributes does not make sense. This is perhaps the best-known book on the subject.

Other books discussed in this chapter are:

- Brümmer, V. *What Are We Doing When We Pray?* (Ashgate, 2008).
- Dummett, M. *Thought and Reality* (Oxford University Press, 2006).

Chapter 2

The nature of God: God, eternity and free will

1 Introduction

Chapter checklist

The chapter begins with an account of some of the issues about human understanding of time and its effects. Attention is drawn to some linguistic aspects of our understanding of time and the ways in which being in time has been considered to lead to inevitable decline. This leads to discussion of whether God can be held to be perfect if he is within the time process. Each of the specified authors, Boethius, St Anselm and Richard Swinburne, is discussed, as is the modern philosopher Alvin Plantinga. Broader philosophical and theological understandings of both timelessness and freedom of the will are examined. Material is illustrated with extensive quotation from original texts. Reference is also made to some recent discussion of the issues. The chapter concludes with study advice, revision pointers and sample questions.

For humans, time is an obsession. We are creatures who have, and know ourselves to have, past and future. Our pasts are ever larger in our experience, and the future, as we age, becomes shorter and perhaps more precious.

This awareness of time may be matched by a sense of decline or regret. Of course, we may look to the future with optimism, look forward to a given event, such as retirement; but at the same time, we have a lively awareness that what remains of our lives becomes ever shorter. Sportsmen and women are very aware that their time of excellence is likely to be brief. Our bodies become less flexible, we cannot run as fast as once we did, and we see other signs of advancing years not only in ourselves but in our friends. Events such as the death of friends, parents and grandparents bring home to us the relative brevity of life and the fragility of mortal existence.

It is not only that we are aware of mortality, but that our whole language is based on being in time. We live now and not then, here and not there – and our language reflects this. Human language is dominated by tenses, as even a cursory awareness of grammar tells us. I *did* that, *am doing* this and *will do* something tomorrow. The past is described in one way, the future another. The way we talk about the past has a certain fixity to it, while statements about the future are more open and provisional.

The obsession with passing time is not a modern one. In past centuries, the sense of the passage of time had a particular urgency. Death was everywhere, public and apparent. Infant mortality was very high, women died in childbirth. To live to be old was rare. In Elizabethan England, old age was assumed to begin at 45. According to the 1662 *Book of Common Prayer*:

> Man that is born from woman hath but a short time to live, and is full of misery. He cometh up, and is cut down, like a flower ...

Time is not only linked to mortality, but to regrets about things we might have done differently, opportunities missed, people who have died, loved institutions that have disappeared, loves lost. Time has its joys as well as its sorrows.

Does God regret as we do? If everything is in his power, and if he knows everything, then he is not prone to human errors. If he is perfectly loving, he will not, as we do, wish he had loved more or loved differently. Even more than this, he will not see in himself the effects of passing time. He will not be less capable with the years, will not suffer lapses of memory, not wonder how many days and years are left to him. Humans wonder what their own deaths will be like, and think about how they will fill their remaining years.

Humans talk of the effects of time, of time leading to decay. We see how living things die, and how our buildings crumble. It is easy to say that 'time decays'. It may be, however, that this is a mistake about language. Time does not operate like a sandstorm eroding a rock. It is not time that rusts an iron bar, for example. We might more accurately argue that 'things, in time, decay'. It is not time that is the agent which brings about the deterioration in things. But everything in creation seems to change and eventually break down, but God does not. It is easy to see how such thoughts lead some to argue that God must be unaffected by time if they see time as the corrosive force.

All talk about time, such as 'time passing' or 'time dragging' is metaphorical. If we forget this, we can get ourselves very confused.

Making mistakes about language has major significance for our understanding of God. To treat God as timeless emphasises how he is always perfect and undamaged by change. It matters to religious believers not to trivialise or reduce the concept of God. He is infinitely different from ourselves and, in conceiving of him, people want to avoid any diminishing of his nature. To see God as outside time preserves the differences between his permanence and our changing – and ultimately dying – lives.

But in preserving the nature of God in this way, we create other problems. Even if God is outside time, we are creatures of time. We live and change in a dimension of time. Our experience has past, present and future; our futures are always open to the unexpected and the unknown. Whenever we express ourselves, our language works in past, present and future tenses. We never speak or think without a sense of time.

If God is timeless, what is his relationship to us? We experience ourselves as people who make choices, who conform to or reject orders. But it does not follow that because we may experience ourselves as free, with **free will**, that this is truly the case. We may be deluding ourselves. Can we truly be free in relation to God if he already knows the choices we make? A timeless God knows from all eternity whether I shall go to heaven or to hell, live a good or a bad life. He made me, anyway, knowing what would be my fate. The question therefore is whether God has already determined my future and whether I am truly free in my choices.

Key terms

Free will The belief that human beings may freely choose their own actions.

Predestination The idea, largely associated with St Augustine and Calvin, that because God knows all our future actions, we have no freedom of the will.

Background

Since the time of St Augustine, the question of free will and predestination has been a vexed issue. It was St Augustine who made most of the idea in ancient times and it became a lively issue at the Reformation. Martin Luther argued that free will was an illusion. In 1524, Erasmus, the greatest Humanist thinker, published a defence of free will, *On the Freedom of the Will*. In 1525, Luther responded sharply with *The Bondage of the Will*. John Calvin, in the *Institutes of the Christian Religion* and elsewhere, took a stronger view of predestination than Luther, rejecting the possibility of free will in very strong terms.

See Year 1, pages 280–1.

Since the time of St Augustine (see background box), the question of free will and **predestination** has been a vexed issue. The philosophical questions raised by the alleged timelessness of God are significant. Various attempts have been made to resolve these, not least by Boethius and St Anselm, and we need to examine the implications of these views.

2 Boethius

Today, Boethius is hardly a household name, and it is easy to overlook his significance to medieval thought. However, his influential text, *The Consolation of Philosophy*, which he wrote in prison awaiting his own execution, contributed a great deal to philosophical thought on the nature of God.

Boethius (480–525): Anicius Manlius Severinus Boethius, Roman aristocrat, commentator on Aristotle, executed at the order of the Emperor Theoderic. Author of the influential *The Consolation of Philosophy* and other philosophical works.

What is said of God, [that] he is always present, signifies a unity, as if he had lived in all past times, is in everything present … and will be in all future times. That way of talking, according to philosophers, can be said about heaven and all imperishable bodies; but cannot be said of God in the same way. He is [exists] *always* in the sense that for him, *always* is about the present time. There is this great difference between the present of our world, which [to us] is *now*, and that of the divine. Our *now* makes time … as if it were running along. But the divine '*now*', remains, not moving, standing still, makes eternity.

Boethius, *De Trinitate*, 20.64–22.77

Background

Boethius

Boethius was an important member of the court of the Emperor Theodoric, arguably the most powerful man in Western Europe after the collapse of the Roman Empire around 500AD. Boethius was a senator, consul and *magister officiorum*, which means he occupied a role analogous to that of prime minister today. Theodoric had Boethius locked up when he became frightened that the Eastern Empire was plotting to overthrow him. Precise details are unclear.

The Consolation of Philosophy was written by Boethius while he was in prison to explain why he, who was believed to be a good Christian, had apparently been abandoned by fortune and God, and left to die by execution. This execution eventually did, rather painfully, take place, probably by slow crushing of the head, followed by a clubbing, a traditional Visigothic method. The book is written as a dialogue between Boethius and 'Lady Philosophy'.

To medieval thinkers, Boethius was a key thinker, and his influence would remain strong. If we can think in modern terms of a bestselling book in the Middle Ages, it was *The Consolation of Philosophy*. Again and again his work is cited as authoritative by other authors, including St Thomas Aquinas. It was translated into Anglo-Saxon at the court of King Alfred and, in the fourteenth century, into early modern English by Geoffrey Chaucer. St Anselm, as we saw in Year 1, made use of Boethius' commentaries on Aristotle in his work, notably in Chapter 3 of *Proslogion*.

For philosophers of the Middle Ages writing before the end of the twelfth century, Boethius provided the principal means of knowing the logic of Aristotle.

See Year 1, pages 82–5.

(a) Divine eternity and divine action in time

Boethius argued for the timelessness of God. He was not the first to do so, as Origen and Augustine had previously done so, but Boethius was the authority to whom later philosophers would appeal.

We see here the influence of the science of Boethius' day. Scientists believed there were necessary beings other than God, such as the stars, moon and sun, things not subject to decay as the things around us are. Here, Boethius is making a very important distinction. (Philosophers sometimes contrast 'eternal' with 'sempiternal' – the latter means being 'always existing', that is, living through all time, while 'eternal' is used to mean 'outside time'). For Boethius, God is eternal – outside time and unaffected by it. God lives in his own eternity, outside time: for him, everything is *now*.

In *The Consolation of Philosophy*, Boethius develops the idea. He argues:

> ### Key quote
>
> That God is eternal ... is the common judgment of everyone who lives by reason. Let us consider what eternity is, because this will make clear to us both God's nature and his knowledge. *Eternity is the complete possession all at once of illimitable life*. This becomes clearer by comparing with earthly things. Whatever lives in time continues as something which is from the past, is now present, and goes into the future. Nothing which is found in time can include the whole of its life, equally. Indeed, it is far from that. It does not now understand tomorrow, and yesterday is already lost. Even in the life of today, you live just in a moving, transitory moment... It follows that any being [God] which includes the fullness of life is a being in which nothing future is missing from it, and nothing past has disappeared. It is necessary that being which has full possession of itself has its full nature always present to itself and that the whole of moving time is present to it.
>
> Boethius, *The Consolation of Philosophy*, Book 5, prose 6
> (our italics)

Key terms

Eternity The idea of timelessness – time does not affect the eternal.
Everlasting existence Existence without end.

See Year 1, pages 33–5.

See Chapter 1, page 7, Dummett's approach to omniscience.

Passages such as these are cited by philosophers who claim that Boethius places God entirely outside the time process (which in turn leads to various considerations about whether God can have true knowledge – an issue as discussed in the last chapter).

It is, however, possible that this is an incorrect interpretation of Boethius.

Boethius (like Aquinas, later) wished to distinguish the **eternity** of God from Aristotle's world of **everlasting** (and beginningless) **existence**.

For Aristotle, God is *unchanging* and quite indifferent to the universe. But Boethius goes much further, distinguishing in an interesting way between our knowledge of God and his own knowledge.

God's eternity is discussed by Boethius in this context. He speaks of God as 'remaining' and 'enduring' and living 'always'. This is a problem. These words imply time, but he wants to deny the idea that time is in God, perhaps a reality beyond our understanding – one whose knowledge is not as ours is, time-constrained, but which is an understanding of an eternal order. But this moves us beyond things we can easily understand.

For many medieval thinkers, the idea that God was timeless became accepted as fact, and the influence remains strong, as we saw in the last chapter when we considered Dummett's approach to omniscience.

Background

Boethius and Aquinas

Later thinkers often cite the authority of Aquinas to claim that God is timeless. However, it is not clear that Aquinas believed that God was wholly outside time, as Boethius believed. In *Summa Contra Gentiles*, Book II, Chapters 32–8, Aquinas deals with the issues of God. But his definition of God is not that he is outside time, but that he is without beginning or end, unlike temporal things. He speaks of God's will and God's actions, each of which are notions that entail time. To will is to wish to bring about something which is not *yet* the case, as the subject of a wish lies in the future, and 'to act' implies movement which suggests duration – a time-bound concept. Aquinas' view of eternity seems to have been less significant in medieval discussion than that attributed to Boethius.

Key question

Is Boethius correct to claim that God is timeless?

Key term

Atemporality The state of being outside the timeprocess.

However we may choose to interpret Boethius on God, it is evident that he means something very significant by the phrase, 'the complete possession all at once of illimitable life'. Nothing in time has this. Lives in time are lived in sequence – one thing follows another, and the earlier state of affairs has gone. For that reason, if God has 'complete possession all at once', then he is not temporal, and yet, if Boethius' wording is correct, has duration (lastingness) *and* **atemporality**.

(i) Criticisms of Boethius' view on divine eternity and divine action in time

Ancient philosophers, such as Plato and Aristotle, when they spoke of something as eternal, were careful not to deny that time exists, or to use 'eternal' to mean timeless. Boethius seems to follow this line. There are two, separate types of existence – the timely *and* the eternal. For Boethius, the eternal is not reducible to time (contrary to Aristotle's view, where the two are interlinked) but is not, in any way, incompatible with time. The problem we are faced with is a double one: is Boethius' notion of eternity coherent and, if it is, how can the eternal interact with the temporal?

A problem in this difficult discussion is that the very notion of time is problematic. The Polish philosopher, Tadeusz Kotarbiński, in his later career, came to argue that time is the duration of objects, and not something separate. Objects for him do not exist within time – there are objects, they last, and what we call time is therefore their lastingness. If there are no objects then there is not empty time and space, but nothing at all. This provides an interesting possibility. If God is not an 'object', then perhaps there is room for saying he would be outside the time process, if time is simply the duration of things.

Other issues are suggested by Einstein's General Theory of Relativity, which leads us to be aware that time may not be the unchanging thing that our everyday experience might suggest. The language we use sometimes treats time as if it were a process, like wave erosion. But if the continuity of time is simply an illusion, what does this mean for our understanding of time?

A key question raised by the idea of a divine eternal being is whether God can change the past. On Boethius' conception, the answer is that he cannot. Because we are temporal beings, we have a past: an eternally present God has no past. In a paper, the philosophers Eleonore Stump and Norman Kretzmann argue:

An omnipotent, omniscient, eternal entity can affect temporal events, but it can affect events only as they are actually occurring. As for a past event, the time at which it was actually occurring is the time at which it is present to such an entity; and so the battle of Waterloo is present to God, and God can affect the battle. Suppose that he does so. God can bring it about that Napoleon wins, though we know that he does not do so, because whatever God does at Waterloo is over and done with as we see it. So God cannot alter the past, but he can alter the course of the battle of Waterloo.

Eleonore Stump and Norman Kretzmann, 'Eternity', *The Concept of God*, 1987, pages 247–8

The difficulty here is that simply saying that God cannot alter the past leaves open how he can act in the present or future worlds in which people live.

It is possible to say a great deal more about God's eternity as considered by Boethius. There is an interesting book to be written, but all we can do here is to indicate some of the issues.

The next section looks at what Boethius' interpretations on the eternal nature of God mean for the idea of God as a benevolent divinity, who is just in his judgement of human actions.

(b) Boethius on divine 'foreknowledge'

Boethius addresses the problem that if God knows what we are going to do, then why do we not hold him, at least partly, responsible for the evil done?

If our behaviour is determined or even foreseen, then it seems fair to assume that God has to take some responsibility for the evil actions brought about by humanity's free choices. We have already considered the nature of God who, for Boethius, is eternal and not temporal.

Boethius makes much of the concept of God's *providence*, a term preferred by Boethius in place of the more customary term 'foreknowledge' (implying as that does 'prior' knowledge, which is contrary to Boethius' view of God as being atemporal).

Boethius poses a question:

Why then, ... [are]... the things which Providence sees in its eternal present, governed by necessity, while the things which ... [humans] see in the present they do not regard as being governed by necessity?

Boethius, *The Consolation of Philosophy*, Book 5, prose 6

The question he considers is clear. God knows what will happen and, in guiding the world, sees what he knows will happen as necessarily about to happen. Knowing everything, he cannot be surprised, and his knowledge of what will happen is fixed and precise. Because he knows the choices I will make, I cannot not make them – they are bound to happen. But, that is not my experience. I find myself making choices, whether to marry or not, or whether to apply for a job. Indeed, my life as I experience it involves continual choosing.

Key question

Is it possible in human words to express what is meant by 'an eternal present'?

But if God knows what my choice will be, it seems that I will inevitably do what he knows I will do. If this were true, it would seem, as Calvin thought, that humans would have no free will. Calvin's view can be seen in the *Institutes*:

> We ascribe both foreknowledge and predestination to God... When we attribute foreknowledge to God, we mean that all things always were, and always continue to be, under his eye. In his knowledge there is no past or future, but all things are present...This knowledge extends to the whole world, and to all creatures. By predestination we mean the eternal decree of God, by which he decided with himself whatever he wished to happen for every man. All people are not created equally, but some are preordained to eternal life, others to eternal damnation; and, therefore, as everyone has been created for one or other of these ends, we say that he has been predestined to life or to death.

John Calvin, *Institutes of the Christian Religion*, Book III, Chapter 21, 5

Calvin puts things in stark terms, drawing explicitly on scriptural references and, in particular, on some of the writings of St Augustine. In this passage, we can see very clearly how reliant he is on the understanding of God's timeless knowledge set out by Boethius, and taken for granted in medieval thought. That the position is so firmly set out by Calvin is a useful reminder that Boethius' argument is not simply a curiosity – an interesting but self-contained puzzle – but touches on issues that remain central to theology.

The Catholic tradition would always seek to defend free will – the idea that we are able to make our own choices. The question is whether, if God knows exactly what the future will be, we can be said to have any true freedom to act as we choose.

Calvin's logic is apparently quite convincing, but Boethius' way round this is ingenious, if not necessarily wholly satisfactory.

(c) Boethius on divine 'foreknowledge': free will (two types of necessity)

The key to Boethius' solution lies in his statement:

> ... when God knows that something is going to happen in the future, he may know a thing which will not happen out of necessity, but voluntarily; God's foreknowledge does not impose necessity on things.

Boethius, *The Consolation of Philosophy*, Book 5, prose 6

Boethius distinguishes here the difference between *knowing* what someone will do and *causing* that to happen. I know that there will be a Presidential election in the USA in 2020; but my knowing that, and the constitutional reasons why that must be so, does not imply that my knowledge is the *cause* of that event. In the same way, even if God *knows* what I might do in 2020, it does not follow that therefore he *causes* my action.

It might seem enough to leave matters there, but Boethius recognises that there remains an issue over the nature of necessity. If, in my future, God knows that I am going to perform a particular act, he knows what I will do, and therefore I cannot do something else. In that sense, it seems as if I will necessarily act in a particular way.

Boethius responds by saying that there are two types of necessity: **simple necessity** and **conditioned necessity**. Boethius says:

> ### Key quote
>
> … the same future event *is necessary from the point of view of Divine knowledge*, but when we think about it in its own nature it seems absolutely free and unconstrained. It follows that there are two types of necessity: one is *simple*, such as that men are mortal; the other type is *conditioned*, so that if someone is walking, he is necessarily walking.
>
> Ibid. (our italics)

Key terms

Simple necessity Something that just *has* to be the case, such as the idea that a mortal simply has to die. It is part of the meaning of mortality.

Conditioned necessity When the necessity follows from choice. If I choose to walk, and then walk, at the moment I am walking then, as a matter of logic, I cannot not be walking. But I could have chosen not to walk: the walking is a necessary consequence of once choosing and now actually walking.

Simple necessity is relatively easy to understand. Some things just are the case, and are necessary in that sense. Boethius' example that humans are mortal is a simple instance – we die, and it is part of the definition of human nature that we are mortal. We might add that there is nothing we can do about it. However much someone might wish not to die or fears death, she is going to die anyway and cannot, by an act of will, change that fact. This necessity is simple (unconditioned).

It is a principle of Aristotelian logic, on which Boethius was expert, that something cannot both be and not be at the same time. *If* I am walking, then I am necessarily walking. I cannot *not* be walking if I am walking. In that sense, I am necessarily walking and God, who knows things exactly as they happen, sees that I am necessarily walking, because I cannot not be walking at that time.

This necessity is *conditional*. *If* I am walking then of course I am necessarily walking. But, this is a case of *if* I am walking. The *if* is the condition of the necessity. I do not have to walk, though I do have to grow older and to die. In the latter cases, it is a necessity of nature that I must grow older and die. But in the case of walking, I only necessarily walk because I have chosen to walk. The necessity is a *consequence* of choice. Boethius says:

> ### Key quote
>
> No necessity compels someone who is voluntarily walking to move forward. But it is necessary for him to go forward at the moment of walking. In the same way, then, if the Providence of God sees anything as present to himself, that must necessarily be the case, although it is bound by necessity of nature.
>
> Ibid.

A useful way to remember the difference between simple and conditional necessity is to remind yourself that the 'condition' in *conditional necessity* is the construction 'if… then…'. In simple necessity, there is no 'if' about it: mortals die, and that's all there is to it.

From this, Boethius concludes that we still have free will. We are the ones who choose, and, of course, have the experience of choosing. The Victorian moral philosopher, Henry Sidgwick (1838–1900) later wrote:

Certainly in the case of actions in which I have a distinct consciousness of choosing between alternatives of conduct, one of which I conceive as right or reasonable, I find it impossible not to think that I can now choose to do what I so conceive, however strong may be my inclination to act unreasonably, and however uniformly I may have yielded to such inclinations in the past.

Henry Sidgwick, *The Methods of Ethics*, seventh edition, 1907, Book I, Chapter 5

Sidgwick's approach seems to coincide with our own experience. For example, I think of myself as someone who makes choices. Sometimes, decisions are quite difficult and I am very conscious of the problem of deciding what I should do. This experience seems to mean that the choices I make are mine and no one else's. In the case of walking, I know that I want to go for a walk – it is sunny outside – and in half an hour or so I will probably decide to stop writing and go out. I experience that as my choice but, of course, once I am walking in the park, I cannot not be walking in the park. In addition to making certain logical points about necessity, Boethius is also appealing to our experiencing ourselves as free persons.

(d) Criticism of Boethius' notion of timelessness – justice and benevolence

An issue with Boethius' notion of timelessness is that it seems to preserve the *greatness* and *otherness* of God at the expense of his other qualities. Believers hold that God is loving in all that he does. Love is seen as his greatest quality – D. Z. Phillips has gone so far as to argue that God *is* Love, and that God and love are equivalent terms.

Is Boethius' God truly just and benevolent? To what extent is it just to know in advance that someone will do great harm, causing actual hurt to others and, perhaps, eternal punishment to himself. Is it loving to allow someone to fall into great harm when you know exactly what will happen? If God eternally knows that a Hitler or a Stalin will do great evil, leading millions to suffer unjustly, how is that either just or benevolent? If God is also omnipotent, then we might ask whether it is either just or benevolent not to use those powers to prevent those evils.

If Boethius is mistaken, and God is indeed not timeless but everlasting, then even a Hitler might be open to redemption – and God might be surprised! A God who accompanies us as a companion into an open future has a different relationship from a God outside our time.

It is interesting to reflect on the idea that, if God is not timeless, there would be a perhaps infinite number of additional possibilities open to him. If his future reality is not fixed in his knowledge then creative opportunities for his action abound.

3 St Anselm

Key person

St Anselm of Canterbury
(1033–1109): major philosopher and theologian of the medieval period. Born in Aosta, in northern Italy, he was a monk of Cluny, in France, until becoming Archbishop of Canterbury in 1093. Major works include *Monologion, Proslogion, De Grammatico, De Fide Trinitatis* and *Cur Deus Homo*.

See Year 1, pages 82–6.

(a) Divine eternity and divine action in time: Anselm's four-dimensionalist approach

When we considered St Anselm's version of the Ontological Argument in the first volume of this series, we drew attention to his reliance on Boethius for his arguments in *Proslogion*, Chapter 3.

There is no doubt that Anselm was fully familiar with Boethius' ideas, and we see elements of this in his own attempts to reconcile the timelessness of God with free will.

St Anselm devoted considerable attention to the issue of free will. For our purposes, his most significant work is *De Concordia: The Compatibility of God's Foreknowledge, Predestination, and Grace with Human Freedom*.

Like Boethius, Anselm insists upon the timelessness of God. For him, this is a consequence of his omnipotence – being 'that than which nothing greater can be conceived'. Anselm argues:

> ... you surely cannot deny that the uncorrupted is better than something corrupt, the eternal than the temporal, and the invulnerable than the vulnerable.
>
> St Anselm, *On the Free Choice of the Will*, 2.10

Notice in the following extract that, for Anselm, God is not merely seen here as eternal but also as *impassible*, that is, not capable of being affected by that which is outside himself. God is simple and outside time to preserve his supremacy:

> This...is the condition of place and time: whatever is enclosed within their boundaries does not avoid having parts, whether they are parts it has to achieve its size, or the type it has in time in relation to duration. Neither can it in any way be contained as a whole at the same time by different places or times. By contrast, if something is not in any way constrained by confinement in a place or time, no law of place or time can force it into a multiplicity of parts or prevent it from being present as a whole all at once in several places or times.
>
> St Anselm, *Monologion*, 22

Anselm insisted on both the eternity and simplicity (he has no parts and is not complex) of God.

Like Boethius, Anselm views God as eternal, and (albeit for different reasons) not constrained by the same laws of place and time. Anselm is therefore faced with the problems that concerned Boethius: whether our timely existence is predetermined, as God knows our future, or whether we have free will.

Anselm treats free will in a distinctive way, though a connection can be made to some comments by St Augustine. In ordinary language, we tend to treat free will as meaning that we can do what we choose to do. This implies a choice between alternatives. I have no freedom not to grow older, because in nature, there is no alternative. But I experience freedom

Compare this with Plato's idea of an eternal soul, as a simple substance – see Year 1, page 44.

to choose between the steak or the casserole on the menu, or to continue writing or not. The freedom lies in the choice.

But for Anselm, freedom is tied to rectitude (doing the right thing). I am free to do the right thing. After all, part of the rightness of my action is the fact that I have *chosen* rightly. If I did the right thing without myself choosing it, I have not really demonstrated my goodness. Choosing rightly is what 'good' people do. For Anselm, who accepts Augustine's notion that evil is an absence, a privation, choosing wrongly is to choose nothing at all – it is to opt for an absence. Thus choosing means choosing something that is good. He argues that God, by his nature, cannot choose evil, but that it would be blasphemy to say that therefore God had no free will. Free will is the ability to choose the right thing because one wants to choose it.

But that still leaves the question of how we are to understand God's 'foreknowledge' of our actions. Like Boethius, Anselm argues that although God knows the future as unchanged (he knows what will happen) we, in time, know it as changeable by our choices:

> ... although that which he foreknows in his eternity is immutable, in time it is mutable before it happens.

St Anselm, *De Concordia*, in *Anselm of Canterbury: The Major Works*, eds Brian Davies and G. R. Evans, 1998, page 451

The distinctive feature of Anselm's work in this area is the detailed account of his understanding of the eternal present. His discussion ventures well beyond Boethius'. After an account of the differences between the necessity of things which are fixed and those which are the necessary consequence of free will (an account which in many respects is much clearer than the original in Boethius, so it is worth reading), he goes on to consider the nature of eternal knowledge.

St Anselm leans heavily – as Calvin would later do, though drawing different conclusions – on St Paul. The passage is worth examining at length:

> ... [God] ... is said to have situated immutably with regard to himself that which is mutable with regard to the human being. St Paul speaks in the same vein about those who, according to God's purpose, are called to be holy: 'Those whom he foreknew, he also foreordained to become conformed to the likeness of his Son, so that his Son would be the firstborn among many brethren. Moreover, those whom he foreordained, these he also called. And those whom he called, these he also justified. Moreover, those whom he justified, he also glorified.' [Rom.1:7; 8:28–9]. Indeed within eternity, in which there is no past or future but only a present, this purpose in accordance to which they are called to be holy, is immutable; but within human beings it is sometimes mutable because of free will. For in eternity a thing has no past or future but only an (eternal) present, though in the realm of time things move from past to future without any contradiction arising. Similarly, that which cannot be changed in eternity sometimes, before it occurs, without involving any incongruity, is changeable because of free will. Moreover, although in eternity

there is only a present, nevertheless it is not a temporal present as ours is, *only an eternal one in which all periods of time are contained. Indeed, just as our present time envelops every place and whatever is in every place, so in the eternal present all time is encompassed along with whatever exists at any time. Therefore,* when St Paul says that God foreknew, predestined, called, justified, and glorified his saints, none of these happen before or after *on God's part. They must all be understood as existing simultaneously in an eternal present.* For eternity has its own unique simultaneity *which contains both all things that happen at the same time and place and that happen at different times and places.*

Ibid., page 442 (our italics)

If we read the passage carefully, we see that Anselm does not build his concept of eternity on our concept of time. For him, the eternal *present* is not the same as our concept of 'the present', which in our experience is contrasted with past and future. 'Eternity' for Anselm becomes a non-temporal concept. It makes sense to speak of Anselm's notion of eternity being in a fourth dimension. The advantage of making this move is that it is no denial of the reality of our temporal world, although we may properly ask how the eternity of God in this other dimension interacts with the world in which we live.

Anselm is very aware of the difficulty of encompassing the fourth dimensional eternity in the language we use. This applies to scripture as well:

… temporally speaking, God had not already called, justified and glorified those whom he foreknew were yet to be born. We can … understand that it was for want of a verb signifying the eternal present that St Paul used verbs of the past tense.

Ibid., page 433

Much of Anselm's most significant work was on logic and the use of language, and so we should not be surprised that he is so careful to remind us that we are using language in a special way when we speak of God. Terms such as 'foreknowledge' or 'predestined' are terms which invoke aspects of time, and so, when we apply them to try to grasp God's knowledge and action – because we have no other vocabulary – we are working at the very edge of their meaning.

4 Richard Swinburne

Boethius and Anselm – and, indeed, medieval philosophy in general – attempt to reconcile our freedom of will and action with the eternal nature of God and his knowledge. They insist on his timelessness, then need to demonstrate how, nevertheless, people in time can have free will. Many modern philosophers of religion, including Richard Swinburne, have come to reject the concept of God as timeless.

Swinburne's argument has many persuasive features. He argues that the concept of God as wholly outside time is unbiblical. After looking at the argument of Boethius, he comments:

Key quote

... , the Hebrew Bible shows no knowledge of the doctrine of divine timelessness; for its authors God does now this, now that; now destroys Jerusalem, now lets the exiles return home. The same applies in general for the New Testament writers, although there are occasional sentences in the New Testament which could be interpreted in terms of this doctrine. Thus in the Revelation of St. John, God is represented as saying 'I am the Alpha and the Omega, the first and the last, the beginning and the end' and 'I am the first and the last, and the Living one'. But it seems to me to be reading far too much into such phrases to interpret them as implying the doctrine of divine timelessness.

Richard Swinburne, *The Coherence of Theism*, (second edition), 2016, page 230

Swinburne goes on to claim that Protestant theologians such as Karl Barth, Paul Tillich and Oscar Cullmann have argued that a timeless God makes no sense. Tillich argues that a God outside the temporal process would be lifeless, yet believers speak of a 'living God'. Barth adds to this that the doctrine of the Incarnation of Christ, the Son of God, is a case of God acting intentionally and decisively in and within human history. Cullmann develops the same point in his *Christ and Time* (1951).

Swinburne believes that the very idea of timelessness in the knowledge of God is radically incoherent:

... God would have to be aware simultaneously of all the events of human history that happen at different times as they happen. But how could God be aware at his one timeless moment of two events happening at different times, unless the two awarenesses are simultaneous with each other, and so two events happening at different times would have to happen at the same time – which is logically impossible. How could God be aware of the destruction of Jerusalem by the Babylonians in 587 BCE as it happens, and of its destruction by the Romans in 70 CE as it happens, when these two times are not simultaneous with each other? Any sense of 'simultaneous' in which this is logically possible would seem to have little connection with the ordinary sense of 'simultaneous'.

Ibid., page 239

Swinburne also argues that believers wish to say many things about God, such as that he brings about this or that, forgives, punishes or warns. These terms lead to questions such as asking *when* God brought it about, or *when* he punished or warned someone. Swinburne argues that it is very difficult to make sense of these terms, which presuppose that God's actions occur at specific times, and at the same time maintain God's timelessness:

> *The God of the Hebrew Bible, in which Judaism, Christianity, and Islam all have their roots, is pictured as being in continual interaction with humans – humans sin, then God is angry, then humans repent, then God forgives them; humans ask God for this, then God gives them this, then they misuse it, then God takes it away; and so on. A totally immutable God is a lifeless God, not a God with whom one can have a personal relationship – as theists have normally claimed that one can have with God.*

Ibid., page 233

Key question

Is Richard Swinburne's view of God as everlasting more consistent with Christian belief than the arguments of Boethius and Anselm?

Swinburne argues that there are no good reasons to insist upon the timelessness of God. To do so is inconsistent with Biblical usage and logically incoherent. No less significantly, there seems to be no good reason to insist upon timelessness. Indeed, we might add that not seeing God as timeless makes more sense of the life of worship and prayer. To think of a God unmoved by the prayers of those who suffer seems to be a denial of faith.

5 Alvin Plantinga

Key person

Alvin Plantinga (b. 1932): analytic philosopher of religion, now Emeritus Professor of Philosophy at the University of Notre Dame, Gifford Lecturer (2004–5). Prolific author, best known for his alternative version of the Ontological Argument, his defence of free will, and his involvement in Reformed Epistemology, which treats God as a basic belief requiring no further justification.

Alvin Plantinga is directly relevant to discussions about God and free will because he is perhaps the most well-known modern proponent of the free will response to the problem of evil, which is the question of how God can be all-loving, all-powerful and yet evil exists in the world. As we saw in Year 1, St Augustine drew heavily on the concept of free will when constructing his response.

Plantinga's approach is based on two ideas – the radical nature of free will and the nature of God's omnipotence.

See Year 1, pages 116–20.

We saw earlier in the chapter how St Anselm sees free will in terms of our acting in accordance with rectitude: it is freedom to do the right thing. But, for Plantinga, it means being radically free:

What is relevant to the Free Will Defence is the idea of being
free with respect to an action. *If a person is free with respect*
to a given action, then he is free to perform that action and free
to refrain from performing it; no antecedent conditions and/or
causal laws determine that he will perform the action, or that
he won't. It is within his power, at the time in question, to take
or perform the action and within his power to refrain from it.
Freedom so conceived is not to be confused with unpredictability.

Alvin Plantinga, God, Freedom and Evil, 1977, pages 29–30

The last point is significant. Jean-Paul Sartre insists that we are radically free, but that no reasons can be given for our choices other than that we have chosen them. Plantinga's version is different, hence his comment that free choice does not entail and should not be confused with the unpredictability inherent in Sartre's version. Indeed, we may question whether we can significantly speak of 'choice' in relation to Sartre – choice implies selecting something for a reason.

Hard choices happen when we have different reasons for different options. But they also remind us that *reasons* are not *causes*. I think it would be a good idea to do something, and have many reasons for doing that thing, but it does not follow that I would do it, for the bad reason that I am deeply idle. If the reasons were causes, then I would be sure to do that thing. The problem is that we often say, 'I did this because ...' where the blank is sometimes a reason ('I did this because I thought it was a good idea'), and sometimes a cause ('I did this because my arm jerked uncontrollably and smashed the glass'). It is important to bear this distinction in mind whenever discussing free will.

Having accepted the idea that we have free will, Plantinga goes on to say that there are morally good choices, and it is the choice that makes the action good. He argues:

> *... I shall say that an action is* morally significant, *for a given*
> *person, if it would be wrong to perform the action but right to*
> *refrain or* vice versa. *Keeping a promise, for example, would*
> *ordinarily be morally significant for a given person ... [W]e say*
> *that a person is* significantly free, *on a given occasion, if he is*
> *then free with respect to a morally significant action.*

Ibid., page 30

Here, Plantinga is arguing two things. On the one hand, he argues that we are significantly free when we can perform a morally significant action, but there is a second point. It is only a genuinely moral action when freely done. To be morally good it must be chosen as good, and freely performed.

From these points, he goes on to detail his version of the Free Will Defence.

Plantinga's Free Will Defence is summed up as follows:

> *A world containing creatures who are significantly free (and*
> *freely perform more good than evil actions) is more valuable,*
> *all else being equal, than a world containing no free creatures*
> *at all. Now God can create free creatures, but He can't* cause or

See Year 1, Chapter 8.

determine *them to do only what is right. For if he does so, then they aren't significantly free after all; they do not do what is right freely. To create creatures capable of moral good, therefore, He must create creatures capable of moral evil; and He can't give these creatures the freedom to perform evil and at the same time prevent them from doing so. As it turned out, sadly enough, some of the free creatures God created went wrong in the exercise of their freedom; this is the source of moral evil. The fact that free creatures sometimes go wrong, however, counts neither against God's omnipotence nor against His goodness; for He could have forestalled the occurrence of moral evil only by removing the possibility of moral good.*

Ibid., page 30

Plantinga agrees with Aquinas' idea that to say that God is omnipotent means that he can do anything *logically* possible. It is no limit to omnipotence not to be able to do the logically impossible, because the logically impossible is meaningless. From this, Plantinga goes on to consider what is logically possible to God. He considers different types of possible worlds, to see whether God did indeed make the best possible world. He concludes that a world that contains moral actions by free creatures is a better world than any alternative. But, as we have seen, for there to be moral action, there must be free choice and the possible reality of bad choices and moral evil. A world with no evil and free choice is, argues Plantinga, logically absurd. The only way to get rid of evil would be by getting rid of free will and morality. A morally good world is one in which there is free co-operation between God and his creatures. If God eliminated the possibility of moral evil, there would be no possibility of the greater good, which is moral (and hence freely chosen) good. This would seem to enable the believer to maintain the omni-benevolence of God in providing what would be the best possible world in the circumstances.

Key question

Is it true, as Plantinga thinks, that a world with free will is superior to one without?

6 Free will, timelessness and God's attributes

Discussion about the relationship of God and free will is largely shaped by the question of whether he is indeed timeless – at least in his knowledge – in the way that Boethius and Anselm assume. If Swinburne is correct, then it is both unscriptural and logically incoherent to treat God in such a way: God's timelessness creates issues around genuine benevolence as well as omniscience. Swinburne represents an important strand in modern scholarly opinion. William Hasker (b.1935) comments:

… it seems much better to take the Bible at face value and to understand God as a temporal being.

The other main difficulty about divine timelessness is that it is very difficult to make clear logical sense of the doctrine. If God is truly timeless, so that temporal determinations of "before" and "after" do not apply to him, then how can God act in time, as the Scriptures say that he does? How can he know what is

*occurring on the changing earthly scene? How can he respond
when his children turn to him in prayer and obedience? And above
all, if God is timeless and incapable of change, how can God
be born, grow up, live with and among people, suffer and die,
as we believe he did as incarnated in Jesus? Whether there are
good answers to these questions, whether the doctrine of divine
timelessness is intelligible and logically coherent, and whether
it can be reconciled with central Christian beliefs such as the
incarnation remain matters of intense controversy.*

William Hasker, 'Does God Change? *Questions About God*, eds Steven M. Cahn
and David Shatz, 2002, page 138

While assuming that God is not timeless resolves some difficulties, this interpretation raises other questions as to God's attributes. In what sense can a God who is in time predict the future yet be considered omniscient? If the future is future to God, and beyond his present action, can he yet be considered omnipotent?

It would be possible to argue, returning to Aquinas' argument that omnipotence means that God can do everything logically possible, that what is logically possible, and, by extension, what is logically knowable, will be different between a timely and timeless God, but complete in itself in terms of what is logically possible. Stephen M. Cahn argues:

*… statements about future choices are neither true nor false,
but, at present, indeterminate. According to this view, it is not
now true you will finish reading this entire book and not true you
won't. Until you decide, the matter is indeterminate.*

*As the medieval Jewish philosopher Gersonides argued, to be
omniscient is to know every true statement. Since it is not true
you will finish reading the entire book and not true you won't,
but true that the matter is indeterminate, an omniscient being
does not know you will finish reading and does not know you
won't, but does know the whole truth, namely, that the matter is
indeterminate and depends on your free choice.*

*Thus, assuming God is omniscient, God knows the entire physical
structure of this universe but not the outcome of free choices.*

Stephen M. Cahn, 'Does God Know the Future? *Questions About God*, eds Steven M.
Cahn and David Shatz, 2002, page 150

Cahn's solution seems to leave untouched the idea of Michael Dummett, noted in Chapter 1, that for every true statement, God knows that it is true, so long as we add a condition about this being every *knowable* true statement. Cahn's formulation, assuming that people are free in their choices, allows a space for them to be genuinely free in their relationship to God. Because they are truly free, if God is in time, then he does not know in advance what their choices will be. In a similar way, we might even make the suggestion that God would not be a truly omnipotent God if he were unable to make creatures capable of free choices of their own, or if he were unable to create a world with space to exercise that freedom.

Ingolf Dalferth has argued that we need to think of God as, above all, perfectly loving. If love is the central truth about God, and this is essential for omni-benevolence, then the everlasting model is the one that makes most sense:

> ... *divine omnipotence is not a divine property alongside or alternative to divine love ... the point of almighty love is not that it can do everything that is not logically impossible but that it will not give up under any circumstances to hope and work for a response of love from those whom it creates and sustains out of love.*
>
> *Second, God's love does not operate uniformly as it does in timeless creation. It adapts to circumstances. It is sensitive to the specific needs of those it loves. It reacts in the workings of the Spirit to the actual state of that which God treats as the object of his love.*

Ingolf Dalferth, *Becoming Present: An Inquiry into the Christian Sense of the Presence of God*, 2006, page 167

If Dalferth is correct, it would seem difficult to reconcile the God of faith with one who is timeless and – to a greater or lesser extent – remote from lived experience of those he loves.

7 Conclusions

It seems at first sight fairly simple to say that God is timeless, as Boethius argued, but the more we examine the idea, the more complex it becomes. Boethius tries to justify his view, while maintaining free will, by making a distinction between simple and conditional necessity. As we have seen, this response seems unsatisfactory. There are linguistic issues of what terms mean: the language Boethius uses is our language, in which the way we talk always suggests time, so that it becomes difficult truly to picture in any helpful way the timelessness of God. Anselm's solution, of putting God into a different dimension, is interesting but suffers from similar problems. Swinburne's solution is important – it suggests, as others have done, that the idea of a timeless God is both religiously improper and logically incoherent. If that is true, it would not be the first time that enormous philosophical effort has gone into an idea that is mistaken. But the concept of a timeless God has been so significant and so much part of philosophical discussion that the concept remains a live issue.

It might be, of course, impossible to ever reconcile apparent conflicts between and among the divine attributes. For a believer, such resolution might well seem unnecessary. When the believer describes her God as all-powerful and all-knowing, is she doing so as a precise scientific description, which can be tested like a description of the constituents of water or volcanic lava, or is she rather concerned to praise and glorify God? Certainly it is unlikely that she experiences the issue as a fundamental dilemma likely to shake her faith, especially as she will be aware that the descriptions she uses refer to things beyond her understanding. She knows that God cannot do evil, because of his nature. In a philosophical moment, she may think about the implications, but it is unlikely in the light of what she experiences as the overwhelming goodness of God, together with his overwhelming power to do that good, that she will fret too much about the technicalities of how that might be possible. The belief she expresses when she describes God as all-knowing, all-loving and so on, seems to be a way of speaking of a quite different order.

Study advice

This may seem a slightly tricky area as we are at the least at the edge of, and perhaps beyond, possible knowledge of the nature of God. It is helpful to bear in mind the points made about language here and elsewhere in this course. Think carefully about possible definitions of terms such as *omniscience* and *omnipotence* as well as the nature of free will. This chapter has concentrated primarily on Boethius, Anselm and Swinburne as they are the names in the current specification, and any or all of these could therefore be named in any question asked, so it is important to be clear about what each brings to the debate.

But there are wider issues, and it is important to think about whether the idea of God's timelessness is essential to faith as well as whether it is logically coherent. Perhaps a good way to do this is to work on the broad issue of timelessness before looking at the relationship of God and human free will. However you choose to deal with the issues, the important thing is – as ever in philosophy – to think through whether the ideas of Boethius, Anselm and the others fully answer the question they have set themselves. In doing so, remember that they – and we – are working at the very limits of what human language can talk about.

Summary diagram: The nature of God: God, eternity and free will

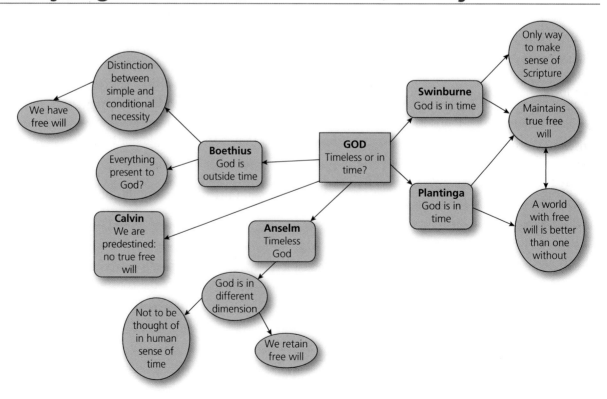

Revision advice

By the end of this chapter you should be able to explain and comment thoughtfully on issues raised by trying to preserve the integrity and greatness of God by conceiving of him as timeless. Above all, develop an understanding of the issues involved in deciding whether we have true free will if God has foreknowledge of our actions. Must we take the route of denying free will, as Calvin does, or is there a philosophically satisfactory alternative? If so, which of the philosophers you have studied might provide this? You should be able to reflect on whether these ideas can ever be usefully expressed in human language and the limits of that language.

Can you give brief definitions of:
- divine timelessness
- free will
- temporality
- predestination
- foreknowledge?

Can you explain:
- the idea of God's knowledge being in an eternal present
- the difference between simple and conditional necessity in Boethius
- Anselm's four-dimensional conception of God's timelessness
- Richard Swinburne's objections to the idea of a timeless God?

Can you give arguments for and against:
- Boethius' conception of a timeless God
- the idea that God's knowledge of the future means the future is determined
- the idea that a God who is in the time process can nevertheless be described as omniscient and omnipotent
- the belief that people have free will even though God knows everything they will do?

Sample question and guidance

Assess the belief that because God knows everything, we cannot have free will.

This question goes to the heart of the issues discussed in this chapter. This question does not specify which philosophers you must write about, but focuses on concepts. Nevertheless, you are expected to use the work of philosophers you have studied – and to make reference to them – in your answer. In looking at concepts, you would find it helpful to consider points raised in the last chapter about omniscience and omnipotence, as well as about the material given here.

In constructing your answer, you need not merely assume that God knows everything, but what that might mean. What is the nature of that

'everything' and is it different for a timeless compared with a timely God? Think also about free will, and make sure you discuss what it might entail. Does Anselm define the idea too narrowly? Was Boethius correct to argue that his concept of conditional necessity is sufficient for us to be able to say we have real freedom to do as we wish? Would it be a limitation of God to say that he could not make humans with genuine free will?

In constructing your answer and reaching your own conclusions about the question, remember that you must not simply assert your conclusions, but rather give reasons for what you say. In doing so, you may choose to remind your reader about the difficulties of all language use about God and his nature.

Further essay questions

'Boethius gives a fully satisfactory account of God's timelessness and free will.' Discuss.

To what extent is it true to say God is outside time?

'Richard Swinburne's account of God and time is unconvincing.' Discuss.

Going further

There is, inevitably, a large literature on the attributes of God and his nature, some of which is outlined in Chapter 1. Richard Swinburne, *The Coherence of Theism* (second edition, Oxford, 2016), is arguably his finest work and not daunting to read. Chapter 12 is especially rich in ideas that develop points beyond those stated here.

Alvin Plantinga's work, *God, Freedom and Evil* (Eerdman's, 1977), though briefer, is a little more testing but repays careful study.

Questions About God, eds. Steven M. Cahn and David Shatz (Oxford University Press, 2002) raises many issues relevant to the present discussion, and there is relevant material in a series of brief essays which form Chapter 3 of *Philosophy of Religion: A Guide to the Subject*, ed. Brian Davies, (Cassell, 1998).

Other books discussed in this chapter are:

- Sidgwick, H. *The Methods of Ethics* (seventh edition, 1907).
- Stump. E. and Kretzmann, N. 'Eternity', *The Concept of God,* ed. Thomas V. Morris (Oxford University Press, 1987), pages 247–8.

Chapter 3

Religious language: apophatic and cataphatic use

> ## Chapter checklist
>
> The chapter begins with a general discussion of the difficulties of writing significantly about God in human language. It looks at some issues in scripture and mystical usage before examining the very important distinction between *cognitive* and *non-cognitive* uses of language. The chapter goes on to consider the *Via negativa,* the belief that nothing positive can be said about God. The ideas of Pseudo-Dionysius, John Scotus Eriugena and Moses Maimonides, among others, are explored, as well as the work of critics, notably W. R. Inge. *Via positiva,* the belief that we can speak positively about God, is then considered. Conclusions consider whether we need to move beyond narrow categories while paying attention to the insights of both.

1 Introduction

We have found ourselves discussing different arguments, whether about the existence of God or the nature of his attributes, in terms of the limits of human language. Any points we make are always limited by the fact that we seem to be stretching words and images to their limit, trying to capture the infinite with finite language, to express the inexpressible and to make sense of the language humans use. There is a continual grasping for meaning, not just by modern philosophers but by the mystics of the Middle Ages, such as St Teresa of Avila, St Hildegard of Bingen, Meister Eckhart and others. In the Bible, we find continual reference to the way in which God surpasses human understanding and the words in which we frame our understanding. In the words of the author of the Book of Job:

> *Can you draw out Leviathan with a fishhook,*
>
> *or press down its tongue with a cord?*

Job: 41:1

In describing God, terms such as 'King', 'Shepherd' and 'Lord' are used of God, only subsequently to be modified in some way to demonstrate that God is not a Lord or a King in the way of earthly kings – he is above all earthly rulers, a better shepherd.

Yet we are left trying not only to find words which enable us to describe the concept of God, but struggle no less when we try to grasp the reality we are trying to describe. Theological language has particular difficulties. Even if we are correct to describe God as 'eternal', we struggle to find any mental picture – to imagine what that reality might mean, especially when we are talking of things of which we – as humans – can have no possible experience.

Some – as we shall see – argue that religious sentences are simply meaningless, while others have different views of both meaning and justification.

Background

The three great ages of philosophy

It is occasionally crudely said that in philosophy there have been three great ages. From the Greeks until the end of the Middle Ages, the principal concern was metaphysical, as philosophers asked what existed (e.g. the Forms, God, and so on). After Descartes, philosophers moved rather to questions of what we can know (epistemological questions). The rise of interest in logic and language in the twentieth century led to a fascination not with what *is*, or what we can *know*, but rather with what we mean by the language we use. It was not that the older problems had been finally resolved but that attention turned elsewhere.

In some ways, this characterisation into three ages has some use when we are learning philosophy. However, it would be quite wrong to imagine that this concern with language was a great modern discovery.

Plato's 'theory of the Forms' is itself an attempt to discern the meaning of abstract terms such as 'truth', 'beauty' and 'goodness'. When Aristotle examines the nature of the good for humans, he looks in detail at how we use terms such as 'goodness' and what we mean by them. He examines at length the meaning of concepts such as knowledge, understanding and judgement. His logical writings are concerned throughout with the correct usage of language. Some of St Anselm's most significant work was concerned with the logical use of names, and other writers of the Middle Ages, including Peter Abelard, St Thomas Aquinas, William of Ockham, Duns Scotus and Hugh of St Victor wrote at length on issues of meaning. The greatest debate among philosophers in the Middle Ages concerned 'that most subtle question', which was whether universal terms such as 'brotherhood' or 'justice' should be considered names of real entities – as the philosophers known as 'realists' thought, or whether they were names only, not referring to real 'things', as the 'nominalists' argued. Such discussions go to the heart of what we truly mean by what we say.

In studying the issues of religious language we need to look quite closely at different theories around meaning and purpose of the language we use. If we think about it, we discover that we do not simply use language to make statements or to describe things. Sometimes we use words as commands, or to form questions, or to express an emotion when we swear or whoop with gladness. Sometimes the words we say perform an action, for instance when we say 'I promise...', when saying the words is the action of promising.

Ludwig Wittgenstein noted this variety in his *Philosophical Investigations* (§23), including making up stories, play acting, guessing riddles, telling jokes, asking, thanking and praying. He speaks of '*countless* different kinds of use' and argues that it is the work of the philosopher to contemplate those usages – 'Philosophy is a battle against the bewitchment of our intelligence by the means of language' (§109).

It is essential then, to investigate the wider uses of language as well as specific meaning in a religious context.

2 Cognitive and non-cognitive sentences

We tend to assume, when we first think about the issue, that the sentences we use either have, or appear to have, some connection with reality. Our first thoughts are that sentences *describe* the world. They are assumed to tell some sort of alleged truth. We think of the things we hear as either true or false.

But not all sentences have this character. Wittgenstein, as we saw, reminds us of the great variety of uses of language.

Suppose, while rushing to get washed (late for the school bus or an urgent appointment), you happen to stub your toe on the corner of the shower. You may exclaim, 'Ouch!', 'Oh, dearie, dearie me!' or 'Oh, golly!' or some such thing (let us not enquire too deeply into your personal habits). Now, if you are overheard by a parent, something that would not be said to you is: 'That's not true'. It is more likely that your mother will say, 'We don't use that language in this house', or, 'Wash your mouth out with soap and water', or even, concerned, 'Are you all right?' Questions of truth and falsity are irrelevant: something different is going on. Your mother may question the *appropriateness* of what you say – you might have frightened the cat, after all – but not the *truth* of what you have said. In the same way, if your mother says, 'Go and wash your mouth out with soap and water', you may reply, 'No, I won't!' but never, 'That's a lie!'

Philosophers pay much attention to two types of sentences: *cognitive* and *non-cognitive*. A **cognitive sentence** is one about which it is appropriate to ask whether it is true or false. A **non-cognitive sentence** is one about which it is not appropriate to ask that question.

Notice – and this is crucial – that a cognitive sentence is not necessarily a true one. For example, the sentence, 'Dublin is the capital of Australia' is cognitive and untrue. If you were to write that in your geography examination the examiner would – we hope – mark it as an error. It is appropriate to ask *whether it is true*, and that is why it is cognitive.

Orders, poetry, commands, curses, prayers, are all – probably – non-cognitive. When I say 'Read this chapter carefully!' it makes no sense to accuse me of being a liar. You may say that you will not, or ask 'Why should I?' – but those are different questions from whether I am truthful.

Sometimes, it is not obvious from the structure of a sentence whether it is cognitive or not. Look at the sentence: 'My grandfather won the Victoria Cross'. It seems cognitive, and it would be if I were claiming to tell you my family history. You might say that I am exaggerating. You might point out that while my grandfather was a soldier in the Boer War – which he was – there is no record of his winning the Victoria Cross. You would be able to research his record as a matter of fact, and suggest that I correct the errors I made when telling his story. In the context in which I was telling you about my grandfather, I was claiming to tell you facts.

Suppose instead that the sentence 'My grandfather won the Victoria Cross' appeared as the opening of my great new novel. In this – as yet unwritten – masterpiece, the story is told through a fictional narrator, whom I have invented. In those circumstances, it would make no sense to ask whether it happened to be true. The book is fiction, and does not pretend to be anything else.

We do not accuse students of literature of being natural liars or enthusiasts for lies. We may even know very honest people studying A Level English or who read novels for recreation. When we describe a novel as a good book, we do not mean it is straightforwardly true, even though we might think it has great insights and reveals much about some aspects of human nature. To ask whether *Pride and Prejudice* or *Harry Potter and the Philosopher's Stone* are true or false is to ask the wrong kind of question. When we watch or read *King Lear*, the greatest of Shakespeare's plays, we do not – or should not – concern ourselves with whether there was a king of England who behaved as Shakespeare describes. But there are great truths here about human nature and the disintegration of a fine and good man.

The question is whether religious sentences are cognitive or not. Many thinkers, such as Richard Dawkins, take the bulk of religious sentences as cognitive but obviously false. For Dawkins, the believer speaks sentences which are untrue. On the other hand, most believers would argue that to say 'God exists' is to utter a true statement, believed to be true, and something they offer the world as a correct account of reality. Believers generally think that when they talk of God's action in the world, it is about a state of affairs they think is true but which atheists believe to be false.

We should, nevertheless, recognise that even for a believer, not all religious sentences are cognitive. When people pray, many sentences are simply greetings – 'Hail Mary, full of grace!' – or have some other function, as in cries of 'Praise the Lord!' or 'Alleluia!'. There is much confusion and argument over how to read scripture. There are those who insist on the literal truth – the verbal inerrancy – of everything in the Bible. But large tracts of the Bible – Psalms, The Song of Solomon, Leviticus, Book of Revelation, for example – seem to have some other purpose. Much hangs on the intention of the original writers – to what extent were they intending to write material that was to be accepted as facts (which might be true or false), or were they trying to show 'truth' as a great writer like Shakespeare might wish to do? To take a simple example, it matters very much whether the first two chapters of Genesis, describing the creation of the world, were to be understood as intended cognitively or otherwise. Origen, in the third century, argued that Genesis made no sense as a statement of fact, but that it was to be understood figuratively as indicating certain mysteries.

In recent years, there have been arguments that suggest that *all* religious sentences are non-cognitive. It is evident that some are, as we have just seen, but there are many twists and turns when we attempt to investigate the **discourse of faith**.

Key question

Is it too simple to treat all religious language as cognitive?

Key term

Discourse of faith Language as used within the religious aspect of life. Its significance and meaning are internal to a given religion.

3 *Via negativa* (the apophatic way)

Given difficulties we have already mentioned of using language to capture a transcendent, non-material God, perhaps the most radical way forward would be to deny that we can say anything about God at all. We can say what God is not – not what he is. So, for example, we could say God is not a bicycle, not temporal, not mortal, not unjust, not ignorant, not in one place, and so on. What we cannot do is to say that God *is* merciful, just, timeless, all-knowing, and so on, because we cannot hope to understand what these terms mean when applied to God. We use them only with our limited *human* understanding as *human* words. Therefore, they cannot be used with any significant meaning. This view seems to concur with a deep religious instinct. In Judaism, the very name of God is not fully articulated, and in Islam God is never portrayed visually.

In the second half of the fourteenth century, an unknown English writer, possibly a member of the Carthusians, a contemplative and strict order of monks, produced *The Cloud of Unknowing*, one of the finest texts in the long history of Christian mysticism. The unknown author speaks of the darkness of our position:

Key quote

The first time when you seek God, you find only a darkness; and as it were a cloud of unknowing ... This darkness and this cloud is, whatever you do, between you and your God, and ... you may [not] see Him clearly by the light of understanding in your reason .... For if ever you shall feel Him or see Him... it is right always to be in this cloud in this darkness.

Anon, *The Cloud of Unknowing*, Chapter Three

When we consider the mystical tradition more widely, we find the same awareness of the ineffable (inexpressible) nature of God. This was mentioned – as we saw in Year 1 – as one of the aspects of genuine mystical experience in William James' *The Varieties of Religious Experience*.

We need to consider, however limited our theological language when discussing God, whether we can ever say more than just negatives.

The *apophatic* way of dealing with theology is often found in Eastern Christian thought, with elements appearing in the work of both Origen (185–254) and Clement of Alexandria (d. *c*.215). The same theme is very strong in the neo-Platonists, especially Proclus (410–485). In late Arianism, Eunomius (d. *c*.394) treated God as directly knowable, but Basil the Great (330–379) and Gregory of Nyssa (*c*.335–*c*.395) pointed to the human inability to know the essence of God. They argue that if we cannot know the mind and essence of an ant, with his (presumably) limited mind and language skills (ants have very tiny brains), we can never begin to understand God. According to Evagrius Ponticus (345–399), the highest understanding is 'pure prayer' – a union with God without words or images, a bare awareness of something beyond anything created. This we find echoed in *The Cloud of Unknowing* and the other mystical writers mentioned here.

Early in the sixth century, Pseudo-Dionysius (Dionysius the Areopagite, *fl*.500) made a distinction between 'cataphatic' (*via positiva*) and 'apophatic ' theology (*via negativa*). The *via positiva* does attempt to use theological language to describe God, using the divine names of scripture like 'The Good', 'Light of the World', 'Life' and so on. These do give us real knowledge of God but, for followers of the *via negativa*, it is provisional knowledge, for God lies far beyond those names. If God is light, he is far beyond that feeble attempt to capture him. The *via negativa*, in contrast, aims to move beyond language altogether to 'the divine darkness' which lies beyond any concept:

See Year 1, page 97.

Key terms

Via positiva (the cataphatic way) The claim that we are able to make certain positive statements about God.

Via negativa (the apophatic way) An approach to religious language which claims that nothing positive can be said about God. We can state only what he is not.

45

Key person

Pseudo-Dionysus (Dionysus the Areopagite) (*fl.*500): anonymous author, probably Syrian, Christian theologian and philosopher. Author of philosophical works known collectively as *Corpus Areopagiticum* or *Corpus Dionysiacum*, incorporating a neoplatonic approach to questions of faith.

Key person

Moses Maimonides (Moshe ben Maimon) (1135–1204): Jewish philosopher, rabbi and physician, born in Cordoba, Spain but moved to Morocco, then the Holy Land and Egypt. Much admired by Aquinas. His *Guide for the Perplexed* remains his best-known work.

Key quote

... in a manner which goes beyond speech and knowledge, we embrace those truths which, in the same way, move beyond them, into a union with God which goes beyond our ability and our use of discursive or intuitive reason. Therefore, we must not dare to speak, or to form any conception of the hidden ... Godhead, beyond those things revealed to us by Holy Scripture.

Pseudo-Dionysius, *On the Divine Names*, Chapter 1:1

This view was strongest in the Eastern Church, but it was found also in Western Christianity, notably in the work of John Scotus Eriugena (*c.*810–*c.*877). He was an Irish monk (the *Scotus* in his name identifies him as Irish), and an expert on Greek language. Apart from his own important philosophical works, which included important developments of the idea of free will, he translated significant parts of the works of the Pseudo-Dionysius, and the influence can be seen strongly in his own treatment of God.

Key person

John Scotus Eriugena (*c.*815–*c.*877): Irish theologian and scholar, who moved to France in *c.*845. He was rumoured to have moved to England where he was murdered by his students stabbing him with their styluses, but this is unlikely. Best known for his translations and commentaries on the work of the Pseudo-Dionysius.

In a sermon, he would argue:

Key quote

God is beyond all meaning and intelligence, and he alone possesses immortality. His light is called darkness because of its excellence, as no creature can comprehend either what or how it is.

John Scotus Eriugena, Homily on the Prologue to the Gospel of St. John, § XIII

The *via negativa* was adopted by the medieval Jewish philosopher, Moses Maimonides (1135–1204). Moses Maimonides (strictly, Moshe ben Maimon) is considered one of the major figures in Jewish thought.

Key term

Anthropomorphise To treat something inappropriately as human.

Maimonides, in both his *Guide for the Perplexed* and his *Commentary on the Mishnah*, a study of the Jewish Scriptures, warns continually of the dangers of **anthropomorphising** God. Though the Scriptures draw – inevitably – on human language, when they speak of 'the mouth of God', 'God's right hand' and so on, we must not think of God in the human terms which these phrases imply. Maimonides warns against literal interpretation of such phrases. In the first part of *Guide for the Perplexed*, he considers the use of various terms in Scripture. He observes that because of who we are, we make comparisons with God:

Because man's distinction lies in having something which no other earthly creature possesses, intellectual perception .... This perception has been compared – though only apparently, not as a matter of truth – to the Divine perception, which requires no bodily organ. For this reason – because of the Divine intellect which man has been given – he is said to be in the image and likeness of the Almighty. But we should not have the idea that the Supreme Being is corporeal, having a material body.

Moses Maimonides, *Guide for the Perplexed*, 1:1

Key question

Can we talk in wholly 'negative' terms without implying something 'positive'?

Key person

W. R. Inge (1860–1954): influential Anglican theologian. Lady Margaret's Professor of Divinity, Cambridge (1907–11), Dean of St Paul's Cathedral (1911–34), prolific author and newspaper columnist. Supported eugenics and nudism. Often described as 'the Gloomy Dean'.

See Year 1, pages 116, 250–1.

Key person

Pierre Teilhard de Chardin (1881–1955): French Jesuit and palaentologist, discoverer of Peking Man. He attempted to develop a new approach to Christian thought, embracing the significance of an evolutionary universe. His posthumous works, especially *The Phenomenon of Man* (1955), have deeply influenced modern theology, especially in the Roman Catholic Church.

St Thomas Aquinas had a deep knowledge of Maimonides' work, frequently citing his sayings and ideas. However, Aquinas was not an exponent of the *via negativa* but was very sympathetic to its proponents and the significance of their insights. To him, the essence of God was infinitely far beyond human understanding or human language. But he did not draw the inference that therefore nothing at all could be done about it. For Aquinas, the *via negativa* was a prelude to understanding God. He took the view that to say God is *not* ignorant or *not* limited by time surely tells us *something* about God even if we cannot know what that something may be. Aquinas' views are explored further in Chapter 4.

(a) Criticisms of *via negativa*

Critics of *via negativa* have argued that any understanding that can be gleaned through this approach is actually negligible (for example, to say that God is not a bicycle gives us no deep insight into the nature of God), though proponents would argue that even to make a negative statement implies some awareness of what is being denied.

A few Christian thinkers have been worried about some aspects of the apophatic way. W. R. Inge, famous for his long service as Dean of St Paul's Cathedral, was concerned that to deny God his descriptions was to lead to an 'annihilation' of both God and humanity. If we strip God of his descriptions, simply because our descriptions are limited and based on finite, human experience, we are in danger of losing the essential link between God and the world. Christian orthodoxy insists on God's involvement in the world, in a God who so loved the world that he gave his only son for its sake. If we can say nothing about God, as our thoughts are formed in words, there is – critics say – a danger not simply that we cannot think significantly about God, but that we will not think about him at all. After all, humans have framed their (inadequate) descriptions in the words they have.

The opposition to Gnostic heresies such as Manichaeanism rested precisely on the insistence that matter comes from God and is not, in any sense, a denial of God.

Some Christian thinkers, notably G. K. Chesterton (1874–1936) and Pierre Teilhard de Chardin (1881–1955), who spoke of the 'divinisation of matter', believed that finding God through our material existence was all part of his divine plan of salvation. It follows then, for Teilhard, that if we can talk significantly about God's relationship with material things, then we are inevitably saying something positive, however limited, about him. For example, it makes sense to say that someone knows the love of God through the love she experiences in her marriage. When we are loved by someone, it is actually very mysterious: human love is never fully understood or grasped. 'Why of all the people did she choose to love me?' is a question to which neither person in a marriage can give a full answer but, as with talking about God, that we cannot properly answer it does not mean either that nothing can be said or that nothing is expressed.

Perhaps a more balanced approach would be to argue that we need both *via negativa* and *via positiva*. The former stands as a constant reminder not to anthropomorphise God; the latter, perhaps, tells us that if we are to say anything at all, that utterance needs some content, however tentative, to say anything worthwhile.

4 *Via positiva* (the cataphatic way)

As will be fairly obvious, those who endorse the *via positiva* believe that it is possible to say something positive about God. Adherents include St Thomas Aquinas and others, including St Augustine and St Anselm.

It should be noticed at once that it does not follow that we are therefore able to be precise in our language about God. What is claimed is that even though what we say is limited, it might be positively indicative. If we are children of God, made in some way by him, then it is possible to have some understanding. An omnipotent God could, we may assume, make creatures capable of some understanding, within the limits of our brains. If we are made to worship God, and the customary mode of human expression is in speech, then it would seem possible to say something more significant than humming aimlessly.

But even if this is so, there is, in the cataphatic way, perhaps a need to retain the insights of the supporters of the apophatic way as a continual reminder of the limits of what may be done.

5 Reconciling *via positiva* and *via negativa*

There is, in the Eastern Churches, a tradition of reconciling cataphatic and apophatic approaches. For the Eastern Orthodox, the aim of human life is *theosis*, which means achieving 'likeness and union with God'. In this tradition, mystical contemplation helps worshippers move towards a greater understanding of God (revelation). In this way, the positive way of speaking about God – with all its limits – becomes possible, but it has to be worked towards.

Rowan Williams is a theologian who has paid much attention to Eastern Orthodox as well as the Western tradition. It is in the Orthodox Churches that the apophatic way has been richly discussed.

In an important essay on the work of Vladimir Lossky (1903–58), the Orthodox theologian, Williams comments:

> *In what way ... is apophasis not the same as the mystical ascent?... It lies ... in the simple recognition that apophasis can never be more than the verbal symbol of the encounter with God. We do not, after all encounter God primarily through language or through the contemplation of words allegedly referring to him, and it makes little difference to the experience of encounter*

whether such words are prefaced with – as it were – a plus or minus sign. In any Christian theology which is serious about the transcendence *of God, there is bound to be present a sense of 'check', of limitation ....*

Rowan Williams, 'Lossky, Via Negativa and The Foundations of Theology', *Wrestling with Angels: Conversations in Modern Theology*, ed. Mike Higton, 2007, page 2

The point made here is that discussion about God, and the attempt to describe him, is not the beginning of faith but rather follows from an original encounter. We meet God, and then, with our limited language, try to express the mystery we encounter. Whether we see our language apophatically or cataphatically, it is always true that it is a mere human attempt to capture something that extends beyond our experience and language, which is always based on that human experience. This is true for both styles of language, and each is to be understood in terms of its limitation.

6 Conclusions

The apophatic way represents an important strand within the thought not only of Christianity but also in all the great religions of the world. Eastern meditative practices strive to go beyond the limitations of human understanding, and the *via negativa* reminds us continually of the impossibility of capturing the divine in our terms. But we need to consider whether it leaves us too little to make sense of what people believe in. Even if the apophatic way falls a little short of what we can achieve with language, it remains a valuable reminder that when we speak of God, perhaps when we think we describe his attributes, we are not truly describing him in himself, but rather providing ourselves with a means of understanding in our terms. It reminds us also that, even if we believe we can speak positively about God, as in the cataphatic way, we must always do so in consciousness of the limits of what we are saying, and never assume that because we have words to describe God, we fully understand the significance of those words.

Study advice

This area is one that requires careful definition as well as appropriate examples. This is why several writers, especially in the apophatic tradition, are introduced. In preparing for the examination, it is helpful to remember that as none of the authors here is directly named on the specification in relation to the *via negativa*, no question can be asked specifically on them. It is helpful, while knowing the names of each mentioned, to pick out one or two for more detailed study. If you are able to do this, then you will be able to write more specifically in answer to any question on the apophatic way, giving clear examples.

When writing, it is important to be clear about just why any use of language is at best limited when describing God. It would be entirely legitimate to refer back to some of the concepts mentioned when discussing problems of attributes such as omnipotence or omniscience.

Summary diagram: Religious language: apophatic and cataphatic use

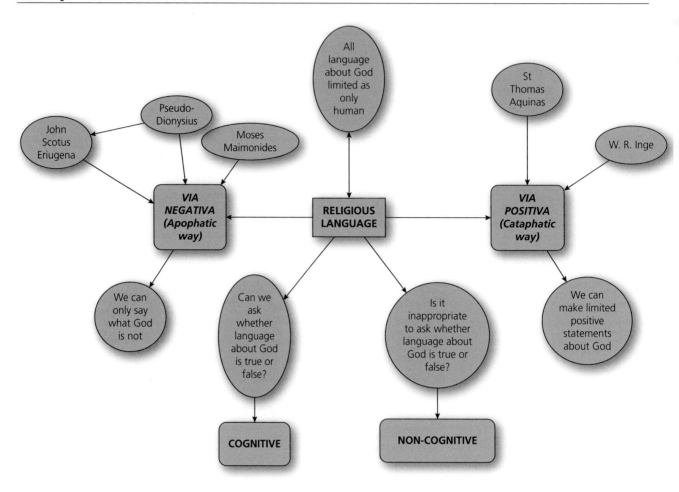

Revision advice

By the end of this chapter you should be able to explain thoughtfully the issues involved in the use of human language about the divine. Reflect on any theories mentioned here – do not just learn them, but think about whether, for example, we could ever say anything of any use about God if all our descriptions were negative. Think also about what positives might be implied by speaking only in negatives. Think through examples for yourself – doing so will give a freshness and originality to your writing.

Can you give brief definitions of:
- cognitive sentences
- non-cognitive sentences
- *via negativa*
- *via positiva*
- *theosis*?

Can you explain:
- the difference between cognitive and non-cognitive uses of language
- why it is sometimes difficult to be certain whether a sentence is cognitive or not
- the difficulties of describing God in human language
- why some thinkers believe that we can only use apophatic language about God?

Can you give arguments for and against:
- the idea that we cannot talk significantly about God
- the use of *via negativa* when talking about God
- the claim that if God created the world, his creatures can have some idea about him
- the claim that Scripture is cognitive?

Sample question and guidance

> Assess the belief that we can say nothing positive about God.

This question could be a trap for the unwary. There is an ambiguity about the word 'positive' and someone might read the question in a colloquial way, as 'we can say nothing *nice* about God'. However, you are expected to be familiar with the specification, and you are expected to understand the question in terms of the *via positiva* and *via negativa*. In this context, 'positive' has a precise meaning. The question points to your understanding of ideas raised in this chapter.

It might be helpful to begin your essay by discussing the difficulties of bridging the differences between God and humankind. It would be valuable to say something about how human language is based on human experience. If you could think of examples of this, your essay would be given greater freshness. You might then go on to consider the claims of supporters of *via negativa* – with some examples of specific philosophers or theologians – thinking about whether these claims are correct or limited in some way.

In wording your essay, notice that the question is worded negatively. Refer back to the wording in drawing your conclusions. You might think that something positive could be said about God, in which case you need to say what might be significantly said, being careful to give at least one example – preferably more – to justify your point.

Remember that this is an essay title which can tempt the unwary into broad generalisation, with no supporting examples. It is good practice – and good philosophy – to support your points with clear instances of how they apply in practice.

Further essay questions

> 'We can never begin to describe God.' Discuss.

> To what extent is it true to say that the use of *via negativa* makes God too remote from his creation?

> 'All religious language is non-cognitive.' Discuss.

Going further

There is a considerable literature on religious language, some of which is touched on in this chapter. Most good introductions to philosophy or religion will incorporate at least one section to the issue. James Ross provides an interesting chapter in *Philosophy of Religion: A Guide to the Subject,* ed. Brian Davies (Cassell, 1998), and John Hick's treatment in *Philosophy of Religion* (fourth edition, Pearson, 1989) is concise and insightful.

Jeff Astley, *Exploring God Talk: Using Language in Religion* (Darton, Longman and Todd, 2004) is brief and readable as an introductory text.

For more on the apophatic way in medieval mysticism, perhaps the best work is Denys Turner, *The Darkness of God: Negativity in Christian Mysticism* (Cambridge University Press, 1998).

An outstanding recent study of religious language, though not quick reading, is Rowan Williams, *The Edge of Words: God and the Habits of Language* (Bloomsbury Continuum, 2014), based on his Gifford Lectures.

Other books discussed in this chapter are:

- Williams, R. 'Lossky, *Via Negativa* and The Foundations of Theology', *Wrestling with Angels: Conversations in Modern Theology*, ed. Mike Higton (SCM, 2007).
- Wittgenstein, L. *Philosophical Investigations* (Oxford University Press, 1958).

Chapter 4

Religious language: analogy and symbol

Chapter checklist

The chapter begins with a reminder of the insights of supporters of the *via negativa*. It then moves on to look at Aristotle's use of analogical thinking before considering Aquinas' treatment of the same issue. A distinction is made between analogical and univocal and equivocal usages, and the two types of analogical thinking, by attribution and proportion, are also considered. A modern version of analogy, by Ian Ramsey, is also explained. There is an examination of Paul Tillich's symbolic use of language, exploring the difference between a sign and a symbol, with some common misunderstandings identified. A non-cognitive use of symbolic language is also examined, in contrast to Tillich.

1 Introduction

When considering how language can be used to describe God, adherents of the cataphatic way have a hurdle to leap. If they wish to say anything positive at all, they need to do so in a way that pays attention to the insights of supporters of the apophatic way, such as Pseudo-Dionysius or John Scotus Eriugena, but that also enables something positive to be said, something which, if not a perfect description, will nevertheless at least be indicative of God's nature.

It is important to religious believers to remain continually aware of the dangers of idolatry, that is, making God in our image and likeness. This can happen easily if we take descriptions about God in their literal, human context. To think of God as a bigger, better version of human beings would be to make him just like ourselves – anthropomorphism – someone who could be manipulated and managed. If we say the right prayers, perhaps sacrifice the right goats, then we can bend God to our own desires, just as we might persuade our parents to let us stay out a bit later, 'if only we ask nicely'. But to look at faith in this way is to reduce it.

Not recognising that language about God cannot be seen as having its ordinary, human use is a problem not only within the discourse of faith communities but also to its opponents. Richard Dawkins, for example, who treats discussion about God as the use of failed scientific hypotheses, tends to take the ideas he attacks according to their normal, everyday meaning – with the result that many believers do not recognise the ideas about God that Dawkins uses as his premise.

But the question remains whether there is a way to talk about God, which is positive, yet avoids the traps of anthropomorphism and failing to do justice to the mystery of God. Perhaps the most well-known approach is that of **analogy**, most famously developed by St Thomas Aquinas.

2 Analogy

(a) Aristotle on analogy

Aristotle developed interesting arguments based on the theory of likeness (*homoites*).

Detailed discussion may be found in *Topics* I, 17 and 18 and later in VIII, 1. Aristotle's idea is that if two things share some sort of attribute, then what will be true of the one should be true of the other. He says:

> We should look at things which belong to the same genus to see whether any identical attributes belong to them all. For example, if we take a man, a horse and a dog, then it would follow that where they have an identical attribute, to that extent they are alike.

Topics, I, 17 108a13

We might, for example, see that all three have hearts that beat, that hearts eventually cease their action, and be able to argue that if horses and dogs die because of the cessation of their hearts, so too will man.

A question Aristotle leaves unanswered is precisely how much we may assume when making an analogy. At what point does an analogy cease to hold? The danger is that we may assume similarities that are not there. We might note that the duck-billed platypus, like the duck, lays eggs and has a bill, and deduce that they are similar creatures, both birds – and so draw completely the wrong conclusion. Apparent similarity should not lead us to think that two things are alike in every relevant respect, and the degree of likeness may vary in important ways.

From Aristotle's writings, we may deduce four ways of making judgements about analogical arguments.

1   The strength of any analogy depends on the number of similarities in the two things being compared.
2   Similarity exists only in identical relations and properties.
3   Good analogies are based on underlying common causes or some general principle.
4   Good analogical arguments do not need to assume acquaintance with the underlying generalisation.

These four points can be further expanded as we use them to consider the validity of the best-known use of analogical thinking in religious language.

(b) St Thomas Aquinas on analogy

St Thomas Aquinas is well known for his Doctrine of Analogy, which tries to deal with the problems of saying anything about God. (This theory is occasionally, but not always helpfully, referred to as the Doctrine of Proper Analogy, as on the specification. There is a technical discussion in *De Veritate*, by Aquinas, of those analogies considered 'proper', but the term is not used in *Summa Theologica*, and for present purposes may be ignored as well beyond the scope of A Level.) In doing so, he is addressing the same issues that created such problems for thinkers like Pseudo-Dionysius, Eriugena and Maimonides. If I were asked to describe my best friend, whom I have known for years, the words I use do not capture her fully. This is partly because there is a convention about the words. If I describe her hair as 'brown', I am aware that 'brown' covers a multitude of shades. If I describe her as having 'short brown hair', then the most I am communicating is *some idea* of what she looks like, and not the whole reality I picture in my mind when I think of her. The phrase will create a picture in your mind, but the picture will not be the same as the one I have, which is based on direct acquaintance. How then can I describe God, whom I cannot begin to comprehend fully, in terms that will make some sort of accurate sense to you?

As we saw in Chapter 3, supporters of the apophatic way argue that language is wholly inadequate to describe God. Aquinas attempts to hold together two points: to accept that human language is indeed inadequate to express the divine, but also that we do not have to assume that it is saying nothing.

St Thomas Aquinas recognises these points throughout his work. In *Summa Theologica* he addresses the issues early in the text. In Part I, Question 12, he devotes 13 articles to our knowledge of God, continually stressing the limitations of our understanding. In Question 13, he deals with the Divine Names, again reminding us of the limitations of our knowledge while developing the idea of description by analogy. In article 12, he concludes:

Key quote

God, however, considered in Himself, is wholly one and simple, but our intellect knows Him by different conceptions because it cannot see Him as He is in Himself. Nevertheless, although our mind understands Him under different conceptions, it knows [intellectually] that one and the same simple object corresponds to its conceptions.

S.T. I, Q.13, a.12c.

Aquinas' argument is that we know God to be one, not least through revelation, and we can say that. We also have the positive awareness that we cannot think of that oneness, conceiving it only in human terms. To know so precisely the limits of our knowledge, and to be able to express that limitation, is itself to be able to say something about God. After all, to describe God as unknowable is to acknowledge our lack of knowledge – but also to give a positive description.

Aquinas argued that there are three types of significant language:

- univocal
- equivocal
- analogical.

Univocal language is when a word or phrase is used in the same way in two different sentences. To say: 'My cat is tabby', 'Your cat is black' is to use the word 'cat' in the same way in two sentences – in each case referring to a domestic feline, commonly referred to as a 'moggy'. The

Key term

Univocal language Words used with identical meaning in different sentences.

Key term

Equivocal language The same word used with entirely different meanings in different sentences. A term like 'bat' may have many different, unconnected meanings.

Key terms

Analogy of attribution We can say something about an author or maker from the product he has created.

Analogy of proportion From a lesser object we can say that something else, such as God, has proportionately more of the same quality.

meaning is the same. Religious language is obviously not like that – we do not use words about God in the way we use them about ourselves. If we did so, we would fall into the trap of anthropomorphising him.

On the other hand, we are not using **equivocal language**. Take the sentences: 'There is a bat in the cave', 'I have bought a new bat for cricket'. The term 'bat' means something totally different in each sentence, and although the terms are the same, they are to be understood wholly differently. The first use describes a rather messy but protected creature, the second a vital piece of sporting equipment. The two have nothing in common beyond the accident of attracting – in English, anyway – the same name. In German, there would be no confusion between *die Fledermaus* and *der Schläger*.

For Aquinas, religious language is not equivocal. If any sentence about God had a wholly different meaning from any other usage, then we would not have religious language that could be understood, but silence.

However, he argues, that when we speak religiously, we do mean *something* if we say, 'God is Love' or 'God is perfectly just'. There is something to be said because there is enough in human behaviour (the love people have for each other, for example) to transfer some of the meaning to God without either emptying the human concept entirely or saying that to speak of God as loving has no meaning.

Aquinas is associated with two types of analogy: **attribution** and **proportion**. There is a question about whether this division was made by Aquinas himself, or was rather an understanding by a later scholar, Thomas Cajetan (1469–1534) in his *De nominum analogia*, but the distinction is commonly attributed to Aquinas himself and plays a substantial role in discussions of Thomist theory.

The first, *attribution,* is based on the Christian belief that God is creator of the universe and everything ultimately comes from him, that creation is not accidental, but based on God's will – it was an intended and deliberate, conscious action. If the world is the product of God as a thinking being, then there is something common between that which is made and the maker – thus apparently satisfying the third of Aristotle's criteria for good use of analogy. How much is common may be disputed, but there is a shared element at least.

From a work of art, even if we know nothing of the artist, we can deduce *something* about him or her from the painting – he has used broad brush-strokes, was better at painting nature than faces, liked bright colours, etc. But the artist is nothing like the work of art, even though we can say limited things about him from the picture. Picasso did not look just like his paintings, any more than we can tell how Beethoven spoke from the sound of his music.

Aquinas gives a different and rather graphic example. From the appearance of a bull's urine, an expert can tell whether the bull is healthy – but it does not follow that the bull is just like a puddle of his urine. Nevertheless, the inference of health is justifiable. If the earth is God's handiwork, then we can *attribute* certain characteristics to him. If there is beauty in nature, then too there is reason to argue that God is in a sense truly beautiful.

Analogy of *proportion* is based on the notion that if something is true of a given person, then it is possible to be more true of another. If you are good, but your friend better at netball, then we can say that she is twice or three times better than you are. Sometimes we can be even more specific; for example, if we compare the number of goals you and your friend score, I may be able to say that she scores twice as many as you do. The problem, of course, is that attribution of proportion doesn't apply to God. If you are just, we can say that God is proportionately more just than you are. God is infinitely more just than you are: we cannot conceive of the extent of that justice, nor can we calculate it as a strict proportion.

Baron von Hügel (1852–1925) tried to clarify the point:

Key quote

The source and object of religion, if religion be true and its object ... real, *cannot*, indeed, *by any possibility, be as clear to me even as I am to my dog.* ... in the case of religion ... we apprehend and affirm realities indefinitely superior in quality and amount of reality to ourselves, and which, nevertheless (or rather, just because of this), anticipate, penetrate, and sustain us with a quite unpicturable intimacy. The obscurity of my life to my dog must ... be greatly exceeded by the obscurity of the life of God to me. Indeed the obscurity of plant life – so obscure for my mind, because so indefinitely inferior and poorer than is my human life – must be greatly exceeded by the dimness, for my human life, of God – of His reality and life, so different and superior, so unspeakably more rich and alive, than is, or can ever be, my own life and reality.

Friedrich von Hügel, *Essays and Addresses on the Philosophy of Religion*, First Series, 1921, pages 102–3

Key person

Baron (Friedrich) von Hügel (1852–1925): Austrian Catholic layman, largely self-taught, who moved to England in 1867, remaining for the rest of his life. Prolific and influential author on Christian themes. Although he had never been to university nor held an academic appointment, he was due to give the Gifford Lectures in the year of his death.

Florrie, the Wilkinson cat

Thinking about von Hügel's example, we recognise some problems. Consider the picture to the left. This is a picture of Florrie, the Wilkinson cat, taken in what I interpret as pleading or winsome mode. But when I attribute certain meanings to her poses, I neither know how her mentality works (though I have a suspicion that she may be bent on world domination) nor have any conception of how such thoughts as she might have are framed in her own terms of reference. Yet I feel just about confident enough to give some interpretation to her glance, and either feeding her or inviting her onto my knee seem appropriate responses, which let me assume I am using language reasonably appropriately when I describe what she might mean by her behaviour.

Key question

Is it possible for analogical use of language to give us precise knowledge about God?

When we speak of God, according to Aquinas, we are saying that God's love, or whatever quality it is, is something like that in humans. There is enough in common that permits us to use the term.

The purpose of the Doctrine of Analogy is not to tell us precisely what the terms we are using about God actually *mean*, because we cannot know. But it does permit us to say *something* positive, restricted though that something must be. The understanding will always be very limited. This is why Aquinas is so insistent on the need for such careful awareness of what we are doing when we talk of God: he insists on the ultimate incomprehensibility of God. We may conclude that what analogy does is to tell us not what the words *mean* but what we are *doing* when we are talking about God: we are finding a way to frame something in our terms, to give us a measure of understanding.

John MacQuarrie (1919–2007), summarises these points well:

Key quote

> ... the way of analogy is the one that has the most positive content. It is not, of course, a literal or direct way of talking about God, and yet it is a way that seems to give us assurance that our talk is not just empty, and that it does somehow impinge upon God and give us some insight into the mystery of Being. Analogy makes possible that language of scripture and liturgy that is at the heart of the Christian religion. ... Unless we can say that it is meaningful, I think honest people would want to get rid of the whole business.
>
> John MacQuarrie, *God-Talk*, 1967, page 214

We should notice that MacQuarrie is very conscious of the need not to claim more for analogy than that it can give us some very dim sense of the positive things that might be made about God. Nothing more can be promised.

(i) Vincent Brümmer on the problems of analogy

However, there are significant issues about suggesting that we can usefully say how we use terms about God without knowing precisely what they mean. Vincent Brümmer develops an argument against the analogy of proportion:

> ... we do not know the nature of God in himself, and we want to define his manner of being wise precisely in terms of his nature. God's nature is not accessible to us, nor therefore is the way in which he is wise. It follows that in using the analogy of proportionality we are saying no more than that God is not wise in the same way as a human person is wise. But then we are still unable to say positively in what sense God is in fact wise .... The analogy of proportionality thus takes us no further than a negative theology.
>
> Vincent Brümmer, *Speaking of a Personal God: An Essay in Philosophical Theology*, 1992, page 46

Key person

Vincent Brümmer (b. 1932): South African-born philosopher of religion and theologian, Professor of Philosophy of Religion, University of Utrecht (1967–97).

Disclosure situation Ian Ramsey's term for an event which reveals something beyond the bare facts of the case.

Qualified model Ian Ramsey's term for a use of human language to 'model' something else. To describe God as First Cause uses 'cause' as a model to give some understanding that everything comes from God, but 'first' qualifies or conditions the term, showing that this is not 'cause' in the normal sense: God as 'cause' is very different from 'cause' as we know it in this world.

Ian Ramsey (1915–72): Anglican philosopher of religion and bishop. Nolloth Professor of the Philosophy of the Christian Religion (1951–66), Bishop of Durham (1966–72). In 1985, the Ian Ramsey Centre at Oxford was created to explore the relationships between religious faith, science and medicine.

See Year 1, pages 67–9.

Brümmer's point is that analogy gives the appearance of saying something significant about God, but that we remain as ignorant as we were before we began our search for something positive to say.

For Brümmer, the case is even worse with attribution, as we have no ability to determine what we might attribute to God if he is unknown to us:

> As creator and cause of everything, he [God] is the source of all the characteristics of his creatures. The analogy of attribution seems to leave us free to call God 'warm', 'multi-coloured' and 'heavy', because he is the source of all warm, multi-coloured and heavy objects! We could add the limitation: not all terms are to be applied to God in this way; only the terms which apply to his nature. But then we would have to know God's nature, and we have already said that we do not know God's nature.

Ibid., page 47

Brümmer is arguing here that when we attempt to use analogy of proportion, we are making assumptions, which we are not entitled to make, as we lack the necessary knowledge to speak with any authority.

(c) Ian Ramsey on analogy

Ian Ramsey, who was Bishop of Durham and author of *Religious Language* (1957) speculated that there must be something in language that we might use to make sense of God. He developed two key notions – the **disclosure situation** and **qualified model**. These are very useful tools in thinking about analogy – Ramsey's approach is ultimately an analogical one.

A disclosure situation happens when we somehow see through and beyond the reality in front of us. To use a favourite example of Ramsey's, a teacher draws and redraws a regular polygon, in which each side is of equal length. He draws it with four sides, then with six, and so on. As he redraws it, we see it with additional sides – sixteen, fifty sides and so on. At some point we see it suddenly *as* a circle, even though close examination would show it to be made up of many tiny straight lines. We would see beyond the lines on the board to the circle that lies beyond its literal shape, a phenomenon which Ramsey describes as a disclosure situation. A similar phenomenon – a *moving beyond* the physicality of this world – can be said to happen when we use religious language.

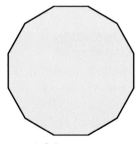

A disclosure situation: At what point does a polygon become a circle?

The second idea that Ramsey developed was the *qualified model*, a term used to explain the way human language is used to 'model' something else. Ramsey uses the religious 'first cause argument' to illustrate this.

Suppose we say that 'God is the first cause'. Those familiar with this concept will understand that this is a model to make sense of how God created the universe.

We use models in our technology. The aircraft designer builds a scale model of the aircraft he has designed and tests it in a wind-tunnel. From the way the model behaves, he makes assumptions about how the full-sized aircraft might behave if built. The model is therefore a means for making a judgement about the greater reality, because it is an analogy of it.

This example raises some interesting questions. However the model works in the wind-tunnel, even with the best modern computer simulations and programs, any aircraft manufacturer will tell you that how a plane behaves in reality will only be known for sure after the full aircraft is test-flown. The best wind-tunnel and the best-made model are not exactly the same as a real aircraft in the real atmosphere. (Film-makers sometimes have this problem when they attempt to depict a sea-battle using models in a small pool. Tiny waves just do not behave like great waves at sea, and the models, as a result, look just like the models they are.)

So, when we say 'God is the first cause', God would not be a cause in any sense that we might understand the term from physics or chemistry: the 'cause' is simply *something like* 'cause' in the normal sense, while the use of 'first' brings home the very special use of 'cause' – it *qualifies* the notion to show both that it is a model and that the term is being used in a very special sense (in this case, we take it to understand that as the 'first cause', God plays a unique role in the creation of our universe). In Ramsey's terminology, *'first'* is the qualifier – the term that *conditions* the idea of the model.

It is not clear that we are being offered here anything which is not part of Aquinas' notion of analogy. The value of Ramsey lies in his explanation and clarification of an old idea – it is not obviously a new one.

(d) Alternative views of analogy

(i) Barth's view

Karl Barth argues that Ramsey's approach, and indeed, analogy in general, is mistaken because we cannot approach God by means of language based on our existing experience: we need revelation.

> **Key quote**
>
> What we can represent to ourselves lies in the sphere of our own existence, and of existence generally, as distinct from [that of] God. If we do know about God as Creator, it is neither wholly nor partially because we have a prior knowledge of something that resembles creation. It is only because it has been given to us by God's revelation to know him....
>
> Karl Barth, *Church Dogmatics*, 'The Doctrine of God', Vol II/I, pages 76–7

If Barth is right, analogy fails, but so too does any other attempt to give meaning to talk about God. If God's revelations, on which Barth relies, can be expressed, then surely these are expressed in human theological language as it is all we can understand. If we cannot

Key question

Is Karl Barth correct to argue that as our existence is 'distinct from [that of] God' that he can only be known by direct revelation?

understand God in our language, then it may be asked how God can communicate with his creatures, as, surely, he would need our language to express himself to us. The Book of Genesis shows God as Creator of all, the cause of all that there is. If we capture that idea by calling God the First Cause, then there is something that phrase tells us. This, however, takes us back full circle to what the words mean in human language. If they are not literal, then what are they, and how can we interpret them?

Key person

Karl Barth (1886–1968): Swiss Reformed theologian, considered by many the most important Protestant theologian of the twentieth century. He was involved with the Confessing Church during the Nazi years in Germany. His 13-volume *Church Dogmatics* is considered a major work in Christian thought. Gifford Lecturer (1936–38).

(ii) Ferré's view

A more fruitful way of approaching analogy is offered by Frederick Ferré, who argues that the value of analogy is that it provides us with a rule for enabling us to use theological language about God. He argues that we should not concentrate on how analogies might be thought to define transcendental ideas such as the idea of God as the 'first cause', as we do not know the nature of God. Instead, we should concentrate on how words need to be used carefully. The meaning has its source in a God beyond our understanding, but we are allowed to use the terms as long as we do so in the right context:

Key person

Frederick Ferré (1933–2013): American metaphysician and philosopher of religion. Based at the University of Georgia, he maintained the significance and meaningfulness of Christian use of language on the grounds that it was consistent, coherent, applicable and adequate.

> *If we insist on the use of the 'material mode' of speech, requiring analogy to provide us with information about the real properties of supernatural entities, little can be salvaged. But if we allow ourselves to examine the logic of analogy as* one means of providing criteria for the disciplined use of ordinary language in theological contexts, *looking for its value on the 'formal' rather than the 'material' mode of speech, much that may be of interest to us remains....*

> *... Analogy ... [explicates]* rules *limiting the use of words drawn from ordinary non-theological contexts in formulae containing the word 'God'... [T]he rules license the use of certain words, properly at home elsewhere, in theological contexts.*

Frederick Ferré, *Language, Logic and God*, 1970, page 115

This approach is a valuable reading of Aquinas, reminding us that analogy tells us what words about God *do,* how they function in our language, without our pretending that we have grasped their full meaning.

3 Symbol

Key person

Key person

Paul Tillich (1886–1965): German-American Lutheran theologian, based at Union Theological Seminary from 1933 until 1955, when he moved first to Harvard (1955–62) and then to Chicago, until his death. Prolific author, best known for *Systematic Theology* (three volumes, 1951–63), connected to his Gifford Lectures (1953–54).

Key terms

Sign For Tillich, something that points to something else by a convention. A road sign is an example.

Symbol For Tillich, something which participates in that to which it points. A flag of a nation represents that nation but also is part of the reality of that nation.

Key question

Is Tillich's idea of symbol any clearer than Aquinas' analogy in telling us what religious language *means*?

Paul Tillich developed an interesting theory of religious language as symbolic. The question about symbolic language is whether this adds anything important to theories of analogy or whether it is simply a different perspective on the same issue.

Tillich distinguishes between a **sign** and a **symbol**. A sign is merely conventional; in the way that a road sign may indicate a hazard, or a bend ahead, or the way a pointing finger may indicate the direction we should follow to find the exit. We know – or quickly learn – the meaning of these signs. Indeed, we glance at the sign quite quickly, but then turn away to look at the thing itself. If a sign indicates that the exit is this way, then I know where to look for the way out, and give the sign itself no further thought. It is a convention – what matters to me is the way out. With a road sign, what takes my attention is the thing signified. The sign tells me that there will be a steep gradient or a hairpin bend ahead. What I then think about is the gradient or the bend – not the sign that indicated to me what I should be thinking about.

If a *sign* is merely a matter of convention, then a *symbol* points towards something and *participates* in that to which it points. Consider the flag of the USA. Certainly it is a sign that tells me that I am encountering something connected with the USA. It puts me in mind of the USA. But it is also part of the USA – without that flag, the reality of that country would be different. It is part of what the USA is. The flag is found in every courtroom and classroom, is placed on the coffins of veterans and those killed in battle, and flies from every public building and many a private one. It is part of the material reality of the USA. It matters deeply to the people, it represents – or acts as a symbol for – the USA abroad.

According to Tillich, religious language has the characteristics of symbol. If I say, 'God is Love', then that utterance is not merely a *sign* of what God is, but is a *participation* in the reality of God. To use the sentence is to participate, to be part of God. Tillich adds that the term is both 'affirmed and negated' by the reality of God. It is affirmed because God really is love, but negated because the human term is so utterly inadequate as a description of God. To see the symbol as participating in God is also to acknowledge its limitations.

The obvious question is whether we are any further forward than with analogy. After all, symbolic language theories tell us what the terms *do*, not what they mean. That is no more or less true than with analogy. A positive feature of Tillich's approach is that by stressing the symbolic nature of religious language, Tillich reminds us starkly of the danger of anthropomorphising God, just as the Doctrine of Analogy does. But what, if anything, does it add to analogy?

Tillich does not explain precisely what he means by 'participation'. Questions have therefore been raised, not least by the British philosopher John Hick, about the idea that a symbol 'participates in that to which it points'. Simply telling us that it does participate does not tell us the nature of that participation. To take an example, what exactly is the symbol in the sentence 'God is good'? Clearly, these words about God do not participate in his nature in the way that a flag is part of the life of a nation. Some questions to consider include:

- If 'God' simply stands for the unknown nature of God, how exactly does it participate?
- Is the symbol the entire proposition, the underlying concept of 'the goodness of God'?
- If an atheist uses the sentence, 'God is love', does that mean that for him it is a *sign* – because he thinks the sentence fictitious – while for the believer it is a *symbol*?

We might also ask whether there are different levels of participation. For example, I belong to and participate in some organisations in the sense that I take the newsletters and once in a while turn up at an event. In others, I play a more active part, go to the meetings and commit more fully by giving time and effort to supporting the organisation. Yet both the nominal adherence and the spending of effort are called participation. If we turn this example to Tillich's idea of symbol, does the religious language become somehow more symbolic the more actively I participate in doing God's work?

A further issue is that there is no way of determining whether my symbolic use of language is appropriate. If I say – and believe – that God is a bad-tempered old woman, then my using the description is participating in God – it is affirmed by the alleged old-womanliness of God, and negated in that my description does not capture the fullness of God's nature as an old woman. Both affirmation and negation are essential to my understanding of God. For me, it is truly symbolic of God: both affirmed and negated. But most believers would argue that my characterisation of God is mistaken, saying that God is not as I imagine her. But it is hard to see how the matter could be decided if there is no criterion for determining the appropriateness of a particular use of a symbol. It seems as if we could describe God in any terms (such as my rubbish about the old woman) with no means of deciding whether ascribing a given symbol is appropriate.

This ties in with a particular danger in symbol. The Confederate States ceased to exist as a separate entity in 1865, with the end of the American Civil War, but their flag, the Stars-and-Bars, retains its resonance in American life. The Stars-and-Bars, however, represents no current political reality: the Confederate States are no longer outside the Union. Their leaders are long dead. A reconstructed Confederacy would not be the Confederation of 1864. What that flag represents is an idea (perhaps an ideal) in the heads and hearts of those for whom it has meaning, but no more. It represents no present reality beyond the creation of the beholders' minds. Symbols are made by people, and we may represent and symbolise Utopia – or a God who existed nowhere but in human minds. We cannot assume that the symbol, however meaningful to the one who uses it, has any truth behind it. If we cannot determine either the truth or the accuracy of a symbol, how useful can it be?

(a) J. H. Randall Jr. and symbols as non-cognitive

Most people would consider Tillich's use of symbols to be cognitive, and he always appears to use them in that way – it is theoretically possible to ask whether they are true or false. Tillich believed in God as the

'Ground of Being', that is, the basis of all reality, on which all else rests. Hence, however problematic they might be for others, for Tillich, religious symbols represent truths. As a result, we may properly ask whether what is offered as true actually is true. To do this is to engage in cognitive discourse.

A **non-cognitive** analysis has been offered by John Herman Randall Jr., based on Tillich's original analysis. He argues that religious symbols are both non-cognitive and **non-representative**. This means that it makes no sense to ask whether they are true or not.

Randall argues that religion is a human activity which contributes to human culture. It speaks to us in a special way.

Think, for example, about music. A great piece of music speaks to us in a way that cannot be translated into anything else. Music also touches parts of our being that nothing else can – it awakens in us emotions that nothing else does. Music in one way expresses nothing beyond itself: it occupies its own world, evoking feelings of its own. It tells us no truths about the nature of things, but works within its own musical language. For Randall, religion is the same: it has its own world, arousing special feelings which nothing else can, but it contains no truths about the world.

Randall says of symbols:

> They make us receptive to qualities of the world encountered; and they open our hearts to the new qualities with which that world, in cooperation with the spirit of man, can clothe itself. They enable us to see and feel the religious dimension of our world better, the 'order of splendor', and of man's experience in and with it. They teach us how to find the Divine; they show us visions of God.

J. H. Randall, Jr., *The Role of Knowledge in Western Religion*, 1958, page 129

For Randall, God is our ideals, an intellectual symbol for what we feel to be the divine, for the religious dimension of our spirituality. In this account, 'God' is just another name for an aspect of our psyche, its spirituality. Just as we have an aesthetic sense, so we have a spiritual sense. Randall argues that it makes no sense to ask whether or not this sense is 'true' – they are non-cognitive symbols. This is just like the world of music; it makes no sense to ask whether a piece of music is true, though we can ask whether it is good or moving.

In other words, Randall's interpretation does not seek to determine the truth or the accuracy of God as a symbol. A religious believer could object that this is not what she means by God, while a non-believer could ask what the difference is between this 'divine' and a figment of our imagination and emotions. For Randall, religion is a human enterprise that performs a valuable cultural function, but no more than that – its symbols are non-representative. The believer would claim that the God in whom she believes is not reducible to an art form or a subjective reality. When she speaks of God, she is speaking of an overwhelming reality. Randall's use of symbol would not relate in any way that mattered to what she meant when she prayed to God, praised him or sought his protection. She would not accept that she was simply praying to herself.

It seems that there can be no wholly satisfactory account of religious language, which should not surprise us given that God would not be like anything in our experience and our language takes its meaning from those things we have experienced. It might seem as if we cannot say that one theory of language is certainly better than another, but there may be reasons why one theory is more useful than another.

Via negativa is a continual reminder not to anthropomorphise God, but seems to achieve this at the expense of saying anything truly informative and of increasing the remoteness of God. It carries also the danger of permitting us to have all sorts of vague and inappropriate notions of God, on the basis that if we have no certain knowledge, anything might be possible.

Analogy seems to allow for a more positive approach, provided we remember that we are simply describing how we use theological language about God, not stating precisely what it means. The advantage of analogy is that it retains the transcendence of God, reminding us that what we say about him is our way of understanding rather than a description of God as he is in himself. We are telling ourselves what God means to us. An advantage of analogy over saying nothing at all is that we can discuss whether a given analogy is appropriate, even if we cannot believe that it wholly grasps God's nature.

Correct use of analogies is far from easy.

Philosophers such as John Hick have questioned whether Tillich's theory of symbol is more than a variant on analogy. The point about affirmation and negation shows that, like analogy, it does not claim to give us certain knowledge about God's nature. Given the lack of clarity about whether symbols do more than encourage particular feelings in us, and of knowing whether we are using symbols appropriately, it is perhaps unsurprising that analogy is the approach most widely used by philosophers of religion.

There is no obvious way of saying that symbol, as understood by Tillich, is a better way of talking about God than Aquinas' concept of analogy. Neither theory is able to offer us a precise quasi-scientific account of God, and neither theory pretends that it is able to do so. Perhaps the value of each theory lies in being able to act as a continual reminder of the difficulty of expressing the inexpressible. Language as symbol perhaps appeals more to the heart in reminding us of how that mystery affects our emotional core – as great art does – while analogy appeals to reason and intellect. Each tries to capture something of the ultimately elusive.

5 Conclusions

However we are to find ways to discuss God, we are continually reminded of the difficulties in doing so. Ideas such as analogy and symbol do not tell us clearly what our descriptions of God mean but, at best, remind us usefully and forcibly of what we are using language to do. It is good to reflect on whether Aquinas' theory of analogy really tells us very much except to say that the nature of God is unknown and we are saying something inadequate about him – but that is itself something essential to consider in all discussion of God. If Tillich's notion of symbol takes us no further than Aquinas, we may wonder about its value as a theory, and yet Tillich is saying something significant about the importance of symbolic thought, even if the application to God – and knowing whether we are using symbolic language appropriately – remains hazy.

Too often, scholars studying the philosophy of religion treat the issue of language as if it were just a separate issue – another item in the list of topics to be learned for the examination. But, if we take the issues seriously, then we need to recognise that the issue of theological language and its meaning matters in every topic studied. When we talk about the attributes of God, we need to be continually aware of the limitations of our descriptions. These are not and cannot be literal usages, and we cannot imagine them as scientifically precise definitions. If we forget this, then we are faced with a multitude of difficulties.

Study advice

As always, careful definition is essential. Learning definitions is useful, but needs to be supplemented by reflection on whether the different theories studied in this chapter really answer the question posed – how language can be used to describe God. You may consider that the question is unanswerable, but in taking such a view you must be clear *why* you think it cannot be answered. Assertion is never a sufficient *philosophical* reason for holding a point of view.

Do not fall into the surprisingly common error of thinking that when Tillich writes of symbols that he means non-verbal things such as rosaries or icons. For Tillich, religious words are symbolic.

Make sure that you are very clear that for Aquinas *all* discussion of God is analogical at best. For him, the nature of God was always strictly unknown. All the writers dealt with in the chapter are conscious that God's own nature is strictly unknowable. It is useful to bear this point in mind not only when writing on the topics discussed in this chapter, but throughout your work in the philosophy of religion. You should, however, also remember Brümmer's argument that, even with the limits Aquinas acknowledges, the notion of analogy still claims more than we have any right to assert.

Summary diagram: Religious language: analogy and symbol

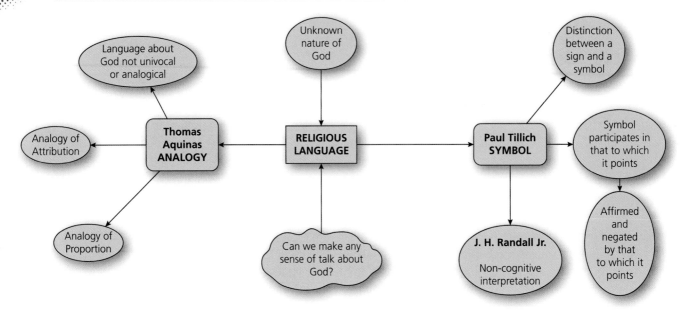

Diagram nodes:
- Language about God not univocal or analogical
- Analogy of Attribution
- **Thomas Aquinas ANALOGY**
- Analogy of Proportion
- Unknown nature of God
- **RELIGIOUS LANGUAGE**
- Can we make any sense of talk about God?
- **Paul Tillich SYMBOL**
- **J. H. Randall Jr.** Non-cognitive interpretation
- Distinction between a sign and a symbol
- Symbol participates in that to which it points
- Affirmed and negated by that to which it points

Revision advice

By the end of this chapter you should be able to explain, with some confidence, the theories of analogy and symbol, but you should also be able to think carefully about why theological language about God is necessarily limited. You should be able to explain the nature of those limits, perhaps considering such issues as the problem of knowing whether other minds exist, when we have no direct experience of them, or discussing the way that human language is always conditioned by human experience. Remember in your revision not just to learn what the theories we have examined say, but think about their relative merits, reaching your own conclusions about these. Remember that examiners might ask you to compare and contrast different theories.

Can you give brief definitions of:
- analogy
- analogy of attribution
- analogy of proportion
- sign
- symbol?

Can you explain:
- how Aquinas distinguishes univocal, equivocal and analogical uses of language
- the idea that human language can never truly encompass God's nature
- Tillich's distinction between a sign and a symbol
- the idea that a religious symbol is affirmed and negated by that to which it points?

Can you give arguments for and against:
- analogy as giving us any clarity about the nature of God
- Aquinas' idea of analogy of attribution
- the claim that religious language is symbolic
- the idea that symbol is a better way of understanding religious language than analogy?

Sample question and guidance

Assess the claim that Aquinas' doctrine of analogy enables us to speak significantly about God.

The question is relatively straightforward provided sufficient attention is paid to the word 'Assess'. You are not being asked to *describe* the idea of analogy but to make judgements and to reach a conclusion about it.

To reach suitable judgements obviously requires you to display knowledge of analogy and its different forms, but it is important to think about – and to write about – what the theory is meant to do. Aquinas appears to say that it lets us speak in a positive way about God, but you should ask yourself whether the theory tells us how we are using words rather than what they fully mean.

Is Aquinas here simply accepting the limitations with God-talk, and trying to make the best of it, or would it be possible to talk about God in a more univocal way? Although the question is specifically about Aquinas' notion of analogy, you may choose to make your assessment in the light of some other theory, such as symbol, which you may think is more or less successful than Aquinas in dealing with the problem of religious language. But you should be careful to avoid a simple descriptive catalogue of every theory you have discovered – only use material that helps you to make the precise assessment required by the question. Throughout, you need to demonstrate awareness that the ability of language to capture the essence of God is very limited.

Further essay questions

'Paul Tillich's symbolic theory of religious language tells us nothing useful about God.' Discuss.

To what extent is it true to argue that we are too remote from God to say anything about him?

'Tillich's claim that religious language is symbolic is more satisfactory than *via negativa*.' Discuss.

Going further

An obvious starting point would be to read carefully the text of Aquinas in the *Summa Theologica*, looking especially at Part 1, Question 13 on the Divine Names. This is not the only point at which Aquinas deals with analogy in his works, but it provides a useful summary.

The literature on religious language is considerable. Jeff Astley, *Exploring God-Talk: Using Language in Religion* (Darton, Longman and Todd, 2004) has some useful material.

John MacQuarrie, *God-Talk* (new edition, SCM, 2012) remains an outstanding contribution to the subject.

Ian Ramsey's work is largely out of print.

On Aquinas and analogy, Ralph McInemy in his *Aquinas and Analogy* (Catholic University of

America, 1998) is a thoughtful challenge to some conventional understandings.

Frederick Ferré, *Language, Logic and God* is now available as a paperback (Forgotten Books, 2012) and is an insightful study.

Other books discussed in this chapter are:

- Barth, K. *Church Dogmatics* (T. & T. Clark).
- Brümmer, V. *Speaking of a Personal God: An Essay in Philosophical Theology* (Cambridge University Press, 1992).
- Randall, J. H. Jr. *The Role of Knowledge in Western Religion* (Beacon Press, 1958).
- von Hügel, F. *Essays and Addresses on the Philosophy of Religion*, First Series (1921).

Chapter 5

Religious language: 20th-century perspectives – verification and meaning

> ## Chapter checklist
>
> Philosophical questions sometimes change their nature. In Aristotelian logic, what matters is whether a sentence is true or false. At the beginning of the twentieth century, the Vienna Circle added a new criterion, that of whether a sentence was meaningful. This chapter begins with an account of the intellectual background to the Vienna Circle before an account of the use of verification theory by A. J. Ayer in his seminal *Language, Truth and Logic*. Reasons why Ayer and others rejected the strong version of the verification principle are explained. Consideration is then given to the logical positivist claim that religious language is meaningless and the idea that theism, atheism and agnosticism are all meaningless positions. The claims of the logical positivists are then critically examined, especially the idea that discussion of types of language is oversimplified by logical positivism. These criticisms should be read also in terms of the criticisms of the Vienna Circle by Karl Popper (explained in Chapter 7).

1 Introduction

Again and again, we have drawn attention to the unknowability of God and the problems of defining him in any obvious or precise way. Even saying that God 'exists' is difficult, because whatever type of existence he might have, it would not be the same as any type of existence with which we are familiar.

The most radical approach to the meaning of religious terms would be simply to dismiss them as meaningless. Such would be the attitude of a group of philosophers known as the Vienna Circle, prominent in the two decades after the First World War, and taken seriously by later philosophers of religion, who in response to them have often felt the need to justify the meaning of not only their sentences but the very activity of studying faith and its claims.

Background

Moritz Schlick was a member of the Vienna Circle

The Vienna Circle (*Wiener Kreis*) was founded as a result of discussions in 1907 among Otto Neurath, a sociologist, Hans Hahn, a mathematician, and Philip Frank, a physicist, all of whom were based at the University of Vienna, in Austria. But its great fame really came after 1922 when Moritz Schlick (1882–1936) assumed leadership. He was Professor of the Philosophy of the Inductive Sciences. Everyone who attended the meetings of the circle was very influenced by modern theories of science. They were interested also in new developments in logic as represented by Frege, Russell and Whitehead.

Close attention was also given to the arguments of Ludwig Wittgenstein (1889–1951). Some meetings were devoted to careful reading of his *Tractatus Logico-Philosophicus* of 1921. However, Wittgenstein was never a member of the Circle, never attended a meeting (attendance was by invitation), and there are clear differences between ideas in the *Tractatus* and the views of the Circle. The Circle itself would break up in the 1930s. Many of its leaders were Jewish, some were Marxist, and with the rise of Nazism, they emigrated to continue their careers elsewhere. Rudolf Carnap (1891–1970), a key figure, joined in 1926 but left in 1931, moving to the USA in 1935. Moritz Schlick was shot dead by a former student while on his way to give a lecture. Otto Neurath (1882–1945) died in exile in Oxford. Each had, in various ways, moved on from the original 'pure' doctrine of the Circle – a doctrine referred to as logical positivism.

2 The development of logical positivism

Key term

Logical positivism Philosophical approach adopted by the Vienna Circle, which avoided metaphysics as meaningless and believed the task of the philosopher was the logical analysis of sentences, separating the meaningful from the meaningless.

The Vienna Circle was past its peak when its ideas were brought to the attention of the English-speaking reader by A. J. Ayer (Alfred Jules Ayer, later Sir Alfred, 1910–89), in the very influential *Language, Truth and Logic*, published in 1936. This book would become a huge bestseller, selling in hundreds of thousands, but, like Stephen Hawking's *Brief History of Time*, perhaps more bought than read, as it is not always transparent to the general reader. There was a great deal of interest in its treatment of ethics and religious beliefs, in Chapter 6. For all its faults, many later acknowledged by Ayer, it remains the classic statement of **logical positivism** for the English-speaking world. Philosophers widely saw the book as a challenge to their subject, and attempted to answer its challenges. The book seemed to make many traditional branches of philosophy, including philosophy of religion, but also ethics, aesthetics, metaphysics and many versions of epistemology both irrelevant and meaningless.

Key person

Georg W. F. Hegel (1770–1831): German Idealist philosopher, perhaps the most influential nineteenth-century thinker, who developed a metaphysics of 'absolute idealism' and the idea of dialectic. Influenced many thinkers including Karl Marx, Karl Barth, Jacques Derrida, and others, but his work was attacked by the Logical Positivists who considered his metaphysical views meaningless.

(a) Logical positivism and the downfall of Hegelianism philosophy

To understand the mission of logical positivism, we need to understand the style of philosophy taught in universities before the First World War. Nineteenth-century philosophy was dominated by the thought of G. W. F. Hegel, who argued all reality is one, a universe in which everything ultimately forms part of a spiritual reality, the Absolute. He emphasised progress, in the sense that the universe is in a continual state of improvement: in *The Philosophy of History*, he argued, 'The history of the world is none other than the progress of the consciousness of freedom'.

What worried logical positivists was that this was a philosophical attempt to state what the universe is like. Surely, they argued, what the universe was like was something to be investigated by scientists, using the tools of science, and not by philosophers constructing grand theories in their studies or armchairs. It is difficult today to appreciate the extent of Hegel's influence but, in the late nineteenth and early twentieth centuries, this was *the* dominant theory in European thought. Not only were most philosophers Hegelians, but the influence spread throughout academic life. Hegelian thought was introduced to Britain by the philosopher and poet, Samuel Taylor Coleridge, and we find its echoes in much Victorian literature and popular writing, for example in the work of H. G. Wells. Wells was not simply a master of science fiction, but looked forward to an age when science would lead to the solution of the issues of earlier times. In his *The Outline of History* (1920), in his lifetime his bestselling book, he presented a view of history as the continual and inevitable ascent from primeval darkness through periods of (religious) superstition towards a future of enlightenment and joy.

Probably the greatest blow to Hegelian optimism was the First World War – for many, it became impossible to believe in inevitable progress after such carnage, when millions were killed by artillery, gas, bombing and barbed wire. The only progress, for many, seemed to be the use of heavy industry to create mass killing. This horror and its effects on humanity were seen in art and literature. Look, for example, at the faceless warriors in the war paintings of the Austrian artist, Albin Egger-Lienz (1868–1926).

Den Namenlosen (The Nameless) by Albin Egger-Lienz

The American Idealist philosopher, Josiah Royce (1855–1916), was emotionally shattered by the torpedoing of the *Lusitania*, seeing it as disproving everything he had taught and believed: he died, a broken man, a few weeks later. Much of twentieth-century philosophy, whether in existentialism, with its attempts to put the individual back at the heart of philosophy, or the emphasis on logical analysis rather than the construction of systems, was a reaction to the downfall of Hegelianism.

In response, the logical positivists offered – or claimed to offer – no world-view of their own. Their concern was not to give an alternative idea of reality. They argued that it was no business of the philosopher to say anything at all about the world, and certainly not to indulge in Hegelian speculations. If you want information about the world, ask a scientist.

3 Verification theory

If philosophers can say nothing about the world, what use are they? Can they say anything significant or useful at all? If they are saying nothing about human life, are they redundant?

Logical positivists argue that the philosopher's task is to analyse the logical structure of sentences. This means that they determine whether a sentence is meaningful, that is, whether it is more than nonsense. The logical positivists thought of themselves as gatekeepers or certification officers for scientists, sorting out various propositions into those worthy of investigation and those empty of meaning. Into the latter category they would place most propositions of ethics, theology and aesthetics. It was not the philosopher's job to decide whether a sentence is true, but rather whether it is sense or nonsense. To assert that Ben Nevis is the world's highest mountain is untrue, but it is not meaningless, because it is a sentence that can be investigated by scientists. Once the philosopher has shown a sentence to say something which the scientist could significantly investigate, her task is over.

For the logical positivists, there are only two types of significant, that is, *meaningful*, propositions.

(a) Tautologies

First, there are **tautologies**, which are *a priori* and true by definition.

The sentence, 'A triangle has three sides' is true because the meaning of the phrase 'a triangle' always includes having three sides. But, of course, this tells us nothing about the content of the world, only about the rules of language. We do not let the word 'triangular' mean anything except something that has three sides. But, whether there are any triangles in the world can only be decided by observation in a scientific way. A tautology is true by virtue of the meaning of the words contained in the sentence, but what we have is a *truth*, not a *fact*. A truth is a sentence that is true, such as 'A triangle has three sides' – having three sides explains the meaning of the word 'triangle'. When we talk philosophically about *facts* we mean to say something about what actually is the case. It would be true that 'triangle' has three sides whether it existed or not, because that is the meaning of the idea of a triangle. However, we say London is the capital of England only if that is indeed the case in the real world. When we talk about something as a fact, we mean that it is the case in the real world.

For Ayer and the logical positivists, tautologies include the whole of mathematics. Mathematics is a set of tautologies. Any sum is ultimately reducible to a straightforward and very simple tautology:

$$x = x$$

After all, when we say '7 + 5 = 12', '7 + 5' is only another way of writing '12'. For every use of '12' in decimal arithmetic, we could write '[5+7]', for it is the same thing.

(b) Empirically verifiable propositions

The second type of significant sentence is the **empirically verifiable proposition**. This type of sentence is one that tells us something beyond itself and not simply about the meaning of its own terms, such as the statement, 'Ben Nevis is the highest mountain'. Such a sentence tells us about something claimed as a matter of fact. To tell whether such a sentence is true, at some point, some sort of observation is needed. The mountain must be seen, measured and compared with others to see whether the sentence is true. Sometimes an observation is direct (such as a statement about the desk at which I am writing these words: I perceive the desk here and now, through my senses). Often our observation is an indirect observation (I cannot directly observe Alexander the Great, I need sense experiences of books, voices, pictures, etc. to give me any knowledge I may have about him). In an indirect observation, I still need direct sense experience of the book or film or other means through which I come to learn facts otherwise hidden from me.

The above are all examples of empirically verifiable propositions – sentences whose truth can be determined by observation. However, not all sentences can be determined as true or false by observation, and so, for a logical positivist, would be meaningless. Suppose I were to say that the universe doubled in size at midnight last night. It sounds like a significant – and meaningful – sentence. A little thought suggests that it is not, because there is no possible observation that could either prove or even make probable the truth of the sentence. If the universe doubled in size, we would notice no difference, because we would be twice the size, our furniture twice the size, our tape-measures twice the size, and so on. Everything would look exactly the same as it does now. In practice, nothing would have changed. To a logical positivist, the claim would be meaningless. As nothing observable would have changed, nothing would look different, and there would be nothing for a scientist to investigate.

For logical positivists, a proposition is meaningful if and only if it is a tautology or it is verifiable through observation. This idea was expressed by Ayer and others as the **verification principle**.

(c) Strong and weak verification

In the first edition of *Language, Truth and Logic*, Ayer distinguished between **strong verification** and **weak verification**:

Key term

Empirically verifiable proposition A sentence whose truth can be determined by observation.

Key terms

Verification principle A sentence is meaningful if and only if it is a tautology or is verifiable by sense experience. There are two forms: strong and weak.

Strong verification principle The *strong* principle requires conclusive empirical evidence. This was *rejected* by Ayer and others as impossible.

Weak verification principle The *weak* principle, adopted by Ayer and others, states that one must be able to state what empirical evidence would make a sentence probable.

A proposition is said to be verifiable, in the strong sense of the term, if, and only if, its truth could be conclusively established in experience. But it is verifiable, in the weak sense, if it is possible for experience to render it probable.

A. J. Ayer, *Language, Truth and Logic*, 1971, page 50

Ayer goes on to point out that strong verification is impossible. We can never conclusively make any statement about the world, as our senses can be mistaken even about what we think is in front of us. I may be mistaken about whether my cat in front of me is really as I see her – I cannot get outside my mind to check whether my perception agrees with the facts. Because of weakness in my eyesight, I might mistake next-door's cat for my own. Sense experience can always be mistaken.

Ayer points out that historical statements and the general conclusions of science would be unverifiable:

It will be our contention that no proposition, other than a tautology, can possibly be more than a probable hypothesis. And if this is correct, the principle that a sentence can be factually significant only if it expresses what is conclusively verifiable is self-stultifying as a criterion of significance. For it leads to the conclusion that it is impossible to make a significant statement of fact at all.

Ibid,. page 51

Key question

Is Ayer correct to reject the possibility of verification in the strong sense?

If we were to ask for verification in the strong sense, *every* factual sentence would be meaningless. It would also be irrational to rule out every sentence when none could reach an impossibly high standard of proof. Ideas such as gravity or any of the things we consider science would become meaningless – we can never experience every possible instance, past, present and future, to be able to say that it is *conclusively* true.

Instead, Ayer chose the weak form of verification outlined above. It is sufficient to state what observations would make the sentence probable. He gives the interesting example of a sentence stating that there are mountains on the far side of the moon. When he was writing, in 1934–35, no one had seen the far side of the moon and the technology capable of creating a rocket or spacecraft to make such an observation did not exist. But, it was possible to state what observations *would* make the statement probable, so it was possible to say that the sentence was significant – it was verifiable in principle, though not in fact. Only in October 1959 would the Soviet probe, *Luna 3* send us the first photographs, which indeed showed mountains. Even if the photographs showed the far side of the moon to be as flat as the fens, on the weak version of the principle, the original sentence, 'There are mountains on the far side of the moon' would still be meaningful, just not true. Given that there are mountains on the side of the moon we can see, it would not be an unreasonable supposition.

4 Implications of Ayer's verification principle on the use of religious language

For a recap on metaphysics, see Year 1, pages 4–5.

The implications of Ayer's view for religion (and ethics and aesthetics) are spelled out in robust terms in Chapter 6 of his book. Although earlier in the book Ayer had rejected metaphysics as meaningless, the examples he gives are of transcendent metaphysics, especially those of Hegel and his followers. That is, he rejects as meaningless any metaphysical language that looks outside immediate sense experience to God or 'the Absolute'. These are not untrue statements, but are quite without meaning, not worth considering.

Ayer argues:

Key quote

'There exists a transcendent God' has no literal significance.

A. J. Ayer, *Language, Truth and Logic*, 1971, page 158

Key question

If people take their beliefs about God seriously, how convincing is a claim that what they are saying is simply meaningless?

It is important to notice that Ayer is not simply arguing that theists are talking nonsense when they say 'God exists'. So too are atheists. If to say 'God exists' is meaningless, then to say 'God does not exist' is no less nonsense. Nonsense does not become sense by adding a negative: if 'floobbodybobodydoo' is nonsense, so too is '*not* floobbodybobodydoo'. Nor would Ayer accept agnosticism as meaningful: an agnostic thinks 'Is there a God?' is a real question, which he cannot answer. For Ayer, the question itself is meaningless. Religious faith is nonsense, genuine religious experience impossible.

Ayer argued that religious belief in God was always without meaning, as was atheism. All discussion of the issue is nonsensical. Richard Dawkins treats religious beliefs as failed scientific hypotheses, devoid of proof. Ayer would not waste his time trying to disprove faith, in the way Dawkins does. For him, there is nothing to be investigated, as religious claims are meaningless, so there is strictly nothing significant to say on the issue.

5 Responses to Ayer's verification principle

Language, Truth and Logic seemed to pose a major challenge to faith, not least because of the immense success of the book; whether it succeeded as a challenge is another matter.

(a) General criticisms

An obvious objection, made by many, is that the verification principle itself is neither a tautology nor empirically verifiable – its truth cannot be known by any process of observation. By its own rules, it seems itself to be meaningless.

Key question

Is the claim that the verification principle is itself unverifiable sufficient reason to dismiss the claims of logical positivism?

Some logical positivists tried to argue for a class of 'protocol statements', that is, arguing that the verification principle was a statement of method. The problem with such an approach is that to invent another class of propositions inevitably undermines the original belief that there are *only* two types of significant proposition, tautologies and empirically verifiable propositions.

Key term

Foundationalism The belief that all knowledge is based on some unarguable, self-evident truth.

Another related problem is that if we adopt the verification principle, we are committing ourselves to a form of **foundationalism**. Foundationalism is the idea that some types of ideas are so self-evidently true that they need no further justification. Descartes thought this of his *cogito ergo sum*. Logical positivists claim that there is an absolute foundation, the verification principle (which itself needs no further justification), on the basis of which we can then go on to assert the rules for determining the meaningfulness of every other sentence. It is not clear that the statement that there are only two types of significant sentence can be justified other than by asserting it. The only permissible reasons to justify the logical positivist project would, by their own rules, need themselves to be either tautologies or empirically justifiable sentences – and that would be circular, question-begging in the precise sense of the term. Many philosophers reject foundationalism, not least because it can lead to a kind of thinking that just knows it is right and has no means of justifying the claim. Is it self-evident that there are only two types of significant sentences? How would we ever be able to say that we 'know' this?

Notice also the underlying assumptions of logical positivism. It argues from what it takes to be the character (and, we shall suggest in Chapter 7, a flawed idea) of science. It assumes that it is scientists who, and scientific statements which, tell us about the world. Of course it is true that science gives us information about the world, and it would be foolish to deny that. But, is that the only informative language? To restrict all information and all understanding of the world to just those points which can be expressed in scientific terms seems to miss something. Poetry reveals to us aspects of human experience that it alone can express. The language of poetry is not cognitive, any more than the language of music is, but it is, at its best, revelatory. A great work of art or a great novel reveals to us new ways of looking at the world; but these are rarely straightforwardly cognitive or – in the logical positivist sense – verifiable scientific sentences. Even in subjects such as political science or economics, theories are never like those in physics and chemistry that can be straightforwardly verified. Judgements and hypotheses are not proven, but are not empty. Logical positivism seems, by reducing all significant language to two opposed categories, to leave no place for valuable and significant contributions to human knowledge.

At the heart of logical positivist beliefs is the assumption that a verifiable sentence is a scientific one – their purpose as philosophers, according to this theory, is to determine what sentences it is worthwhile for scientists to investigate. But a Shakespeare sonnet is not a scientific hypothesis. It would be a bold literary critic who thought a great sonnet to be without meaning. To reduce sentences to two classes – the meaningful, and hence open to scientific investigation, or the meaningless – seems absurdly to misrepresent the fullness of either the range of possible sentences or of meaning. It is not a self-evident truth that the many uses of sentences can be so easily reduced to just two classes. (Aspects of the variety of sentences will be explored in Chapter 7.)

Most philosophers of religion argue that religious sentences are of a quite different order from scientific sentences.

Key question

Does logical positivism fall into the trap of trying to reduce everything to a scientific question?

(b) Brümmer's response

Theologian and philosopher Vincent Brümmer has recently argued that to treat the sentences of faith as if they were scientific sentences – as the verification theory does – is to commit an error of understanding. He, like D. Z. Phillips before him, believes that we make a mistake if we treat religious sentences in terms set by Enlightenment thinkers, such as Hume (and, more recently, Dawkins), who look at them as (failed) scientific sentences. This is a mistake: just as the methods of scientific analysis are inappropriate to poetry, so they are to the experience and utterances of faith.

Professor Brümmer comments, writing about the atheism of Flew and Dawkins:

> The success of science has had the effect that for many of us today the search for knowledge has become the paradigmatic model for all our thinking. Today many of us intuitively assume that all *thinking is aimed at extending our knowledge, that human beings are mere knowing subjects and that reality is merely the object of knowledge. The effect of this mindset for the way religious faith is understood has been disastrous.*

Vincent Brümmer, *What Are We Doing When We Pray?* 2008, pages 141–2

Brümmer argues that we have, in modern times, tended to assume that if something is not scientific or measurable that it is somehow not very significant. But even to think like that is to make an assumption we cannot possibly justify: it is not self-evidently true and it is difficult to see what could be evidence to demonstrate that the modern view is correct.

Indeed, it is sometimes said that when the supporters of logical positivism reject metaphysics, they are constructing an 'alternative metaphysic' of their own. To dismiss the very possibility of God seems to necessitate a particular world-view. Their stance towards the world, the assumption that things are only significant if open to scientific investigation, seems to be based on a metaphysical assumption about the way things are: that the entire contents of reality are those possibly known to science, and that there is nothing beyond this.

There are, however, also good grounds for arguing – as we shall see in Chapter 7 – that the logical positivists presuppose a deeply flawed vision of science.

(c) Emmet's response

It has also been argued that the logical positivists fail to understand the nature of metaphysical thinking. Such a view was taken by Dorothy Emmet, more than 70 years ago. She argues that it was an error of Enlightenment thought to treat natural theology and its claims univocally, that is, as scientific propositions equivalent to those of conventional science. For Emmet, the claims of natural theology should be understood as analogies, not as scientific accounts. This idea may be referred back to our discussion of the analogical nature of religious language in Chapter 4.

Emmet argues that it is a natural human inclination to see our attempts to make sense of the mysteries of existence as if what we know is all there is to be known. We look for a complete explanation of the

Key person

Dorothy Emmet (1904–2000): British philosopher who worked with Alfred North Whitehead. She was Professor of Philosophy at the University of Manchester (1946–67), having been preferred over Paul Tillich. Author of *The Nature of Metaphysical Thinking* (1945) and many other works, especially in Philosophy of Science and Philosophy of Religion.

kind that we want science to provide. She suggests that faith is not about having a complete explanation. Instead, it is an attempt to express and understand:

> ... the character of thought itself, as seeking coherence, tempts us to present our explanatory ideas as a closed system, instead of as interpretations of a relation in which we stand to a reality other than our ideas. It is for this reason that a sound theology should, I believe, be analogical in character; it should be an elucidation of the analogies in terms of which people have expressed their relation to the transcendent, and should exhibit the nature of this relation, recognising that we can only say so much about the nature of the transcendent itself as can be indirectly indicated in these ways...

Dorothy Emmet, *The Nature of Metaphysical Thinking*, 1945, page 118

This view suggests that metaphysical thinking is analogical in character. It fits with the ideas of Aquinas explored in Chapter 4, but also raises interesting issues about logical positivism. Emmet's account suggests that the logical positivist characterisation of religion (and metaphysics more widely) fails to understand not only the type of language involved but the modes of thinking which our sentences represent. Analogical thinking is not scientifically verifiable, but we use analogies to help us understand the world. To say that the world is like a single organism is not scientifically verifiable but might be a way for someone to understand the ecosystem. If it helps, it makes a difference to that person, and is not an empty concept. It can also be debated, not in terms of being true or false, but whether it is an *appropriate* or helpful analogy.

Confusion may occur because we do not normally begin our conversations by saying, 'my next sentences represent discussion in religious and not scientific terms'. In our ordinary sentences we move between jokes, statements of fact, speculations, opinions and so on without preface. Sometimes, a humorous suggestion is taken seriously by our listener, and misunderstanding follows – we find ourselves rather lamely having to explain that 'it was only a joke'.

It is not only other people who get this wrong: sometimes we do not fully understand the way our own sentences should be taken. Think about someone who says, 'I was literally petrified', which means that she was actually turned to stone. By adding 'literally' she is saying that what followed is not a metaphor, but should be taken at face value as precise fact. But what was said actually was a metaphor. The fact she is still speaking rather implies that she is not a stone. She has misunderstood – or not thought about – the precise character of the sentence she has used. Getting things wrong, and misunderstanding the character of what we say, is part of the human condition. Part of our living is – for many people – the religious life. If Aquinas and Emmet are right, when we talk about God, we do so analogically, but even then, our account of religious language would be incomplete. Prayers, hymns, and many other types of language, deeply significant within the context of faith, are used by believers. To reject all this as simply meaningless seems to pay insufficient attention to what people mean.

Key question

Does logical positivism treat the variety of propositions too simplistically?

6 Swinburne's solution and the nature of sentences about God

Richard Swinburne, in *The Coherence of Theism*, argues against logical positivism. He claims that there are sentences which obviously have meaning, describing states of affairs, but which are not verifiable in any way. He gives a much-quoted example of a sentence that he holds to be unverifiable but nevertheless meaningful:

> *Some of the toys that to all appearances stay in the toy cupboard while any humans in the house are asleep come out of their boxes and dance in the middle of the night without disturbing any detecting devices, and then go back to the cupboard, leaving no traces of their activity.*

Richard Swinburne, *The Coherence of Theism*, (second edition), 2016, page 43

One can understand why Swinburne thinks his point useful. He is aware of the enormous variety of possible significant sentences, as used by people in their discussions, and he is pointing us to the possibility of genuinely significant sentences that fall outside the over-simple demands of logical positivism.

(a) Objections to Swinburne's solution

However, his example is much more problematic than Swinburne seems to realise. Obviously, it does not satisfy the weak verification principle. As no human observation is possible in the circumstances, we cannot specify an observation which would make the event probable.

However, it does not follow that the weak verification principle fails (as Swinburne claims) as a criterion for genuinely meaningful statements, because we would need to demonstrate that this sentence is a genuinely factual and meaningful statement by means *other than* the verification principle. Think about this for a moment. If it is not meaningful in terms of the verification principle, then it must be meaningful in terms of something else. Swinburne needs to tell us what that alternative might be. The truth of the sentence cannot be empirically grounded, because we cannot state any observations that would enable us to say we are justified in holding that this is a genuinely factual sentence.

Swinburne appeals to the fact that we *understand* the sentence because we understand all the words contained in it. The understanding of the words is based on our ability to make conceptions of things, such as toys, feelings, and so on. We can picture the event he describes. But it does not follow that *because* each word is understood, that a sentence made up entirely of words we can understand, is itself, *as a sentence*, coherent or genuinely factual. 'We are sitting in the train' has a factual possibility and coherence quite different from: 'The train is sitting in us', even though we understand every word in the sentence. When Ayer looks at a sentence such as 'God exists' he is not denying that we can have some understanding of the words. He denies that the sentence *as a whole* is verifiable or meaningful.

In any case, even if Swinburne were right that the sentence about the toy cupboard is meaningful, it would not follow that sentences about God were meaningful, because they are not of the same kind as sentences about toys. I know very well what a toy is. I can describe it in factual terms and understand fully the sentences I use. I do not know the mind or nature of God, and my understanding is, as St Paul says, 'through a glass darkly'.

Believers such as D. Z. Phillips argue that a sentence such as 'God creates and sustains the earth' is a sentence of a quite different type from 'water is made of hydrogen and oxygen'. The first sentence looks a bit like the second in structure, but it is very different. God is not a creator in the same sense as a potter is creator of the clay jug, nor would he be a thing like an element such as hydrogen. Whatever God's existence may be, it would be nothing like anything in the universe. Phillips always insisted that the search for God is a *religious* rather than a scientific quest. Such an approach opens the question of what it means to be a religious quest, but, whatever the answer to that might be, the logic of the quest would be different.

(This point is applicable against a thinker such as Dawkins, who argues that God fails as a scientific hypothesis. To say that 'God made the world' is to say something different from 'The Big Bang made the world'. The second sentence is a genuinely scientific sentence where 'made' refers to processes which are in principle open to scientific investigation, because they would be something like other scientifically known processes. God's making of the world would be nothing like that, because God would not be like any known – or knowable – scientific process.)

Think of this another way. When we are on a scientific quest, we understand both the subject and object terms in a sentence. Take, for example, the sentences:

I am seeking the Loch Ness Monster.

Scientists are looking for the cure for cancer.

In both cases, we understand the whole sentence, both the subject ('I', 'Scientists') *and* the object ('the Loch Ness Monster', 'the cure for cancer'). We know the conditions and tests that would enable us to say 'I have found the monster'. We can state with great precision what would convince those who believe the monster to be a consequence of an over-active imagination (or too much whisky) that they were wrong. If someone hauled a great dinosaur-like creature from the inky depths of Loch Ness, I could say confidently that there really was a monster there. I do not know what the cure for cancer would be, but I know exactly what clinical results would follow if it were ever found.

Think about this sentence:

I am seeking God.

The sentence looks identical in structure to the sentences about the cure for cancer and the Loch Ness Monster, but it is very different. I cannot define the object term, 'God', in that way. I cannot tell you the tests which would demonstrate that I had indeed found God, because I do not know what the God is that I seek. The term 'God' represents something of a quite different and incomprehensible order. But it does not follow that because I cannot understand a given term in a sentence that the sentence is, in itself, meaningless, any more than the fact that I know the meaning of all the words in a sentence entails the factual possibility of the sentence as a whole.

Swinburne's sentence about the toys in the cupboard is quite unlike any sentence in which 'God' is a term. In Swinburne's case, I can understand every name in the sentence because I am familiar with the concept from other sense experiences. I know what a toy is, what a cupboard is, from other contexts. That is why the words in the sentence have meaning for me. But 'God' is not the object of a sense experience in any ordinary way, nor by any way achievable by the methods of science – there is no Godometer to measure him by. So, the meaning of 'God' is not a measurable or quantifiable concept any more than it is based on normal sense experience. We cannot go from Swinburne's assumption – perhaps mistaken – that a statement about toys in a cupboard is meaningful to assuming that a sentence about God is meaningful in the same way.

(b) Another objection to logical positivism

If logical positivists are right, then it seems that much of what people say every day would be meaningless. But is it true of what we say in conversation?

Suppose I said to you: 'Shut that door!' Obviously this is not a scientific sentence. It is an instruction, perhaps even an order. It is not a tautology and not even verifiable. But it is *significant*, and something that is not nonsense. If I continually spoke to you in that bossy tone of voice, it would affect our relationship, probably very quickly. But notice something else. It is appropriate to *respond* to what is said. You might say, 'Of course I will!' and close the door, or say something to refuse the instruction. Even to ignore what I tell you to do is a response.

One cannot *respond* in any significant way to what is nonsense, except to say that it is nonsense. If I say 'floobbodybobodydoo', you might *characterise* my statement as nonsense, but no *response* to what I say is possible. There is nothing to be done, no actual state of affairs to alter. Nonsense is just that.

If someone says, 'Praise the Lord!', a response can be made: one can behave differently, perhaps by choosing to join the praise, or by ignoring it. Prayer and other forms of religious life enable *response*: they change things. So too would a statement, 'I do not believe in God'. Others may respond to it, and, if I believe what I say, my own form of life – the way I spend Sunday mornings, and the way I think about meaning and value in the world – will be a response, and, I think, a significant one.

The logical positivist's approach is binary – either a proposition is meaningful in the sense he wants, or it is meaningless. There is no other option. But speech is surely richer and more complex – and interesting – than that.

In the next chapter, we will see how Wittgenstein showed the immense variety of the ways in which we use language, with each possible form having its own significance.

7 Conclusions

The challenge of logical positivism to religious belief was undoubtedly an important one, in that it forced philosophers to reconsider the basis of their claims, to determine whether they were indeed saying something which had meaning. The challenge, as we shall see in Chapter 8, was not only to faith, but to an entire range of discourse, including the claims made in ethics.

The issue is the *binary* nature of the logical positivist challenge. The question posed is one set out in terms of *either/or. Either* a statement is scientifically verifiable (and meaningful) *or* it is not (and so meaningless).

The claim is that this characterisation is too simple. Language has many forms, and a wealth of uses. And the great philosophers of the Vienna Circle – including Ayer, Carnap and Neurath – themselves came to the view that the original project was overly simple. They did what good philosophers do as they and others tested their claims: they changed their minds.

Study advice

It is very helpful to read the original text of Ayer, especially as a number of writers have made significant mistakes in understanding, especially over strong and weak verification. Familiarity with the text will help you to avoid mistakes.

This chapter lists a number of objections to logical positivist arguments. It is important to take time not simply to *learn* some of the points but to *think* about whether they are damaging or even fatal to the logical positivist perspective. In your own notes, remember to make comments which reflect your own ideas and reasons for judgements.

Summary diagram: Religious language: 20th-century perspectives – verification and meaning

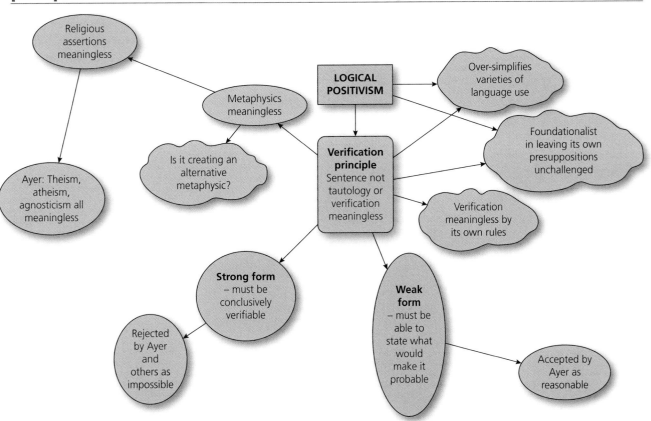

By the end of this chapter you should be able to explain thoughtfully the issues involved in logical positivism and to have reflected on objections to this view of philosophy. Here, as always, you need to practise precise definition of ideas and to give appropriate examples to illustrate your points.

Can you give brief definitions of:

- logical positivism
- metaphysics
- empiricism
- tautologies
- the verification principle?

Can you explain:

- what logical positivists believed to be the true role of the philosopher
- the idea that a sentence is meaningful
- the difference between *strong* and *weak* forms of the verification principle
- the reasons why logical positivists considered it meaningless to ask whether God exists?

Can you give arguments for and against:

- the verification principle
- the idea that there are only two kinds of significant sentences
- the claim that God must be understood in scientific terms
- the claim that the task of philosophy is simply the logical analysis of sentences?

Sample question and guidance

Assess the belief that talk about God is meaningless.

This question is one that looks simple but could be a trap. Many candidates might use it as an opportunity to write about every theory of religious language they have studied. A wiser student will spot the word 'meaningless' in the question. Whenever the words 'meaningful' or 'meaningless' are used, you are being pointed towards the philosophical notion of verification. Examiners would otherwise specify a theory, such as analogy, and ask about how these help us to 'understand' God or religious language.

Asking you to assess the concept means that you need to consider very carefully whether the concept is coherent – that is, makes some sense –

and what it might entail. To do this, you need to be able to outline the claim made by Ayer and others, looking at both the approach to statements about the world and, especially, the verification principle. Be careful to explain precisely what this says and do not just *refer* to it. You need to demonstrate your understanding.

It is worth discussing whether the approach of logical positivism is simply too limited in its approach to language. Is true significance applicable only to a single category of sentence? Think about the nature of scientific understanding. If you look again at this question after reading Chapter 7, you may wish to include some of Karl Popper's objections to treating language as meaningless. Material there is also relevant here.

Further essay questions

'The verification principle is too flawed to be useful.' Discuss.

To what extent is it true to say that the existence of God is a scientific question?

'Atheism is meaningless.' Discuss.

Going further

It is very useful to look at the text of *Language, Truth and Logic* (Penguin, 1971), Chapters 1 and 6 in particular. In the first, Ayer explains the outlook of logical positivism and his reasons for rejecting the strong form of verification and accepting the weak.

Rupert Shortt, *God is No Thing: Coherent Christianity* (Hurst and Co., 2016) is useful for reflection on the idea of God as 'not a normal' subject of scientific enquiry.

J. L. Austin in a justly famous book, *How to Do Things With Words* (Clarendon, 1962), developed in various ways ideas about the different uses we have for language, and their various meanings, ranging far beyond the scientific and the narrow boundaries of the logical positivist claims.

Other books discussed in this chapter are:

- Brümmer, V. *What Are We Doing When We Pray?* (Ashgate, 2008).
- Emmet, D. *The Nature of Metaphysical Thinking* (Macmillan, 1945).
- Swinburne, R. *The Coherence of Theism* (second edition, Oxford University Press, 2016).

Chapter 6

Religious language: 20th-century perspectives – Wittgenstein and language games

> ### Chapter checklist
>
> The background to Wittgenstein's theories is outlined, explaining the distinction between the early Wittgenstein of the *Tractatus* and the later Wittgenstein who developed the idea of language games in the *Philosophical Investigations* and *The Blue and Brown Books*. The idea and significance of language games for philosophical enquiry is explained, drawing extensively on Wittgenstein's own words, and their religious implications. The non-cognitive analysis of Don Cupitt in his idea of *theological non-realism* is explored, together with the rejection of such a view by critics. There is then discussion of how twentieth-century Thomists have used Wittgenstein's language games in their understanding of Aquinas' Doctrine of Analogy. Implications for understanding religious texts are also considered. Objections to language game theory, such as claims of circularity, or that in religious terms they lead to fideism, are also explored.

1 Introduction

Key person

Ludwig Wittgenstein
(1889–1951): Austrian-born philosopher, largely based in Cambridge. In his lifetime, his only published work was the *Tractatus Logico-Philosophicus*. Now considered one the greatest thinkers of the twentieth century.

Ludwig Wittgenstein himself wrote little directly about religion, although he did discuss it in tutorials, but various followers and disciples, including Elizabeth Anscombe, Gareth Moore, Peter Winch, Rush Rhees and D. Z. Phillips have developed his ideas.

Perhaps the greatest problem with Wittgenstein's work is that his statements were frequently very obscure and much that we have from him consists of edited versions of scattered notes and notebooks, published after his death by various pupils and followers. Philosophers also have to deal with 'two' Wittgensteins, the early and the late: we must not confuse the earlier with the later. It is in the later Wittgenstein, perhaps especially in *The Blue and Brown Books,* as well as *Philosophical Investigations,* that we find the bones of language game theory.

Background

The 'two' Wittgensteins

Ludwig Wittgenstein was born in 1889 to a wealthy and incredibly talented Viennese family (his brother, Paul, was a concert pianist who in the First World War lost his right arm and used family wealth to commission piano concertos for the left hand from composers such as Prokofiev and Ravel). He studied engineering, first in Berlin, then in Manchester, but felt increasingly drawn to philosophy. He moved to Cambridge in 1912, where he worked closely with Bertrand Russell. On the outbreak of war, in 1914, he went home to join the Austrian army, fighting on the Italian front, where he was captured and became a prisoner of war. During this time, while held in a camp, he wrote his *Tractatus Logico-Philosophicus*. This was the only book by him published in his lifetime.

In the *Tractatus*, Wittgenstein argued that many of the traditional problems of philosophy were actually problems of language. If only we could construct an appropriate logical language on the lines he set out, it would be quite easy not to *solve* traditional problems, but to *dissolve* them. They would be seen not to be problems, but simply the result of errors in language. He accompanied this notion with his *picture theory* of language, arguing that language is a kind of pictorial representation of the world, though we often rearrange the pictorial elements in ways which do not directly represent what is actually there. He completed this short but very difficult book with the words, 'whereof we cannot speak, thereof we should be silent'. This was taken by logical positivists as a declaration that things such as religious and ethical propositions were meaningless. That is almost certainly a misreading. It certainly seems not what Wittgenstein meant.

Wittgenstein returned briefly to Cambridge, but believed he ought not to draw his salary – as he thought he had dissolved all the problems of philosophy, there was nothing left to say. He returned to Austria, and worked as a primary school teacher in the Tirol from 1920 until 1926. His disciplinary methods were considered too robust, and he resigned after knocking a pupil senseless. He then worked as an architect in Vienna, building a modernist mansion for his sister (today it houses the cultural department of the Bulgarian embassy, in Kundmanngasse). Even this he described in philosophical terms: he said of it, 'I am not interested in erecting a building, but in [...] presenting to myself the foundations of all possible buildings', and he showed an obsessive concern with detail, even to the design of doorknobs.

In 1929 he returned to Cambridge, becoming Professor of Philosophy: he remained there until 1947, dying in 1951. During the Second World War, after becoming a British citizen in 1939, he worked as a hospital porter at Guy's Hospital. His work became known mainly through word from his pupils and his rather odd personal life (he lived without furniture, Bertrand Russell having sold his stored furniture to send him the money to leave the prisoner-of-war camp and return to Britain) and strong character gave him guru status. The publication of his *Philosophical Investigations*, posthumously, in 1953, was a major event in disseminating his ideas.

After his return to Vienna, in 1926, Wittgenstein met and discussed ideas with members of the Vienna Circle, but was not invited to, and did not attend, any of their meetings. He was never a member of the Circle, and did not endorse their views.

His discussions included religion, which the Vienna Circle had dismissed as meaningless. He is recorded as saying:

Is speech essential for religion? I can quite well imagine a religion in which there are no doctrines and hence nothing is said. Obviously the essence of religion can have nothing to do with the fact that speech occurs – or rather: if speech does occur this is a component of religious behaviour and not a theory. Therefore nothing turns on whether the words are true, false, or nonsensical.

Quoted in Patrick Sherry, *Religion, Truth and Language-Games*, 1977, page 1

This suggests that his idea of silence does not indicate that religious sentences are meaningless, as well as revealing something of his fundamental disagreements with the Vienna Circle. He is not even entering on discussion of whether religious sentences are meaningful.

By this time, he was moving away from the views of the *Tractatus*. He gave up his belief that we could construct one master logical language. He rejected the picture theory of meaning and developed the work we know as that of the *later* Wittgenstein.

2 Language games

'Uncle Pantagruel is not as well as he might be.'

Consider this sentence, and ask what it means. If you looked in a dictionary, you might understand all the words in the sentence and understand the speaker to be saying that Uncle Pantagruel was 'feeling under the weather', 'a bit peaky', 'not quite the ticket' or any other variant you could think of for being unwell. Suppose all the knowledge you had of English came from a dictionary. Would a Martian understand 'not quite the ticket' from the literal meanings of the words?

The answer is clearly that the Martian would be baffled. But even an English speaker might misunderstand the sentence as spoken by me. In the Wilkinson household, 'not as well as he might be' is used to mean 'dead'. A former neighbour would word the same sentiment differently: Bert would say, 'Uncle Pantagruel is brown bread'. Our Martian friend would have real fun with that one.

To understand what is being said, we need not only to know the dictionary meanings of words but how words are used in practice.

We live our lives in parts. For instance, an important part of life may be spent with our families, while at other times we are students, or with friends. In another part of our lives we may be members of a church, synagogue or mosque, in another a member of a club or society, in another as customers of a bank, in another at a part-time job. Each of these aspects of life has a certain way of speaking. In our families, we often have turns of phrase that would make little sense to those outside the family group, such as my example of Uncle Pantagruel. The language we use with our friends is not identical to that which we use in more formal situations – such as in the classroom or when giving evidence in court, or even with our parents. When we learn a new subject, what we are doing is to learn a new language. When a computer novice hears computer buffs in conversation he does not begin to understand their language, and the language of astro-physics makes no sense to many of us. Once we understand the language used, then we can become part of the conversation, joining in in an appropriate and informed way.

This idea is at the heart of **language game** theory. When I learn the language of a subject, I am learning the rules of a game – the language game. I am learning how a given type of language is being used.

For Wittgenstein, I am always a player of games. Each game has its own rules, and one does not play one game by the rules of another. The rules of rugby and those of cricket are different. To speak of a ball in cricket is to speak of a cork, leather and twine spherical object, which is small and hard with sewn seams. A rugby ball is very different. A 'bat' is very different in talk of the animal kingdom from what it is in cricket or baseball. A 'slip' is something different in an office, in cricket, in fashion, in a theatre, in descriptions of my attempts at ice-skating, and so on.

For the later Wittgenstein, we cannot ask the absolute meaning of any word – only its meaning *in use*, that is, its meaning in a particular game.

> **Key quote**
>
> What we call 'sentence' and 'language' has not the formal unity that I imagined [in the *Tractatus*], but is the family of structures more or less related to one another … 'What is a word really?' is analogous to 'What is a piece in chess?'
>
> Ludwig Wittgenstein, *Philosophical Investigations*, §108

> **Key question**
>
> What is meant by saying that to understand the meaning of a term we must look at its use?

There are important things to notice here. To ask the meaning of a piece in chess is to ask what it means in the board game: it is not an absolute definition. Without understanding chess, the meaning of the piece we call a *rook* makes no sense. It is not the same as a birdwatcher's *rook*, any more than a *bishop* in the context of chess refers to an episcopal figure with responsibility for a diocese.

We should notice also a feature of language games often overlooked. There are relationships and similarities. The inspiration of the *bishop* in the game of chess is presumably the actual bishops in society, but that meaning has been modified, adapted, altered on the way to its use in chess. Games are not wholly isolated – there are families of language games. But we cannot just put things into a simple category:

> *Consider for example the proceedings we call 'games'. I mean board-games, card-games, ball-games, Olympic games and so on. What is common to them all? … look and see whether there is anything common to all. – For if you look at them you will not see something that is common to* all, *but similarities, relationships and a whole series at that.*
>
> Ludwig Wittgenstein, *Philosophical Investigations*, §66

Wittgenstein goes on to list some different types of games. Some games we play involve winning and losing, such as football, but this is not true of all – he gives the examples of the card-game patience or a child throwing a ball against a wall and catching it. If we go through the range many things follow:

> *We can through the many, many other groups of games in the same way; we can see how similarities crop up and disappear.*
>
> *And the result of this examination is: we see a complicated network of similarities overlapping and criss-crossing.*
>
> *I can think of no better expression to characterize these similarities than 'family resemblances'; for the various resemblances between members of a family … overlap and criss-cross in the same way. – And I shall say: 'games' form a family …*
>
> Ibid., §66, 67

(a) Conceptual clarity and the difficulties of finding 'meaning'

As philosophers, it is our task to analyse these differences and similarities, to make sense of the activities that people are doing when they engage in the language of each game. The philosopher's task is to seek conceptual clarity.

In what way might we not know the way about? By not reflecting on the meaning of language as we use it (in context), perhaps, or by not recognising when language is being used metaphorically or analogically. Think about the examples earlier, such as 'not the ticket', 'brown bread' or 'peaky'. If we treated these terms as used by their speakers literally we would be in a real mess.

In the last chapter, there was discussion of whether the question 'does God exist?' should be treated as an ordinary scientific question. According to Wittgenstein, the danger of our understanding this question incorrectly is engagement in the wrong sort of discussion – leading to further muddle and further problems.

We must understand that for Wittgenstein *there are only the games*. We cannot get 'outside' the games to ask the 'real' meaning of words. We can only play another game. To ask for the real meaning – perhaps the dictionary meaning – of a word is not to step outside the world of games, but rather to play the lexicography game – the game played by the writers of dictionaries.

This has important consequences. We cannot get outside games – we can only play more games, or play them more competently: I may confidently play a greater or smaller number of games than you; and they will almost certainly not be precisely the same sets of games. I can only contemplate the nature of the games I play, seeking to describe with accuracy what is meant by what is said, and grow in understanding. Wittgenstein calls this process conceptual clarity, which he argues is the only task that philosophers can perform.

Even when we speak about meaning, we are playing a game: the term 'meaning' plays different roles in different games.

When we speak of the meaning of something, the very term 'meaning' is itself conditioned by the language game we are discussing. If Wittgenstein's theory is correct, this is a useful reminder that when we discuss 'meaning' within the context of a religious form of life, that use of 'meaning' is not synonymous with the use by someone asking the 'meaning' of a term in a poem or a scientific textbook.

Importantly, we should note that the language games do not *reflect* reality: they *make* it. We need to get beyond the idea that language pictures the world:

> A picture *held us captive. And we could not get outside it, for it lay in our language and language seemed to repeat it to us inexorably.*

Ludwig Wittgenstein, *Philosophical Investigations*, §115

The world as we know it is the world expressed in our games. I cannot play a 'real-world' game that is superior to any other game I play: it remains still a game – another game among games. What the world means to me – what it *is* to me – is determined by the games I play. Wittgenstein has moved away from any notion that language involves pictures of reality, or that there is any one master form of language. Therefore, we cannot ask what reality is like – we only play another form of language game – the 'reality' language game.

Background

Language games and Forms of Life

The term 'Forms of Life' has entered discussions about Wittgenstein, and it is evident that there are many different interpretations of Wittgenstein on offer. (Broadly speaking, philosophers have taken *form of life* to refer to some particular type of activity, such as playing games or the world of banking, where we use language in different ways and, indeed, behave very differently – the way an athlete talks about and participates in sporting activities is quite different from the way a sporty accountant might live and talk when in her office.)

Everything depends on what different thinkers mean by a 'Form of Life'. For some, language games are very broad, so the language game of physics would be one 'Form of Life', medicine another, poetry another, and so on. On this interpretation, religious faith would be a form of life, perhaps subdivided by denomination or faith, with, for example, Islam as a form of life with subdivisions such as Sunni or Shia. Atheism and agnosticism would be their own forms of life.

The question is whether reading Wittgenstein this way is too broad. His own remarks are not clear, either in *Philosophical Investigations* or in *On Certainty*. In *Philosophical Investigations*, he imagines someone asking him a question:

> 'So you are saying that human agreement decides what is false and what is true?' -- It is what human beings say that is false and true; and they agree in the language they use. That is not agreement in opinions but in form of life.

Ludwig Wittgenstein, *Philosophical Investigations*, §243

It is difficult to decide in this context exactly what a 'Form of Life' is, whether something broad like a religion or something more narrow. Things become even more complicated when we think about the varieties of usage within the language of something like religion, with language use moving through the poetry of the Psalms, the precise philosophical and theological formulations of someone like Aquinas, the distinctive language of worship and so on.

It seems that the problem lies in the texts from which we attempt to understand Wittgenstein's views:

> The *Philosophical Investigations* is not organized systematically: it has no chapters and no simple sequence of thought: it is even disputed whether it contains arguments. Much of it has the form of a probing conversation of the author with himself: Wittgenstein raises a worry – often on behalf of a more traditional approach to philosophy – responds to it, responds to the response, and so on. It's often not clear which of the things which are said represent Wittgenstein's own view ... In this respect, the text asks to be read more like a literary work than a scientific treatise.

Michael Morris, *An Introduction to the Philosophy of Language*, 2007, pages 292–3

At times, we are working with best guesses of what was, for Wittgenstein, very much a work in progress. It may well be that the notions of the language game

→

and the forms of life have been over-interpreted as being wholly self-contained and filled with their own reality, a reality which cannot be compared with the reality of another game. It may be that 'forms of life' should be understood not as categories of things in the world, but rather as a poetic way of expressing the variety of different linguistic usages.

Fergus Kerr argues, in *Theology After Wittgenstein* (1997, pages 29–31), that it is an over-interpretation of Wittgenstein to think of a religion as 'a form of life' or a language-game. Wittgenstein himself appears to have thought of games much more narrowly: a joke is a form of life, rather than 'humour' as a whole. If Kerr is right, then the idea of a form of life should rather be seen as referring to specific situations, such as comforting an injured man. This interpretation suggests that Wittgenstein simply wants us to pay attention to the particular use of language, and is not attempting to make a grand statement:

> ... it is impossible to apply the expression ['form of life'] to any phenomenon on the scale of 'religion' – which must include innumerable language-laced activities. As a very specific exchange that normally involves talking, comforting someone cannot be isolated ... from encouraging him, explaining, promising, calling a doctor and many other different from obviously related activities. The notion that any language game functions in isolation from others has no basis in Wittgenstein's work.

> Fergus Kerr, *Theology After Wittgenstein*, (second edition), 1997, page 31

This reading seems consistent with Wittgenstein's own examples of language games:

Giving orders and obeying them –

Describing the appearance of an object, or giving its measurements –

Constructing an object from a description (a drawing) –

Reporting an event –

Forming and testing a hypothesis –

Presenting the results of an experiment in tables and diagrams –

Making up a story; and reading it –

Play-acting –

Singing catches –

Guessing riddles –

Making a joke; telling it –

Asking, thanking, cursing, greeting, praying.

Ludwig Wittgenstein, *Philosophical Investigations*, §23

Each of these examples is particular, none as grand as 'religion' or 'science'. Each also is related to other things, and not just something occupying a world of its own. Telling a joke or play-acting takes place in a wider context. Meaning is not wholly self-contained, but we need to pay attention to both the particular and the context to understand the meaning in use.

It is useful to remember this in any thinking about 'Forms of Life'. Wittgenstein is a rich but elusive thinker, whom some see as poetic in his approach, rather than literal. Even after half a century of study, views of what he meant remain unsettled and disputed. That is part of his richness, but also his elusiveness.

3 The religious significance of language games

As noted previously, Wittgenstein himself wrote little directly about religion. He gave three lectures on religion in 1938. The only record of these lectures is some 20 pages of notes by one or more of his students. Certainly in his life he was not an observant member of the Catholic Church. Yet, he was fascinated by religion. He often refers to St Augustine, and there is little doubt that his disposition had many of the qualities of religious life – his asceticism, his personal generosity and his sense of the mystery of things. His executors made sure he had a Catholic funeral. Perhaps we should see him as having a religious disposition, rather than being a believer in a particular faith. His comments on the idea of a religion without doctrines seem to support this reading of his beliefs.

Nevertheless, many of his followers, including Elizabeth Anscombe, Rush Rhees, and, later, D. Z. Phillips, were devout believers. They argued that this analysis had a profound effect on the understanding of religious belief and faith.

An obvious area would be the question of the debate between theists and atheists. If Wittgenstein is right, the believer and the non-believer are playing different language games. In the case of the believer, 'God exists' is a sentence filled with meaning: God is essential to the reality created by the language game she played. It is not simply a theoretical question, but rather changes her sense of both herself and her world: it is transformative. But to the non-believer, playing the atheist game, the term 'God' would be an empty phrase, perhaps stripped of meaning.

The consequences of this understanding are significant. If we say God is a reality in the theist language game and a non-reality in the atheist game, we seem to be guilty of holding a contradictory position, that is, saying that God both really is and really is not, which looks absurd. (There are questions also about how we understand the idea of 'real', as the term might mean different things in different language games.)

We can go further. The Wittgensteinian philosopher, engaged simply in the contemplation of language games, is in a position to point out areas of conceptual confusion. She can show us where the differences between the language use occur. The atheist may be playing a scientific game, treating God as a scientific hypothesis, as Dawkins does, while the believer may perfectly well see God as a religious concept, not reducible to an ordinary hypothesis, as God is not a 'being among beings'.

Having a religious belief involves *faith*. To hold to a faith involves many things – and many forms of language. To *understand* faith it is necessary – in Wittgensteinian terms – to contemplate all those many uses, the language games of praise, of prayer, of being in a given faith community, a particular mosque, church, religious institution. These games are not fixed and once-and-for-all: they change over time, as new believers and new ideas come and go (this is an important consideration when we consider the failed attempt of logical positivism to reduce all language to two categories, as we argued in the last chapter).

If we contemplate the meaning of 'faith' as used by different speakers, then we may see that they are not necessarily in direct contradiction. Their usage can be quite different, even though they are using the same meaning. Someone may see faith as good, entailing life-changing devotion

Key question

Why is it mistaken to see 'God' as a scientific term?

See Chapter 5, Section 3 (Verification theory).

to God. To someone else the term might simply be used to mean 'superstition' or 'foolishness'.

Unless we take care to analyse how terms are used by a speaker or writer, we may misunderstand what is meant and perhaps attack them for the wrong reasons. It might well be possible for a believer to say that she also does not believe in the God Richard Dawkins rejects, because the God he rejects is not what she means by the word 'God'.

4 Language games and sacred texts

Central to faith is the status of sacred texts and there is much that can be said about how to understand these. Even within the great faiths, there is no consensus about this. Texts are written at particular times in human history, written in particular languages and always with human language. To maintain the integrity of faith, some argue that their texts are authentic only in the original language. But even if this integrity is justified, each language has its limitations. We sometimes say 'the Greeks had a word for it', but the Greeks had no word for 'will', Polish speakers struggle with articles ('a', 'the') when speaking in languages that use them, Chinese has fewer tenses than some other languages, and so on. Even when we use the same word in different cultures and contexts, meanings shift. The mental picture conjured up by the simple noun 'home' will be different in different parts of the world, and even among the citizens of the same nation.

Beyond that, there is no agreement about the status of either scripture as a whole or the different parts of it. Within Christianity, there are several approaches. A common way to see these approaches to scripture is to divide believers into:

- *Literalists*, who treat every sentence as true and cognitive
- *Conservatives*, who accept the general message as from God – thus treating scripture as the Word of God – but accepting the role of Biblical scholarship. This approach does not argue that every word is factually true, but believes the message to be authentic – this is roughly the position of the Roman Catholic Church, which has never taken the Bible literally.
- *Liberals*, who take a very open approach to scripture, seeing it as fundamentally a human document, to be interpreted in the light of our times.

Literalists represent a minority within the Christian tradition. It seems to have been a reaction to the apparent threat to faith offered by the discoveries of nineteenth-century science. Fundamentalism insisted on the literalness and inerrancy of the Bible in ways not previously encountered in scholarship. The term 'Fundamentalist' came first from the Niagara Bible Conference (1878–97), which defined certain notions as 'fundamental to faith'. A set of twelve books published in 1910 by Milton and Lyman Stewart was known as 'The Fundamentals', and the 1910 *General Assembly of the Presbyterian Church*, an American body, declared five 'fundamentals' of faith:

- The inspiration of the Bible by the Holy Spirit and the absolute accuracy of scripture.
- The virgin birth of Christ.

- The belief that Christ's death was the atonement for sin.
- The bodily resurrection of Christ.
- The historical reality of Christ's miracles.

Most controversial is the belief in the absolute accuracy of scripture. An older tradition doubted this: as early as the third century, we find Origen, one of the greatest early Christian thinkers, arguing:

> For who that has understanding will suppose that the first, and second, and third day, and the evening and the morning, existed without a sun, and moon, and stars? And who is so foolish as to suppose that first day was, as it were, also without a sky? And who is so foolish as to suppose that God, after the manner of a husbandman, planted a paradise in Eden, towards the East, and placed in it a tree of life, visible and palpable, so that one tasting of the fruit of the tree with bodily teeth obtained life? And again, that one was a partaker of good and evil by masticating what was taken from the tree? And if God is said to walk in the paradise in the evening, and Adam to hide himself under a tree, I do not suppose that anyone doubts that these things figuratively indicate certain mysteries.
>
> *De Principiis*, IV, 16

There is no hint of Fundamentalist literalism here, and many – most – Christians are not literalists. The Roman Catholic Church rejects literalism as do most others.

But this leaves open a fundamental question. How then is scripture to be interpreted? The Bible is a collection of writings of many different types. It contains sets of laws, poetry (such as *Psalms* or *The Song of Songs*), allegories (*Job, Apocalypse*), history and other forms of teaching. The question is not made easier by saying that the historical elements are the true, cognitive parts. Conventions for writing history change.

If today I were to publish a history book without good evidence for the factual material I included, I would rightly be criticised. If I made up parts to fit what I thought a historical character might have said or done, even though I did not know if he truly did or said those things, I would be thought to be dabbling in fiction. If I included things just because they made a good story or a moral point, I would be thought unreliable. Yet ancient historians did all those things. Herodotus seemed unable to resist a good story, Thucydides puts into the mouths of major characters long speeches, of which he could have had no record, in his own style, and the writers of Genesis provide not one but two inconsistent accounts of creation (Genesis 1 & 2). Even within the Gospels, there are inconsistencies between one gospel and another. In the Gospel of Mark, both thieves crucified with Jesus mock him; elsewhere we have the morally uplifting tale of one of the thieves recognising the innocence of Jesus, repenting his own sin and given the promise of paradise.

It would seem absurd to treat the entirety of scripture as straightforwardly cognitive or non-cognitive.

These considerations rather seem to lead to the conclusion that the best approach to sacred texts is the kind of critical Wittgensteinian understanding of the meaning of sentences in terms of the way they are being used, not imposing on terms a single, univocal meaning. If we are to attend to meaning in use, then what a Wittgensteinian approach demands is a sensitivity to such matters as intention, form of a text, and proper understanding – the same things sought by scriptural criticism. The straitjacket approach seems bound to fail.

5 Language games: cognitive or non-cognitive?

Key term

Expressivism The non-cognitivist view that moral (or religious) statements simply express an evaluative attitude but correspond to no objective reality.

Don Cupitt (b. 1934): Cambridge-based Anglican priest and radical theologian, best known for his theological non-realism. His best-known works include *Taking Leave of God* and a 1984 TV series and accompanying book, *The Sea of Faith*, which has led to the creation of a movement and magazine of the same name.

There is a question about whether Wittgenstein's theory of language games should be interpreted cognitively or non-cognitively. In many circles, it has become almost an article of faith that Wittgenstein's theory should be understood non-cognitively. Peter Vardy has argued strongly for this interpretation in various books and addresses. Among theologians, Don Cupitt has argued strenuously for such a view. But others, including D.Z. Phillips, have argued that this is a misinterpretation. This latter interpretation has become more common among Wittgenstein scholars, so we should consider the evidence.

Remember that a cognitive sentence is one about which it is appropriate to ask whether it is true or false.

If a non-cognitive view is taken, it would seem to mean that no sentence is true or false, but something in a game which does little more than express a feeling, a view sometimes described as **expressivism**. But if there are only language games – that is, every use of language takes place within a language game – then what do we mean in any language game in which we use the terms 'true' or 'false'? In most usages, perhaps all, the word 'true' means something like: 'I use the word "true" when I mean that such-and-such is the case in reality'. If Wittgenstein argues that all we are doing is to analyse usage – what words mean as they are used – it seems odd to say to the user of language that he does not use the word 'true' in the way he thinks he is using it, and that he is just expressing a positive emotion.

A few scholars, such as Don Cupitt and Peter Vardy, have insisted on non-cognitivist interpretations of Wittgenstein, but the overwhelming weight of scholarly opinion rejects that reading.

They argue that Wittgenstein is using language non-cognitively as conventional categories of *true* or *false* seem not to apply to language games. This approach has been adopted by Don Cupitt and his followers in the Sea of Faith movement, at least as far as the language games of religion are concerned. This has meant denying God as a reality in himself.

(a) Don Cupitt's non-cognitive analysis of Wittgenstein

For Cupitt, God is not something that exists but simply a reality within the community of faith. Cupitt argues that Christianity involves a special form of life, with special values and meanings. He recommends his own non-metaphysical approach as the best way to live.

Theological non-realism Term used by Don Cupitt for the belief that 'God' refers to no objective reality but refers simply to spiritual meaning in our own lives and discourse. Should not be confused with the epistemological idea of *antirealism*, which is a notion developed in epistemology by Michael Dummett, and irrelevant here.

His view is often called *non-realism* (or **'theological non-realism'**), which is concerned not with asserting the objective existence of God (which Cupitt calls 'theological realism'), but with the meaning of God in people's lives. For Cupitt and his followers (many in the Sea of Faith movement) God exists in us – faith is a stance on life. Cupitt opposes theological realism to 'expressivism'. For him, God has no objective reality:

The Christian doctrine of God just is Christian spirituality in coded form, for God is a symbol that represents to us everything that spirituality requires of us and promises to us.

Don Cupitt, *Taking Leave of God*, 2001, page 15

What matters for Cupitt is what the God-concept *expresses*. For Cupitt, our lives on earth are transformed by our sense of the meaning of God. Cupitt claims that there is no God 'out there'. We have only the meaning within the community of belief and its significance in our lives, but *there is nothing else that is God*. Non-realism is not about any reality but the personal and spiritual. As Cupitt says:

The main interest of religion is in the conquest of evil by the transformation of the self...The emancipation of consciousness that religion seeks makes possible, and gives worth and stability to, all the other concerns of civilization such as science and art... God is the pearl of great price, the treasure hidden at the centre of the religious life... But we should not suppose God to be a substance, an independently-existing being who can be spoken of in a descriptive and non-religious way. Religious language is not in the business of describing really-existing super-sensible objects and their activities. We do not nowadays have sufficient reason to suppose that there are any such beings or influences, and in any case religion is not concerned with them. No external object can bring about my inner spiritual liberation. I must will it for myself and attain it within myself. Only I can free myself.

Ibid., page 178

His point, too often erroneously described (by Vardy, among others) as 'antirealism' (a term not used by Cupitt himself), is based on reading Wittgensteinian language games as non-cognitivist. In this reading, everything which is uttered is completely within the language game being played, with no connection to other language games outside itself. This seems contrary to Wittgenstein's claim that we need to study the relationships between games. If words do not reach in any way outside the game in which they are used, then it seems difficult to discuss their relationships.

Cupitt's reading of Wittgenstein as non-cognitive, simply expressing feelings – such as a spiritual sense to which we give the name 'God' – is controversial, both for its non-cognitivism, which is attacked by both religious thinkers as not capturing what they mean by 'God' which they see as a name for an overwhelming reality, as well as by Wittgensteinian scholars such as D. Z. Phillips who believe that Cupitt has misunderstood Wittgenstein. There are also questions about whether something as broad

Key person

D. Z. Phillips (1934–2006): Welsh Wittgensteinian philosopher of religion and ethics. Prolific author who believed the purpose of philosophy was the contemplation of the meaning of terms in use. Fierce critic of the work of Richard Swinburne and others.

Key quote

Philosophy may in no way interfere with the actual use of language; it can in the end only describe it.

For it cannot give it any foundation either.

It leaves everything as it is.

Ludwig Wittgenstein,
Philosophical Investigations, §124

as 'religion' can rightly be interpreted, according to Wittgenstein, as a 'form of life' (see Background box, page 89), as it is too wide-ranging – within religious discourse there are too many different types of language games to put under a single heading.

(b) D. Z. Phillips's cognitive analysis of Wittgenstein

D. Z. Phillips, perhaps the most significant Wittgensteinian philosopher of religion, argued differently (Phillips himself developed his work from that of Rush Rhees, with whom he worked closely. When Rhees died, Phillips bought for himself the plot at Rhees' feet in Swansea cemetery.) Phillips builds upon an idea from Wittgenstein about forms of life. It is not always clear whether he treats religion as a whole as a 'form of life' or rather uses particular terms as forms of life (See Background box page 89). Both elements appear in his work.

For Phillips, as for Wittgenstein, the philosopher's task was not to comment on the truth of religious statements, but to question and clarify their meaning within the discourse of faith. The task of philosophy is not 'to settle the question of whether a man is talking to God or not, but to ask what it means to affirm or deny that a man is talking to God' (D. Z. Phillips: *The Concept of Prayer*, 1965, page 37).

Unlike Cupitt, Phillips does not deny the objective existence of God. He simply denies that it is part of the philosopher's task to determine God's existence. Phillips argued that to ask whether God exists is a question in the religious form of life, rather than a scientific one. It is a question beyond the philosopher's remit:

> We resist mystery because we tend to give the primary place to explanation. But religion brings to our attention the limits of human existence, limits for which no further explanations can be found. Religion, in this context, asks us to die to the understanding. … In religion, meeting what confronts us is a form of acceptance in terms of the grace of God.

D. Z. Phillips, *From Fantasy to Faith*, 2006, page 228

This position is very different from Cupitt's. Phillips argues that *as philosophers* we can only look, coolly, at the meanings and grammar of sentences in religious sentences. For him, there is a reality beyond the game with which we are confronted, whereas for Cupitt the only reality of God is found *within* the language game.

Phillips thought emphatically that God was real. On the realism/non-realism debate, he commented:

Key quote

Theological non-realism is as empty as theological realism. Both terms are battle-cries in a confused philosophical and theological debate.

D. Z. Phillips, *Wittgenstein and Religion*, 1993, page 35

Writing of modern faith, Phillips says:

Our problem, it seems, is not how to escape God, but how to find him. There are even theologians who say that God cannot be found on high. They insist that we should speak of him as deep inside us, but secular psychiatric and psychoanalytic explanations threaten to monopolise explanations of what can be found there.

D. Z. Phillips, *Faith After Foundationalism*, 1995, page 11

For Phillips, 'God exists' is not a scientific proposition. But for him, the doubt is over the form of the sentence. If we ask 'Does God exist?', it is not reducible to the same form as other existential sentences. 'God' is not a name like another.

Phillips doesn't deny that God exists, just that whatever God is cannot be measured using the same rules of language, or reduced to a form of words.

A similar idea is supported by Father Gareth Moore. Arguing within a Wittgensteinian perspective, he says:

I do not want to deny the reality of God, that God really exists. But it is not yet settled what the reality of God consists in.

Gareth Moore, *Believing in God*, 1988, page 101

Here, Moore is obviously denying the non-cognitive reading of those like Cupitt. The question is, which reading is truest to Wittgenstein's intention?

(c) Criticisms of non-cognitive readings of language games

Remember Wittgenstein's own comment: 'It leaves everything as it is'. A non-cognitivist interpretation changes things, because it would mean that a believer is not using language in the way she thinks she is using it. And that would change everything.

After Wittgenstein's *Lectures on Religious Belief*, a student asked an important question. Were religious statements simply expressions of the feelings of the believer? The student gave the example of someone who was convinced he might never see a friend again, telling him, 'We might see one another after death'. The student asked whether this simply expresses a certain attitude, a feeling towards that friend, rather than a factual belief. Wittgenstein rejected that interpretation:

I would say 'No, it isn't the same thing as saying "I'm very fond of you" – and it may not be the same as saying anything else. It says what it says. Why should you have to substitute anything else?'

Ludwig Wittgenstein, *Lectures and Conversations*, ed. Cyril Barrett, 1999, page 71

A recent study says that the non-cognitivist approach misreads Wittgenstein (and Phillips):

In contrast with the Cupittian non-realist, who is busy instructing religious believers how their words should be understood, the Wittgensteinian finds that there is more than enough to be

Key quote

The main reason for these differences is that God's reality is not one of a kind: He is not a being among beings. The word 'God' is not the name of a thing. Thus, the reality of God cannot be assessed by a common measure which also applies to things other than God.

D. Z. Phillips, *Wittgenstein and Religion*, 1993, page 62

getting on with in just exploring the meanings that are already there, open to view, before our eyes ... not trying to innovate or reform, but just to look, see and describe.

Mikel Burley, *Contemplating Religious Forms of Life: Wittgenstein and D. Z. Phillips*, 2012, page169

If we follow Wittgenstein's idea that we should just look at our language, seeing and describing, some interesting things happen.

Remember that a cognitive sentence is one about which it is appropriate to ask whether it is true or false. If we think about the language game of physics, or the language game of geography, it is absolutely appropriate to ask whether a sentence within those subjects is true or false. It matters to physics, properly understood, whether Ptolemy's theory of the earth as the centre of the universe is true: meanings in the rest of the activity rest on whether the theory is correct. A geographer asks whether it is true that Paris is the capital of France. Surely, in these language games, truth and falsity matter.

But this is not true of all language games. In the language game of poetry, it is usually inappropriate to ask whether a poem such as Wordsworth's *The Daffodils* or Tennyson's *The Lotus-Eaters* is true, even though we may properly ask what it means.

To argue that some language games are cognitive and some not, makes more sense of the material than arguing they are all of one type. There is no evidence at all that Wittgenstein is saying any more than instructing us to examine all we say *in its own terms*.

Cupitt insists that all religious language is non-cognitive. His critics would see this as reductionist. Religious language is used in so many ways. Believers use the Nicene Creed to state what they believe to be true – it is more than a poem. It matters as a statement of beliefs they think are true, and they would argue that a non-Christian holds that the statements in the Creed are not true. Truth matters. But the Christian does not deny that some religious sentences, such as those in a prayer or a hymn, are non-cognitive. A careful study, such as a Wittgensteinian seeks, of religious discourse reveals the use of all kinds of very different sentences.

6 Analogy or language games?

So, how well does the theory of analogy put forward by Aquinas marry with the language game theory of Wittgenstein? In some ways, they are complementary.

Remember that in his theory of analogy (outlined in Chapter 4), Aquinas points out that the descriptions of God – and many within religious discourse – are being used in a particular way, as analogies which enable us to say something positive about God.

He tells us how terms are used, and points to the variety of usages. What this indicates is the idea that there is not one 'right' use – we have to seek meaning in the context of our discussion of God, but also to be aware that our analysis is faulty if we think we grasp precisely those meanings. Aquinas points to the limitations of our understanding and tries to get us to think carefully about what we are doing when we talk of God: he reminds us continually of the *use* of language.

On Aquinas' theory of analogy, see Chapter 4, page 53.

What is a Wittgensteinian philosopher doing when he asks us to examine the *use* of our language in the context? He is no less concerned than Aquinas with identifying the boundaries of meaning. For both, the concern remains careful textual analysis within its proper context.

We can usefully look again at something we said about Aquinas' notion of analogy, when we said that what Aquinas was doing was not to explain the meaning of terms used analogically about God, but rather to show *how they are used*. Wittgenstein's interest is in usage, so we should not be surprised if we find great similarities between Aquinas and Wittgenstein.

It is also little surprise that many modern Thomist scholars make so much use of Wittgenstein in their work. Both were concerned about conceptual clarity, and both wanted to understand how terms were to be understood in their use. David Burrell in *Analogy and Religious Language* (1973) and a range of subsequent works has used the insights of Wittgenstein to find conceptual clarity about Aquinas' intentions, and in the United Kingdom, scholars such as Herbert McCabe and Anthony Kenny have followed similar pathways. In an Introduction to Herbert McCabe's posthumously published lectures on Aquinas, Kenny says of McCabe:

> *He was indeed an admirer of Wittgenstein, and he sought to graft the insights of the twentieth-century thinker on to those of the thirteenth-century thinker ... because he recognised a genuine affinity between the two masters.*

> *Undoubtedly, Aquinas and Wittgenstein shared a conviction that it is through an unconstrained attention to the operation of language that we achieve philosophical understanding. ... Whereas Aquinas himself undoubtedly believed that every thought we have can, in principle, be expressed in language, he did not, McCabe says, fully grasp that human thought just is the capacity to use language. 'We analyse understanding and thinking in terms of human communication, whereas Aquinas analyses communication in terms of understanding and thinking.'*

> Anthony Kenny: 'Introduction', Herbert McCabe, *On Aquinas*, ed. Brian Davies, 2008, pages viii–ix

The difference between Aquinas and Wittgenstein, identified by McCabe, was one of whether it is language which creates thought or the other way round. For Aquinas, language reflects our ideas, while for Wittgenstein it is the precondition.

(a) Similarities and differences

It is not clear whether differences are great enough to say that Aquinas and Wittgenstein are doing something completely different. It might be possible to argue for differences if we accept Cupitt's non-cognitive approach to language games, but any argument along these lines needs to pay attention to the very different views of scholars such as Moore and Phillips.

More convincing as a difference is the point made by McCabe and reinforced by Kenny, that there are differences in assumptions made. For Wittgenstein, it is the use of language which makes thought and activity: it is their precondition.

Aquinas in his theory of analogy takes language as a given. We just have language, and use it to express ideas, as well as we can – in the case of God, analogically. We use language to express a thought, whereas for Wittgenstein it is the language games we play that determine the thoughts we are able to formulate.

The other difference is that Aquinas is very specifically writing as a philosophical theologian. He develops the idea of analogy – though it has significance in relation to other uses of language – specifically to deal with the problem of the terms we use about God. The question he is answering is different from Wittgenstein: for Aquinas, it is 'How can we use our language to find some way of speaking significantly about God', while for Wittgenstein the question is not a specifically religious one: he asks more generally what language does and how we are to perceive it.

Nevertheless, it is important not to lose sight of the central point, which is that the question for both philosophers is how we *use* language, determining any meaning in relation to that use.

7 Objections to language games

The very notion of language games has been the subject of much heated debate in the past 50 years. A major critic was Ernest Gellner, whose *Words and Things* (1959) is a blistering and often very funny attack on Wittgensteinian assumptions, with a preface by Bertrand Russell who likens the obsession with meaning to those who are always sharpening their tools but never using them. He compares the obsession with the meaning of words with someone who takes apart a perfectly performing clock and then wonders why it no longer works.

Gellner has compared the obsession with the meaning of words with someone who takes apart a perfectly performing clock – then wonders why it no longer works. Is this a fair comparison?

(a) Circularity

Probably the most significant criticism of language games is that they are circular. Where do we find the meaning of a word? From the language game from which it takes its meaning. But where does the language game get its meaning? From the words that make it up. It seems that for a given language game to make sense, there has to be some external link to give meaning to the whole. The question is whether language games can have the autonomy which some attribute to them. If it is correct to say that Wittgenstein does assume that the world is real and his constant reminders to look at what is there makes us think that he does – then there is presumably some link (i.e. they are not autonomous), though Wittgenstein does not, and perhaps cannot, tell us what that link is.

(b) Choosing between language games

If all language games are autonomous, we may very properly ask how we can justify paying attention to one rather than another. I may describe the differences between the game of Christianity and the game of atheism, but part of the religious life is making a judgement about the relative merits of the two. The believer – and the atheist – experience their choices as meaning more than simply opting for playing one game over another.

As we saw earlier, for Phillips, science and religion are different types of discourse, and we can *justify* neither. The game is basic, in the sense that we cannot get behind it to justify it: the game is played and that is why as philosophers we should seek to understand it. Because it is a reality as a game played, it needs no further justification.

This creates an interesting problem. It looks as if, if this is indeed the case, science and theology could say nothing to each other, as each occupies its own realm. However, in reality, as we know from thinkers such as Swinburne and Dawkins, religious believers and supporters of science very often want to engage with each other. If we say simply that theology and science are different basic games, then what can we say about that discourse in which they attempt to debate with each other? (For an interesting discussion of this with particular reference to language games, see: William H. Austin: *The Relevance of Natural Science to Theology*, 1976, especially Chapter 5.)

Patrick Sherry develops the point, looking at the question of *why* we should choose to play one game rather than another. He argues that:

> ... *whilst it may be silly to ask for a* general *justification of religion or science, we can certainly discuss* particular *ones, e.g. Christianity or astrology (incidentally, although the question 'Is science true?' is absurd, the question 'Why pursue science?' is not.)*

Patrick Sherry, *Religion, Truth and Language-Games*, 1977, page 30

Sherry is making a very important point. Between Christianity and astrology we may, and probably do, want to discuss reasons for playing one game rather than another. The Christian would want to argue that her game is better than astrology, which she may characterise as 'mere superstition'. An atheist might dismiss both as superstitious, but still take the claims of one more significantly than the other. He might say that Christian views need to be argued against while thinking astrology complete rubbish, and not worth the effort.

Key person

Patrick Sherry: British philosopher of religion with special interests in language games, the relationship of aesthetics and religion, and Catholic thought in general. Emeritus Professor at the University of Lancaster.

(c) The question of truth

The question of what those in a community believe *and whether those beliefs are true* matters within the game. To develop Sherry's point, in the faith community, 'God' is not simply a given term, with meaning to the community. It is central to the very notion of faith that God might not exist – his non-existence is a real possibility, which the true, thoughtful believer (as opposed to an unthinking zealot) accepts. She recognises that she might be wrong. That is why she has *faith* rather than certainty. Again, truth matters.

There may be another circularity in the theory of games. If there are only games, each with equal legitimacy, how then are we to treat the entire theory of language games? Is this just the 'Language Game language game', no more significant or important than any other? Why should this be privileged over any other? There is nothing outside the language game – on the theory nothing could be outside – to legitimate its claims.

8 Wittgensteinian fideism

An interesting question was raised by A. J. Ayer in his inaugural professorial lecture at Oxford (A. J. Ayer, *The Concept of a Person and Other Essays*, 1963, page 18). If each language game has its own reality, are not Wittgenstein followers committed to accepting talk about fairies and witches? Just because someone describes someone else as 'bewitched', it does not follow that there actually are demons in the world, and there are good reasons why one might want to characterise that entire language game as untrue, and not simply to say that a given sentence is true or false only within the game. Surely, thinks Ayer, we would want to argue the superiority of physics over talk of magic spells and potions.

These ideas led to a long-running argument, principally between Phillips and Kai Nielsen, with others joining in. Following the publication of Phillips' *The Concept of Prayer*, in 1965, Nielsen wrote an essay in *Philosophy* called 'Wittgensteinian Fideism'. The ins and outs of the debate may be enjoyed in Kai Nielsen and D. Z. Phillips, *Wittgensteinian Fideism* (2005). The argument between the two ceased only on Phillips' sudden death in 2006.

Nielsen's charge was that according to language game theory, ideas of reality, intelligibility and reason become ambiguous as their precise meaning can only be determined *within their given discourse*. There is therefore no outside position from which a philosopher or anyone else can criticise a given discourse. If this is the case, then to be within the game of faith seems to mean that faith becomes simply **fideism**. Remarks by Phillips, such as those quoted on page 96, about religion being beyond understanding or explanation, appear to give evidence to strengthen Nielsen's case, though the majority of faith denominations (notably the Catholic Church) would dispute fideism.

> **Key term**
>
> **Fideism** The belief that all that is required in religion is faith, which has and needs no justification. This belief is considered heretical by the Catholic Church.

Is a Wittgensteinian view of
religion fideist?

Phillips replied that the work of a Wittgensteinian analyst is not simply one of blind faith. He argued that much religious belief is confused and muddled and that finding true meaning requires intellectual rigour and is arduous – it is neither blind nor simple. It is in that way that justice can actually be done to competing views on religious belief. Phillips' last words on the subject were:

> *Philosophical contemplation seeks to do justice to belief and atheism, to the confusions and the sense that can be found in each. An atheism that holds that* all *religious beliefs are either false or incoherent will be unable to do that. But, then, it has always been recognised that one's own beliefs can get in the way of the kind of attention called for by a contemplative conception of philosophy.*

Kai Nielsen and D. Z. Phillips, *Wittgensteinian Fideism*, 2005, page 371

Does that really answer the claim that Nielsen makes? It is one thing to argue that the language game approach does justice to atheism and belief in that it resolves conceptual muddles *within* those claims; but it cannot settle, as Phillips acknowledges, the *external* question of whether the forms of life themselves are true. Of course, it may be that the Wittgensteinian claim that there are only the forms and nothing outside that can justify them, is correct; but if there is no possible external justification, how can we justify the claim? A justification must lie outside the claim to be justified, but language game theory rules out the possibility of the means of external justification – we can only really talk about what goes on within the game.

9 Conclusions

Wittgenstein was one of the greatest of all philosophers, but was far from the most precise in his views. In this chapter we have seen how some, for example Don Cupitt, have interpreted him in non-cognitive terms, while others, such as D. Z. Phillips, take a wholly different view. As we have seen, the idea of language games has been hotly debated, with arguments about what Wittgenstein meant by a 'form of life', as well as ongoing discussion of how we can significantly justify playing one game rather than another.

There is wider agreement among scholars that non-cognitive interpretations of Wittgenstein, as espoused by Cupitt and some others, are probably mistaken and distant from his intentions. It is interesting, in this context, that Thomist scholars, such as McCabe, Gareth Moore, Kenny and Burrell, none of whom would interpret 'God' as just an expression of personal feeling or spirituality, all believe that Wittgensteinian insights are invaluable in finding conceptual clarity in Aquinas' theories of language.

Whatever the reality of what Wittgenstein truly meant, the need to attend to the grammar, to *look*, is a lesson for anyone engaged in the business of clear thinking.

Study advice

This is not the easiest topic you will study, but the key to success is to be very clear about what is meant by Wittgenstein in his argument that we should concentrate on meaning in use (in its context). Think of your own examples of different kinds of usage. In an essay of this type, within the context of the Philosophy of Religion, you might find it very helpful to use examples from sacred texts. Once you are reasonably clear and confident about this idea of language in use, then – and not before – you can concentrate on the significance of Wittgenstein's theory for language games. Think about the issue that more may have been claimed for language games than Wittgenstein intended. Be aware that while non-realists such as Don Cupitt have argued for a non-cognitive reading of Wittgenstein, others such as D. Z. Phillips have taken a different perspective.

Summary diagram: Religious language: 20th-century perspectives – Wittgenstein and language games

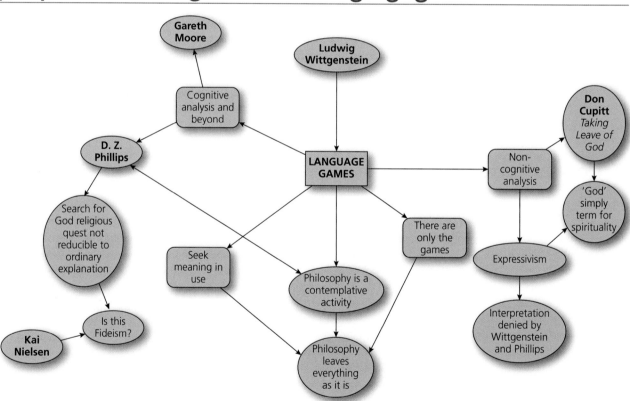

Revision advice

By the end of this chapter you should be able to explain, with examples, the idea of language games. You should also be able to reflect on how the idea might be used to clarify our understanding of religious language and the implications for studying the nature of both God and religious faith.

Can you give brief definitions of:
- meaning in use
- language games
- philosophy as contemplation
- fideism
- expressivism?

Can you explain:
- Wittgenstein's conception of the purpose of philosophy
- non-cognitive approaches to discussion of religion
- the alleged circularity of language game theory
- the problems of deciding what is meant by a language game?

Can you give arguments for and against:
- the idea that there are only language games
- the idea that language game theory leads to fideism in religion
- the claim that religious language should be understood non-cognitively
- the claim that the language game of physics is not superior to that of witches and warlocks?

Sample question and guidance

'Wittgenstein's theory of language games is very helpful to any study of sacred texts.' Discuss.

This question should remind you that your study of given ideas does not happen in a self-contained box marked 'religious language'. If what philosophers say about language is significant, that significance can only be understood in context. Scripture has a fundamental role in faith, and all faiths have a tradition of textual understanding, with disagreements not only about the meaning of individual sentences and passages, but also about the relative weight to give to each part of the texts. Many Christians have debated whether the Old Testament should be understood as leading to the fullness of the New, or whether – as Calvin appeared to have thought – all books of the Bible should be treated as equally the Word of God. In Islam, scholars argue about whether Surah 96 is more or less important to Islam than Surah

1. Similar debates occur in Judaism and other faiths. Some argue that texts are only authentic in the original languages, but even if this is true, understanding of terms within a language changes. When a text in Sanskrit or Syriac uses the word for 'home', my mental picture will not be identical to that of the original writer.

For this essay, you need to be aware of textual issues. It is unlikely you will be familiar with every religion's sacred writings and you would be wise to refer only to those writings with which you are familiar. You need to be clear about what Wittgenstein says in his theory of language games, with its emphasis on meaning in use. If you can give examples of different types of writing and intention within scripture – parts which are allegorical, historical, law-making, poetic and so on – you may wish to use these to demonstrate the value of paying close attention to definition in use.

Further essay questions

'Wittgenstein's theory of language games is too unclear for it to be useful.' Discuss.

To what extent is Wittgenstein's theory of language games helpful in clarifying Aquinas' idea of analogy?

'Language game theories lead us to fideism, not to faith.' Discuss.

Going further

Wittgenstein is a notoriously difficult philosopher and, as we have seen, there are significant issues in interpreting what he meant. Of recent works, Mikel Burley's *Contemplating Religious Forms of Life: Wittgenstein and D.Z. Phillips* (Continuum, 2012) is as useful an introduction to the themes of this chapter as any. Patrick Sherry's excellent study is, unfortunately, out of print.

Anthony Kenny, *Wittgenstein* (revised edition, Wiley-Blackwell, 2005) is very clear, and A. C. Grayling, *Wittgenstein: A Very Short Introduction* (Oxford, 2001) gives a brief overview.

For D. Z. Phillips, perhaps his most complete account may be found in his *Religion and the Hermeneutics of Contemplation* (Cambridge University Press, 2001) but he gave an excellent outline of his philosophy in the introductory chapter of his *From Fantasy to Faith: Morality, Religion and Twentieth-Century Literature* (second revised edition, SCM, 2006).

The ins and outs of the debate on fideism may be enjoyed in Kai Nielsen and D.Z. Phillips, *Wittgensteinian Fideism* (SCM, 2005).

Although the distinction between antirealism and nonrealism is not required for this examination, if you wish to look at the topic, it is covered in Michael B. Wilkinson, *Philosophy of Religion: An Introduction* (Continuum, 2010), pages 285–96.

Other books discussed in this chapter are:

- Austin, W. H. *The Relevance of Natural Science to Theology* (Macmillan, 1976).
- Ayer, A. J. *The Concept of a Person and Other Essays* (Macmillan, 1963).
- Burrell. D. *Analogy and Religious Language* (Wipf, 1973).
- Cupitt, D. *Taking Leave of God* (SCM, 2001).
- Gellner, E. *Words and Things* (Routledge, 1959).
- Kerr, F. *Theology After Wittgenstein* (second edition, SPCK).
- McCabe. H. *On Aquinas,* ed. Brian Davies (Burns and Oates, 2008).
- Moore, G. *Believing in God* (T. & T. Clark, 1988).
- Morris, M. *An Introduction to the Philosophy of Language* (Cambridge University Press, 2007).
- Phillips, D. Z. *Wittgenstein and Religion* (1993).
- Phillips, D. Z. *Faith After Foundationalism* (1995).
- Sherry, P. *Religion, Truth and Language-Games* (Macmillan, 1977).
- Wittgenstein, L. *Philosophical Investigations* (Oxford University Press, 1958).

Chapter 7

Religious language: 20th-century perspectives – the falsification debate

Chapter checklist

The main focus of this chapter is the famous *University* debate of Antony Flew, R. M. Hare and Basil Mitchell. The chapter begins with discussion of the original intention of Karl Popper's falsification as a principle of **demarcation** between science and non-science, and not, as interpreted by A. J. Ayer, as a principle of meaning. Flew's contribution to falsification is discussed, as are the views of Hare, Mitchell and subsequent comments by John Hick. Throughout, arguments are supported by close textual reference, to avoid common misunderstandings.

1 Introduction

Key term

Falsification Karl Popper's theory that a proposition is scientific if one can state what evidence would prove it false. This is a principle of demarcation between science and non-science, *not* between the meaningful and the meaningless.

One of the most interesting, but also most misunderstood, debates in the second half of the twentieth century was about the relationship between religious language and the ideas of **falsification**. Attention focused above all on the falsification symposium, first published in the journal, *University*, and republished in the 1955 collection, *New Essays in Philosophical Theology*, edited by Antony Flew and Alasdair MacIntyre. The purpose of these essays was partly to move philosophical discussion of religion beyond the logical positivists, who dismissed religious language as meaningless. Since the publication of *New Essays,* the falsification symposium has been repeatedly anthologised and much discussed.

The idea of a symposium goes back to Greek times. Plato's *Symposium* is a major dialogue in which the various speakers attempt to answer the question, 'What is Love?' A symposium has all the advantages of a conversation, in which a question is put, others respond and, in the case of the falsification discussion, the original questioner then responds. In the falsification debate, the question is about the status of religious language. Flew, using Popper's idea of falsification, asks what would count as a disproof of religious beliefs. The discussion then follows.

The discussion is very brief and is entirely in ordinary language – Flew and the two other philosophers in the debate were each noted for the clarity of their writing. Taking the half hour needed to read the whole discussion is an invaluable use of your time. There is much to think about, and it is always valuable to develop the habit of reading original texts to see what writers actually say – which is sometimes very different from what people imagine they say.

Background

Falsification and logical positivism

Logical positivism has, as we saw two chapters ago, had many problems. Its claim to determine the distinction between meaningful sentences and others was much criticised. As we saw, Dorothy Emmet in *The Nature of Metaphysical Thinking* (1945) suggested that the logical positivists misunderstood the character of metaphysical sentences. Younger philosophers, most notably Antony Flew, also found much wanting in the assumptions of verification theory. But the most significant opponent of logical positivism was Karl

Popper (later Sir Karl Popper), one of the greatest philosophers of the twentieth century.

While studying in Vienna, Popper became friendly with many leading figures in the Vienna Circle, but because of his disagreement with the conclusions of logical positivism, he was never invited to their meetings. Otto Neurath described Popper as 'The Official Opposition'. His approach to science, and his opposition to the principle of verification, were set out in *Logik der Forschung* of 1934 (translated as *The Logic of Scientific Discovery*, 1959).

> **Key person**
>
> **Karl Raimund Popper** (1902–94): born in Vienna and was educated at the University of Vienna, where he received his Ph.D. in 1928. After the rise of Nazism, he emigrated in 1934 first to London, then to New Zealand, where he lectured for a decade before moving back to London in 1946, first as Reader, then as Professor of Logic and Scientific Method at the London School of Economics, from 1949 until 1969. He was knighted in 1965, by which time he had been fully recognised as perhaps
>
>
>
> the most significant figure in the Philosophy of Science, as well as a major contributor to political thought. His seminal *The Open Society and Its Enemies* had been written in New Zealand. Popper is always worth reading – the clarity and elegance of his English style provide a model of good writing.

2 Popper and the falsification debate

Popper opposed the basic assumption of the Vienna Circle that what mattered was to be able to prove scientific propositions true. He pointed out that if we believe that science is about proving our views to be true, we would make no progress at all. We would also have the wrong approach to experiment and research.

When we do experiments, we should not look to verify theories, but to falsify them: we must test, test and test again, even to destruction. Theories require robust scrutiny. Only in that way does science progress – we find, through continual criticism and testing, weaknesses in our existing theories, discard them, and try to produce better ones. If we conducted all our experiments on the assumption that they would prove our theories true, we would try to explain away anomalies and exceptions. But it is the anomalies and exceptions that tell us that there is something wrong with our original theory. Popper, who was sometimes rather peppery in manner, would become cross with those who took the lazy view that it is the exception that proves the rule: he would point out that it is the exception that *disproves* the rule.

Thus, for Popper, the key activity is that of *falsification*. The mark of a genuinely scientific statement is that it is possible to state what would falsify it.

Antony Flew explains the point very clearly:

Key quote

Popper's contention was ... that, whereas no theory and no proposition may be accounted scientific even when it is known to be false, no theory and no proposition can be properly presented as even a possible contribution to science unless its proponents are prepared to specify what would have to happen, or to have happened, for it to be falsified; that is, shown to be false.

Antony Flew, *An Introduction to Western Philosophy*, (revised edition), 1989, page 482

So, the method of science is not of proving things true but one of falsification, testing theories to destruction to see where we need to devise better ideas. Real science is highly falsifiable, for, if it were not, then it would not be informative.

Imagine a meteorologist who wanted never to be caught out with a wrong forecast. His forecast is: 'It will rain, somewhere, sometime.' That is very likely to be true, but it does not tell me whether I will need my umbrella tomorrow. A truly useful forecast would be: 'It will be raining at 4.00 in Milton Keynes tomorrow.' That forecast is much more informative and much more likely to be wrong, because it could be mistaken in so many details – time, place and so on. If we give more information, our theories become more improbable – but that is why they are valuable. Each new piece of information added gives another possibility of error. As Popper often remarked, high probability does not count in favour of a theory: its high probability means it is not very informative.

A key advantage of falsifiability is, according to Popper, that some statements can be conclusively falsified when they cannot be conclusively verified. To say all giraffes have long necks cannot be more than highly probable – it could only be verified beyond doubt by checking the necks of every possible giraffe, past, present and future. Just because every giraffe so far noted has had a long neck, it does not follow every giraffe will do so. But, the moment I have found just one short-necked giraffe, I have falsified the original **hypothesis**.

Key term

Hypothesis A supposition or proposal offered as a possible explanation, but which needs further exploration and experiment.

Background

Falsification: Ayer's misinterpretation

It is sometimes said that a lie is halfway round the world before truth has got its boots on. The same is also true of an honest error.

As we saw in Chapter 5, logical positivism holds that all talk of God is simply meaningless, a position outlined by Ayer in *Language, Truth and Logic*. Having outlined his theory of verification on page 19 (Penguin Modern Classics), he goes on to criticise the idea – which he attributes to Karl Popper – that a sentence must be meaningless if it cannot be falsified.

In saying this, Ayer seriously misrepresents Popper, as we shall see. For Popper, falsification was not a principle for the division between what was meaningful and what was not; in the way that verification theorists had said anything not verifiable was meaningless. Rather, it was the criterion of demarcation between the scientific and non-scientific. For Popper, a myth or a legend, such as the tales of King Arthur, cannot be proven false, so we do not count it as science, but that doesn't make stories of King Arthur meaningless – they are just not scientific.

Ayer's mistake is understandable. Although Popper's great book *Logik der Forschung* (*The Logic of Scientific Discovery*) was published in German in 1934 – while Ayer was formulating his ideas – it would not be published in English until 1959. It is not clear that Ayer had time to read Popper's book closely, or indeed whether he knew of it only by report, but his mistake has been taken as fact rather too often.

The misreading of Popper seems to have been not uncommon in the Vienna Circle:

> *... in 1933 I published a letter ... in which I tried to compress into two pages my ideas on the problems of demarcation and induction. In this letter I described the problem of meaning as a pseudo-problem, in contrast to the problem of demarcation. But my contribution was classified by members of the Circle as a proposal to replace the verifiability criterion of meaning by a falsifiability criterion of meaning – which effectively made nonsense of my views....*
>
> *... Neither falsifiability nor testability were proposed by me as criteria of meaning ...*

Karl Popper, 'Science: Conjectures and Refutation' in *Conjectures and Refutations*, 2002

The mistaken reading was, unfortunately, given further currency by John Hick in his book *Faith and Knowledge,* but again, before the publication of the English translation of Popper's work. The mistaken view still has currency in some popular works, but it would be absurd and unscholarly to base an understanding of falsification on Ayer's brief remarks, given the current awareness of Popper.

It is essential to recognise that falsifiability is not a criterion to determine whether a statement is meaningful or not, only whether it has the status of a scientific assertion. As Flew says:

> **Key quote**
>
> ....Popper proposed his Falsification Principle. Unlike the Verification Principle of the Logical Positivists, this was put forward as *a criterion not of meaning but of scientific status.*
> Antony Flew, *An Introduction to Western Philosophy*, (Revised Edition), 1989, page 482 (our italics)

Popper pointed out that much of our science originated in unfalsifiable myth, thought significant enough to gradually be replaced with genuinely scientific theories. He would not deny that there was *meaning* to utterances such as prayer, ethical commands or poetry: his point was that they were not science. He attacked Marxism and psychiatry as unscientific, because their claims were unfalsifiable, but it does not follow that they have no meaning for him. He discusses both at great length in his works – whereas writers like Ayer do not engage with the views they think are meaningless, but rather dismiss them in a few sentences.

Popper was interested in the weaknesses of logical positivism, and his intention was to delineate the nature of science. He did not develop a detailed theory about the different types of sentences which were non-scientific – and their meaning. To say that these are not devoid of meaning, however, leaves open the question of degrees and types of meaning that they might have. He said very little in his works about religion, but it is clear that for Popper, there would be no suggestion that religious sentences were meaningless, though the vast majority would not be genuinely scientific.

3 The falsification symposium: Antony Flew and the *University* debate

Key quote

It has often been asserted ... that 'Theology and Falsification' expresses Flew's view of the meaning, or rather the meaninglessness, of all religious language; while many have wanted to dismiss that view, and anyone so unfashionable as to continue to harbour it, on the grounds that verificationist accounts of meaning have long since been discredited. But I have never held that all religious utterances either possess or lack some single sort of meaning. That is a silly view, because so obviously false.

Antony Flew, 'Apologia pro Philosophia Mea', *Philosophy in Britain Today*, ed. S.G. Shanker, 1986, page 84.

The most discussed use of falsification in relation to religion was the *University* debate, 'Theology and Falsification: a symposium', which involved Antony Flew, Basil Mitchell and R. M. Hare. The piece first appeared in a short-lived journal, *University*. Its prominence rests to a large degree on its re-publication in Flew and MacIntyre's *New Essays in Philosophical Theology*. The entire symposium is very brief and non-technical and should be read by any serious student of the subject.

Flew's intention in the symposium to move beyond the debates of the logical positivists is clear in the Introduction that he and Alasdair MacIntyre contributed to *New Essays*:

Key quote

It should be sufficient ... simply to repudiate the popular misconception that 'all the philosophers are Logical Positivists nowadays', and to ask that this volume be judged on its arguments, and not be forced into some preconceived matrix of misunderstanding. The second thing which the contributors share is a concern with theological questions, and a conviction that these call for serious and particular treatment. (Whereas the Logical Positivists used to reject all theology holus-bolus as so much meaningless metaphysics.)

Antony Flew and Alasdair MacIntyre, *New Essays in Philosophical Theology*, 1955, page ix

111

Antony Flew (1923–2010): born in Berkshire, the son of a Methodist minister. Flew studied Japanese at the School of Oriental and African Studies at the University of London, joined the RAF and served as an intelligence offer at Bletchley Park. After philosophical studies at Oxford, he lectured at Christ Church, Oxford (1949–50) and Aberdeen (1950–54). He then served successively as Professor of Philosophy at Keele (1954–71), Calgary (1972–73) and Reading (1973–83). His religious position was atheist for most of his career, though he announced in an interview in 2004 that he had become a deist with some belief in an Aristotelian God, though emphatically not in Christianity. In later times he endorsed the idea of Intelligent Design. Some critics have argued that dementia played a part in his late views.

Flew begins his contribution to the symposium by referring to John Wisdom's parable of the gardener, from his article 'Gods' (Proceedings of the Aristotelian Society, 1944–45, reprinted as Chapter X of Antony Flew, ed., *Essays in Logic and Language*, 1951). The parable itself is simple. Two explorers come upon a clearing in the jungle. Some parts look well cared for, but others do not. In the original, one man takes the view there is a gardener who comes to look after the ground, while the other thinks there is not (the point being that the world is rather like that, capable of different interpretations of the same observations). Neither can find the gardener, neither experiences anything the other does not, yet their belief about the clearing is very different. Wisdom suggests from this that the difference between the believer and the non-believer is not a difference about the facts of the world but a disagreement about how those same facts are to be interpreted.

Flew draws a slightly different conclusion. He asks what is the difference between the apparently invisible, intangible, scentless, soundless gardener and no gardener at all? It looks as if what seemed a genuinely scientific hypothesis, that a gardener comes to the clearing, is actually not a genuinely scientific hypothesis because the believer in the gardener does not accept any falsification of his views, and, of course, no conclusive disproof seems possible – he makes justifications, but still believes in the gardener because he allows nothing to falsify his view.

Flew then applies the question to theological assertions:

> *And in this, it seems to me, lies the peculiar danger, the endemic evil, of theological utterance. Take such utterances as 'God has a plan', 'God created the world', 'God loves us as a father loves his children'. They look at first sight very much like assertions, vast cosmological assertions. Of course, this is no sure sign that they either are, or are intended to be, assertions. But let us confine ourselves to the cases where those who utter such sentences intend them to express assertions.*

Antony Flew *et al.*, 'Theology and Falsification', *New Essays in Philosophical Theology*, eds Antony Flew and Alasdair MacIntyre, 1955, page 97

You will notice that Flew explores the status of the sentences, as genuine assertions. Flew goes on to say that for an assertion to be genuine as an assertion, it must be falsifiable: 'if there is nothing which a putative assertion denies then there is nothing which it asserts either: and so it is not really an assertion' (ibid., page 98).

He notes that it sometimes seems as if for the believer nothing seems to falsify his belief. If the problem of evil is cited as denying God's love, believers resort to sayings such as 'God's love surpasses understanding' or 'God's love is not merely human'. (This, incidentally, is why Popper argues that the views of Marxists or psychiatrists are unfalsifiable and not scientific. According to Popper, if critics point to the USSR as a failed Communist state, defenders will say that it was not truly communist and so does not falsify the theory. In the same way, if a psychiatrist tells a patient that he must have been abused by someone then even if the patient then denies any recollection of such an event, his denial is taken as itself evidence of the truth of the diagnosis. Critics have argued that Popper was too sweeping in his criticisms.)

Flew gives an example:

> Someone tells us that God loves us as a father loves his children.
> We are reassured. But then we see a child dying of inoperable
> cancer of the throat. His earthly father is driven frantic in his
> efforts to help, but his Heavenly Father reveals no obvious sign
> of concern. Some qualification is made – God's love is 'not a
> merely human love' or it is 'an inscrutable love', perhaps – and we
> realise that such sufferings are quite compatible with the truth
> of the assertion that 'God loves us as a father' (but of course, ...).
> We are reassured again. But then perhaps we ask: what is this
> assurance of God's (appropriately qualified) love worth, what is
> this apparent guarantee really a guarantee against?
>
> Antony Flew *et al.*, pages 98–9

Following these considerations, Flew issues this challenge:

Key quote

Just what would have to happen not merely (morally and wrongly) to tempt but also (logically and rightly) to entitle us to say 'God does not love us' or even 'God does not exist'? I therefore put to the succeeding symposiasts the simple central questions, 'What would have to occur or to have occurred to constitute for you a disproof of the love of, or of the existence of, God?'

Antony Flew *et al.*, page 99

As always in philosophical matters, we should attend to the detail of what is said. Nowhere does Flew say that religious beliefs are meaningless, as Ayer does. We should notice also that Flew does not state that religious believers all treat their beliefs as unfalsifiable. He says:

Now it often seems to people who are not religious as if there was no conceivable event or series of events the occurrence of which would be admitted by sophisticated religious people to be a sufficient reason for conceding 'There wasn't a God after all' or 'God does not really love us then'.

Antony Flew *et al.*, page 98

He carefully does not say that religious people do not accept anything against their beliefs. He says simply that it often seems that way. Hence the question to his fellow philosophers about whether there is anything which would count as disproof of their beliefs. He asks for evidence of something that would be a falsifying instance. We should also notice that to a logical positivist such as Ayer, the question Flew asks would itself be meaningless – but clearly Flew thinks he is saying something significant. Remember how for Ayer the question 'Is there a God?' is meaningless, because, for Ayer, there are no possible significant questions that could be asked. Flew obviously thinks otherwise.

Key question

What precisely is the question asked by Flew?

4 The falsification symposium: R. M. Hare and *bliks*

The first response to Flew is given by R. M. Hare.

Key person

R. M. Hare (1919–2002): born in Somerset and educated at Balliol College, Oxford. During the Second World War, he served in the Royal Artillery and was captured by the Japanese at the Fall of Singapore in 1942. His suffering as a prisoner was central to his deep interest in morality. His teaching career was almost entirely at Oxford. He taught at Balliol from 1946–96 and was White's Professor of Moral Philosophy (1966–83). He was also Graduate Professor of Philosophy at the University of Florida (1983–94). His best-known works are *The Language of Morals* (1952), *Moral Thinking: Its Levels, Method and Point* (1981) and *Essays in Ethical Theory* (1989).

Hare's response to the question is that Flew is right on his own ground, that religious beliefs are unfalsifiable. Hare says that religious statements have a different logical status.

He says that religious beliefs are what he calls '*bliks*'. He gives the case of an insane university student who believes all the dons are out to kill him. No evidence will dissuade him – if presented with a gentle and kindly don, he will see this as evidence only of the diabolical cunning of a professor trying to give him a false sense of security. Hare notes that while the lunatic's view can neither be proven nor disproven, it profoundly alters the lunatic's life. Think about how such a paranoid view would affect the way the lunatic would see the world and live his daily life. He argues:

Key term

Blik R. M. Hare's term for a belief which is life-changing but cannot be verified or falsified.

Let us call that in which we differ from this lunatic, our respective
bliks. *He has an insane* blik *about dons; we have a sane one. It is
important to realize that we have a sane one, not no* blik *at all;
for there must be two sides to any argument – if he has a wrong*
blik, *then those who are right about dons must have a right one.*

Antony Flew et al., page 100

Hare goes on to say that we all have *bliks* and they profoundly affect
our lives. Hare gives the example of driving a car – we assume that the
structure we drive will remain solid while we do so: we do not and cannot
know this, as we can neither prove nor disprove it.

Hare argues that the concept of *blik* shows what we are doing when
we make a religious statement. It is not merely a sort of explanation of
the world, but is completely life-changing, even though unfalsifiable. It is
a matter of the very deepest concern to us, and the world and our lives
are different for believing it.

Hare's position is superficially convincing, but is vulnerable to many
criticisms.

Flew, in his response to Hare, argued that *bliks* do not account for the
way in which religious believers think of themselves as speaking. He says
believers surely see themselves as making genuine assertions, which they
see as true facts about the world.

*Religious utterances may indeed express false or even bogus
assertions: but I simply do not believe that they are not both
intended and interpreted to be or at any rate to presuppose
assertions, at least in the context of religious practice.*

Antony Flew et al., page 108

Flew justifies his argument with various examples:

*... I nevertheless want to insist that any attempt to analyse
Christian religious utterances as expressions or affirmation
of a* blik *rather than as (at least would-be) assertions about
the cosmos is fundamentally misguided. First, because thus
interpreted they would be entirely unorthodox. If Hare's religion
really is a* blik, *involving no cosmological assertions about the
nature and activities of a supposed personal creator, then surely
he is not a Christian at all? Second, because thus interpreted, they
could scarcely do the job they do. If they were not even intended
as assertions then many religious activities would become
fraudulent, or merely silly.*

Antony Flew et al., pages 107–8

John Hick argues that Hare's notion of *bliks* contains a fundamental
inconsistency, as Hare provides no criterion for distinguishing between
right and wrong, sane or insane *bliks*:

*We want to distinguish, in Hare's terminology, between right and
wrong* bliks. *... Hare assumes that one can make this distinction;
for he identifies one* blik *as sane and the contrary* blik *as insane.
But there seems to be an inconsistency in his position here, for*

a discrimination between sane (=right) and insane (=wrong) bliks *is ruled out by his insistence that* bliks *are unverifiable and unfalsifiable. If experience can never yield either confirmation or disconfirmation of religious* bliks, *there is no basis for speaking of them as being right or wrong, appropriate or inappropriate, sane or insane.*

John Hick, *Philosophy of Religion*, (second edition), 1973, pages 88–9

Hick's point here is that Hare has said fairly bluntly that this man is a lunatic because he has an insane *blik*, yet as *bliks* can be neither verified nor falsified, it is difficult to see how we can justify characterising a *blik* as insane.

We can, I think, go even further than Hick. It is a sign of madness that someone refuses to entertain the possibility that he might be wrong. Nothing counts against his belief because *he will not permit anything to count against it*. It is surely a mark of sanity to admit that one might be wrong, to be open to the possibility of a need to re-think a position.

True faith is not fanaticism. A religious person holds a belief, and there are fanatics who simply will not entertain the possibility that they might be wrong. But it would be wrong to assume that every believer is like this. The very notion of *faith* implies the possibility of error: it means holding to and living by a commitment that is not established beyond doubt. There is a gulf in both belief and living between faith and fanaticism. When evil happens, believers, including some considered the greatest saints, attest to their faith being tested. They speak of the difficulties of belief. Hare's lunatic has no such doubts: that's why he is a lunatic.

Key question

How useful is Hare's concept of a *blik* as a response to Flew's question?

5 The falsification symposium: Basil Mitchell and the partisan

Key person

Basil Mitchell (1917–2011): educated in Birmingham and Oxford. He served as an instructor in the Royal Navy (1940–46), principally in the Mediterranean. He taught at Keble College, Oxford, from 1947, moving to Oriel College in 1968 as Nolloth Professor of the Philosophy of the Christian Religion, until 1985, when he was succeeded by Richard Swinburne. His Gifford Lectures (1974–76), *Morality, Religion and the Secular* attracted much attention.

Basil Mitchell responded to Flew in a more interesting, and perhaps more successful, way. Unlike Hare, he wanted to maintain that religious statements are genuinely factual though not straightforwardly falsifiable. He tells his own parable. This would have been readily understandable in the immediate post-war years when the debate took place, but today it possibly requires a word or two of explanation.

During the Second World War, when the Resistance was created in occupied countries like France or Holland, secrecy was essential. The Gestapo would use torture absolutely without mercy to gain information which would enable them to round up other members of the Resistance. To minimise casualties, remembering that even the strongest will crack under torture, the Resistance organised itself into small cells, of perhaps a dozen or so men and women. Ideally, only one member of the cell would know the identity of one member of the next cell in the chain. The idea was that if one cell member should be caught and tortured, the Gestapo could not just roll up the entire Resistance network.

Mitchell's parable talks of the resistance fighter who meets a stranger who impresses him deeply. They spend a night in conversation, during which the Stranger claims to be the head of the entire Resistance. The fighter believes him, but is warned by the Stranger that his faith will be sorely tested — that at times he will find the man he trusted apparently working with the enemy. Despite this, and although they never again share such a conversation, the partisan persists in his belief that the Stranger is who he claims to be. He maintains his belief even when he sees the Stranger in the uniform of the occupying force.

Mitchell's argument is that the partisan does not deny that there is strong evidence against his belief that the Stranger is who he claims to be. Mitchell argues that to remain sane, the partisan *must accept* the reality of the evidence against his belief. If he does not, he is 'guilty of a failure of faith as well as logic' (Antony Flew *et al.*, page 105).

In the same way, if a believer does not accept that there is strong evidence against the belief in a loving God, then she is guilty of self-delusion: if the believer does not accept the strength of the argument, her beliefs become '...vacuous formulae (expressing, perhaps, a desire for reassurance) to which experience makes no difference and which make no difference to life' (ibid., page 105).

But Mitchell does not argue that the believer has blind faith — she has reason for her faith, just as the partisan has. In this case, it is a belief in the personal character of the Stranger. Mitchell says:

> *It is here that my parable differs from Hare's. The partisan admits that many things may and do count against his belief: whereas Hare's lunatic who has a* blik *about dons doesn't admit that anything counts against his* blik. *Nothing* can *count against* bliks. *Also the partisan has a reason for having in the first instance committed himself, viz. the character of the Stranger; whereas the lunatic has no reason for his* blik *about dons — because, of course, you can't have reasons for* bliks.

Antony Flew et al., page 105

The point here is that Mitchell, as a believer, accepts that faith can be mistaken. To have faith is not to deny that a believer cannot accept that her faith might prove to be false, and her reasons for believing it irrational. He agrees with Flew that theological statements must be understood as assertions — the partisan is making a factual claim when he says, 'The Stranger is on our side' (ibid., page 105). After all, the partisan is claiming that one interpretation of the facts — that the Stranger is indeed who he claims to be — is correct, against those who assert that the man is a liar.

Mitchell goes on to say while 'God is love' cannot be conclusively falsified, it is essential to recognise that it could be false and that there is a point (unspecified) beyond which it would be rationally impossible to support the view. Indeed, for proper faith the pull of the contradictory evidence must be acknowledged – blind faith would be absurd:

> It will depend ... on the manner in which ... [the partisan] ... takes the Stranger's behaviour. If he blindly dismisses it as of no consequence, as having no bearing upon his belief, it will be assumed that he is thoughtless or insane. And it quite obviously won't do for him to say easily, 'Oh, when used of the Stranger the phrase "is on our side" means ambiguous behaviour of this sort.' In that case he would be like the religious man who says blandly of a terrible disaster 'It is God's will'. No, he will only be regarded as sane and reasonable in his belief, if he experiences in himself the full force of the conflict.

Ibid., pages 104–5

Key question

Is Mitchell's cognitive response more convincing than Hare's *bliks*?

Here we note some sympathy with Flew's original concern about the 'vast cosmological assertions', which some believers seem to make. Mitchell agrees that some religious believers occasionally slip into vacuous remarks – he talks of this as 'a constant danger' (ibid., page 105). For him, a mature belief is not blind faith.

6 The falsification symposium: John Hick and eschatological verification

John Hick has added to Mitchell's parable. Hick argues:
- Presumably the Stranger himself knows whether he is telling the truth, even though the partisan is not in a position to make the judgement, so there is a truth to be known about the statement.
- When the war is over the truth will come out. Either the Stranger will be hailed as a hero, awarded with medals, or he will be led away and (one assumes) shot as a traitor.

Hick uses these ideas to develop his own response to both falsification and verification. These appear to have validity even allowing for his error about falsification, noted on page 119.

He contends, in arguments which can be found in slightly different forms in different places (initially in his essay 'Theology and Verification', *Theology Today*, XVII, No. 1, April 1960, further developed in *Faith and Knowledge*, 1967 as Chapter 8, and found also in his *Philosophy of Religion*), that Christianity has certain specific afterlife beliefs which mean that it is possible to meet at least the conditions of weak verification. Weak verification, as noted in Chapter 5, holds that a sentence is verifiable if one can state what would enable us to state what observations would make it probable. Christians who believe in an afterlife can state some experiences which would render their beliefs probable (remember, as with Ayer's example of the mountains on the far side of the moon, that one has only to state what position one would need to be in to make the observation possible; no present observation is needed).

Suppose I believe that, when I die, I will see Christ in heaven. Suppose further that I die, know I have died, and experience the things I have always believed I would experience. In those circumstances I can verify my original belief and say I was right all along.

The problem with this solution is that it is, to use Hick's term, an **asymmetrical** solution to problems raised by verification and falsification. As Hick says:

> *The hypothesis of continued existence after bodily death provides ... [an]... instance of a proposition* which is verifiable if true but not falsifiable *if false. This hypothesis entails a prediction that one will, after the date of one's bodily death, have conscious experiences, including the experience of remembering that death. This is a prediction that will be verified in one's own experience if it is true but that cannot be falsified if it is false. That is to say, it can be false, but* that *it is false can never be a fact that anyone has experientially verified.*

John Hick, *Philosophy of Religion*, (second edition), 1973, page 91 (our italics)

Hick, as we noted, equates falsification with verification theory. This is an error, because although he has demonstrated very clearly how certain specifically Christian beliefs might satisfy the demands of weak verification, and are thus meaningful, he has failed to demonstrate, against the claims of falsification theory correctly understood, that Christian claims are genuinely falsifiable propositions. He argues that they cannot be falsified. It seems to be a consequence of his argument that the claims of faith are not scientific hypotheses at all. This leaves open what he believes their status might be.

There is a difference between the claims of **eschatological verification** – which we are never able to falsify – and Hick's comments on Mitchell's parable. In the case of the Stranger, we can state the conditions of falsification. If, when the war is over, those in the position to know whether he was telling the truth are adamant that he did not, then we can confidently assume he was indeed a traitor and the partisan's judgement was wrong.

This suggests that we cannot say that eschatological verification meets the same conditions as Mitchell's parable of the partisan. For Mitchell, there is always the potential that *in this life* we can say that we were wrong in our beliefs. True falsification is available to the believer and, if she has true faith, she accepts that limitation.

Key terms

Asymmetrical Having aspects which are not equal or equivalent. In the case of eschatological verification, this is Hick's term for a case in which verification is possible but falsification is not.

Eschatological verification John Hick's theory that believers with specific afterlife beliefs will, after death, be able to verify those beliefs if true, but not falsify them if they are false.

7 The falsification symposium: some final considerations

There is, in the symposium, an interesting issue touched on by R. M. Hare and not really explored. Speaking of his parable of the lunatic, Hare comments:

> *There is an important difference between Flew's parable [of the gardener] and my own which we have not yet noticed. The explorers do not* mind *about their garden; they discuss it with interest, but not with concern. But my lunatic, poor fellow, minds about dons; and I mind about the steering of my car; it often has*

Antony Flew *et al.*, 'Theology and Falsification', *New Essays in Philosophical Theology*, eds Antony Flew and Alasdair MacIntyre, 1955, page 97

Here, whatever the reservations about *bliks*, Hare seems to touch on, but does not develop, something very important. While it is essential to examine the grammar of a sentence, to examine its meaning, it is also necessary, as Wittgenstein argued, to look at the use, that is, the context and meaning attached to what is said by the speaker.

If a scientist says that he believes in the Loch Ness Monster, it is an intellectual assent to the claim that the Loch Ness Monster exists. He might even be quite excited by the claim, and perhaps be impatient with those who believe him mistaken. His belief might be life-changing if his college think him mistaken and deny him promotion, or refuse to fund his quest (leaving Nessie happily undisturbed), but that change is limited in other ways. A belief in the Loch Ness Monster is not a belief for which someone is likely to be martyred; it does not alter every detail of daily life. A believer offers prayer to her God, and tries to live in constant awareness of God's presence. But there is a further difference. The believer in the Loch Ness Monster is assenting to a proposition he believes intellectually to be true. The religious believer does not simply say enthusiastically that her belief is true. There is much more to it than that.

It is possible to argue, as a Wittgensteinian might, that the debate over falsification simply misunderstands the nature of belief in a loving God. She would be surely right to argue that there is more to her belief than accepting that a religious proposition is true.

However, Flew is surely right to argue that the truth of a religious proposition matters to a believer, and that they are intended as genuine assertions. Hare's notion of a *blik* seems to be a very pure form of non-cognitivism, as it is not appropriate to ask whether a *blik* is true or false. But one of the things a believer *minds* about is that what she asserts is indeed the case. She intends to say that the religious outlook is factually the right one, and not simply that she gets some sort of comfort or psychological prop from her beliefs. In making that assertion, she must, if she is rational, surely accept that she might be mistaken, and that she is living her life on the basis of a mistake.

8 Conclusions

The falsification debate has, as we have noted, been much misunderstood, despite the enormous interest and literature it has created. Problems are avoided by a return to the sources and by close attention to what scholars themselves say, rather than what others say about them. It is essential to be clear about Popper's ideas and Flew's use of them. A Wittgensteinian would also remind us to 'attend to the grammar', which, in this case means noticing that Flew asks a question to which his fellow philosophers respond. Their responses to his question are interesting indeed, though perhaps Mitchell's response is stronger than Hare's notion of *bliks*.

Study advice

It is obviously central to any study of falsification to be very clear about Popper's intention in developing his theory of falsification as a criterion of demarcation between the scientific and non-scientific. Additionally, to avoid misconceptions, be careful to read the very brief *University* symposium so that you are familiar with what it actually says and not what some have mistakenly claimed it says. If you are clear about what the participants say for themselves, errors will be avoided and you can approach any question on the subject with confidence. As always, remember not simply to learn what the different philosophers say, but also to reflect on their views. Is Mitchell's response to Flew more or less satisfactory than that of Hare? You might also wish to reflect on whether Flew's question is a good one or whether it provides more or less of a challenge than that provided by Verification theory.

Some students in the past have used the term *blik* as a synonym for 'belief' in essays *not* on falsification. Do not fall into this trap. Hare himself seems to have made no further use of the term in later writings, and it has no philosophical currency outside the context of the debate itself.

Summary diagram: Religious language: 20th-century perspectives – the falsification debate

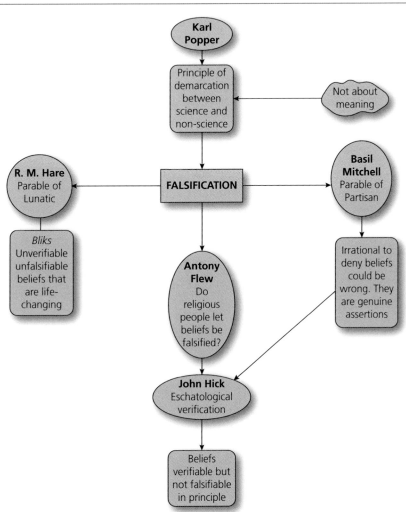

By the end of this chapter you should be able to explain the issues involved in the falsification debate. As everywhere, careful definition is essential. Look at the precise question asked by Antony Flew and reflect on whether Hare, Mitchell – or Hick – satisfactorily answer the question he asks.

Can you give brief definitions of:
- falsification
- demarcation
- non-science
- *bliks*
- eschatological verification?

Can you explain:
- how Popper distinguishes between science and non-science
- the Parable of the Gardener
- *bliks* and the Parable of the Lunatic
- Mitchell's argument in the Parable of the Partisan?

Can you give arguments for and against:
- falsification as the mark of genuine science
- the theory of *bliks*
- the claim by Mitchell that faith is not irrational
- the claim that falsification is a significant challenge to religious belief?

Sample question and guidance

Assess the claim that religious belief is unfalsifiable.

As always, concentrate on the precise wording of the question. This is not an invitation to write everything you know about religious language. Nor is this asking you simply to *describe* the debate about falsification but rather to make judgements about the various claims made. As always, it is important to make – and to support – judgements as you work through (this is the mark of real engagement with the question and the topic).

It is important to remember that any philosophical discussion is always an attempt to answer a question. Assessment of theories requires consideration both of whether theories adequately answer the question posed, but also whether it

was an appropriate question in the first place. You might want to argue that religious assertions should not be considered scientific in the first place, in which case it would be inappropriate to use a criterion intended as one of demarcation between science and non-science. On the other hand, what other criteria might be appropriate if Flew is right in his belief that believers do mean their beliefs as genuine assertions? You might also consider whether the challenge of falsification is stronger or weaker than that of verification theory, or you might consider both irrelevant, as religious statements could be considered differently from ordinary scientific ones. If you consider this possibility, be very clear that falsification is not about meaning.

Further essay questions

'Falsification presents a weaker challenge to faith than that offered by the Verification principle.' Discuss.

To what extent is it true to say that the claim God loves us is unfalsifiable?

'R. M. Hare's theory of *bliks* provides the best response to Flew's challenge.' Discuss.

Going further

At the centre of this chapter is the debate about falsification between Flew, Hare and Mitchell. There is no substitute for reading the debate for yourself. It may be found in many anthologies, and there are various editions of *New Essays in Philosophical Theology*. The debate is also freely available online.

Bryan Magee's little book, *Popper*, in Fontana Modern Masters, remains an admirable and very clear introduction to Popper's thought. Popper himself provides an example of very clear philosophical writing. A good place to begin would be with his own intellectual autobiography, *Unended Quest* or his essay collection, *Conjectures and Refutations* (both published by Routledge). There are many excellent works on Popper: as good a collection as any is *Karl Popper: Philosophy and Problems* ed. Antony O'Hear (Cambridge University Press, 2008).

Other books discussed in this chapter are:

- Ayer, A. J. *Language, Truth and Logic* (Penguin, 1971).
- Flew, A. *An Introduction to Western Philosophy* (revised edition, Thames and Hudson, 1989).
- Hick, J. *Faith and Knowledge* (Macmillan, 1967).
- Hick, J. *Philosophy of Religion* (second edition, Prentice Hall, 1973).

2 Religion and ethics

Chapter 8

Ethical language: meta-ethics

Chapter checklist

Initial discussion outlining the difficulties in justifying the meanings of terms such as 'good', 'right', 'moral' is followed by examination of the classic 'fact/value' problem set out by Hume, among others. There are three key theories covered in response to this problem: naturalism, intuitionism and emotivism.

- First, there is analysis of the solution offered by **naturalists**, such as Epicurus and Bentham who attempt to identify the good with some natural quality, such as pleasure. Refutations of this move, by Plato, Moore and others are explained. Reasons are given for rejecting the idea that naturalism necessarily entails some form of moral absolutism.
- Second, there is an examination of **intuitionism** as advanced by Moore (among others) and the claims that we somehow have the ability to know good, a non-natural quality, by a simple, given awareness.
- The third theory, **emotivism**, as represented by Ayer and Barnes is then discussed. This approach argues that moral statements simply evince (but do not necessarily express) certain moral feelings. There is discussion of whether, and in what ways, emotivism might lead to a form of moral relativism.

Conclusions consider the adequacy of these responses, whether the original question raised by Hume is well formed, and whether the justification of moral terms is one not of logic but of living, thus requiring different types of justification.

1 Introduction

'What do you mean by that?'

The use of language seems natural to human beings – indeed, we might properly say that to use language is part of what it means to be human: we are language-using creatures. For much of the time, we use language unreflectively and with relatively little ambiguity. If I ask you to close the door, there might be a discussion about which door I mean, or about why I should want you to do this, or why I do not close the door myself, but our dialogue is relatively straightforward. Meanings can be determined and agreed quite quickly and with no great difficulty.

But not all language is that simple. When we looked at issues of religious language, we saw that terms such as 'God', 'omnipotence' or 'eternity' are anything but simple in their meaning. People might imagine the words to be uncomplicated, but it takes little analysis to realise that their meaning is far from simple. It seems almost as if the more we seek precision in defining meaning, the more elusive that precision becomes.

The same fuzziness applies to ethical terms, and many of the same problems apply. What is goodness? The problems associated with clear definitions of moral terms are explored in the following sections.

2 Defining ethical terms

See Year 1, page 24.

Consider the term 'good'. As we saw when we considered Aristotle's criticisms of Plato's Form of the Good, the term 'good' has many possible meanings.

If we think about how we usually speak, we notice that some of our uses of 'good' are *non-moral*. We sometimes say that something is good simply to indicate appreciation. To describe a meal as 'good' is not to comment on a moral quality – a tasty meal is not generous, kindly, charitable or just and fair – but rather to say that it pleases us in a particular way. The *moral* use of 'good' seems to apply only to human actions and intentions. If I say of someone that she is good, then I am making, I think, some sort of judgement about her actions but also about her intentions and dispositions.

We might go further. If I describe something as 'good', am I making a factual claim? If I say: 'St Paul's Cathedral in London is 365 feet high and has 528 steps if you want to climb to the Golden Gallery at the top of the dome', then I am offering something as a matter of fact which could be checked, at least in theory, by anyone in the right position, to say nothing of the appropriate stamina, to climb all the way up. The thing to notice here is that we know very clearly how to check this and we can agree very quickly – *and in a public way* – how this might be checked by anyone who wished to do so.

But compare this with a suggestion that something is 'good', Someone may disagree with me, and say that it is not 'good'. Think about the disagreement between us. My questioner is not only disagreeing with whether the something we are discussing is 'really good', but also questioning the methods I might use for claiming something is good. On matters of fact we can agree appropriate methods, fairly straightforwardly. It is much easier to agree on the height of St Paul's than on whether it is a good piece of architecture.

But that leaves further questions. If I describe something as 'good', is there any way in which I am being factual, in the sense of saying that there is something which anyone can check in the way that they might check the number of steps in a building? Is the goodness of something a simple matter of fact (and presumably objectively checkable), just a vague feeling, private opinion, or something in between? If I say something is 'good', am I just saying 'I like it', or even 'You ought to like it too, which is why I am telling you that it is good'?

The fundamental problem is not merely that there is no apparent certainty about agreement on the questions of whether things are good, but that there seems to be no agreement on how the question could be resolved.

Aristotle distinguishes many uses of the term 'good':

> *Things are called* good *in as many ways as we say they exist. They are called* good *in the categories of Substance (such as God or mind), in Quality (the virtues), in Quantity (a moderate amount), in Relation (what is useful), in Time (opportunity), in Place (the right habitat for what we want to do) and so on. It is clear there cannot be one universal use.*

Aristotle, *Nicomachean Ethics,* Book I, vi

Here we have an admirable example of a great philosopher thinking about the nature of the good, in opposition to his mentor, Plato, who had attempted, in his theory of the Forms, to fix the meaning of the term 'good' in a simple, universal way.

The peculiar difficulty of defining the 'good' is that we all have a vague sense of what we mean by describing something as good – otherwise we would not use the term at all – but greater precision is difficult. Part of the problem is similar to the issues in defining 'happiness'. As Aristotle noted, if we are asked our goal in life, we are likely to say 'happiness' but it is difficult then to decide what happiness is. It is an oddity of human life that we are very conscious of being unhappy, of the pains and miseries that we feel, but often with happiness, we are not conscious that we are in the state. Sometimes we look back and say that we were happy at a given time in our lives, but we didn't fully realise it at the time. It is rather the same with health: when we are healthy, we do not think about it, but we are very conscious of our ailments when we are ill. Perhaps there is something similar about good and evil – that which we call evil strikes us more directly and with more certainty. We notice cruelty towards ourselves and others and – most people, most of the time – have little difficulty in proclaiming cruelty as evil. We would, I suggest, find something very odd with someone who thought cruelty good, and we would seek from him a justification we would probably not demand from those who condemn cruelty.

Notice two things: we have outlined some issues with the meaning of the term 'good' and have attempted also to touch on the issue of justification. If someone argues in favour of cruelty of child abuse, we would seem correct to ask for a convincing justification of those actions. But he might in turn ask us for justification for our (to him) soft-heartedness and woolly-mindedness.

Such issues of meaning and justification are the subject matter of **meta-ethics**.

Key term

Meta-ethics The study of the meaning and justification of moral ideas. Normative ethics looks at how we should live while meta-ethics focuses analytically on the underlying concepts.

Background

What is meta-ethics?

Your main encounter with ethics will have been the theories of normative ethics you studied in Year 1, which concerned how we should behave and the sorts of people we should be.

For normative ethics, see Year 1, page 138.

In meta-ethics we need to look beyond this to consider what the good *is* that we should pursue through those actions, and why we should be moral in the first place. As we shall see, it is important not to confuse normative with meta-ethical questions. An easy, if somewhat crude, way to think of the difference would be to see normative ethics as concerned with *what* we should do or be, while meta-ethics asks *why* we should behave in those ways as well as the *meaning* of the language we use. In this chapter, we are essentially continuing Plato's discussion in *The Republic,* which is both normative and meta-ethical – he considers the meaning of the good as well as how we should live and what we should do in the light of that true awareness.

Key terms

Normative ethics Theories of ethics that give guidance (norms) on how we should behave and/or the character traits we should develop.

Fact/value, is/ought problem The problem, identified by Hume, among others, of finding any logical justification of ethical judgements from the facts of the world. We cannot derive what we ought to do from a statement of the facts of the case.

See Year 1, pages 5–6.

3 The *fact/value, is/ought* problem

We remember that any philosophical theory is an attempt to answer a philosophical question or problem. The question at hand is a particularly clear one in meta-ethics and is expressed in the question of fact and value, first raised by David Hume.

The **fact/value problem** (also called the **is/ought problem**) is one of logic. To remind ourselves, the basic unit of Aristotelian logic is the syllogism, for example:

(i)	All men are mortal	(Major premise)
(ii)	Socrates is a man	(Minor premise)
(iii)	**Therefore** Socrates is mortal	(Conclusion)

Now, it is illegitimate to put into the conclusion anything which is not contained in the premises. We cannot conclude from the premises stated:

(iv) **Therefore** Socrates is mortal and is a keen follower of the Olympic games.

The bit about the Olympic games was not part of the original information or argument, and has been sneaked in dishonestly.

The fact/value problem is based on this principle – any factual proposition about the world is *reducible* to one involving the verb 'to be':

For example:

- Socrates *was* a philosopher.
- Paris *is* the capital of France.
- Maturity brings grey hair (which may be re-expressed as: 'Grey hair *is* brought by maturity').

The verb 'to be' does *not* contain any idea of 'ought'. From 'Socrates is mortal' we cannot derive 'Socrates **ought** to be valued'. To do so contravenes the rules of logic.

According to David Hume:

Hume's argument is that in moral discourse authors speak about certain facts, perhaps about human nature, and then make an illegitimate leap to tell us how we should behave. He argues that we have no justification for making this jump.

The consequence is profound. In the final sentence of this quotation, Hume seems to put any moral judgement about what is right or wrong beyond the possibility of either factual descriptions about the world or the abilities of human reason.

It may be that Hume is too pessimistic about human morality, but his comments about the impossibility of any firm grounding of moral judgements provide the question that other philosophical approaches have attempted to answer. Often called the fact/value problem, this is essentially the question of what basis we have for making moral judgements.

4 Naturalism

Perhaps the most apparently attractive response to Hume's problem would be to argue that there is something factual about goodness. If the good were somehow some feature of the world, then it would follow that the good is simply another natural fact. This branch of philosophy – which claims that 'the good' describes a quality that is inherent in nature – is called **naturalism**.

(a) Plato's Form of the Good

This type of resolution to the problem is offered by Plato's concept of the Form of the Good. Plato attempts to fix the meaning of Good by taking it as a singular, spiritual being. (Although the Forms are spiritual, not physical, they are nevertheless natural parts of nature in its widest sense, which is why we can describe Plato's approach as naturalistic.) The Form of the Good is argued to have even greater reality than the objects of our perception. That such a Form exists is, for Plato, a given: it is, for him, rationally necessary that it is there to make sense both of our ability to describe things as good and to ground our perceptions of reality. But, as we saw when we discussed Plato's theory, there is such a weight of criticism against his ideas, principally but not only from Aristotle, that it is difficult to accept his ideas.

Plato's approach is one which finds the good as a natural fact, but a fact outside the world of our everyday experience. As we have seen when we considered the Form of the Good in Year 1, Chapter 2, the idea of the Form of the Good is deeply problematic. But suppose the good were something much more 'natural' in the ordinary sense of the term.

(b) Hedonism

One of the commonest views that takes a very 'this world approach' is **hedonism**, the view, held by Jeremy Bentham, among others, that pleasure – a naturally occurring phenomenon – is the good. In this view, *good* and *pleasant* become synonyms. At first sight, this seems intuitively a sensible approach. After all, we naturally tend to seek pleasure and to avoid pain, so treating pleasure as the good would seem to fit commonsense assumptions.

But things are not quite so straightforward. We are often quite fickle in our pleasures. Suppose you buy a CD of music you enjoy. You may play it endlessly, day after day – then, all-of-a-sudden it loses its appeal. That which you played endlessly is left, scarcely noticed, on the shelf. Again, we find that things we found pleasant as young children no longer appeal. We may lose our taste for sticky sweets, dodgem cars, *Tracy Beaker* or other things as we grow older. New pleasures replace old ones. It becomes difficult to say of something that it is, indubitably, pleasant for everyone, everywhere, all the time.

Despite the difficulties, hedonism as a philosophy has a long history, back to ancient Greece. Aristippus of Cyrene (*c*.435BC–*c*.356BC) was a pupil of Socrates who developed a philosophy based on finding the pleasure in every aspect of life. Fellow students of Socrates thought he had moved too far from the teachings of his master and repudiated his views.

More famous today is Epicurus, a philosopher much misunderstood. When we hear today of an epicure, we think of someone devoted to the pleasures of the table. But for Epicurus himself, what truly mattered was to have a happy and contented life, lived in tranquility. If pleasure is the good, then the unpleasant is evil. What we must seek therefore are true pleasures, that is, those which contain no mixture of pain. Over-indulgence leads to pain, so one should avoid things such as excess of food, drink or anything else that could lead to the experience of pain. One should live simply and wisely, and the philosopher himself seems to have lived according to these precepts (incidentally, it might then be argued that, for hedonists, the good is the right attitude to pleasure rather than pleasure itself – different hedonists take different views). Such an outlook seems to have been common among Greek philosophers. Aristotle, who lived before Epicurus was born, wrote of Eudoxus (*c*.406 –355BC), a pupil of Plato, but a man who also came to the view that pleasure is the good:

For more on Plato's Form of the Good, see Year 1, pages 19–22.

Key term

Hedonism The belief that pleasure is the good and nothing else is the good. 'Good' and 'pleasure' are interchangeable terms.

Key person

Epicurus (341–270BC): born in Samos but lived in Athens from 306BC until his death (from kidney stones). A hedonist philosopher, his school, known as 'The Garden', was the first philosophical school to admit women as a policy, and not just as an exception. His atomic theory influenced the thought of Hume and Nietzsche, among others.

His arguments seem to have been accepted on the basis of his excellent character rather than because of their own merits: he was considered exceptionally self-controlled. People concluded that he held his views not because he was a pleasure-lover but because true pleasure really was the Good.

Aristotle, *Nicomachean Ethics*, Book X, ii

Aristotle's arguments are useful, because they help us to see something very important about the claim of the hedonists. A hedonist is not someone who believes that pleasure is good, and a non-hedonist is not someone who thinks that pleasure is bad. A hedonist holds that pleasure is the good *and nothing else is the good* – that qualification is crucial to the hedonist claim. That is what it means to say that for the hedonist, 'good' and 'pleasure' are synonyms: they are interchangeable terms.

When Aristotle discusses pleasure, in Book X of *Nicomachean Ethics*, he does not argue that pleasure is not good. He argues that it is not *the* good. He notes, as Plato had done, that people do seek pleasure, just as we avoid pain. Given that reality, it would be absurd to deny the significance of pleasure in our lives. For Aristotle, what we seek is a life of fulfilling activity. Such activities are, if they are good, also pleasant, but we seek them for their own sake. Think about an activity others find pleasant but that you do not. It doesn't matter how happy they are, whether it is trainspotting, playing jazz or bungee-jumping, if the activity has no appeal for you, you will not want to do it. Activities you do want to do are pleasant to you, but it is the activity that appeals – pleasure is something that accompanies and reinforces the activity. Pleasure is also difficult to quantify – Aristotle says that pleasure accompanies good activities like 'the bloom on the cheek of youth'. We do not first calculate the amount of pleasure then choose the activity which creates the maximum amount of pleasure. We do not say to ourselves that trainspotters seem to get more pleasure than other people so therefore we must take up trainspotting, if to us it looks a rather dull and pointless activity.

(c) Naturalism and absolutism

It might initially seem that if we adopt naturalism as a meta-ethical theory that we are also committing ourselves to some form of **absolutism** in our normative theories of how we should conduct ourselves and the actions we perform. After all, if the nature of the good is fixed, whether as pleasure, or some other natural quality, then it might seem as if we should always pursue that (fixed) good, and that we have an absolute duty to do so. If pleasure is the good, then it is the good for everyone and we must absolutely maximise it. Bentham seems to have thought in this way in his defence of his hedonic version of utilitarianism.

Key question

Is it possible to have a bad pleasure?

Key term

Absolutism The view that there are some things which are always obligatory. Examples of absolutist theories include utilitarianism, Kantianism and situation ethics, each of which assumes some underlying principle, whether utility, duty or love, which should always be applied.

See Year 1, pages 193–5.

Key person

Jeremy Bentham (1748–1832): utilitarian, lawyer, political thinker, deeply influential in developing utilitarianism in ethical and legal thinking but also a significant social reformer. His auto-icon is in University College, London, on permanent display.

Background

What is absolutism?

We need, at this point, to remind ourselves that absolutism should be seen as the claim that there is at least one (perhaps more) principle or principles which should always be followed. Absolutism is a denial that ultimate moral values are relative. Absolutism is not opposed to situationalism. Fletcher's situation ethics, rather like Act Utilitarianism, is an absolutist theory because it is based on the principle that we have an absolute duty to be conscientious and to perform the most loving act in every circumstance.

At first sight, then, it seems as if a naturalistic account of the good necessarily leads to some version of absolutism in practice. But such a reading would be a false inference. There are versions of naturalism which would support relativism.

A relativist naturalism is quite simple to construct. Suppose we take the view that the right thing to do is that which my society takes to be the right. It would follow that in a society that practised cannibalism, cannibalism would be the norm – a natural fact of that society. The good would be the following of that norm. But in a non-cannibal society, the norm would be different. If one's ethical belief is that the good is 'that which is approved by my own society', then what the society believes is a simple natural fact of the world which can be easily discovered by the normal methods of social science – it would be a fact that in society X, eating people is good, while in society Y, eating people is bad. And because the assumption is that 'the good is that which is approved by my society', there can be no appeal to a criterion outside the beliefs of the society which we can consider as an absolute. Cultural relativism is itself a naturalist theory, because it takes the views of a given society as a straightforward fact.

We cannot deduce absolutism from naturalism, even though some naturalist theories are absolutist in implication.

(d) The Naturalistic Fallacy

The most famous objection to naturalism is offered by the great British philosopher, G. E. Moore (1873–1958) in perhaps his most famous work *Principia Ethica*, published in 1903.

Here he identifies the **Naturalistic Fallacy**, which is the error of assuming that the good is identical with some natural quality, such as pleasure. Moore's argument is appealing, and refreshingly simple to understand. He makes use of the **Open Question Argument**.

Take, for example, the hedonist account of pleasure as the good. Remember that the claim is not that pleasure is good, but that pleasure is *the* good *and nothing else is*.

Consider the following question:

X is pleasant, but is it good?

Does this question make sense? Suppose we take the following version of the sentence:

Bear-baiting is pleasant, but is it good?

Undoubtedly there have been many people in the course of history who have enjoyed this activity and found it pleasant, perhaps as a diversion after a performance of *Hamlet* at the Globe Theatre in Jacobean Southwark. But consider the hedonist claim that pleasure is the good (and nothing else is). This means that 'pleasure' and 'good' are synonyms: pleasure = good. So, we can rewrite our sentence, substituting our terms:

Bear-baiting is good, but is it good?

But that makes no sense at all, whereas I would argue that 'Bear-baiting is pleasant, but is it good?' is an intelligible and significant question. If, as the hedonists think, 'good' and 'pleasure' are identical, then any sentence in which one term is substituted for the other would be absolutely equivalent in meaning.

Moore's insight is not a new one. Plato and Aristotle both pointed out that we can properly speak of a 'bad *pleasure*' while it makes no sense to talk of a 'bad *good*', so that the two terms cannot be synonymous. In the dialogue *Gorgias*, Plato (Socrates) in an extended discussion with the questioner Callicles, defends the idea that pleasure and the good cannot be synonyms in an argument very similar to those used by Moore more than two millennia later. For Plato, pleasure should be pursued to the extent that it leads to good.

Key question

If a natural quality can always be bad, should we give up hope of justifying good?

5 Intuitionism

Key term

Intuitionism The belief that the good is real but not a natural fact, grasped by an intuition of the mind. An ethical theory supported by Moore, Ross and Prichard, among others.

Key question

What is a non-natural quality? Does the idea make sense?

Moore's conclusion from his argument that the good cannot be a natural quality is an interesting one, but perhaps not altogether persuasive, in the theory known as **Intuitionism**, a notion further developed by W. D. Ross in *The Right and the Good* (1930) and H. A. Prichard in *Moral Obligation* (1949).

The underlying idea is that we know the good – it is a simple perception of a non-natural but simple property, rather like yellow. We see at once that something is yellow, we know it with great certainty, yet there is no one *thing* which is yellow. But when we perceive yellow, it is an undeniable feature of the world. We know it when we see it.

Moore was much influenced by the German philosopher and psychologist Franz Brentano (teacher of Freud and Husserl among others). Brentano developed the idea of intentionality, the idea that our minds are never neutral observers of the world: it is natural to perceive the world in terms of love and hate (we might prefer the term 'preference'). This preferring, this seeing things as good or bad, is what the mind naturally does. In an enthusiastic review of Brentano's *The Origin of our Knowledge of Right and Wrong*, Moore notes:

> *His main proposition is that what we know, when we know that a thing is good in itself, is that the feeling of* love *towards that thing (or* pleasure *in that thing) is* right *('richtig'). Similarly, that a thing is bad, is merely another way of saying that* hatred *of that thing would be* right.

The great merit of this view ... is its recognition that all truths of the form 'This is good in itself' are logically independent of any truth about what exists. No ethical proposition of this form is such that, if a certain thing exists, it is true, whereas, if that thing does not exist, it is false. All such ethical truths are true, whatever the nature of the world may be. ... Brentano recognizes fully the objectivity of this fundamental class of ethical judgments.

G. E. Moore, 'Review: The Origin of the Knowledge of Right and Wrong', *International Journal of Ethics*, Vol. 14, No.1, October 1903, page 116

According to Moore, this view is not subjective – things are not right and good because I say so. The good is there, to be perceived. If our minds are rightly ordered, then we will perceive correctly.

The use of the term *intuition* can be misleading. In common use, the word 'intuition' is sometimes used as a synonym for a guess, or a feeling, something non-rational. An intuitionist does not quite mean this, because, as Brentano had argued, we can through reason justify our awareness of the goodness recognised by the mind.

Moore himself was aware of the special use of the term 'intuition'. In the Introduction to *Principia Ethica* he notes:

> ### Key quote
>
> ... I would wish it observed that, when I call such propositions 'Intuitions,' I mean *merely* to assert that they are incapable of proof; I imply nothing whatever as to the manner or origin of our cognition of them. Still less do I imply ... that any proposition what[so]ever is true, *because* we cognise it in a particular way or by the exercise of any particular faculty: I hold, on the contrary, that in every way in which it is possible to cognise a true proposition, it is also possible to cognise a false one.
>
> G. E. Moore, *Principia Ethica*, 1922, page x

Key question

What happens if your intuition is different from mine?

This is important. Moore is not claiming that the good is a purely psychological phenomenon, nor is he asserting that the recognition of the good is something like a guess or a hunch. The mind is still able to reason about whether a proposition is true; but what the mind cannot do is to prove the truth of the proposition. In other words, the mind can recognise something as true even when it lacks the means to demonstrate that it is true.

Given the difficulties with the term 'intuition', it is unsurprising that later philosophers such as W. D. Ross would rarely use the term, but it is difficult to work out a natural English substitute. Nevertheless, it is important to be continually aware of the special character of the term when used by Moore.

(a) Objections to intuitionism

The advantages of intuitionism are that it appears to avoid some of the issues of naturalism, especially the problems of definition exposed by the open question argument. For many recent philosophers, non-naturalism, if not full-blown intuitionism, has appeal. After all, it seems natural to us to use terms such as 'good', 'bad', 'right' and 'wrong' as part of our basic vocabulary, and when we discuss things with friends, we assume that we can bring them to perceive things as good in the way we do. We also believe that we are saying something with an understandable meaning, something that they can relate to and perhaps come to agree with. Our debate assumes that there is *something*, however elusive, that it means to be good.

The question, however, is whether Moore's intuitionism is the answer. Three objections are perhaps worth considering, but many others might be added.

1 Intuitionism seems to assume some odd faculty of mind, different from ordinary perception. Knowledge of material objects in the world is gained from sense experience, by known physical means. But Moore is claiming that we are able to recognise non-natural qualities. How can we do this, if our senses are not attuned to non-natural properties? How are we to know that the 'good' we perceive is not simply a creation of our minds?

One possibility might be to argue that this perception is *a priori*. This was Bertrand Russell's approach for a while (he and Moore were close friends and Moore's influence can often be seen in Russell's remarks on ethics). Russell argues in his early (1912) *The Problems of Philosophy* that not all *a priori* knowledge is mathematical and logical:

> Perhaps the most important example of non-logical *a priori* knowledge is knowledge as to ethical value... In the present connexion, it is ... important to realise that knowledge as to what is intrinsically of value is *a priori* in the same sense in which logic is *a priori*, namely in the sense that the truth of such knowledge can be neither proved nor disproved by experience.

Bertrand Russell, *The Problems of Philosophy*, Oxford, 1967, pages 42–3

What Russell asserts here is highly questionable. If, as many philosophers believe, a priori knowledge is simply tautologies – self-evident truths, which give us no factual information – then it is contentious to include statements about ethical sentences, which many wouldn't deem to be self-evident. But Moore and Russell are both claiming an understanding which is a priori. A tautology's truth can be demonstrated by careful explanation of all the terms in the tautology: once these are correctly understood, the truth of the tautology can be understood. But that is not the case with good, as the purpose of the theory of intuitionism is not based on a previous definition of good, but rather that the perception of something as good somehow will reveal just what 'good' means.

It is unsurprising that Russell seems later in his life to move from including ethical statements as a priori knowledge, and that the view of the good as knowable a priori is not widely shared.

2 A second, and much simpler objection, is that if we simply know the good by a process of intuition, how can we properly discuss our views? If the criterion of 'good' is that it is that which is known by intuition, then how is it possible to reach a coherent judgement that your view is better or worse than mine? If you think Snowdon is a taller mountain than Everest, then there is a factual dispute, which is resolvable by a public process of measurement. There is an outside

Key term

a priori Knowledge which is not dependent on sense experience, such as 'a circle is round', which is true by definition.

See Year 1, pages 7–8, where *a priori* is explained more fully.

criterion by which your statement can be judged right or wrong. But Moore's view, as both he and Russell admit, is not resolvable in that way. We are left no wiser about *how* precisely we are to have any clear way of knowing what the good is.

In an epigram, the poet, Hilaire Belloc wrote:

Pale Ebenezer thought it wrong to fight,

But Roaring Bill, who killed him, thought it right.

Hilaire Belloc, *The Pacifist*

Intuitionism seems to offer no obvious way of resolving the question of who was truly right. Of course, it may be that such questions cannot be answered in any objective way. However, intuitionism claims to answer the question of what the good is, but by assuming that we just have some moral sense different from the ordinary five senses, seems to offer no clear way of determining or agreeing what that good is. The philosopher G. J. Warnock used to argue that intuitionism was simply a sense of bewilderment got up to look like a theory (see G. J. Warnock, Contemporary Moral Philosophy, 1967, especially Chapter 2).

3   A further point is the whole question of non-natural properties. What can such a concept mean? Something non-natural is not measurable nor detectable by ordinary sense experience. How is it recognisable or described, given that our language is based on the experience of things? According to the Principle of Parsimony (Ockham's Razor), we should not multiply entities beyond necessity or, in simpler terms, when there are competing hypotheses, the simpler or simplest is most likely to be correct.

For an explanation of the Principle of Parsimony (Ockham's Razor), see Year 1, page 66.

Intuitionism posits adding a category of 'non-natural qualities' to the world to explain the good. If we use Ockham's Razor, then a competing theory which manages without having to assume a new category of things, in this case the non-natural properties, is more likely to be correct.

6 Emotivism

In Chapter 5, we considered the claims of logical positivism that a proposition is meaningful if and only if it is either a tautology, and thus true by definition (such as in mathematics), or could be verified by experience. A proposition which does not meet those criteria is, by definition, meaningless and – strictly – nonsensical. (It would be helpful to look back at Chapter 5, as Emotivism depends on the same reasoning as the denial of significance to questions of religious language.)

If this is true, the question relevant to our present discussion is around the status of ethical sentences. Ethical sentences make judgements about the world, and clearly are not simply definitions. We might argue that some sentences could be constructed which are tautological such as 'Murder is wrong', but only because by the word 'murder' we mean 'wrongful killing' (therefore 'wrongful killing is wrong', hence the tautology) but doing this gives us absolutely no justification for the wrongness of murder. If Hume is right, then there can be no factual justification of rightness and wrongness, which leads to the conclusion that no factual, empirical information could serve to verify an ethical judgement.

This is precisely the conclusion drawn by A. J. Ayer in Chapter 6 of *Language, Truth and Logic*:

> ## Key quote
>
> If … I … say, 'Stealing money is wrong,' I produce a sentence which has no factual meaning – that is, expresses no proposition which can be either true or false. It is as if I had written 'Stealing money!!' – where the shape and thickness of the exclamation marks show, by a suitable convention, that a special sort of moral disapproval is being expressed. … in saying that a certain type of action is right or wrong, I am not making any factual statement, not even a statement about my own state of mind.
>
> A. J. Ayer, *Language, Truth and Logic*, 1971, page 110

Key term

Emotivism The theory, promoted principally by logical positivists, that ethical sentences simply evince emotions, though strictly they are meaningless. Characterised by Winston Barnes as the 'Killing-boo!' theory.

Ayer describes his theory as 'emotive'. We should notice certain features of his theory. Ayer himself is sometimes slightly careless in his use of language. His carelessness is evident in the above passage, where he says that an emotion is expressed. Elsewhere, he uses the word 'evinced', which is more precise and closer to his meaning. If we say – as some have done – that **emotivism** holds that emotions *express* a feeling, then the problem arises that expressing an emotion is the expression of something the speaker has felt as an emotion. Ayer denies this interpretation. I may say something is right even though I do not feel it, perhaps because I think it would be wise in a given set of circumstances to say it. If I were a vegetarian who found myself captured by a cannibal tribe who said 'Eating vegetarians is right, and they taste better', I might well say with them, 'Vegetarians, yum-yum!' on the not unreasonable grounds that I preferred to stay out of the stew-pot.

Ayer argues that as ethical judgements have no factual content, there can be no genuine arguments between people about which is the 'right' ethical conclusion. If ethical sentences were seen as *expressing* beliefs that the speakers held or felt, then there would be factual content, which could be verified. If I were to say 'Vegetarianism is right!' that would be a verifiable statement if it could be shown that it did (or did not) express my feelings. If I said 'Vegetarianism is right!' and you saw me tucking into sausages, black pudding and bacon for breakfast, then you could say that 'Vegetarianism is right!', as spoken by me, was an untrue statement as an expression of my feelings. This is where emotivism is different from the meta-ethical theory of subjectivism. Subjectivism holds that '*X* is right because I say so/have chosen it' (Sartre was a subjectivist as he held that my choosing something was its right-making feature), and it is, at least in principle, possible to investigate whether that truly is my belief or choice. Subjectivism is verifiable (and cognitive), whereas emotivism is not.

... the orthodox subjectivist does not deny, as we do, that the sentences of a moraliser express genuine propositions. ... His own view is that they express propositions about a speaker's feelings. If this were so, ethical judgements clearly would be capable of being true or false. They would be true if the speaker had the relevant feelings, and false if he had not. For if I say, 'Tolerance is a virtue,' and someone answers, 'You don't approve of it,' he would, on the ordinary subjectivist theory, be contradicting me. On our theory, he would not be contradicting me, because, in saying that tolerance was a virtue, I should not be making any statement about my own feelings or about anything else. I should simply be evincing my feelings, which is not at all the same thing as saying that I have them.

A. J. Ayer, *Language, Truth and Logic*, 1971, page 112

Ayer denies the possibility of any *philosophical* discussion of ethical value:

Key quote

We find that ethical philosophy consists simply in saying that ethical concepts are pseudo-concepts and therefore unanalysable. The further task of describing the different feelings that the different ethical terms are used to express, and the different reactions that they customarily provoke, is a task for the psychologist. There cannot be such a thing as ethical science, if by ethical science one means the elaboration of a 'true' system of morals. For we have seen that, as ethical judgements are mere expressions of feeling, there can be no way of determining the validity of any ethical system, and indeed, no sense in asking whether any such system is true.

A. J. Ayer, *Language, Truth and Logic*, 1971, page 116

Key question

If it is true that we cannot prove moral judgements, does this mean that they are completely impossible to argue about?

Key term

Relativism The theory that there are no absolutes in ethics and that every judgement is relative, perhaps to culture or other beliefs. This denies any claim to universalism. The term should not be confused with 'situationalism'. A theory such as situation ethics is situational in application but absolutist in the moral demand of love.

We can see why the philosopher Winston Barnes characterised the theory as the 'Killing-boo!' theory, as words such as 'right' or 'wrong' are strictly outside the field of meaningful words. If someone shouts *boo!* because he does not like something, he is offering nothing to discuss – a yelp of dislike is not an argument which we can debate. However, the danger of Barnes' formulation is that, as a simplification, it could lead us to think of emotivism as a kind of subjectivism.

We have already noted some carelessness in Ayer's use of language. He sometimes refers to his view as 'subjectivism'. This is misleading, because a subjectivist believes 'X is right *because I say so*'. In emotivism, as no reason can be given and the claim is strictly unverifiable, it makes no sense to describe someone's expression of a belief as untruthful. Emotivism and subjectivism are different.

(a) Emotivism and relativism

Does the theory of emotivism lead to support of ethical **relativism**? It seems an inference of this kind would be an error.

A relativist holds that no ethical judgement can be proven beyond doubt, and/or that an ethical judgement is relative to a given culture, whether that is a nation, tribal group, religion or something else, or that any ethical sentence is no more valid or invalid than any other. She might say, 'If it's right for you, then it is right'. It is perfectly possible then to make factual judgements – as Ayer acknowledges – about whether one truly holds the judgement one claims to believe.

A relativist believes her account to be superior to that of a non-relativist, because she believes that she can justify it by pointing to different beliefs sincerely held by different people. She thinks her approach is better, either because it can be shown to be accurate, while others are inaccurate, or because any non-relativist account fails.

For emotivists, the relativist claim is simply meaningless. No factual information could demonstrate the superiority of a relativist judgement over a non-relativist one, because there is nothing factual or verifiable which could be adduced in support of the claim. In exactly the way that we saw atheism, theism and agnosticism were meaningless to logical positivists, so too would be a moral claim, whether absolutist or relativist. The meta-ethical debate simply makes no sense – it is beyond discussion.

(b) Objections to emotivism

Many of the doubts about logical positivism expressed in Chapter 5 are relevant here. The biggest issue is that, for emotivists, all ethical judgements are outside the scope of reason, being strictly meaningless.

The question this raises is serious. At the philosophical level, emotivism seems to confuse two issues. There is a difference between being able to *prove* something and being able to give *reasons* for thinking it.

Emotivism seems to set the bar too high. It suggests that because I cannot *prove* a moral judgement, that any justification becomes meaningless. But there are all sorts of things I cannot prove, yet I can give reasons for thinking as I do. I cannot *prove* that the music of Bach or Beethoven is superior to the tuneless humming I produce in the bath, but I can give all sorts of reasons, in terms of harmonic subtlety, design, melody, structure and development and so on for suggesting that there is something better about their music than my meanderings. In the same way, I can think of a host of reasons, in terms of outcomes, pain, psychological damage, effects on the agents, etc., for arguing that incest, torture, child abuse or cruelty are wrong, and I can think of no good reasons for thinking that these are good actions. Even if the reasons are not the same as those which constitute normal scientific or geometric proofs, it does not follow that there are no reasons at all. If the claims of emotivism are correct, it follows that there is no possibility of moral or value judgement at all, as there are no possible moral *reasons*. The emotivist cannot even justify his judgements, as a relativist can, by saying that something is justified because it follows the ideas of a particular cultural viewpoint: there is, strictly, nothing he can use in justification.

This has a consequence not immediately apparent that many, perhaps most, people would not wish to accept. If *no* reason offered has any moral validity, then *any* reason for a point of view may no more be condemned than any other. Suppose someone wants to change your views about an idea someone else has. He says that third person should not be believed because she is 'a filthy, stinking Jew/black/Catholic/Irish person'. I would want to say that such an 'argument' is *ad hominem*, racist or bigoted, and has no place in debate or persuasion. A racist bigot might, however, use just such an argument to work on your emotions. It is in just such a way that racism works, by creating negative feelings.

Emotivism offers no defence against such tactics. Any reason offered, being beyond rational argument, is as good as any other. I cannot complain about the racist or bigoted arguments, because I can have no reason and no possible justification for thinking my views superior or justifiable. Nor can the victim of this abuse, the person you are being encouraged to look down on, give any reasons in her own defence.

It can be argued that emotivism, if true, simply destroys the possibility of rational ethical discourse. It also seems counter-intuitive, given that we really have experience of reasoning about the morality of actions. I might say 'it is wrong to do something such as murder because...' Some reasons I choose to give can be prudential or self-serving: 'I should not murder *X* because I do not want to go to prison or be hanged', but not all reasons people offer are of this type. 'I should not murder *X* because he has rights as a human being' is reasoning of a different kind, which we call moral, but it is neither an unnatural way of thinking nor indicative of no reasoning process. To argue like this is not to go beyond reason, as emotivism suggests, but is experienced by us as (however difficult) a reasoning process. Emotivism seems at odds with what we actually mean when we think about our actions.

7 Alternative viewpoints

It is always valuable to interrogate the question to which different theories are put forward as an answer. This seems especially true of the meta-ethical theories discussed in this chapter.

People have sought an answer to the logical question proposed by Hume, the fact/value, is/ought problem as outlined by Hume. This question is posed as one of logic, a question of how we can legitimately move from a statement of facts about the world to the justification we make about what is to be valued or judgements of what we should (ought to) do.

But it is possible to suggest that the questions we are considering are not ones of logic, but of living. The need to behave in particular ways does not occur to us as a logical question but from our living as people in the world, in interaction with others. If there were no other people, I would be aware of no moral demands.

The American philosopher, Alan Gewirth, in a major work, *Reason and Morality* (1978, revised 1980), suggests his **Principle of Generic Consistency**. The thesis is based on the idea that humans are not self-sufficient. We have needs, which can only be met with the help of other people, so we make demands upon them, to provide food, education and so on. But there is need for some return – we need to do things for them if we are to receive the things we need. If we treat people badly, they will feel little requirement to do things for us. The consequence is that mutual dependence creates a world of contracts, duties and obligations, a world of rights. The Principle of Generic Consistency grows out of this nexus of needs, duties and obligations. We contract with each other and can only

> **Key term**
>
> **Principle of Generic Consistency** Gewirth's term, in *Reason and Morality*, for the principle that human life necessarily requires treating everyone else as having the same rights and duties as I find necessary for myself.

Key person

Alan Gewirth (1912–2004): American philosopher, based at the University of Chicago. He worked principally in ethics and political philosophy. His major work is *Reason and Morality* (1978), in which he introduced the influential idea of the Principle of Generic Consistency to overcome questions about the legitimacy and justification of ethical judgements.

Key question

Is moral justification a question of logical justification, or of living?

do so effectively by recognising that others should be treated similarly to the ways we seek for ourselves – hence the need for Generic Consistency. In Gewirth's analysis, therefore, being moral is a reality of living, not a logical question.

In a similar vein, Karol Wojtyła, the future Pope St John Paul II, in his major philosophical work, *The Acting Person*, wrote:

> *In each of his actions the human person is eyewitness of the transition from the 'is' to the 'should' – the transition from 'x is truly good' to 'I should do x.'*

Karol Wojtyła, *The Acting Person* (*Analecta Husserliana* Vol. X), 1979

Wojtyła's argument is that the ethical demand grows out of human encounter. It is in encounter that we experience the emotions of love, liking, need, desires, hopes and demands – the very things that make us face the need to be moral.

If analyses like these are correct, then perhaps the good and being moral need a different type of justification from the scientific/logical one which Hume and others seek.

A second question perhaps worth considering is whether there is a mistake in trying to pin down the good to a single thing, whether Plato's Form of the Good or Moore's non-natural qualities. As Aristotle and others have pointed out, good has many forms, both moral and non-moral, and what is good for one person is not necessarily wholly good for someone else. A difficulty is that the bad, in terms of pain, suffering and mental anguish is instantly recognisable, in ways that the good is not. We want to define good in terms that are stronger than the mere absence of harm – there seem to be goods, such as delight in things, which are more than merely the absence of the painful and unpleasant. Perhaps the good is not capable of being defined, even though it is known – and enjoyed – when experienced.

8 Conclusions

It sometimes seems as if the questions of meta-ethics are abstract, but, if we think about them, we recognise that, even if we have never studied any philosophy, we are continually asking why we think as we do. That we think this way, often without fully realising it, becomes apparent when someone tells us that he finds something good while we cannot share that perception. As teachers, parents and concerned citizens we might want to ask how people can justify behaving in anti-social ways. Faced with a law we do not like, we might ask why it is wrong to behave in the way the law forbids. Justification matters.

As we saw when we considered hedonism or Plato's theory of the Forms, the question of what we mean by good is as old as the academic discipline of philosophy. In this chapter we examined several main approaches, notably emotivism, naturalism and intuitionism, suggesting that none is wholly satisfactory as an answer to the original questions asked. This does not mean that studying them is, in any sense, pointless. Here, as elsewhere, possible mistakes in reasoning, carefully identified, can develop many very productive lines of thought.

Study advice

Meta-ethics is not the easiest ethical topic, but the question of why we should be moral and how we justify our judgements is an important part of life, especially in a climate of ethical uncertainty and fundamental differences between various peoples, faith groups and individuals.

As ever, pay close attention to the accurate definition of terms such as 'absolutism' and the various theories named here. Wherever possible, check your own definitions against original texts to make sure that you fairly represent authors' views. Make sure that, as with any theory, you set different views, such as naturalism, against the questions they are designed to answer. Take time to think through and think about the issues. Examination questions always move beyond mere description to ask you to *consider* the issues set out here and elsewhere.

Summary diagram: Ethical language: meta-ethics

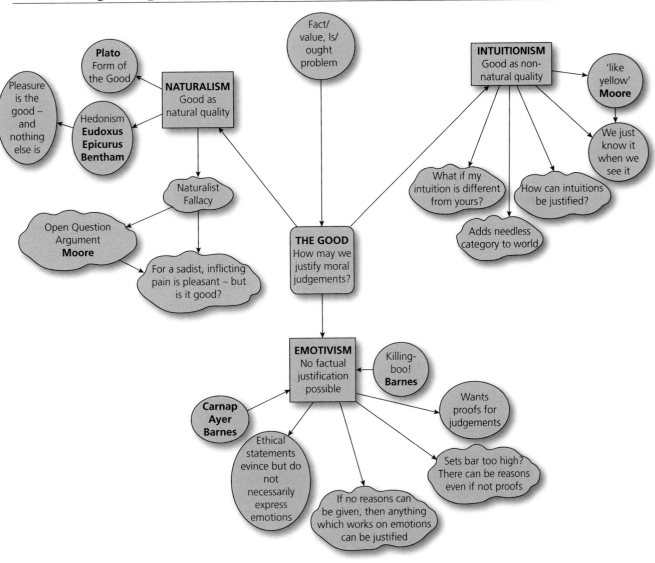

You should be able to be confident in your understanding of key terms and the three theories developed in this chapter in answer to the challenge to ethical justification posed by Hume and others. You need to be very precise in your understandings of naturalism, intuitionism and emotivism. You should be able to reflect on whether any meta-ethical theory is doomed to fail, either because of the challenge of relativism or because the dilemma posed by Hume is insoluble.

Can you give brief definitions of:
- naturalism
- intuitionism
- emotivism
- hedonism
- absolutism?

Can you explain:
- the fact/value, is/ought problem
- Moore's arguments against what he sees as the naturalistic fallacy
- the difference between expressing and evincing an emotion
- the problems of denying the claims of relativism?

Can you give arguments for and against:
- hedonist accounts of the good
- the claim that moral judgements are ultimately meaningless
- intuitionism
- the possibility of an absolutist approach to ethical judgement?

Sample question and guidance

Assess how well emotivism resolves the problem of justifying ethical judgements.

This question looks at just one attempt to resolve the fact/value problem. It is important to notice that there is no comparative element in the wording of the question. It does not ask whether emotivism is better or worse than any competitor view, so you are being invited to consider just this theory. This suggests that the examiner would wish to see a reasonable range of detail and identification of more than one aspect of emotivism.

Clearly you need to be very clear about the challenge to which emotivism is a response. You may wish to observe that Ayer considers the dilemma posed by Hume as insoluble and a fact which must be accepted in any attempt to think philosophically about morality. You would almost certainly find it very useful to your essay to consider – and not just to state – how emotivism relates to the other claims made by logical positivism. This might suggest interesting lines of argument, because if the claims of logical positivism and verification theory are flawed, then it is quite possible that the theory of ethics derived from those claims is deficient also.

You may wish to consider whether the distinction made in emotivism between evincing or expressing emotion adds anything useful to the theory. You will almost certainly want to explore the question of whether emotivism leaves an important part of life without any justification at all, and it would probably be useful to consider whether in demanding proofs for judgements, emotivists ignore the possibility that there might nevertheless be good reasons for them. You might choose also to consider the objection that if no moral argument is justifiable, then any kind of argument, however racist, sexist or unpleasant, might be used to change someone's mind.

The usual points about justification, careful definition and thinking through issues apply with special force in this essay.

→

Further essay questions

'The good is not a natural quality.' Discuss.

To what extent is it possible to argue that we just know what the good is?

'No moral judgements can ever be reasonably justified.' Discuss.

Going further

The literature on meta-ethics is, understandably, vast. There are useful introductions by Andrew Fisher (Routledge, 2011) and Simon Kirchin (Palgrave, 2012), both called *Metaethics*, while *An Introduction to Contemporary Metaethics* by Alex Miller (Polity Press, 2003) may also be recommended.

There is a wealth of useful material in *A Companion to Ethics*, ed. Peter Singer (Blackwell, 1993) and, in the same series, *A Companion to Ethical Theory*, ed. Hugh LaFollette (Blackwell, 2000).

It is useful to read Ayer's comments on ethics in Chapter 6 of *Language, Truth and Logic* (Penguin, 1971) to get a basic grasp of emotivism, and G. E. Moore,

Principia Ethica is widely available in various editions, and David Mills Daniel, *Briefly: Moore's Principia Ethica* (SCM, 2011) is a useful, brief guide. *Ethics: The Fundamentals* by Julia Driver (Blackwell, 2007) has a useful overview of intuitionism.

Other books discussed in this chapter are:

- Gewirth, A. *Reason and Morality* (University of Chicago, 1978).
- Hume, D. *A Treatise of Human Nature* (1739).
- Russell, B. *The Problems of Philosophy* (Oxford University Press, 1967).
- Warnock, G. J. *Contemporary Moral Philosophy* (Macmillan, 1967).

Chapter 9

Conscience – Aquinas and Freud

> ## Chapter checklist
>
> The chapter begins with a discussion on the nature of conscience and its relationship to human thought. There is then a detailed account of Aquinas' theory of conscience, noting its relationship to prudence as practical reason and considering also how Aquinas develops the ideas of Aristotle, especially on the question of moral responsibility. Particular attention is paid to the ideas of *ratio, synderesis, conscientia* and vincible and invincible ignorance.
>
> This is followed by a section on why we must always follow conscience. Some comparisons are drawn between Aquinas and the ideas of the God-given nature of conscience as argued by Newman and Butler. Discussion of Freud considers whether he is dealing with the same issues as Aquinas. Freud's ideas of *id, ego, super-ego* and *libido* are explained and discussed, and the alleged origins of the Oedipus Complex – and its relation to the *super-ego* – are also discussed. Study guidance, suggestions for further reading and sample essay titles are provided at the end of the chapter.

1 Introduction

The relationship of mind to action is an extraordinary one in human beings, and not easily reducible to simple terms. It would be easy to say that we think about a possible action, work out how to do it, then decide to get on with performing it. But even this is far from simple – choosing to act is not like pressing a button to put an electric motor into motion. The process of deciding to act is complex. We do not think in straight lines, but often double back on ourselves and decide to investigate a different action or a different way of doing the same action. We wonder not simply about whether an action *can* be done, but also about whether it *should be done*. That idea of 'should be done' can be a 'should' which has an ethical quality as the morally right and proper thing to do, or a 'should' which is purely prudential, as when I look at the sky and the weather forecast and decide that I would be wise to take an umbrella with me. Sometimes, of course, a decision to act has both prudential and moral aspects, and these are not always easy to disentangle. And even if I can conclude (without changing my mind too much) what I ought to do – and have the will and means to do it – there are still questions such as those about when and where those actions are to be performed.

If thinking about decision-making is hard enough, there are further complications: we are not only people who decide and act but also people who reflect on our lives and on actions we have performed. Often we look back on past actions with regret and embarrassment, occasionally with pleasure. We often wish we had acted differently and, sometimes, have no understanding of why we acted in a particular way. We make judgements not only about our actions, but also our motivations and feelings at a given time. But this is not a once-and-for-all process. We sometimes change our judgements about those past decisions, thinking what we did was worse or better than we thought either at the time or later.

Often we discuss these feelings, judgements and thoughts in terms of *conscience*. We may use the term in a variety of ways: 'I have a bad conscience about what I did', or 'I cannot in good conscience do that'. It has both a reference to past events and a connection with future possible actions. Sometimes a religious person may speak of 'examining her conscience', reflecting on the judgements and actions (or inactions) she has performed. Sometimes we speak of a 'crisis of conscience' when we mean that we simply have no idea of the right thing to do, or the pressures of doing what seems to us the right thing appear overwhelmingly difficult. Sometimes we speak of heroic human beings as 'prisoners of conscience', undergoing punishment for standing up for what they believe to be right, while in another way we may permit someone not to fight in a war or not to assist in certain operations or activities because of 'conscientious objection'.

The word 'conscience' simply means 'with knowledge', and is connected to people knowing what they are doing. There are interesting questions about whether animals have any faculty which approaches what we mean by 'conscience'. Certainly, some animals seem to demonstrate regret – at least of a prudential sort – but there is much to be done on animal psychology and we have enough to do, for this enquiry, with the complexities of human psychology.

2 Conscience – Thomas Aquinas' views

Perhaps the most thoroughgoing account of conscience is given by St Thomas Aquinas; his account is detailed and developed and is interesting in its attempt to do justice to the complexity of human experience of reflection on conduct.

Aquinas' view of conscience is sometimes described as a 'theological approach', but we must be careful not to see his idea as 'the voice of God' or some version of divine command theory.

For an explanation of divine command theory, see Year 1, pages 139–40.

It would be equally wrong to see his idea of conscience as some sort of intuitive little voice, which just knows what is the right thing to do.

(a) Aquinas and *ratio*

Aquinas' approach is always reasoned, as may be seen from his treatment of the intellect as a fundamental part of the soul, which itself is closely tied to reason (*Summa Theologica*, I, Q79, a1, c.).

For more information about Aquinas' idea of *practica ratio*, see Year 1, pages 155-6.

Aquinas makes use of the concept of *ratio,* which means rather more than its literal translation as 'reason': it also contains a notion of a concept or an idea. This is important, because of Aquinas' idea of *practica ratio*, that is, the use of reason in practice, which inevitably is always situational in application. *Practica ratio* entails not merely being able to know what should be done, but also the practical way of thinking through *how* that which should be done can be done by the agent with the means available.

Like Aristotle, Aquinas distinguishes between the theoretical or speculative parts of reason, such as those we use in drawing up scientific hypotheses, and the practical.

The moral life is a practical life – we have to work out carefully what it is right and proper to do. There is not an invariable right answer, and so there is a relationship between the skills of acting well and an artist's doing well. Like Aristotle, Aquinas sees a distinction between the skills of an artist ('right reason of things to be made') and those of prudence ('right reason of things to be done'). Both operate in the world of variables. Both Aquinas and Aristotle argue that an artist, such as an architect, has to reason through how to use the materials he has at hand to achieve some particular artefact – this is practical reasoning. There is not one absolute right building to be built: questions need to be asked about what the building is for, and then accommodate that need according to the means, such as space, money and materials, which are available. Circumstances cannot be ignored, and the architect has to work within those constraints.

The same is true for the individual in life. It is not enough to think of what should be done, but to ask also about what I can do from where I am with the means I have available. To do well, we need more than the theory of what is good but the skills in practical reasoning to get good results. Decisions about what to do in our lives have to begin from the reality of our here and now. If someone asks us how to get to London, it would be useless to say, 'I wouldn't start from here', as here is where we must begin. Aquinas is always insistent on the practical and immediate aspect of moral decision-making, which necessarily entails close attention to circumstance. For him, there is always close connection between conscience and practical reason (*practica ratio*).

(i) Conscience and prudence

There are close links between Aquinas' theory of natural law and his treatment of conscience. As we saw (Year 1, Chapter 10, pages 146–63), Aquinas was insistent on the importance of careful judgement of what it is right and proper to do in the circumstances. One size does not fit all situations. The practical question of moral life means understanding the general principle, but also being able to apply it in particular circumstances. The same is true in cases of conscience, both when we are judging what we need to do, but also when we judge the past actions of ourselves and others. This is the realm of conscience. We ought not, Aquinas thinks, to feel guilty for every action we have ever done which has turned out wrongly. Sometimes we could not have done differently; sometimes our motives were for the best; sometimes we could not possibly have foreseen particular consequences, which occurred despite our best intentions.

There is a close link between prudence and conscience. In his treatment of natural law, Aquinas, like Aristotle, insisted on the need for the intellectual virtue of prudence.

For Aquinas' treatment of natural law, see Year 1, especially the account on pages 155–6.

As Aquinas tells us:

Prudence entails not only consideration of the reason but also the application to action, which is the goal of practical reason.

S.T. II-II, 9.47, a. 3c.

Prudence involves three intellectual skills: *Understanding*, *Judgement* and *Good Deliberation*. The last of these is the practical business of working out how, in the situation in which we find ourselves, to achieve what our judgement tells us we ought to do. Notice that in the use of conscience, whether in deciding what we should do or in examining previous actions, judgement is an essential part – did we perform the right action in the circumstances? Conscience, like action, is always to be examined circumstantially.

The great Thomist scholar, Servais Pinckaers has noted:

… it is clear that St. Thomas saw conscience and prudence as two converging lights coming from the same source. Both are prompted by our aspiration to the truth and both share the object of the discernment between good and evil.

Servais Pinckaers, 'Conscience and the Virtue of Prudence', *The Pinckaers Reader: Renewing Thomistic Moral Theology*, eds John Berkaman and Craig Steven Titus, 2005, page 353

This connection between prudence and conscience must never be forgotten as they are a useful caution against those who have attempted, on rather thin evidence, to interpret Thomist moral thought as indifferent to circumstance.

(b) Conscience – Aquinas' view

The simplest summary of Aquinas' view of conscience may be found in *Summa Theologica*. This summary should be studied closely as it is rich in its implications:

Key question

Why is it important to understand Aquinas' theory of conscience in the light of his teaching on prudence?

Key quote

Properly speaking, conscience is not a power, but an act. … The word 'conscience' comes from 'cum alio scientia,' that is, knowledge applied to an individual case. But the application of knowledge to something is done by some act of the mind. So, from this explanation of the name it is clear that conscience is an act.

This is obvious from those things which are attributed to conscience. For conscience is said to witness, to bind, or incite, and also to accuse, torment, or rebuke. All these involve the application of knowledge or science to what we do. This application is made in three ways. One way happens when we recognise that we have done or not done something; 'Your heart knows that many times you have yourself cursed others' (Ecclesiastes 7.22). In this case, conscience is said to witness what we have done. In another way of speaking, we say – through

the conscience – that something should be done or not done. In this sense, we describe conscience as 'inciting' or 'binding'. In the third way, through conscience we judge that something done is well or badly done. In this sense, conscience is said to excuse, accuse, or torment us for our actions. Now, it is obvious that all these things follow the actual application of knowledge to what we do. So, properly speaking, conscience is the name of an act. But as habit is a principle which creates an act, sometimes the name conscience is given to the first natural habit – that is, synderesis. Jerome calls synderesis 'conscience' (Gloss. Ezekiel 1:6). Basil [Hom. in princ. Proverb.] calls it the 'natural power of judgment,' and Damascene [De Fide Orth. iv. 22] says that it is the 'law of our intellect.' For it is customary for causes and effects to be called after one another.

S.T. I, Q79, a.13c.

We notice at once that this view of conscience is based on a principle of reason. It is important that it entails an action of mind, because an act is always particular – it is this act, performed in the here and now.

There is something in common with Joseph Fletcher's idea when he treats 'conscience' as a verb, to refer to an action.

But Aquinas' version is richer than Fletcher's in that it continues by considering the ways in which we make judgements not just about the actions we are now to do, but also about those we have done (or not done). Notice how Aquinas, always sensitive to language in use, is concerned to demonstrate how his description of conscience fits with the way people use the term in ordinary language.

(c) *Synderesis* and *conscientia*

Aquinas' view of conscience is quite subtle, with many different strands within it, but it forms a coherent whole, not just in itself, but also in relation to his entire understanding of morality. His account always pays attention to the intellectual and rational nature of human choices as well as to how we should judge our actions. As always with Aquinas, we find how he gives close analysis of the terms we use when we speak about ideas such as conscience or prudence.

In the previous passage, we find Aquinas making reference to *synderesis*. This is a concept with an interesting history, as Aquinas acknowledges. The term, which is not an original Greek word, is first found in a passage in St Jerome (347–420), when he comments on the vision of Ezekiel, in which he sees a human, a lion, an ox and an eagle (an eagle was traditionally seen to represent reason and the ability to reflect on our own actions). As Aquinas rightly notes, for Jerome, 'synderesis' and 'conscience' are interchangeable terms.

See Year 1, pages 170–1.

Key question

What is the scope of conscience, according to Aquinas, and how does it differ from the view of Joseph Fletcher?

Key term

Synderesis An inner principle, implanted by God in all persons, directing a person towards good and away from evil.

Background

From *syneidesis* to *synderesis*

The Latin, *conscientia* is a direct translation of the Greek *syneidesis*, which has several meanings, including being aware of something (close to our idea of 'consciousness') or also sharing understanding with someone else, perhaps knowing her secret. As a result, in Greek, *syneidesis* came to have a legal meaning, meaning 'to bear witness'. Aquinas refers to conscience as *bearing witness* in the sense of a faculty of thought which judges our own thinking processes. It is a feature of our minds that with part of our brains we can, as it were, watch our own thinking processes, and reflect not only on the process of thought but on the reflections we have about those processes. Not only do we know things, but we know that we know them, and we know that we know that we know that we know them. In certain usages, *syneidesis* came also to mean the state of knowing one's own mind, and so it referred to making judgements about oneself.

The origin of the word *synderesis* as a synonym for *conscientia* is perhaps no more than an original transcription error, a miscopying of *syneidesis*. But by the time of Aquinas and Scholastic thought in general, it would have a useful technical function.

For Aquinas, *synderesis* is the natural inclination to do good and avoid evil, a desire which is universal, infallible and part of God's will for the creatures he created. There are questions in Aquinas and other writers about whether *synderesis* is a habit, a power, or a disposition, but these arguments can, for present purposes, be laid to one side. The infallibility of *synderesis* is, for Aquinas, self-evident: it could never be wrong to wish to do good and avoid evil.

Just because we have the desire to do good and avoid evil, it does not follow that this infallible desire leads to right action. *Conscientia* is the name Aquinas gives to the intellectual process of forming our particular moral judgements in individual circumstances, which of course includes the skill of prudence. Here, errors can be made, either because we are mistaken about the facts of the case or for some other reason, perhaps because we are blinded by desires, feel pressures from outside or are simply too hasty in our judgements.

(d) A theological account?

This distinction between *synderesis* and *conscientia* is valuable for considering whether we should see Aquinas as essentially theological in his approach to moral questions. In an important sense he is theological in that he believes we are the creatures we are because of the will of God, and because God chose that we should be the people we are, with the skills of intellect and the potential for good will that we have. In that sense, the ability to do right and avoid evil is God-given.

Nevertheless, as we have suggested, the actual business of choosing the right thing and making right judgements is, for Aquinas, absolutely to be understood in terms of a rational use of our minds (*ratio*).

Background

Difficulties in defining conscience

Aquinas would not speak of conscience, as Cardinal Newman would, in Section 5 of his *Letter to the Duke of Norfolk* (1875), as 'the aboriginal vicar of Christ'. (An aborigine is the original occupant of the country – in this phrase, Newman uses the term 'aboriginal' to mean 'original or 'primary'.) For Newman, when we feel ashamed, we are hearing the voice of God speaking to us, just as Christ may be held to speak through his Church in the person of the Vicar of Christ, the Pope. For Aquinas, God gave us reason, but it is reason that speaks to us.

Neither would Aquinas quite agree with the great Anglican thinker, Bishop Butler, in the Dissertations that appear as appendices to his *The Analogy of Religion* (1736), that conscience is a God-given

principle of reflection which enables us to achieve the right judgements in particular circumstances. The difficulty with both Butler and Newman is that they find it less straightforward than Aquinas to account for errors in the application of conscience. Newman attempts to deal with this by arguing that we sometimes have false conscience, by listening to our own desires and telling ourselves that this is our conscience speaking, but that still assumes that a conscience properly listened to would always get things right. Butler, similarly, assumes that if we only attended to it, our God-given conscience would give us the right answers. For Aquinas, we can make mistakes in good conscience, just as we can make mistakes in any kind of reasoning. If Aquinas is correct, any error in conscience is very obviously a human mistake.

Aquinas is very clear that, while reason is God-given, it is, like any use of thought, capable of error. Just as we can make mistakes in scientific reasoning, artistic judgement and any other use of our minds, so too the same, as we shall see, is true of that type of thinking which we think of as conscientious.

If, as Aquinas thinks, particular judgements of conscience are neither merely feelings nor the voice of God, it would be possible to construe his ideas on conscience in secular terms, as something that minds are capable of doing. Aquinas, as a believer, thinks that the mind is God-given, but his analysis would seem to work equally well even if the mind were simply a surprising natural fact.

Key question

To what extent is the Thomist view of conscience dependent on belief in God?

(e) Moral responsibility

A central concern for Aquinas, as for many medieval thinkers, was the question of when we can ascribe moral responsibility. Plato notoriously believed, as Greek thought in general had done, that we do wrong only as a result of ignorance. For Plato, everyone desires the good, but most people (other than true philosophers) are more or less ignorant of what the true good is. Plato held the common Greek view that if we know the good, we are bound to do it.

Aristotle disagreed. He thought that we can know the good but fail to do it, perhaps because we have fallen into bad habits or lack the courage to do what we know we should. In *Nicomachean Ethics*, Book III, Chapters 1 and 2, Aristotle considers the nature of moral responsibility, in terms which have had deep influence on later discussion. Aquinas, both in his *Commentary on Nicomachean Ethics* (*Sententia Libri Ethicorum* (1270–71)) and in the *Summa,* is explicit about his debt to Aristotle, and his ideas should be seen as a development of Aristotle's theories.

Aristotle considers two factors which might excuse someone from being blamed for an action. One of these is *ignorance*, the other, *lack of choice*. In Aquinas, these ideas are developed, and Catholic moral theology, following Aquinas, still teaches that to commit a sin, one needs full knowledge and full consent.

As Aristotle notes, 'full consent' is a difficult notion. When does one freely choose? Aristotle notes that it is not always easy to decide:

> *When we think of the things that are done from fear of greater evils or for some noble reason (for example if a tyrant were to order one to do something wicked, having one's parents and children in his power, and if by doing the action they would be saved and not be put to death), it may be debated whether such actions are involuntary or voluntary. Something similar happens if the captain of a merchant ship throws goods overboard in a storm; for in the abstract no one throws goods away voluntarily, but to secure the safety of himself and his crew, any sensible man does so. Such actions, then, are mixed, but are more like voluntary actions. They are chosen at the moment they are done, and the purpose of an action is relative to the occasion. Both the terms, then, 'voluntary' and 'involuntary', must be used with reference to the moment of action. In these circumstances the man acts voluntarily because the choices that move the body*

to act are in him. Those things which are choices of the man are in his power to perform or not. Such actions, therefore, are voluntary, but in the abstract are perhaps involuntary because no one would choose any such act in itself.

Aristotle, *Nicomachean Ethics*, Book III, Chapter 1

We should notice here that we can only determine the degree of responsibility case-by-case: particular practical judgement is always situational. So too for Aquinas: someone might be under such pressure that his choice cannot be said to be free, nor is he truly consenting to the action. The voluntariness of an action can be affected by many things, depending on the individual and circumstances. There might be force applied to the agent; for example, if a bank employee has a gun pointing at him, or there could be some problem in the agent, such as mental illness, which creates a compulsion to act in a particular way. In law, we assume that people below a certain age do not have full consent in their actions, and do not penalise very young children. Even with adults, we may think someone not responsible for his actions. As in the courtroom, there is a clear need to look at each individual case before ascribing responsibility.

(f) Vincible and invincible ignorance

There is a close connection between consent and knowledge. It seems impossible to give proper consent – 'informed' consent – if we are ignorant of the facts. For Plato, ignorance was a reason for blame: he advocated punishing the person who acted through ignorance to teach her to know better next time. For Aristotle and Aquinas, on the other hand, forgivable ignorance gives good reason not to punish the wrongdoer.

Aquinas distinguishes **vincible ignorance** from **invincible ignorance**.

If someone is vincibly ignorant, then he is potentially blameworthy. This is ignorance, which is avoidable and correctible. There are things which I should be expected to know. If I visit another country and murder someone, it is no excuse for me to say I was brought up in Britain and could not be expected to know that killing people was illegal in Austria. My own common sense should tell me that it is wrong to murder, anywhere. If I were unaware of Austrian law, there are always opportunities to ask (though I suspect my Austrian friends would be a little taken aback at a question about whether I could murder someone in Vienna without breaching some law). Aristotle, in his original account, explains the point very well:

we punish a man for his ignorance, if he is considered responsible for the ignorance, for example when penalties are doubled in the case of drunkenness; as ... in the man himself: he had the ability not to get drunk and his getting drunk was the cause of his ignorance. And we punish those who are ignorant of anything in the laws that they ought to know that is not difficult to find out. The same is also true in the case of anything else that they are thought to be ignorant of through carelessness.

Aristotle, *Nicomachean Ethics*, Book III, Chapter 5

Key terms

Vincible ignorance Ignorance which we could easily overcome and for which we are blameworthy. If I ask to be excused for my bad driving because I didn't know what I was doing, because I was drunk, that is really no excuse and adds to the offence.

Invincible ignorance Ignorance which cannot be overcome by my own efforts and for which I cannot be blamed.

153

Aquinas makes similar points. These ideas seem to match our commonsense understanding. A court would be unlikely to take seriously the driver who offered his drunkenness as an excuse for his dangerous driving.

Some ignorance is not of this kind. In some cases a person cannot be reasonably expected to foresee the unfortunate consequences of her actions. If I give someone a holiday as a gift and he is killed in a plane crash, then I might – and probably would – feel a sense of guilt and responsibility, but no reasonable person would hold me *blameworthy* for something I could not foresee and in which I had played no part and certainly had not wished. I could not possibly be expected to have foreseen the tragedy. This, for Aquinas, is *invincible* ignorance, an ignorance which in no sense was in my control.

Invincible ignorance has many forms. We do not hold people responsible for their actions when they are insane. Insane people, because of their illness, accept things as true that others recognise as erroneous. Of course, it is not always possible to determine precisely when people are insane, and courts sometimes have difficulty in individual cases, but Aquinas' principle seems a just one.

Other forms of invincible ignorance could be the result of being too young to know right from wrong. Even for adults, sometimes we are unable to get the necessary facts, and our actions are forgiven. Sometimes we are able to look back on an event and say honestly that we meant well – our intentions were the best – but we would have acted differently if only we had known something we could not have known at the time. In those circumstances, we feel *regret* about what happened but cannot hold ourselves to be *guilty* of a moral offence. We are sorry that we got things wrong, and we wish things had turned out differently, but we cannot say that our judgement was in any way wicked at the time. To be *guilty* is to act in a way that was clearly wrong at the time the offence was committed.

Key question

Is it ever truly possible to determine guilt?

(g) The demands of conscience

Aquinas is insistent that we have a duty always to follow conscience. He was explicit about this primacy. Even if we are objectively wrong in the decisions we make, he argues that we must still do as conscience dictates. If we happen to do what is objectively the right thing, but do it against what our conscience told us to do, we commit the sin of not following conscience.

His argument for always following conscience can be simply summarised:

1   We should always seek what is good and are naturally inclined to do so (this is *synderesis*).
2   Reason decides what is good.
3   Part of the definition of 'good' is 'rationally chosen'.
4   Therefore, what our reason (which of course can be wrong) tells us is good is the good to be pursued.
5   Therefore, if we do not follow our reason, we are seeking something which our reason tells us is not good.
6   Therefore, we must always follow our reason (otherwise called 'conscience').

This is linked to Aquinas' belief that we have free will and are agents capable of rational decisions. In the circumstances of life, we are the people who have to make decisions, and our actions are ours, to be judged in specific circumstances. God expects us to use our reason to the best of our abilities and not simply to be creatures of whim driven by irrational urges.

3 Conscience – Sigmund Freud's view

Sigmund Freud wrote at some length about the phenomena of guilt and conscience, and his views are interesting, if often controversial.

(a) Freud and Aquinas

For present purposes, it is essential to notice that in his account, Freud is trying to answer very different questions from those addressed by Aquinas. Aquinas asks what conscience is, its relation to proper decision-making and how we should use it. He assumes that it is essentially a rational function.

Freud, on the other hand, is attempting to answer a different question, looking to provide a naturalistic account of how moral responsibility and guilt feelings could occur. He is asking why we feel guilty and responsible, not, as Aquinas does, seeking a rational account of the proper use of conscience.

For Freud, conscience was essentially the process of internalising parental prohibitions and demands, so that they seem to come from within ourselves. This experience creates an aspect of our minds known as the *super-ego*.

For Freud, there are three parts of what he calls the psychic apparatus – the *id*, which is our instincts, disorganised and a bit chaotic; the *ego*, which is the organised and more realistic part of the mind; and the *super-ego*, which criticises the rest and is the moralising function. (Incidentally, the terms used here were not part of Freud's vocabulary, but were used by the translator into English. Freud could be more accurately translated as 'the It', 'the I' and the 'Over-I'. Had the translator used Freud's terms, connections with some other aspects of German thought would have been much more clear.)

(b) *Id* and *libido*

For Freud, the new-born child is all *id*, with basic drives such as those for food, aggression and sex. This part of the mind is amoral, egocentric, pleasure-seeking. A fundamental part of the *id* is the *libido*, commonly described as the sex-drive. Freud defined *libido* as the energy of those instincts which have to do with all that may be meant by the word 'love'. As physical beings, we have sexual drives.

According to Freud, the child, sexually driven, goes through the *oral stage*, based on his love of being nursed at the breast. Next comes the *anal stage*, when he delights in his own ability to control his bowels, followed by a *phallic stage*, in which he becomes fascinated by his sexual organs. These stages can, Freud believes, all be seen in the infant. There is then a period of latency, when the child largely ignores his sexual nature, only for everything to re-emerge at puberty. But, when this re-emergence happens, there is also the subconscious recollection of parental and other authoritative warnings to the infant to ignore his sexual feelings. These early childhood stages where the child develops awareness of his libido are also known as stages of **psychosexual development**.

By the time of puberty, the child has gone beyond being all *id* and *libido*.

(c) *Ego* and *super-ego*

Unlike the *id*, the *ego* is rational, capable of controlling the *id*. Freud gives the analogy of a horse and rider. The rider (*ego*) controls the way the horse (*id*) goes. Sometimes, control fails and the horse goes the way it wishes to go, over rocky terrain.

But the *ego* has to battle with the external world and the *super-ego* as well as with the *id*. When this happens, the *ego* tends to be more loyal to the *id*, avoiding conflict, excusing problems.

The *super-ego*, however, watches the *ego's* actions like a hawk, punishing it with feelings of inferiority, anxiety and general guilt. The *ego* does have defence mechanisms, such as fantasy, rationalisation, repression and others, but is in continual battle with the *id* (and *libido*).

(d) The *super-ego*

The *super-ego* develops as a result of socialisation and growth, largely through the effect of parents and authority figures on us. It is the clash between *super-ego, id* and *ego* that leads to the phenomena of conscience and guilt. The voice of the *super-ego* is what makes us feel guilty about having the basic sexual drives that are fundamental to our being.

The *super-ego* symbolically internalises the sense of a father figure and the regulations found in society. It tends to oppose the *id*, giving us a sense of the moral and sets up taboos against certain types of feelings and actions, especially the sexual. The more the Oedipus Complex (which inclines men to sleep with their mothers and kill their fathers, see below), is particularly repressed, through parents, schooling and authority figures in general, the stricter will be the rule of the *super-ego* over the *ego*, and the stronger the sense of the moral and of conscience rejecting – and making us feel guilty for – our urges.

Key term

Psychosexual development For Freud, we are innately sexual beings who go through various stages of development, which he calls oral, anal, phallic, latent and genital.

Key question

How convincing are Freud's theories of personality? How well does Freud justify them?

Key term

Oedipus Complex Freud's notion, borrowed from Greek legend, that boys for inherited reasons subconsciously wish to sleep with their mothers and kill their fathers.

(e) The Oedipus Complex

The **Oedipus Complex** is one of the most disputed aspects of Freud's very controversial theories, and is rejected by many psychologists, both for its rather shaky historical basis and for doubts about its explanatory power.

Background

The Oedipus Complex and the theory of the Primal Horde

The Oedipus Complex is named after the mythical Oedipus, King of Thebes, of whom it is prophesied that he will kill his father and sleep with his mother. His father, Laius, hearing the prophesy, abandons the infant Oedipus to die on a mountainside, but Oedipus is rescued by shepherds and brought up by King Polybus and Queen Merope. As a young man, he hears the prophecy at Delphi, so leaves the home of Polybus and Merope, because he thinks the prophecy refers to them. On his journey he meets a stranger, argues and kills him (the stranger, of course, unknown to Oedipus, is King Laius). When he arrives at Thebes, he hears the king has recently been killed, and that Thebes is at the mercy of the Sphinx (a mythical creature – part lion, part human). Oedipus is able to defeat the Sphinx, because he alone can answer the Sphinx's riddle, and the people acclaim him king. He marries Laius' widow, Jocasta, and then, a year later, discovers that Laius was the stranger and his father, and that Jocasta is therefore his mother. Jocasta, driven by guilt, kills herself by hanging and Oedipus punishes himself by putting out his own eyes with two pins from her dress.

Freud found in the legend the themes of unconsciousness – Oedipus lacked knowledge of his incest and of forbidden desires in general. Freud based his ideas on material which he drew from *The Golden Bough* by Sir James Frazer (1854–1941). In its time, this was an immensely influential work on anthropology and religion. It was first published in two volumes, in 1890; by its third edition (1906–15) it had stretched to twelve. Freud was not the only thinker influenced by the work: Wittgenstein was fascinated by it, and often discussed it.

Freud drew on the theory of the Primal Horde. Once, in primitive times, the theory says, there was the Primal Horde, a tribal group dominated by the Old Man. He was stronger and more cunning than any of the other males, and exercised total rights over the females, denying other men any opportunity to release their sexual urges. The young men were deeply angry and frustrated, but if any one challenged the Old Man, he would be beaten off. In the end, the young men realised that while no single one of them could beat the Old Man, if they got together they would be able to overwhelm him. So together, they ambushed the Old Man, killed him, ate him (they were cannibals) and started to have their way with the women, able to indulge their desires.

But, disputes broke out over the women. Men do not usually wish to share their partners. One woman might be the object of desire for more than one person. To maintain any kind of balance in things, some sort of discipline has to be imposed. Gradually, the young men started to think there was a point in some of the Old Man's rules and began to feel regret (at least a prudential regret) at his death. This leads to a sense of guilt, both in that giving in to their urges led to chaos and because of the recognition that society needs to create rules, especially to regulate sexual behaviour.

Much of Freud's thinking in this area has been subsequently discredited or ignored, but it still contains valuable insights.

Freud drew on the theory of the Primal Horde (see Background box above). From that set of events we get our taboo against incest, which according to Freud is about the proper limits of sexual relations, one of the deepest and strongest of all instincts about human behaviour. Freud believes that the men's collective guilt about their sexual instincts and behaviour is the origin of the guilt we feel. If we feel guilt, then this is not really just about ourselves but the buried memory of that primeval guilt experienced by our forefathers. It was on that basis that Freud constructed his notion of the Oedipus Complex.

Unfortunately, for the arguments of Frazer and Freud, there is not a shred of historical or other empirical evidence for this deeply moving tale, which might form the basis of a fantasy film. It is almost as if Freud has constructed these past events as an explanation which seemed to fit the data, paying insufficient attention to the possibility of other explanations. A common criticism of Freud is that his record-keeping was slapdash and that he constructed his theories with insufficient empirical evidence, based on the cases of a few of the patients (mainly middle class and frequently neurotic) encountered in his practice in Vienna. But it was on that basis that Freud constructed his notion of the Oedipus Complex.

Key question

Is the idea of the Oedipus Complex credible?

(f) Guilt, conscience, environment and God

Freud was atheist in his religious views, and this might be argued to affect his judgement about our sense of guilt. Yet there are important aspects of his theories which have abiding interest.

In his writing about primitive mankind (I use the term deliberately, as Freud's theories tend – as in the Oedipus Complex – to be male dominated), Freud is concerned to demonstrate how the senses of God and guilt are related. He notes how in primitive times nature would appear terrifying and massive in its effects. Our pre-historic ancestors were at the mercy of a nature that rose up against them, with its storms, earthquakes, droughts and floods, quicksand, bogs and avalanches. Man must have lived in a state of fear, with a deep sense of helplessness. To be helpless is to have no control and no ability to know how to control the terrors which assail us.

But there is in human nature a recognition that we are less afraid if we find an explanation for the things which terrify us. The consequence is a desire to explain. What we can understand is human actions. I can understand an earthquake if I can see it as the personal action of some God of the underworld or of the earth. And, if I can so personalise the action, then I feel more able to do something about it. If a member of my family is angry, I can do something about it, such as by some appeasement or by taking his mind off whatever caused the rage. Most people eventually calm down. I can exercise control – or at least influence – by my words and gestures. We use our voices and we give gifts. Hence, we find the origin of prayers, hymns and religious ceremonies in these attempts to appease the gods we have imagined. We try to please them by way of gifts, through sacrifices of animals, young girls or whatever we think might be sufficient appeasement. Our behaviours are reinforced when the prayers and sacrifices seem to work. Storms and earthquakes eventually stop, the rain comes and we find measures of respite. We draw the wrong conclusion through the ***post hoc, propter hoc* fallacy**. This is the logical error of thinking that because an event follows another, that the latter event was necessarily caused by the former. Because the earthquake stops when the sacrifice is complete, it does not follow that the sacrifice caused the earthquake to end. Earthquakes do end, but for other reasons.

Key term

***Post hoc, propter hoc* fallacy** Literally, 'after this, because of this'. The logical error of assuming that because one event follows another that therefore the first event caused the second.

This initial argument explains polytheism, and certainly has persuasive elements. John Hick has argued that Freud might – inadvertently – not have explained God away, but rather shown us how the experience of nature might be a way of God revealing his power and his connections with the human.

Freud explains the development of monotheism by referring to our childhood experiences. As babies, we are dependent for our thriving on our fathers who provide the means of our sustenance through their efforts and work. Because he works, he is a distant but also powerful figure, on whom all else depends, at least in our world. He is a figure of authority who sometimes visits us as we lie in our cots. When he leans over the cot to see us, his face dominates and fills our vision. Later we project the buried memory of our fathers onto our universe – hence the seeing of God as Father and Sustainer of all things (and, perhaps, God as a bearded older man). For Freud, the entire enterprise of religion was an error, with no basis in the reality of the world, something constructed out of our own needs and desires.

There is here an explicit link to the arguments of Ludwig Feuerbach, who had argued for an anthropological understanding of religion. For Feuerbach, religion is a dream of the human spirit. God, for him, is a projection of the human mind – we give our own values cosmic significance and see them in the universe as a whole. The danger of this projection is that we may be false to ourselves. While Feuerbach did not describe himself as an atheist, unlike Freud, his views would very much influence not only Freud – who acknowledged his debt – but many others who see faith as simply the consequence of wishful thinking.

Couple the sense of being answerable to our father with the Oedipus Complex and we have a clear picture of how Freud explains the consciousness of guilt, our sense of responsibility and unworthiness, and their implications for our living a more contented life. These views would seem to provide a basis for providing a naturalistic explanation for Cardinal Newman's idea that when we feel the pangs of conscience, we do so because we are actually conscious of being in the presence of God, with conscience itself as the 'aboriginal vicar of Christ'.

(i) Freud and moral responsibility and decision-making

An important question here is whether Freud's account leaves any room for the possibility of moral responsibility, as discussed by Aquinas. If our behaviours and judgements are simply the result of conflict in our subconscious and the collective unconscious, could we ever justly hold someone responsible for our action, especially if our act of judging is itself the consequence of similar dark urges? The difficulty of adequately answering this interesting and controversial question is also held by some as a criticism of Freud's theory.

(g) Criticisms of Freud's theories

The scientific basis of Freud's theories is disputed by many psychologists, scientists and philosophers. Freud himself tended to construct theories on relatively little empirical evidence, and it is not easy to see how some of these might be tested. There is no evidence for the Primal Horde, and no certainty about either the collective unconsciousness (if it is unconscious, how can we speak authoritatively about it?) or the Oedipus Complex, which seems to be devised as a theory to fit the facts. Using Ockham's Razor (see Chapter 8, page 137), we might well argue that if we could find a theory to explain guilt using fewer guesses and hypotheses, it would be more likely to be correct.

Karl Popper argued that much psychology – and he had theories such as these very much in mind – was not scientific as it involved hypotheses that were not falsifiable – that is, it was not possible to say precisely what would prove them incorrect. According to Popper, real science is always falsifiable. If we say that pure water always boils at 100 degrees Centigrade, we can see precisely what would falsify it – an instance of pure water boiling at a different temperature. But it is difficult to see what would falsify the claim that the *super-ego* acts in the way that Freud suggests. If I say I do not feel an overwhelming sense of guilt and responsibility then a Freudian might well claim that I was in denial – that I felt it really but blocked it out. Indeed, my very denial would be evidence for its reality.

A major issue, as noted earlier, was the very limited experimental basis on which Freud constructed his theory. His largely female, largely well-off, Viennese patients were self-selected and not necessarily typical of the whole of society. A middle-class family in Vienna at the turn of the twentieth century might well have nursemaids and nurseries, but not everyone has that upbringing, nor do all fathers live in that way. Different times and societies – and families – have different norms and ways of living. Some children have no contact with or knowledge of fathers, and those who do may well have a different conception of God from the way they see their fathers. Someone might have an abusive father yet seek solace in the perceived love of God.

A potent criticism is the very male-oriented ideas of the entire theory. Men might have Oedipus complexes, but that does not account for the sexual drives of women. Freud suggested they have an Elektra Complex, in which they wish to sleep with their fathers and kill their mothers, but the argument for this is thinner than that offered for the Oedipus Complex. Women seem to be passive victims, especially in the Primal Horde.

Whatever the faults of Freud, he provided a theory that explained the moral sense in a plausible way, by pointing to the notion that we get our sense of guilt and responsibility from our upbringing or authority figures. This seems significant, even if we reject some of the more fanciful elements of Freud's theory. There is no doubt that our early experiences shape our world picture, even if there is argument over precisely how this shaping takes place. Above all, Freud shook many people's belief that God is our only explanation for the conscience.

4 Aquinas and Freud's theories: a comparison

(a) The concept of guilt and the process of rational decision-making

As suggested earlier in this chapter, Freud seems to be answering questions very different from those considered by Aquinas in exploring issues of conscience, though each explores the concept of guilt, the process of moral decision-making, and the workings of the conscience (or, for Freud, *super-ego*).

Aquinas does not concern himself with addressing psychological reasons for feeling guilt and responsibility as Freud does. His account presupposes that humans are above all rational creatures, or at least, creatures capable of reason when we function well. He agrees with Aristotle that feelings are things we share with animals, and what matters is that we direct our feelings in accordance with reason. For Aquinas, when we think of conscience we are exploring a particular use of reason: for Freud, conscience is the name of a non-rational feeling. Freud is interested in the origins of feelings such as shame, guilt and desire: for Aquinas, they are not phenomena to be explained, but just facts about how we are. He is concerned with the reality of ourselves as rational creatures capable of judgements and applying them. His is essentially a project of clarifying our use of conscience in action. Though he sees our conscience as God-given, because reason is God-given, he sees it also as an essential tool to be used with prudence in our lives. Like many medieval thinkers, he is concerned with questions of blame and responsibility. After all, if, as he believes, we all face God's final judgement, then it matters that we are justly treated. By using the ideas of consent and knowledge we can have some idea of whether we are truly blameworthy and responsible for particular actions. A just judge does not condemn a child for something he did not and could not be expected to understand.

Freud equates conscience with guilt, as we can see in this key quote, where conscience and guilt seem to be used as synonyms. He goes on to argue that 'The reproaches of conscience in certain forms of obsessional neurosis are … distressing' (ibid., page 30), which again suggests that conscience is dangerous for us, as it is simply guilt. Freud goes on to discuss the cruelties that this inflicts on the human psyche.

For Freud, guilt is a psychological issue to be overcome: like God, it might be maturely rejected as an infantile fantasy. The question of blame and responsibility is not an issue for Freud: he asks only why we feel these things. For him, there is no question of final judgement. Similarly, Freud is not concerned, as Aquinas is, with the reasonableness of our thoughts about our actions, but rather about the origin of certain feelings. For this reason, it is easier to contrast Freud's account with Aquinas' than to compare them, as we are not comparing like with like.

In summary then, Aquinas does link conscience very specifically to the rational mind: it is an act of rational thought. He does not treat it as a feeling, in the way it is used in common parlance, simply meaning guilt, but for Freud it is very much a social and psychological construct, with links to both conscious and (especially) unconscious mind.

Key quote

An interpretation of the normal, conscious sense of guilt (conscience) presents no difficulties; it is based on the tension between the ego and the ego-ideal and is the expression of a condemnation of the ego by its critical agency. The feelings of inferiority so well-known in neurotics are presumably not far removed from it.

Sigmund Freud, *The Ego and the Id*, 1923, page 28

Background

Freud and Fromm

A significant critic of Freud, within the development of psychology, was Erich Fromm (1900–80). Fromm, a Hasidic Jew, was, like Freud, a refugee from Nazi Germany, living much of his later life, from 1934, in the USA and Mexico.

While respecting much of Freud's work, he dissented from his teachings, claiming that Freud was misogynistic and too limited in his approach. Fromm was very influenced by his own strong humanistic and socialist views, considering that many psychological issues arose not because of psychological repression, but because of the inherent injustices of political circumstances.

The authoritarian conscience

People are all influenced by external authorities, such as teachers and parents, but also by the legal and coercive forces of wider society. We are punished for breaking rules. We internalise these fears and rules, and call it our 'conscience'. The effect of this is that we think of 'obedience' as virtuous and disobedience as wicked.

This has serious political and social consequences. Authoritarian conscience makes us submissive to authority – which accounts for why Germans were submissive to Nazism. This submissiveness leads to a loss of autonomy, which means distrusting our reason and thinking rigidly. Authority is then idealised as infallible.

Fromm goes on to argue that this sort of conscience can lead us into evil. He thought that the Nazi authorities played on this sort of submissiveness to get ordinary Germans to despise Jews and other minorities.

Humanistic conscience

Later in his career, Fromm considered a second view of conscience, which considers what is truly human and what is inhuman, seeking what is good for human flourishing, through self-development, and rejecting what destroys it. This enables us to develop personal integrity and to oppose groups such as the Nazis.

If we are to grow, we need conscience of this type – but it needs the right environment in which to grow and develop.

Freud v. Fromm

A Freudian might argue that Fromm is looking at conscience too superficially. To say that we are all influenced by external authorities does not look deeply enough into the internal conscious and subconscious reasons for being susceptible to these environing pressures. If we are so subservient, there must be internal reasons why this is so.

Other critics have argued that Fromm was too influenced by his strong socialist views and active involvement in left-wing politics, giving not a psychological account of conscience but rather a sociological one.

Fromm provides an alternative account to Freud, though his concept of the authoritarian conscience seems to be a development of conscience-as-guilt, while his humanistic conscience presents an ideal to which, as humans, we should aspire.

5 Conclusions

See Year 1, page 170.

In studying the views of Aquinas and Freud, as well as Fletcher, we might ask whether there is a single definition that can be given to 'conscience'. The conception of each thinker is so different: for Aquinas, conscience is about rationally judging human actions, past and present; for Freud it is a synonym for 'guilt', in the sense of feeling ashamed; for Fletcher it is 'merely a word for our attempts to make decisions creatively, constructively, fittingly' (Joseph Fletcher, *Situation Ethics*, 1966, page 53).

Given the varieties of understanding, it might be possible to argue that the term means just whatever an author wants it to mean.

This might be too trite. It is clear, from our study of Aquinas and Freud, that the word may be given various meanings. We might argue that, while we use the term 'conscience' in many different ways – as

Aquinas and Freud, Fromm and Fletcher obviously do – each usage is attempting to capture something fundamentally important about human life. This may be, for Aquinas, how we rationally and morally choose our actions, for Freud about why we feel guilt and shame, for Fromm how we should relate to political and social structures, for Fletcher how we determine our actions. Each thinker picks out important facets of human experience, related to the central questions of what it means to act 'with knowledge' – conscientiously.

Study advice

It is always useful to go back to the original sources. This is very valuable here, especially for Aquinas, as his writings on conscience are some of his most accessible.

Throughout this book and its predecessor (Year 1), we have stressed the need to think about what questions thinkers have been attempting to answer. Think very carefully about whether Freud and Aquinas are answering the same questions and – if not – what were the questions to which they were responding. In relation to Freud and Aquinas, a useful exercise is to examine your own experience, to see how accurately their accounts reflect your own experience of making decisions and reflecting on your own actions. If an account does not match our introspective experience, we have good reason to question it.

As always, take time to reflect on, and not simply to learn, the ideas you have studied.

> The same test can usefully be applied to Joseph Fletcher's theories of conscience, see Year 1, pages 170–1.

Summary diagram: Conscience – Aquinas and Freud

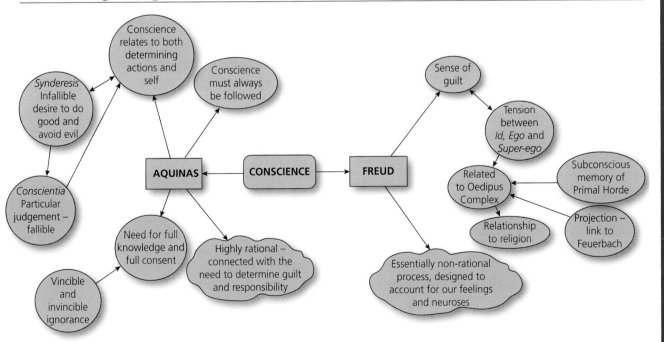

By the end of this chapter you should be able to explain the issues involved in understanding conscience. You should be able to reflect on the differences between Freud and Aquinas, always in the light of consideration of the purposes of their theories.

Can you give brief definitions of:
- *synderesis* and *conscientia*
- prudence
- vincible and invincible ignorance
- *id* and *libido*
- *ego* and *super-ego*?

Can you explain:
- how Aquinas argues that we must always follow conscience
- the relationship of prudence and conscience in Aquinas
- the Oedipus Complex and its relation to conscience
- Freud's idea of the relationship of *id, libido, ego* and *super-ego*?

Can you give arguments for and against:
- the idea that conscience is God-given
- the idea that, according to Aquinas, we are not always blameworthy for our actions
- the claim that conscience is simply the consequence of unconscious desires
- the Freudian account of guilt and conscience?

Sample question and guidance

'Aquinas' account of conscience is less convincing than that of Joseph Fletcher.' Discuss.

This question is a useful reminder that in the examination you might be asked about material drawn from any part of the course over the last two years, and a reminder to think about Fletcher's account of conscience as well as those of Freud. Fletcher has an account which treats 'conscience' as a verb, not a noun, seeing it simply in terms of its relationship to action. It is therefore useful to think about whether Aquinas' treatment is more comprehensive and truer to the ways in which we actually use the word in our ordinary language. In doing this, it might be useful to consider the

passage in which Aquinas speaks of conscience rebuking us for our actions. If you are asked to discuss the different views, as in this question, it is very important to take care to describe – accurately but briefly – what these views actually are, judging their respective merits not just in your final paragraph but as you work through the essay.

This title is a good example of a title with which the examiner might not agree, and a useful reminder that you are at liberty to use any justified and supported argument. Such an argument would not include asserting that Fletcher's ideas must be superior as more modern: you would need to demonstrate in what ways they are superior to those of Aquinas, if you wanted to make this case.

Further essay questions

'Freud's account of conscience is mistaken.' Discuss.

To what extent is Aquinas successful in arguing that we must always follow conscience?

'"Conscience" is just a fancy name for old-fashioned guilty feelings.' Discuss.

Going further

Much relevant material on Aquinas is to be found in the *Summa Theologica*, notably II-I, Q. 57, a.4 & 5, II-I, Q96, a4, and II-II, Qq 47-51. The last of these deals with the question of prudence.

Freud's more speculative theories may be found in *Totem and Taboo* (Routledge, 2001).

In Paul Strohm, *Conscience: A Very Short Introduction*, (Oxford University Press, 2011), chapters 1 and 3 have some useful material, without digging very deeply: its value is as an overview, but much of the discussion is around the historical development of the idea and its political significance.

A useful collection of Freud's works, including *The Ego and the Id* may be found in a very cheap edition: Sigmund Freud, *Collected Works* (PacificStudio, 2010), while *The Ego and the Id* may be accessed free of charge at www.sigmundfreud.net/the-ego-and-the-id-pdf-ebook.jsp. Eli Sagan, *Freud, Women and Morality* (Basic Books, 1988) touches on many points raised here.

Erich Fromm's 1947 book, *Man for Himself: An Enquiry into the Psychology of Ethics* (Routledge, 1947) has useful material if you wish to look at his thought – though no examination questions will be asked on this – but needs to be supplemented by *The Sane Society* (Routledge, 1955), arguably his most systematic and important book.

Other books discussed in this chapter are:

- Aristotle *Nichomachean Ethics*.
- Fletcher, J. *Situation Ethics* (SCM, 1966).
- Frazer, J. *The Golden Bough* (third edition, 12 volumes, 1906–15).

Chapter 10

Sexual ethics

Chapter checklist

The chapter begins by outlining traditional and contemporary Christian teaching on marriage, premarital and extramarital sex. It then considers traditional and contemporary Christian teaching on homosexuality and the ongoing debate between conservative and liberal Christians about gay and lesbian relationships. The chapter then focuses on the impact of non-religious secular views of sexual ethics, especially the impact of Mill's liberty principle. The chapter concludes by reviewing sexual relationships from four normative ethical standpoints: natural law, situation ethics, Kantian ethics and utilitarianism.

1 Introduction

Should the young woman carry out patriotic prostitution by sleeping with the enemy in order to blackmail him?

Joseph Fletcher, the moral philosopher, describes the time in the Second World War when he met and discussed with a young American woman a moral dilemma she was facing: whether she should sleep with a foreign married agent so he could be blackmailed.

Her problem? "O.K. This is it. One of our intelligence agencies wants me to be a kind of counterespionage agent, to lure an enemy spy into blackmail by using my sex." To test her Christian sophistication, I asked if she believed Paul's teaching about how our sex faculties are to be used, as in First Corinthians. Quickly she said, "Yes, if you mean that bit in the sixth chapter – your body is the temple of the Holy Spirit. But," she added, "the trouble is that Paul also says, 'The powers that be are ordained of God.'"

The defense agency wanted her to take a secretary's job in a western European city, and under that cover 'involve' a married man who was working for a rival power. Married men are as vulnerable to blackmail as homosexuals. They did not put strong pressure on her. When she protested that she couldn't put her personal integrity on the block, as sex for hire, they would only say: "We understand. It's like your brother risking his life or limb in Korea. We are sure this job can't be done any other way. It's bad if we have to turn to somebody less competent and discreet than you are."

So. We discussed it as a question of patriotic prostitution and personal integrity. In this case, how was she to balance loyalty and gratitude as an American citizen over against her ideal of sexual integrity?

Joseph Fletcher, *Situation Ethics*, 1966, pages 163–4

Fletcher's case study illustrates the power and contradictions of human sexuality. On the one hand, preserving her sexual purity is essential to the young woman's sense of personal integrity, but on the other hand, using her body sexually just as a means to an end is fine because sex in this case is just a physical act and the ends justify the means.

The case Fletcher describes also indicates the enormous power sex has in human relationships: it can be used to exploit; it can be an expression of love; it defines a person's identity; it is the foundation of family and social life.

2 Christian teaching on premarital and extramarital sex

Key question

What are the religious reasons for marriage?

Traditional Christian teaching about sexual practices focuses on marriage. Because sex is primarily concerned with the procreation of children, and because children need to be cared for and nurtured, then marriage ensures that both parents remain with each other. Marriage is not a specifically Christian institution; it is to be found in every society from antiquity to the present day.

But, for Christians, the significance of marriage is more than this. Marriage, as the union of man and woman, also mirrors the union of God and the world. Marriage is therefore one of the most important and significant institutions of society. Marriage gives rights, responsibilities and protection to the couple.

(a) Christian teaching on marriage

See pages 180–2 on sex and natural law.

The main reasons for marriage in the West rest on natural law arguments, especially those developed by Augustine and Aquinas.

Both theologians begin with the observation that humans the world over pair off for the primary purpose of procreation: this is the primary

Goods of marriage The three goods (or purposes) of marriage are traditionally: the procreation of children; faithfulness of the couple to each other; and control of the sex drive.

Monogamous Being married or in a relationship exclusively with one person.

purpose of marriage. From this, other secondary purposes are then derived. Together, these are called the **goods of marriage**, and comprise:

- **procreation** (primary purpose or good): marriage is for the procreation of children
- **nurture** (secondary purpose or good): children need to be nurtured, so marriage is about companionship and love of the couple to each other
- **control of sex** (secondary purpose or good): as sex outside marriage would result in children being brought into non-stable relationships, then marriage is there to control the sex drive. Marriage is **monogamous**, heterosexual and life-long.

Key quote

The vocation of marriage is written in the very nature of man and woman as they came from the hand of the Creator.

Catechism of the Catholic Church, para. 1603

The natural law basis for marriage does not in itself suggest that the institution of marriage is religious. The specifically Christian dimension of marriage is that marriage is a sacrament or a covenant.

(i) Marriage as sacrament or covenant

In traditional Christian theology a **sacrament** is a holy or highly significant religious moment. A ceremony which is a sacrament has various outward and visible signs which represent inward spiritual changes brought about by God's grace. This means that marriage is more than a contract and is morally and spiritually binding. Traditional Christians vary in their understanding of the sacrament of marriage, which has implications for divorce.

The key passage in the New Testament where Jesus discusses the nature and purpose of marriage is as follows:

> Some Pharisees came, and to test him they asked, 'Is it lawful for a man to divorce his wife?' He answered them, 'What did Moses command you?' They said, 'Moses allowed a man to write a certificate of dismissal and to divorce her.' But Jesus said to them, 'Because of your hardness of heart he wrote this commandment for you. But from the beginning of creation, "God made them male and female." "For this reason a man shall leave his father and mother and be joined to his wife, and the two shall become one flesh." So they are no longer two, but one flesh. Therefore what God has joined together, let no one separate.'

Mark 10:2–12

Key term

Sacrament A holy or highly significant religious moment. A ceremony which is a sacrament has various outward and visible signs which represent inward spiritual changes brought about by God's grace.

Key term

Fidelity Faithfulness, loyalty and commitment. In sexual terms it means being sexually committed to one person.

The significance of the test by the Pharisees is that the rabbis at the time were divided over what constituted legitimate grounds for divorce (permitted according to the law given to Moses in Deuteronomy 24:1). Jesus' response establishes that:

- marriage is a transformation brought about by God as a new creation
- as 'one flesh' the couple are not two single people living together but spiritually one. This implies life-long **fidelity**, an idea that is not widespread in the Old Testament.

To the married I give this command – not I but the Lord – that the wife should not separate from her husband (but if she does separate, let her remain unmarried or else be reconciled to her husband), and that the husband should not divorce his wife... But if the unbelieving partner separates, let it be so; in such a case the brother or sister is not bound.

St Paul: 1 Corinthians 7:10–15

But I say to you that anyone who divorces his wife, except on the ground of unchastity, causes her to commit adultery; and whoever marries a divorced woman commits adultery.

Jesus, speaking in Matthew 5:32

Indissoluble Literally means 'cannot be dissolved'. An indissoluble marriage is one that cannot be undone or 'dissolved' through divorce.

Annulment An act of law releasing both partners from their marriage duties by recognising that for technical reasons (such as lack of consent, misunderstanding of commitment) the marriage was invalid and never formally took place.

However, immediately afterwards when discussing marriage with his disciples (Mark 10:12), Jesus appears to allow for divorce but forbids remarriage. There is much debate among scholars whether Jesus completely ruled out divorce. St Paul permits divorce in a mixed marriage where a Christian has married a non-Christian (1 Corinthians 7:10–15) but not for a Christian husband and wife. Jesus does appear to have permitted divorce on the grounds of *porneia* (Matthew 5:31). The Greek word *porneia* has been translated variously as: 'adultery', 'unchastity' and 'unfaithfulness'. It is not clear whether Jesus permitted divorce purely on sexual infidelity (such as adultery) or relationship break-down (unfaithfulness). It is ambiguous whether he permitted remarriage after divorce.

The New Testament teachings on marriage are interpreted in two ways by different Christian traditions: as sacrament or as covenant.

■ **Sacrament**. For Roman Catholics and some Anglicans, a sacrament is composed of two parts: the external symbols and the internal spiritual essence. The externals in marriage might include the spoken words by the couple (promises to be faithful, the intention to have children), the exchange of tokens (rings for instance) and the blessing by the priest. All these signify that an essential spiritual change has taken place and the couple have become 'one flesh' (Mark 10:8). This view of marriage is **indissoluble** and excludes divorce. Official separation is possible based on Jesus' adultery clause and Paul's teaching. Only **annulment** can end a marriage if it can be shown that for technical reasons (such as lack of consent, misunderstanding of commitment) the marriage was invalid and never formally took place.

■ **Covenant**. For many Protestant Christians, sacrament signifies the establishment of a binding two-way promise or covenant. For Protestant Christians, no essential change takes place but there is a spiritual change in the relationship. This suggests that marriage is intended to be a union of minds and bodies in the creation of a loving and stable environment in which children may flourish. In a covenantal marriage divorce is a possibility when a relationship has broken down but there is considerable disagreement as to whether remarriage is permitted.

(ii) Companionate marriage

Historically, marriage has served many purposes, from the exchange of property between families to the establishment of treatises between nations to producing an heir to carry on the family line. For many women getting married was the primary aim in order to secure a home and income. But over the past two hundred years, with women's independence, contraception and shifting attitudes to relationships, the emphasis on marriage is now more on companionship, friendship and love. Companionate marriage fulfils the Christian teaching on love and friendship. Indeed, marriage depends on these qualities for its success.

Even though women's roles have shifted, ideas of marriage for companionship and friendship has long been a characteristic of Christian marriage. For example, the great Anglican **Jeremy Taylor** argued that, 'Christian charity is friendship', and friendship is generous, sacrificial and equal. Unusually for his time, Taylor presents marriage as the 'queen of

Read pages 229–33 on changing views of sexuality, gender and gender roles.

friendships' because it is the expression of the whole human – physically, emotionally, spiritually and morally. All friendships are in a sense 'marriages', however imperfect they might be, because Christianity is a 'religion of friendship'.

Contemporary Christian companionate marriage has to take into account secular shifting gender roles, attitude to divorce and sexual practices.

Key person

Jeremy Taylor (1613–67): Anglican theologian best remembered for his influential *Holy Living* and *Holy Dying* (1650–1). His essay 'A Discourse of the Nature and Offices of Friendship' (published 1657) combined Christian and classical thinking about friendship.

Key terms

Premarital sex Where two unmarried people have sex before marriage.

Consummation of marriage The first act of sexual intercourse between husband and wife after marriage.

(b) Premarital sex

In traditional Christian teaching **premarital sex** is forbidden, as both sacramental and covenantal ideas of marriage require an act of sexual intercourse to complete the marriage. This is referred to as the **consummation of marriage**. New Testament teaching is reasonably consistent that premarital sex or sex before marriage is considered immoral. St Paul tells the members of the church at Corinth that it is better to marry than to be consumed by sexual lust:

For it is better to marry than to be aflame with passion.

1 Corinthians 7:9

See Year 1, pages 253–6 for more about Augustine, sex and transmission of original sin.

But while Christian teaching remains firm on its teaching on premarital sex, the realities are that a combination of effective contraception and contemporary views that sexual intercourse is not associated with the transmission of original sin (as Augustine taught) have altered many Christians' view of premarital sex. Whereas in the past cohabiting was usually regarded as 'living in sin', this is not so today.

(i) Premarital sex and cohabitation

Cohabitation or 'living together' has become increasingly the norm in contemporary Western societies. Whereas in the past, marriage offered emotional and financial stability, women today have more autonomy sexually (through contraception) and financially (through equality in the workplace) and therefore the need for marriage is far less obvious. Cohabitation also reflects the more informal nature of modern living, which doesn't see the need to formalise relationships. Moreover, with the taboo on premarital sex largely removed, living together for a short period of time or for a lifetime has now become a common part of modern life. Cohabitation can broadly be divided into three categories:

- **Casual cohabitation**: The least formal cohabitation relationship is characterised by a lack of long-term commitment. It might begin with a casual sexual relationship and develop so that by living together both partners share a common sexual and social life.

Key question

Is cohabitation good for society?

- **Trial marriage cohabitation**: Many couples today regard living together before marriage to be important if not essential. They argue that before taking such a serious step as marriage both partners should be sure that they are compatible to ensure that the marriage will last. This form of cohabitation is seen as a short-term arrangement and a form of preparation for the next stage, marriage.
- **Substitute marriage and ideological cohabitation**: Increasingly, there are those who never marry but who opt for a long-term relationship without marriage. There are two main types: those who are excluded from marriage (e.g. one partner may not be allowed to divorce for religious reasons) and those who choose for ideological reasons not to marry (i.e. because they disagree with the institution of marriage).

(ii) Christian responses to cohabitation today

How are Christian Churches to judge cohabitation? The official position of all mainstream Churches is that marriage is the most stable and satisfactory basis for family and sexual life. Cohabitation is unacceptable. However, trial marriage is treated by more liberal Christians as being an acceptable part of the process of marriage. Their argument is that marriage has never been a single event, i.e. a marriage ceremony, but a moment in a number of stages, which might begin with a commitment to marry (engagement), sexual relationship, the marriage ceremony and then children. Whether it likes it or not, the Church has to take into account secular attitudes to sex otherwise it will find itself out of step with what ordinary people think. The Church can still encourage marriage as the ideal. This was the line taken controversially by the Archbishop of York, John Sentamu, when he publicly supported Prince William and Kate Middleton's cohabitation as a sensible means of testing their desire to marry (which they did in 2011).

(c) Extramarital sex

Extramarital sex has always been regarded by the Christian Church as grossly immoral. Extramarital sex includes adultery (having sex or a sexual relationship with someone who is not your husband or wife) and prostitution (having sex with a prostitute). It has carried the severest of penalties because as Anthony Harvey comments, 'the social consequences of adulterous relationships were seen to be too damaging to be tolerated' (*Strenuous Demands*, 1990, page 83).

(i) Biblical teaching on extramarital sex

According to Old Testament law, both the offending men and women could receive the death penalty for adultery:

> *If a man commits adultery with the wife of his neighbour, both the adulterer and the adulteress shall be put to death.*

Leviticus 20:10

However, the punishments for women who had extramarital affairs reflect the view of the time that women were regarded as temptresses and therefore always at fault. A man who had an extramarital affair was not punished (unless it was with a married woman or a virgin), whereas

Christ and the woman caught in adultery (John 8:1–11)

a married woman who had an extramarital affair could be immediately divorced by her husband.

Jesus did not condone adultery but he did consider punishment by death to be unwarranted. In the incident where an adulterous woman is about to be stoned, Jesus says to her accusers, 'Let anyone among you who is without sin be the first to throw a stone at her' (John 8:7). As none of them is perfect then they are unable to condemn her. However, Jesus did not overlook her behaviour and told her, 'Go your way, and from now on do not sin again' (John 8:11).

(ii) Christian responses to extramarital sex today

Churches today continue to regard adultery as a serious breach of marriage vows, but would place blame and responsibility equally on a husband who has had an affair as a wife who has done the same. Adultery continues to be a justification for divorce (or even annulment).

However, Churches are also conscious that, as in the story of the adulterous woman, forgiveness and understanding are needed to understand why a partner has failed to keep to his or her marriage promises. This is particularly critical where a person has divorced because he or she has committed adultery (perhaps because the relationship has broken down) and wishes to remarry in church. Liberal Christians argue that depending on circumstances, and with intentions to fulfil marriage promises, that they should be allowed to remarry in church (i.e. in a Christian context). Conservative Protestants take the biblical teaching on adultery very seriously and do not allow a Christian remarriage in a church. There is no 'remarriage' in the Roman Catholic Church as annulment recognises that a couple were never technically married.

Some Churches consider Jesus' apparent ban on divorce and remarriage not to be an absolute ban but a reinforcement of the seriousness of marriage. So, in a case where a divorced husband or wife whose partner has committed adultery wishes to remarry in church, the Church should show love and generosity and allow them to do so.

Key question

How should Christian churches today judge those who have had extramarital affairs?

3 Christian teaching on homosexuality

(a) Traditional Christian teaching on homosexuality

Traditional Christianity, that is conservative Protestants and the Roman Catholic Church, teach that the Bible condemns all forms of homosexual practice because it breaks the covenant relationship between God and his people.

Key quote

Where are the men who came to you tonight? Bring them out to us, that we might know them.

Genesis 19:5

- The towns of Sodom and Gomorrah were destroyed by God because of their practice of homosexual rape (Genesis 19:1–8). This story in particular has become synonymous in Christian tradition for the evil of homosexual sex.
- Leviticus 18:22 states that 'You shall not lie with a male as with a woman; it is an abomination.'
- In 1 Corinthians 6:9–11 St Paul makes a list of 'wrongdoers' who cannot enter the Kingdom of God. The list includes male prostitutes and sodomites. The two Greek words used here are *'malakoi'* and

Key quote

Their women exchanged natural intercourse for unnatural, and in the same way also men, giving up natural intercourse with women, were consumed with passion for on another.

St Paul, *Letter to the Romans* 1:26–7

Key terms

Unitive sex Sex for loving purposes.
Chastity Refraining from sex.

Key quote

That teaching, often set forth by the magisterium, is founded upon the inseparable connection, willed by God and unable to be broken by man on his own initiative, between the two meanings of the conjugal act: the unitive meaning and the procreative meaning.
Humanae Vitae, para. 12

'*arsenkoitai*', which some translations combine and translate with a single word 'homosexuals'.

■ Paul condemns homosexual and lesbian practices, which he uses to illustrate Gentile (not Jewish) depravity in Rome and the reason for God's judgement. He argues that these practices go against the natural order and against conscience (Romans 1:18–32).

In addition to the biblical teaching against homosexuality, traditional Christians also teach that as marriage is the proper place for sexual relationships and one of the primary purposes of marriage is to have children, then homosexuality by definition cannot be acceptable.

The contemporary Roman Catholic teaching on marriage is set out by Pope Paul VI (1968) in *Humanae Vitae*:

> Nonetheless the Church, calling men back to the observance of the norms of the natural law, as interpreted by their constant doctrine, teaches that each and every marriage act must remain open to the transmission of life.

Humanae Vitae, para. 11

In other words, sex is to be **unitive** but must also intend to be 'open to the transmission or life', that is, to be procreative and result in children. Any separation of the unitive and the procreative undermines the sacramental dimension of marriage and degrades the relationship of husband and wife.

It is for these reasons that the Roman Catholic Church regards homosexuality as contrary to both Scripture and natural law. Homosexual sex is regarded as an improper and misdirected use of the sexual organs given the impossibility of conception. Homosexuals are called to **chastity**, disinterested friendship and self-mastery of their sexual urges. The Church has declared that even though 'homosexual acts are intrinsically disordered' (*The Catechism of the Catholic Church* para. 2357), homosexual people must be treated with 'respect, compassion and sensitivity':

> The number of men and women who have deep-seated homosexual tendencies is not negligible. They do not choose their homosexual condition; for most of them it is a trial. They must be accepted with respect, compassion and sensitivity ...

The Catechism of the Catholic Church, para. 2358

The Church teaches that there is a vocation or place for the single life. For example, a priest, monk or nun is called to the celibate single life because they can contribute to the life of the Church and to society in special ways. Likewise, a gay or lesbian person may also 'approach Christian perfection' by developing his or her gifts as a single person.

Key quote

Homosexual persons are called to chastity. By virtues of self-mastery that teach them inner freedom, at times by the support of disinterested friendship, by prayer and sacramental grace, they can and should gradually and resolutely approach Christian perfection.
The Catechism of the Catholic Church, para. 2359

(b) Liberal Christian teaching on homosexuality

For liberal Christians two arguments shape their approach to traditional teaching on homosexuality. First, they argue that the Bible must be read in its historical context and from the perspective of what it means to be in a gay relationship and not focus solely on the physical aspects of sex. Second, they argue that Christianity from its earliest times has had a strong sense of justice, supporting the marginalised against the prejudices of society. So, it is only right and proper to value all human relationships as all people are made in the image of God and have intrinsic worth. Being gay (lesbian, bisexual or transgender) is not something which is chosen but given and should be valued.

With these arguments in mind, they interpret biblical teachings on homosexuality as follows:

- Sodom and Gomorrah are condemned because of all kinds of social wickedness, including violence against strangers and rape (both homosexual and heterosexual). Ezekiel 16:49–50 cites Sodom as a place whose abominations included failure to help the poor and needy, and in the New Testament Jesus chooses Sodom's notorious lack of hospitality as an example of the events which will be particularly judged on the Day of Judgement (Matthew 10:14–15).
- Leviticus 18 condemns all things which upset the natural order of things – a field must contain one kind of seed and a garment one kind of fibre. The law is also to make sure the Israelites don't do what their enemies the Canaanites do, such as homosexual prostitution. What is not being condemned, however, are gay *relationships*.
- In 1 Corinthians 6:9 St Paul is referring to two practices of masturbation (*malakoi*) and male prostitution (*arsenkoitai*), not gay relationships. Furthermore, to put this in context, Paul also includes this in a list of sins that contains drunkenness and robbery.
- In his letter to the Romans, Paul chooses homosexuality as a way of persuading Jews to convert to Christianity by assuring them that the 'unclean' Gentile practice of homosexuality is condemned. However, his argument then goes on to show that all Jewish cleanliness laws have been superseded by Jesus' death – including the Jewish food laws. This implies that homosexuality is also acceptable.

Liberal Christians are inspired by the presentation of Jesus the liberator, whose message was to 'let the oppressed go free' (Luke 4:18).

Jesus preached to all kinds of people and did not distinguish between them because of their sexual orientation. For liberal Christians, it is the role of the Church to be inclusive and to accept that it must also adjust itself to society as well as contribute to it. But more than that, as **Alan Wilson** (a Church of England bishop) argues, the Church should support same-sex marriage in church as an enrichment and healthy development of marriage. Wilson is, however, a minority voice among Anglican bishops in his overt call for same-sex marriage.

Key quote

Condemnation of violence, even where it appears likely that it would have included homosexual rape, can hardly be equated with a universal condemnation of homosexuality or even homosexual acts...

L. William Countryman, *Dirt, Greed and Sex*, 1989, page 31

Key quote

I know and am persuaded in the Lord Jesus that nothing is unclean in itself.

St Paul, *Letter to the Romans* 14:14

Key question

How might same-sex marriage be an enrichment of the Christian teaching on marriage?

For more about Jesus the liberator see Year 1, pages 310–13.

Gay marriage poses a challenge to the Churches.

(c) The middle way

Is there a Christian middle way between the traditional gay but chaste position and the liberal full acceptance of homosexuality and same-sex marriage? The issue presents all the Churches with a considerable moral and spiritual challenge because as the following extract from the Church of England report *Issues in Human Sexuality* (1991) illustrates, the biblical view is that heterosexual marriage is the normative place for sex:

> *There is, therefore, in Scripture an evolving convergence on the ideal life-long, monogamous, heterosexual union as the setting intended by God for the proper development of men and women as sexual beings. Sexual activity of any kind outside marriage comes to be seen as sinful, and homosexual practice as especially dishonourable.*

Issues in Human Sexuality, 2.29

On the other hand, the report goes on to say that God does not condemn homosexuality because 'God loves us all alike':

> *This leads directly to our second fundamental principle, laid upon us by the truths at the very heart of the faith; homosexual people are in every way as valuable to and as valued by God as heterosexual people. God loves us all alike, and has for each of us a range of possibilities within his design for the universe.*

Issues in Human Sexuality, 5.4

While *Issues in Human Sexuality* remains the official teaching of the Church of England, over the years the Church's bishops have become less content with its ambiguous conclusions. As set out in *Issues in Human Sexuality,* the Church of England goes beyond a mere toleration of gay and lesbian people, and yet it stops short at a commitment to knowingly ordaining someone to the priesthood who is in an openly gay or lesbian sexual relationship (although it allows a priest to be in a celibate same-sex relationship). The Church permits prayers to be said after a civil partnership ceremony but a priest is not allowed to bless a same-sex union.

However, there has been increasing pressure from lesbian and gay Christians, both lay and ordained, that *Issues in Human Sexuality* is not only unhelpfully ambiguous but contrary to a Church which ought to be welcoming, hospitable and open for all. In January 2017, the bishops acknowledged that shifting attitudes in the UK and across the globe to lesbian and gay sexuality have changed dramatically since the 1990s and especially since gay marriage was made law. The bishops' request for a review of *Issues in Human Sexuality* was out of a sense that the Church had failed to be inclusive in accordance with fundamental Christian teaching:

Our cultural context is one in which human isolation is a major scandal and an evil which neither state intervention nor commercial contracts can begin to resolve. The sustenance of viable, warm, reciprocal and loving human relationships is too often neglected. The family, and the communities to which we belong, have been left to struggle with the task of keeping us all human – and matters of sexuality cannot be separated from the family, from friendship or, ultimately, from community.

Marriage and Same Sex Relationships after the Shared Conversations: A Report from the House of Bishops (23 January 2017) para. 6

However, despite the bishops' call to review *Issues* the meeting of the Church's synod (government) in February 2017 was not supported by traditionalist clergy. The discussions continue.

4 The impact of secularism on sexual ethics

Secularism is a broad term and describes the world outside religion and the Church. Since the late eighteenth century, the close relationship of Church and society has widened due in part to diverse religious beliefs, the development of science and technology and self-conscious humanist philosophies, which deliberately distanced themselves from religious practices and teaching. One particularly significant figure in this respect is that of **John Stuart Mill**, a philosopher known for his secular utilitarian ethics and in particular his principle of liberty. His liberty principle has had considerable influence on legal, moral and religious thought.

Key person

John Stuart Mill (1806–73): a philosopher and political theorist. He was a Member of Parliament and member of the Liberal Party. As an atheist and secularist he was influenced by Jeremy Bentham and Auguste Comte and wrote several influential books including: *A System of Logic* (1843), *On Liberty* (1859) and *Utilitarianism* (1863). He was married to Harriet Taylor and was greatly influenced by her feminist principles.

(a) Mill's liberty principle

In Chapter 1 of *On Liberty*, Mill describes his liberty principle as follows:

The only freedom which deserves the name is that of pursuing our own good in our own way, so long as we do not attempt to deprive others of theirs or impede their efforts to obtain it. Each is proper guardian of his own health, whether bodily or mental and spiritual. Mankind are greater gainers by suffering each other to live as seems good to themselves than by compelling each to live as seems good to the rest.

John Stuart Mill, *On Liberty*, 1859, page 72

Liberty can be defined in two ways:

- **Negative liberty** is the least interference of the state or anyone else to restrict individual behaviour.
- **Positive liberty** is the freedom to fulfil one's potential by being actively involved in government.

Mill's position, expressed in the quotation an page 176, is largely a defence based on negative liberty. Mill supports negative liberty, especially when it comes to different sexual practices on the basis that:

- a variety of lifestyles enhances the richness and enjoyment of society
- liberty allows individuals to 'flourish and breathe' according to their own sexual wishes and rational choices
- no one can have a monopoly on morality; people should be allowed to make their own moral choices (even wrong ones)
- tolerance makes for a happier society.

There are many responses to Mill's notion of liberty, and in particular to different libertarian lifestyles, which would today include cohabitation, non-marital sexual relationships and gay and lesbian practices:

- Variety does not necessarily make for a happier society. A community working within common values and aims and sense of purpose might feel freer.
- A profusion of different sexual lifestyles may simply lead to confusion, distrust, anxiety and unhappiness.
- It does not follow that freedom of all forms of sexual expression makes society a richer and more cohesive place.
- Mill's negative liberty presumes that people are their own best judges. But even he acknowledges that this is not the case and we need 'competent judges' who have better and more expert knowledge to decide what is best for society as a whole. Some forms of sexual behaviour are deliberately subversive and should not be recognised by law.

(b) Tolerance and harm

A good example of the use of Mill's liberty principle in revising the law was Lord Wolfenden's report on homosexuality, which led to the decriminalising of homosexuality. Despite his own Christian objections to homosexuality, Lord Wolfenden adopted Mill's liberty principle as the only rational means of judging whether it was right for the state to interfere with a person's own private sexual behaviour. Not long before **The Wolfenden Report** was published, the Enigma codebreaker and Cambridge mathematician Alan Turing had been charged under the Criminal Law Amendment Act (1885) and chemically castrated for 'gross indecency', i.e. homosexual acts.

At stake here was the question of whether homosexual practices were a cause of harm to society sufficient to interfere and restrict those practices through criminal law. According to Mill's liberty principle, harming one's self is no reason for the state to intervene, but harm to others is reason to interfere with someone's autonomy:

Alan Turing was chemically castrated under the Criminal Law Amendment Act (1885) for his homosexual relationships.

The only purpose for which power can rightfully be exercised over any member of a civilised community, against his own will, is to prevent harm to others.

John Stuart Mill, *On Liberty*, page 68

The question is whether self-harm *alone* is a sufficient reason for the law to intervene. Mill states that self-harm might be a necessary condition for intervention but in most cases we should respect the autonomy of the individual; there is an exception for cases involving children or people with severe mental disabilities who may lack the ability to make a rational choice. So, there is no sufficiently good reason to interfere in adults who participate in unusual forms of consensual sexual activity such as sadomasochism, however morally questionable we might consider this to be. On the other hand, if we could show that self-harm of this kind is irrational, then and only then would we have reason to intervene even if it did no harm to others.

(i) Public and social harm

Harm might also occur because it offends other people's moral values and sense of decency. This is far more elusive and judging when this actually threatens public stability is notoriously hard to define. Some particular challenges are as follows:

- Mill argued that causing moral *offence* to others is not a sufficient reason for the law to outlaw it. However, this begs the question: if many people are offended then might not this be a necessary condition of harm? If it could be shown that homosexuality causes widespread offence, then some have argued that there is good reason for the law to make it illegal.
- Can one really claim that private consenting acts have no effects on public morality? Some argue that all our actions and attitudes affect society. So, for instance, if I enjoy watching hard-core pornographic videos at home, many argue that this will inevitably alter the way I think and treat others. This view challenges Mill's notion of private morality.

There has been a long-standing view that some same-sex relationships cause harm to public decency. For example, St Paul cites homosexuality as a reason why Roman society had degenerated morally. Similarly, in the eighteenth century the 'Societies for the Reformation of Manners' was instrumental in the raids and closure of many 'molly houses' or gay clubs because it considered such places undermined public decency.

Because of the effectiveness of contraception, premarital sex and cohabitation have largely lost their moral stigma because they are not regarded as being morally harmful. Nevertheless, there are boundaries to be drawn. Underage sex is defined by law to be under the age of 16, which is also the age of consent, and yet many teenagers have sex without fully understanding the psychological effects this might have on them.

Adultery is less clear. The key factor here is consent. Where both partners in marriage (or cohabitation relationship) consent to the other having a sexual relationship outside marriage, then this might not be considered problematic according to the liberty principle. But many would

2 Religion and ethics

178

regard all cases of adultery or extramarital sex (i.e. with a prostitute) with or without consent of a partner as harmful to the promises made in marriage (or the implicit promises made in a cohabitation relationship) and therefore something which society should consider morally unacceptable. Indeed, the law supports adultery as grounds for divorce.

(c) Law and morality

It is recognised that 4 to 5 per cent of the population consider themselves to be gay men or lesbian women. Since 1967 the Sexual Offences Act has permitted homosexual relationships in private for consenting adults over 21; in 1994 the law was amended to reduce this to 18 and reduced again to 16 in 2000. The basis for the 1967 law was the liberty principle that the state should not interfere in an individual's freedom in a private relationship, though more recent legislation has sought to ensure equality of rights regardless of sexual orientation. Many people in Britain today are supportive of the rights of gay men or lesbian women, and while there are some people who might personally dislike homosexuality, there are few who would deny that as a matter of basic human rights, a lesbian, gay or bisexual person should be able to express their sexuality. Even so, there is still dispute about whether gay relationships should have exactly the same rights and privileges as heterosexual ones, namely the right to marry and have children. Over the past decade the law on same-sex relations has undergone substantial changes.

(i) Civil partnerships

In the UK the Civil Partnerships Act (2004) became law in 2005. A civil partnership means giving legal recognition to same-sex relationships. A couple is required to register their partnership at a registry office or other approved place. The documentation enables the couple legally to adopt a common surname. Civil partnerships are ended in the same way as a divorce in marriage and, as with marriage, couples between the ages of 16 and 17 are required to give written consent from parents.

Civil partners have the same right as married couples in a range of legal matters, including:

- tax, including inheritance tax
- employment benefits
- most state and occupational pension benefits.

A civil partnership is different from marriage because in a civil marriage, registration takes place when the couple exchange spoken words whereas a civil partnership is registered when the second civil partner signs the relevant document. But in all other respects it is equivalent to marriage.

(ii) Same-sex marriage

However, for many lesbian and gay couples, civil partnership does not have the same social respect and status as marriage. As a matter of equality and fairness, the Marriage (Same Sex Couples) Act became law in 2013 and gives gay and lesbian couples in England and Wales the right to marry and have the same rights and responsibilities as a heterosexual married couple. Out of respect for religious traditions the Act permits clergy in the Church of England or Church in Wales not to carry out same-sex marriages. Same-sex couples may convert their civil partnerships to marriage.

5 Application of ethical theories

Key question

Are normative theories useful in what they might say about sexual ethics?

For a recap on natural law ethics, see Year 1, Chapter 10, pages 146–61.

For Aquinas' primary and secondary precepts, see Year 1, pages 154–55.

(a) Natural law sexual ethics

Although natural law does not need to be a religious ethic, the form it has taken in the West has largely been through Christianity and, in particular, Catholicism.

(i) Marital, premarital and extramarital relationships

As we have seen, traditional natural law, as presented by Augustine and Aquinas, argues that all humans naturally pair off.

This reflects Divine Law where humans are instructed by God to 'be fruitful and multiply, and fill the earth' (Genesis 1:28). In accordance with Aquinas' primary precepts, marriage allows the proper 'ordering' of sex for the good of society, to ensure reproduction and to provide the right environment in which to raise and educate children.

Marriage as a sacrament is ordained by God, but enshrined in Human Law throughout the world in terms of legislation and local customs. The secondary precepts in Christian terms are that marriage is lifelong, monogamous and for companionship.

Roman Catholicism today continues natural law teaching. Marriage is the basis of a healthy life and family and the building block of human relationships and a strong society. It provides the moral basis for the development of children by providing fellowship, love and grace. Roman Catholics highlight the fact that sex within marriage fulfils both a unitive and procreative function. Marriage is a sacrament. The couple administer the sacrament of marriage to each other when they consent to live together in faithful union for the rest of their lives. A new and indissoluble bond is formed.

Natural law cannot condone extramarital relationships as these undermine Divine, Natural and Human laws. For example, in the case of patriotic prostitution given in an example by Fletcher at the start of this chapter (see pages 166–7), even though the intention was good, the misuse of sex from a natural law position cannot be justified.

Premarital sex in a committed relationship might though be acceptable if the intention is to fulfil the primary precepts. In specifically Christian terms, if the couple intend to fulfil the secondary precepts but without the formality of the marriage ceremony, these might be sufficient for the Church to regard the relationship as effectively marriage. This would only be true in more liberal Christian traditions, for in traditional and official Church teaching the intention can only be expressed through the marriage vows; as cohabitation lacks the commitment of those vows, it is to be regarded as an **apparent good** and not an actual good.

Key term

Apparent good In natural law, an action which may appear to be good but through ignorance or lack of knowledge is not fully good as it doesn't enhance the purpose of being human as a whole.

(ii) Homosexual relationships

Although natural law has traditionally rejected homosexuality, there are some today who argue that this takes an unduly biological view of human relationships and they consider that natural law does support full sexual gay and lesbian relationships.

According to traditional Christian natural law homosexual sexual relations are explicitly rejected because the purpose of sex must always be procreative:

> It is evident from this that every emission of semen, in such a way that generation cannot follow, is contrary to the good of man. And if this be done deliberately, it must be a sin. Now, I am speaking of a way from which, in itself, generation could not result; such would be any emission of semen apart from the natural union of male and female...Moreover, these views which have just been given have a solid basis in divine authority. That the emission of semen under conditions in which offspring cannot follow is illicit is quite clear. There is the text of Leviticus (18:22–23) 'thou shalt not lie with mankind as with womankind...'

Thomas Aquinas, *Summa Contra Gentiles*, 3.2. 122, quoted in Robin Gill, *A Textbook of Christian Ethics*, pages 484, 466

As we have seen, *Humanae Vitae* supports Aquinas' main argument that the purpose of sex is to be procreative. It does though add that sex should also be unitive and for many natural law proponents the distinction importantly suggests that there is more than one purpose or *telos* of sex, but they don't need necessarily to operate at the same time every time.

At the heart of the homosexuality debate is the central issue of what constitutes normal sexual behaviour. Michel Foucault's analysis is that 'normal' is usually an idea established by those who have a vested interest in controlling society and especially its sexual practices.

For example, the Church for centuries controlled marriage but as this institution has developed and (some would say) become unnecessary, so gay relationships and practices have been freed from the control of institutions such as the Church. According to Foucault as there is no 'normal' sexual nature, there is no homosexual nature, there is just sexuality. For these reasons Foucault is suspicious of the very limited procreative purpose of sex used by traditional natural law proponents. His secular view poses a major challenge to natural law.

However, for some theologians, natural law can still provide an important moral basis for gay relationships once the purpose of being human is expanded to be more than merely procreation. The theologian **W. Norman Pittenger**, for example, argued that it is inhumane, unloving and un-Christian to condemn gay sex, because full sexual relations are part of the created order:

> We do not know the 'origins' of homosexuality: neither do we know those of heterosexuality. Both are present in every culture; both are found, by those who are involved, to be fulfilling and satisfying; lack of opportunity to accept one's primary inclination, and the rejection of the possibility of acting thereupon, can only be recognized as inhuman and inhumane. To deny opportunity

Key question

Is it meaningful to claim that there is normal sexual behaviour?

Read page 232 for more about Michel Foucault and his analysis of sexuality.

and to condemn acting upon it would be tantamount to asking someone to reject something basic to his or her nature and hence to live an inhuman life... I suggest that the 'controls' for homosexual expression of human sexuality are the same as those for its heterosexual expression. They are based upon the centrality and primacy of love – love which is mutuality, sharing giving-and-receiving, life together in the most radical sense of the phrase.

Norman Pittenger, *Towards a Theology of Gay Liberation*, 1977, pages 87–8

In support of Pittenger's argument, other natural law arguments to back gay and lesbian relationships include:

- The notion of a *telos* is ambiguous. Sex may equally be regarded as purposeful for recreational and loving ends. If the lack of intent to reproduce does not condemn a heterosexual relationship, it could equally be applied to a gay or lesbian one.
- Aquinas' argument is a judgement on all sexual genital acts which are conducted without the intention to reproduce. This is not a judgement on homosexual orientation or relationships as such but all – and that includes heterosexual – anal/oral sex practices and the use of artificial contraception.
- Modern scientific consensus does not regard homosexuality to be a deviant pathology. Being in a minority is not in itself contrary to any natural law any more than being left-handed or of a different race than the majority.

Contrary to the traditional natural law position, the liberal natural law arguments give many lawful or licit reasons why gay and lesbian Christian couples may marry and have children if they wish.

(b) Kantian sexual ethics

For a recap of Kantian ethics, see Year 1, Chapter 12, pages 181–4.

Kantian sexual ethics are based on Kant's fundamentally important principle of the categorical imperative. The imperative is based on the notion that all humans have a 'good will', which seeks to treat each other with respect. He called the principle of respect the 'moral law'. The tests for whether one is acting according to the moral law is whether an action can be applied consistently to all human beings and whether it treats people as people and not as objects.

(i) Marital, premarital and extramarital relationships

Kant gave many lectures on sexual ethics so these act as usual starting points for contemporary discussion on marriage, premarital and extramarital relationships, but modern Kantians often rework his arguments and arrive at different conclusions.

Marriage is based on promise keeping and duties, the two fundamentals of Kantian ethics. What is important is the nature of duties of husband and wife to each other. Kant argues that sex either out of a sense of duty or from lust fails to treat either husband or wife with the respect which moral law requires. So, sexual relations must be freely given, absolutely equal and mutually consenting and if any of these are infringed then the couple become no better than animals. Most important, as both would be treating each other as a means to an end, neither would truly respect each other as persons. Finally, marriage must be companionate and not merely for sex. If it were merely for sex then as soon as people became too old for sex they would cease to have a reason to be married. This is to misunderstand the nature of the promise on which marriage is predicated which is permanent, unconditional and life-long.

The primary Kantian criticism of all forms of cohabitation and especially casual cohabitation is lack of commitment. From a Kantian perspective, the danger is that couples are using each other as a means to an end – and as an important reason for sexual relationships is to have children, then a stable and committed environment is a necessary condition for children's welfare.

However, for Kantians today there is stronger case to be made for substitute marriage cohabitation. If the intention in this kind of relationship is faithful and committed, then it is difficult to see what additional moral benefits marriage offers. However, as this kind of cohabitation lacks the same kind of legal protection as marriage then many couples draw up **cohabitation contracts** setting out the terms and obligations of their relationship to each other. The question then is how is this so different from marriage?

Premarital sex such as prostitution, one-night stands and casual cohabitation are unsupportable because the relationship is not between equals and based on mutual respect. A relationship based on lust treats the other person as a means to an end; it demeans both people.

> *It follows from this that nobody can make themselves into an object of the other's enjoyment if it is injurious to their personality, and that strictly incumbent obligation to consummate a promise of carnal intercourse cannot be admitted.*

Immanuel Kant, *Lectures on Ethics*, page 378

Key term

Cohabitation contract (or agreement) Sets out the terms of agreement for cohabitation, for example who is responsible for childcare, who owns what and how assets will be divided if a couple separates.

Key quote

In general, a promiscuous desire with unfettered inclination to choose any object for satisfaction of its lust, cannot be allowed to either party.
Immanuel Kant, *Lectures on Ethics*, page 380

Kant argues that adultery breaks the promise on which marriage is based and indicates that 'one party thereby seeks to withdraw from the primal duty' (*Lectures on Ethics*, page 379). It is a fundamental reason for divorce.

(ii) Homosexual relationships

As Kant argues that sexual intercourse may only take place within marriage and between husband and wife it follows that homosexuality falls into the same category as adultery and premarital sex: it lacks mutual commitment. In fact, Kant is much more outspoken than this and states that homosexual sex 'demeans man below the beasts' (*Lectures*, page 381).

But why does this follow? If we consider that gay and lesbian people are rational autonomous beings capable of living by the Kantian 'moral law' then there is every reason why gay sex can be expressed in a loving, exclusive, mutually committed manner and there is no contradiction in accepting the validity of homosexual relationships.

For a recap of utilitarian ethics, see Year 1, Chapter 13, pages 193–200.

(c) Utilitarianism

Utilitarianism, more than the other ethical theories we have looked at so far, is thoroughly secular in its approach to sexual ethics. The basic utilitarian maxim is that of the greatest good for the greatest number. One of utilitarianism's great strengths is that it questions whether a law or tradition actually maximises good or happiness for society: if it doesn't then it needs to be reformed. Utilitarianism shares many of the same aims as the liberty principle (see pages 176–7 above on the liberty principle) that a good life is when a person is happy, free from pain and able to satisfy their preferences.

(i) Marital, premarital and extramarital relationships

There is no normative utilitarian view of marriage. The analysis of marriage by an act utilitarian is more likely to judge marriage in terms of the quality of relationship. Increasingly today, people don't distinguish sharply between cohabitation and marriage and the trend is for couples to live together before marriage with children and for many years. As utilitarians don't share the Christian view that marriage is a sacrament or covenant with God, then it is for the couple to decide on the quality and commitment of their relationship.

From a preference and rule utilitarian point of view, what matters is the mutual sharing of interests. For some, marriage may be preferable to cohabitation because it offers better protection of rights and duties by the state and its formality offers long-term security. But for others who have no long-term view of a relationship their interests are best served by the informality, flexibility and open-endedness of cohabitation.

Finally, there is much controversial sociological evidence as to whether cohabitation or marriage produces happier people. Some argue that in cohabitation relationships there is a higher rate of alcoholism, an increased death rate due to cancer, a higher abortion rate and a greater frequency of sexually transmitted diseases. But the evidence is inconclusive.

As there is no firm evidence, the utilitarian therefore does not give priority of cohabitation (i.e. premarital sex) over marriage.

But how does the utilitarian regard adultery or an affair outside a committed relationship? The utilitarian does not consider adultery to be intrinsically wrong, rather it is for the couple to decide. Some might have an **open marriage**, which is non-exclusive and where both agree that the other can have extramarital sexual relationships. Whereas this may work for some, many find this unsatisfactory as it can cause mistrust and jealousy.

For the rule utilitarian, the observation is that if monogamy has a tendency to bring about greater satisfaction, then there is a good reason to justify having a rule that prohibits adultery or extramarital affairs. This is the conclusion of the film *Indecent Proposal* (1993) where the husband allows his wife to sleep with a multimillionaire for one night in exchange for one million dollars. Although she says that the end justifies the means (the money pays off their debts) his jealousy jeopardises their relationship.

Key question

Does marriage generally lead to happier lives than cohabitation?

Key question

Does utilitarianism necessarily consider adultery to be wrong?

Key term

Open marriage An arrangement where both partners agree to allow extramarital relationships without being considered unfaithful.

Indecent Proposal (1993). Would you allow your partner to sleep with another person for one million pounds if the money paid off your debts?

(ii) Homosexual relationships

The key requirement for all utilitarians is that both partners consent to the relationship and avoid harm. Utilitarians argue that rejection of homosexuality is frequently based on irrational homophobic prejudice, superstition and religious tradition, none of which take seriously the happiness or interests of same-sex couples.

Moreover, as Michel Foucault has argued, satisfying preferences for different types of sexual expression does not cause society to collapse. In a liberal society, according to the liberty principle, people have the right to rule their own bodies as they wish. A society which encourages a wide range of different lifestyles is good because diversity gives individuals greater scope to express themselves according to their sexuality.

However, as in all utilitarian calculations an assessment has to be made of pain or harm caused. Some argue that if a sufficient number of people are morally outraged by the idea of homosexuality, then based on the greatest number principle it should be made illegal.

Some, as we have seen, consider that some homosexual sexual behaviour is socially harmful and others have sometimes argued that children brought up by a gay or lesbian couple are likely to suffer from prejudice or be emotionally confused. But those who reject these criticisms argue that if homosexuality is wrong because of certain sexual practices (such as anal and oral sex) then many heterosexual relationships should also be criticised for using the same acts. Finally, there is no conclusive evidence that children suffer by being brought up by same-sex parents; what matters is the quality of the relationship.

(d) Situation ethics

Many of Fletcher's situation ethical ideas are developed from a combination of Kantian and utilitarian as well as liberal Christian ideas. The four working principles (pragmatism, relativism, positivism, personalism) are designed to place the needs of people before laws and rules and to be judged by the Christian principle of love (*agape*). Very much like Mill's secular liberty principle, Fletcher's 'new morality' is designed to allow people more autonomy and give them greater **permissiveness**, that is to say permission to live freer happier lives and to question the traditions they have been brought up in. But for his critics, sexual permissiveness just means a licence to have sex without commitment.

(i) Marital, premarital and extramarital relationships

Situation ethics does not set out to undermine traditional Christian teaching on marriage, but it does question the absolute teaching of the Church. According to Fletcher, marriage is not an intrinsic good. Marriage suits some people and not others. What matters is that the couple treat each other as companions and friends (much as Jeremy Taylor taught – see page 169). Situation ethics challenges the sacredness which is sometimes given to sex. As the example at the beginning of this chapter illustrates, the young woman was giving too much irrational value to her body. Premarital sex is a means of exploring one's sexuality and providing it is not treating a person as a means to an end but is out of mutual respect, then it cannot be wrong.

For a recap of situation ethics, see Year 1, Chapter 11, pages 167–70.

Key term

Permissiveness Enjoying the freedom to behave in ways others might consider unacceptable, especially in sexual matters.

Key quote

The Christian ethic is not interested in reluctant virgins and technical chastity.
Joseph Fletcher, *Situation Ethics*, 1966, page 140

Read Joseph Fletcher, *Situation Ethics*, 1966, pages 164–5 for the account of 'sacrificial adultery'.

In another of Fletcher's examples, entitled 'sacrificial adultery' set in the Second World War, a woman who has been separated from her husband and children and held in a concentration camp in the Ukraine learns that if she becomes pregnant she could be sent back to Berlin to be with her family. She therefore sleeps with one of the guards and when found to be pregnant is sent to Berlin. A possible justification according to the four working principles might be:

- **Pragmatism**: as the end justifies the means, the benefits of being reunited with her family outweigh the adultery
- **Relativism**: the facts of the situation demand that the most loving thing to do is help her family; the Commandment 'do not commit adultery' is not an absolute and only relevant if the adultery causes harm and suffering
- **Positivism**: there is no intrinsic law against extramarital sex. As the motive is positive and loving then this situation is not deceitful and adulterous
- **Personalism**: the child who is born from the adulterous relationship is much loved and accepted as part of the family; the wife's sacrificial act was done out of love and respect for her husband and children.

Key question

How convincing is Fletcher's argument for sacrificial adultery from a Christian point of view?

(ii) Homosexual relationships

According to the principles of situation ethics developed by Joseph Fletcher and which are characteristic of the views of other liberal or radical Christians, the Bible is not to be treated as a source of commands but is indicative of the most loving and fulfilling human relationships. We also have to take into account the context in which the writers were developing their ideas. Viewed in this way, it is clear that while the Bible does condemn certain homosexual practices, homosexual relationships are not condemned because the main concern of the writers was to distance themselves from non-Jewish and later non-Christian pagan practices.

Revision advice

By the end of this chapter you should be able to explain how and why contemporary conservative and liberal Christians differ over their interpretation of traditional Christian sexual ethics. You should be able to discuss how secular views of ethics influenced by Mill's liberty principle have challenged religious teaching on ethics and altered laws on consent and same-sex relationships. You should be able to apply natural law, Kantian, utilitarian and situation ethics to all the sexual ethical issues raised in the chapter.

Can you give definitions of:
- fidelity
- monogamy
- sacrament of marriage
- companionate marriage
- adultery
- chastity?

Can you explain:
- what Christians mean when they describe marriage as a covenant
- the difference between divorce and annulment
- the problems over defining consent and harm in sexual relationships
- the liberty principle?

Can you give arguments for and against:
- cohabitation
- the view that there is no 'normal' view of human sexual behaviour
- liberal Christian teaching on homosexuality
- adultery being always morally wrong?

Summary diagram: Sexual ethics

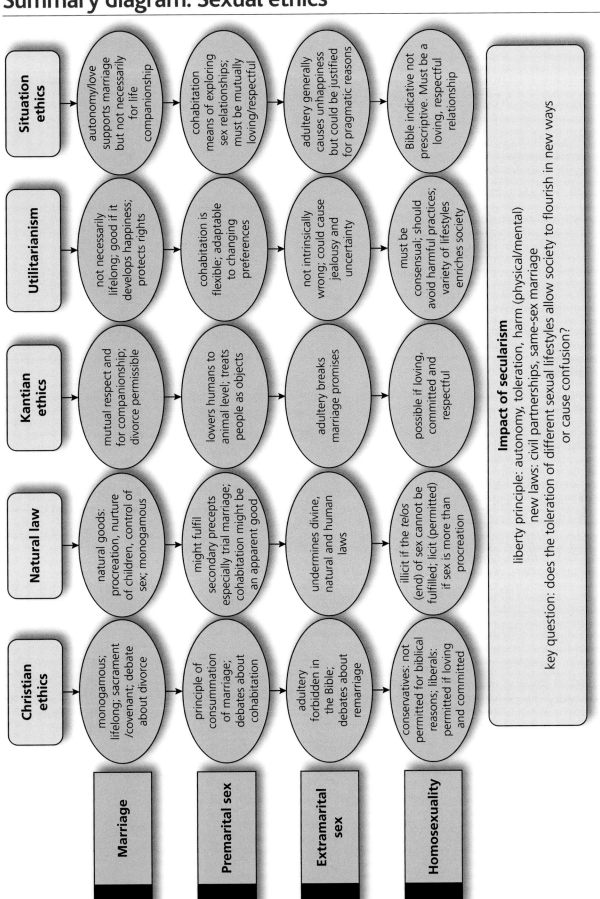

Situation ethics
- autonomy/love supports marriage but not necessarily for life companionship
- cohabitation means of exploring sex relationships; must be mutually loving/respectful
- adultery generally causes unhappiness but could be justified for pragmatic reasons
- Bible indicative not prescriptive. Must be a loving, respectful relationship

Utilitarianism
- not necessarily lifelong; good if it develops happiness; protects rights
- cohabitation is flexible; adaptable to changing preferences
- not intrinsically wrong; could cause jealousy and uncertainty
- must be consensual; should avoid harmful practices; variety of lifestyles enriches society

Kantian ethics
- mutual respect and for companionship; divorce permissible
- lowers humans to animal level; treats people as objects
- adultery breaks marriage promises
- possible if loving, committed and respectful

Natural law
- natural goods: procreation, nurture of children, control of sex; monogamous
- might fulfil secondary precepts especially trial marriage; cohabitation might be an apparent good
- undermines divine, natural and human laws
- illicit if the *telos* (end) of sex cannot be fulfilled; licit (permitted) if sex is more than procreation

Christian ethics
- monogamous; lifelong; sacrament /covenant; debate about divorce
- principle of consummation of marriage; debates about cohabitation
- adultery forbidden in the Bible; debates about remarriage
- conservatives: not permitted for biblical reasons; liberals: permitted if loving and committed

Marriage

Premarital sex

Extramarital sex

Homosexuality

Impact of secularism

liberty principle: autonomy, toleration, harm (physical/mental)

new laws: civil partnerships, same-sex marriage

key question: does the toleration of different sexual lifestyles allow society to flourish in new ways or cause confusion?

187

Sample question and guidance

'All forms of sexual behaviour should be tolerated providing no one is harmed.' Discuss.

The essay might begin by setting out Mill's liberty principle and considering the advantages and disadvantages of negative and positive liberty. The argument might then review what is meant by tolerance and what kinds of harm are permissible and which ones are bad for society and individuals.

The essay might review certain sexual practices such as marriage, cohabitation, extramarital sex and homosexuality in the light of the liberty principle. It might refer to Michel Foucault's controversial view that there is no 'normal' sexual behaviour and contrast this with traditional and conservative Christian teaching that there are standards of behaviour which are required for society to flourish morally, spiritually and physically.

Further essay questions

Assess the view that according to natural law, homosexuality is always wrong.

'Utilitarianism is of little use when considering the morality of extramarital sex.' Discuss.

Critically assess traditional religious ethical teaching about sexual ethics.

Going further

John Stuart Mill, *On Liberty and the Subjection of Women* (Penguin Classics, 2006), Chapter 1. Mill sets out his influential notion of liberty and its relationship to harm and limits of autonomy.

Pope Paul VI, *Humanae Vitae* (1968). This is the classic statement by the Roman Catholic Church, which touches on sanctity of life, marriage and human relationships. This is a prescribed text.

Duncan Dormor and Jeremy Morris (eds), *An Acceptable Sacrifice? Homosexuality and the Church* (SPCK, 2007). Covers a wide range of topics from interpretation of scripture to gay priesthood.

Issues in Human Sexuality. A Statement by the House of Bishops (Church House Publishing, 1991). This is the statement issued by the bishops of the Church of England on sexual ethics and in particular on homosexuality. It represents the official teaching of the Church of England. This is a prescribed text.

Other books, articles and websites discussed in this chapter are:

- *Catechism of the Catholic Church* (Geoffrey Chapman, 1994).
- Countryman, W. *Dirt, Greed and Sex* (SCM Press, 1989).
- Fletcher, J. *Situation Ethics* (revised edition) (Westminster John Knox Press, 1997).
- Gill, R. (ed.) *A Textbook of Christian Ethics* (T&T Clark. 1985).
- Harvey, A. *Strenuous Commands* (SCM Press, 1990).
- Pittenger, N. in *Towards a Theology of Gay Liberation*, ed. Malcolm Marcourt (SCM Press, 1977).
- *Marriage and Same Sex Relationships after the Shared Conversations. A Report from the House of Bishops* (23 January 2017) can be found at: www.churchofengland.org/media/3863472/gs-2055-marriage-and-same-sex-relationships-after-the-shared-conversations-report-from-the-house-of-bishops.pdf

3 Developments in Christian thought

Chapter 11

Religious pluralism and theology

Chapter checklist

This chapter begins by looking at plural societies today and what theological issues these raise for religious truth claims. The chapter then considers three possible responses to Christianity's relationship to the truth claims of non-Christian religions: theological exclusivism, theological inclusivism and theological pluralism.

1 Introduction

The liberal democracies of contemporary Western European society are characterised by the ideology of **liberalism**. Liberalism considers that two notions are important. First, liberalism tolerates the freedoms of the individual, providing there is no direct threat to the wellbeing of society. Second, liberalism permits the individual or individual groups to believe what each wishes – providing those beliefs don't undermine the rights of others to believe what they consider to be true. Liberalism inevitably allows and even welcomes **plural societies** because it considers that a variety of beliefs and lifestyles make for happier, culturally richer and diverse societies.

Key terms

Liberalism An ideology which develops its laws based on the principle that humans flourish when given maximum freedoms and minimum control by governments.

Plural society A society which tolerates many different beliefs and lifestyles.

2 Religious pluralism

Key term

Religious pluralism The varieties of beliefs and practices within a particular religion, as well as varieties of different religions and their beliefs and practices.

One aspect of a plural society is **religious pluralism**. Religious pluralism can refer to the varieties of beliefs and practices within a particular religion such as Anglicanism, Methodism, Presbyterianism, Orthodoxy, Roman Catholicism within Christianity, as well as varieties of different religions and their beliefs and practices such as Judaism, Islam, Buddhism, Hinduism, Sikhism and Christianity.

Religious pluralism poses two distinctive but related problems for Christian theologians:

For the idea of truth claims, see Year 1, page 96.

Key terms

Epistemology The study of knowledge.

Soteriology The study of salvation or liberation according to Christian teaching and the different ways in which humans achieve this.

Phenomenology Phenomenological existence refers to the experience of things as we encounter them and the structures of consciousness (as opposed to abstract or theoretical ideas of existence).

Key question

Why would a loving and benevolent Christian God ultimately deny any human being salvation?

On Knowledge of God's Existence, see Year 1, Chapter 18.

On Universalism, see Year 1, pages 281–2.

Key term

Theology of religions Primarily concerned with Christianity's theological, philosophical and practical relationship with non-Christian religions.

- The **epistemological** problem: to what extent may the truth claims of non-Christian religions also be considered true within Christian theology?
- The **soteriological** problem: can people of non-Christian religions or who hold no religious belief receive God's salvation?

Why do humans believe what they do? Some argue that the debate is really a cultural or **phenomenological** one. Different cultures have developed their lifestyles based on belief-systems adapted to a particular environment. It is natural to assume, therefore, that religious belief is connected in some way to society but is not in itself exclusive or unique.

Established religions don't traditionally use the phenomenological argument. Their response is that beliefs are true regardless of culture as they have special access to the truth.

To some extent, the epistemological problem has already been discussed at length in Year 1 in the chapter, Knowledge of God's Existence.

For natural theology Christian theologians, knowledge of God is not exclusive to Christianity and non-Christian religions may develop truth claims that are compatible with Christian beliefs about salvation. On the other hand, while revealed theology Christian theologians consider something may be known of God through a *sensus divinitatis*, religious experience or conscience, this is insufficient to bring us into full relationship with God (i.e. salvation); that can only be achieved fully through Jesus Christ.

The question of whether salvation is possible for non-Christians is an ancient one. One solution, as proposed by Origen and Gregory of Nyssa, was that of universalism: everyone would eventually be reconciled with God after death.

The soteriological problem, in simple terms, is this: why would a benevolent Christian God of love ultimately deny any human being salvation?

(a) Theology of religions

There are three kinds of **theology of religions**: theological exclusivism, theological inclusivism and theological pluralism. In practice these are not clearly defined and some scholars find the distinctions unhelpful and misleading. However, each position is useful as a starting point for consideration of one of the most important Christian theological questions of our times.

(b) Necessary and sufficient conditions

An important distinction in the theology of religion is the philosophical relationship between necessary and sufficient conditions. A **sufficient** condition is one where it is *enough* for something to be the case; whereas a **necessary** condition is *required* for something to be the case.

Baggini and Fosl give the following two examples of necessary and sufficient conditions:

- It is *necessary* for the prime minister to be a UK citizen but it is not *sufficient* because he also needs to be chosen by the party, win the election and have other personal credentials.

Gavin D'Costa (1958–): Professor of Christian Theology at Bristol University. He is a Roman Catholic but works also with The Church of England and Roman Catholic Committees on Other Faiths. He has written many books on the theology of religions including *Christianity and World Religions* (2009).

From a Christian perspective, is it necessary or sufficient for a person to believe in God to receive salvation?

- Giving a large sum of money and having no criminal record are *sufficient* to gain US citizenship but these are not *necessary* because there are other means of gaining citizenship.

From a Christian perspective the key question in the theology of religions debate is: what are the necessary and sufficient conditions for salvation? **Gavin D'Costa** argues that the answer to this question will depend on what he calls the 'controlling beliefs' of a specific Christian tradition or community.

From a Christian perspective, is it necessary or sufficient for a person to believe in God to receive salvation? Different Christian responses might be that:

- although belief in the one God is necessary, it is not sufficient for salvation. For it to be sufficient a person would also have to believe in Christ
- belief in Christ as God's Son alone is necessary *and* sufficient for salvation
- belief in Christ is sufficient for salvation but it is not necessary because there are many other conditions (such as the practice of loving-kindness) which may also enable salvation
- although there are many necessary conditions (such as love and respect for neighbour, overcoming egoism, openness to God), no one condition is sufficient for salvation.

The controlling beliefs which D'Costa refers to include the following:

- **Sola Christus**: the belief that God's grace is possible only through Christ.
- **Extra ecclesiam nulla salus**: the belief that salvation is not possible outside the Church as the Church is the continuing mediator of Christ's presence on earth.
- **Fides ex auditu**: the belief that true faith is only possible through hearing the Gospel as witnessed in the Bible and preached by the Church.
- **God and creation**: the belief that God alone created the world; the belief that although God is one, he is also trinity or triune (comprising Father, Son and Holy Spirit).
- **Eschatology**: the belief that God promises a future state of bliss or 'beatific vision' after death for the elect or damnation for the wicked.
- **Sin and election**: the belief that humans are fallen and incapable of knowing God fully by themselves; God calls or elects some to salvation and some to damnation.

The particular controlling beliefs will depend on which Christian tradition a person belongs to. For example, whereas Calvinism and Roman Catholicism teach all six conditions, the Catholic Church does not think that the Fall has made humans 'incapable' of knowing God. As we shall see, theologians of other Christian traditions modify and interpret controlling beliefs based on what they consider to be the necessary and sufficient conditions of Christian salvation.

3 Theological exclusivism

Key question

As a matter of logic can only one religion be true (or all untrue)?

(a) Only one religion can be true

In a famous lecture, **Bertrand Russell**, the philosopher and atheist, commented:

> *I think all the great religions of the world – Buddhism, Hinduism, Christianity, Islam, and Communism – both untrue and harmful. It is evident as a matter of logic that, since they disagree, not more than one of them can be true.*

> Bertrand Russell, *Why I Am Not A Christian* (1927)

Key person

Bertrand Russell (1872–1970): mathematician and philosopher. He delivered his lecture *Why I Am Not A Christian* on 6 March 1927 to the National Secular Society.

Whereas Christians would disagree with Russell that all religions are 'untrue and harmful', many would agree that if one religion is in fact true then the others must necessarily be untrue. This is the traditional Christian position and is the position known as **theological exclusivism**.

Theological exclusivism raises two important issues about the nature of God:

- Can God be known outside Christianity?
- Is knowledge of God the same as receiving salvation?

The answer to these questions depends on which version of exclusivism is being referred to. D'Costa distinguishes two kinds of theological exclusivism:

- **Restrictive access exclusivism** (RAE)
- **Universal access exclusivism** (UAE).

Key terms

Theological exclusivism
The view that only Christianity fully offers the means of salvation.

Restrictive access exclusivism
The view that salvation is only possible by directly hearing the Gospel (*fides ex auditu*) and accepting baptism into the Church.

Universal access exclusivism
The view that God wills the redemption of everyone (universal salvation).

(b) Restrictive access exclusivism

Restrictive access exclusivism (RAE) is often considered to be the most traditional version of the theology of religions. The controlling beliefs of this school of thought place particular emphasis on the sinfulness of human nature and therefore the uniqueness of Christ as the only means of salvation (*sola Christus*). Salvation is only possible by directly hearing the Gospel (*fides ex auditu*) and accepting baptism into the Church. RAEs support their position with reference to biblical texts such as the following:

> *Jesus said to him, 'I am the way, and the truth, and the life. No one comes to the Father except through me.'*

> John 14:6

> *There is salvation in no one else, for there is no other name under heaven given among mortals by which we must be saved.*

> Acts 4:12

> *All this is from God, who reconciled us to himself through Christ, and has given us the ministry of reconciliation; that is, in Christ God was reconciling the world to himself.*

> 2 Corinthians 5:18

For more on limited election, double predestination and the antelapsarian divine decree see Year 1, pages 279–81.

Key term

Middle knowledge The knowledge which God has of all possible events in the world as performed by free agents. It is so-called because it is midway between natural knowledge (the state before God wills to act) and free knowledge (knowledge of the way things are as God has created them).

Key question

If Christ is the 'truth' can there be any other means of salvation?

But what of those who have not heard the Gospel either before the coming of Christ or because they have lived in a non-Christian culture? Is it impossible for them to receive salvation? Superficially it would seem to be contradictory for a just and loving God to condemn those who through no fault of their own have not encountered Christianity.

The response to these questions as given by Calvinists is that as humans are inherently sinful then God is under no obligation to save anyone. However, as he is a just and loving God there are some whom he does elect because of their virtuous and devoted lives. Most other denominations have tended therefore to support the doctrine **of limited election** and **double predestination** and at the most extreme the **antelapsarian divine decree** – the belief that God selected the good for heaven and wicked for hell at the moment of the creation.

Some contemporary scholars justify the criticism that double predestination limits human freedom and the purpose of faith by appealing to the **middle knowledge** argument. The middle knowledge argument states that although God is omniscient and humans have some free will, God knows all that could happen. Thus, for example, it is possible that God knows who would truly receive the Gospel had it been preached to them – and that would include those who were born before the Gospel was revealed in Christ.

(c) Universal access exclusivism

A key difference between restrictive and universal access exclusivism is that when St Paul writes 'in Christ God was reconciling the world to himself', the RAE interprets 'the world' to mean the elect (in its limited sense) whereas the UAE considers it to mean everyone. An important supporting New Testament passage is:

> *This is right and is acceptable in the sight of God our Saviour, who desires everyone to be saved and to come to the knowledge of the truth. For there is one God; there is also one mediator between God and humankind, Christ Jesus, himself human, who gave himself a ransom for all – this was attested at the right time.*
>
> 1 Timothy 2:3–6

UAE is supported by both Roman Catholics and Protestant theologians. The problem posed for theologians is that if God does indeed will the redemption of everyone (universal salvation), how are those born before Christ or into non-Christian societies to be saved if they lack *fides ex auditu*. There are two broad answers to this:

■ **Preparation**. The following qualities might be considered good preparation for a person to receive the Gospel when it is finally preached to them: living the moral life according to conscience and natural law; practice and devotion to God through a non-Christian religion; having a *sensus divinitatis*.
■ **Life after death**. In hell, purgatory or in an intermediate state a person may encounter the Gospel and accept God's redemption in Christ.

Importantly, most UAEs distinguish between universal salvation and **universalism** (which they reject) because there can be no salvation outside the Church (*extra ecclesiam nulla salus*).

(i) The Roman Catholic Church

The official teaching of the Roman Catholic Church is that:

> *The Catholic Church rejects nothing of what is true and holy in these religions. She has a high regard for the manner of life and conduct, the precepts and teachings, which, although differing in many ways from her own teaching, nonetheless often reflect a ray of that Truth which enlightens everyone.*

Pope Paul VI, *Nostra Aetate*, 1965

So, while there is every reason to be respectful and non-judgemental of non-Christian religions as they 'often reflect a ray of that Truth', these religions lack the necessary 'controlling beliefs' as defined by the Catholic Church and cannot be means of salvation. In **Dominus Iesus** the Church makes it quite clear that the position of theological pluralism or relativism undermines the **unicity** of the Church and the 'fullness' of Christ's salvation.

Background

In line with its version of universal access exclusivism (UAE), the term unicity is used by the Catholic Church in preference to the older term 'uniqueness' as this limits God's revelation and fails to describe satisfactorily the single and total nature of Christianity for salvation while not excluding revelation in other Christian traditions and other religions. Furthermore, unicity suggests that the Church satisfies the necessary and sufficient conditions for salvation, whereas other religions may satisfy some necessary conditions but they cannot fulfil them all; in that sense non-Christian religions (and many non-Catholic Christian churches or denominations) are 'deficient'.

> *If it is true that the followers of other religions can receive divine grace, it is also certain that objectively speaking they are in a gravely deficient situation in comparison with those who, in the Church, have the fullness of the means of salvation.*

Congregation for the Doctrine of Truth, *Dominus Iesus*, 2000, para. 22

Many consider that the Catholic Church's position is not exclusive but in fact inclusive because it recognises the rays of truth in non-Christian religions. This not only indicates the ambiguity and limitations of using the 'exclusive-inclusive model' but the problems inherent in the theology of religion of wishing to respect the integrity of each religion (a characteristic of exclusivism) while not wishing to limit God by human standards (a characteristic of inclusivism).

Key term

Universalism The belief that God will restore the whole of the world to perfection; it rejects the belief that hell is eternal.

For more detail on universalism, see Year 1, pages 281–2.

Key terms

Dominus Iesus Also called *The Lord Jesus*, the Dominus Iesus is a Roman Catholic declaration made by the Congregation for the Doctrine of Faith in 2001. Its subtitle is 'On the Unicity and Salvific Universality of Jesus Christ and the Church' and it reasserts and clarifies that the Catholic Church is the one true Church of Christ.

Unicity Oneness or singleness.

For different ideas of hell read Year 1, pages 273–6.

Key question

Is Karl Barth a theological exclusivist or inclusivist?

For a summary of Barth's key ideas, see Year 1, pages 295–7, 282.

Karl Barth.

Key question

Is universal access exclusivism more respectful of non-Christian religions than restrictive access exclusivism?

(ii) Karl Barth

A good example of exclusivist/inclusivist ambiguity is to be found in Karl Barth's discussion of Christianity and other religions. Although writing in the Calvinist exclusivist tradition there are many points where he departs from the RAE position and challenges even the UAE position.

At the heart of Barth's theology is the argument that God may be known only when he reveals himself to those people whom he chooses. From this point of view Barth appears to support the RAE position; this is supported by a passage from his *Church Dogmatics* I.2 section 17 entitled: 'The Revelation of God as the Abolition of Religion' where he discusses if God's truth can be found outside Christianity. One interpretation of what Barth is arguing is that as only Christian revelation is true then the truth claims of non-Christian religions should be 'abolished' or treated as untrue. To support this view further, Barth considers that the Christian teaching on the Trinity is uniquely Christian – no other religion expresses God in this way. Barth makes it quite clear that Christianity alone has exclusive access to this knowledge:

> It is the doctrine of the Trinity which fundamentally distinguishes the Christian doctrine of God as Christian – it is it, therefore, also, that which marks off the Christian concept of revelation as Christian, in face of all other possible doctrines of God and concepts of revelation.
>
> Karl Barth, *Church Dogmatics* I.1, 1969, page 346

But other scholars offer a different interpretation of Barth as that of an UAE or even an inclusivist. First, they disagree that the German word translated 'abolition' means to destroy but to 'transform'. They argue that what Barth meant was that God's revelation transforms all religions, including Christianity, because all religions are human attempts to understand the divine and none can claim to know the truth of God. Second, they argue that Barth's teaching on the Trinity doesn't necessarily imply that only believing Christians have access to God's saving grace.

For example, God as the Holy Spirit is the means by which each human mind is opened to accept the reality of the incarnation and the teaching of the Word found in the Bible and Church tradition. But there is no restriction on whom the Spirit might operate because for Barth 'election' does not mean a select predestined few but anyone who is open to God's grace and called by him. So, as Barth considers 'church' to mean all those who live guided by the Holy Spirit then it might be better to go even further and describe Barth as an inclusivist.

This brief analysis of Barth indicates first how difficult it is to categorise the different theological positions and second, that as even traditional Christians cannot know the mind of God, no one is in a position to judge the fate of other people. This is why, as Barth encourages himself, Christians must be tolerant and understanding of all non-Christian religions.

(d) Criticism of exclusivism

One of the great strengths of theological exclusivism as far as Christians are concerned is that it gives a reason for believing in Christianity. The weaknesses of inclusivism and pluralism are that they undermine the notion of specific or unique truth claims by suggesting that these may be shared by other non-Christian religions or indeed that Christianity has no such claims. Advocates of UAE argue that exclusivism is more respectful of non-Christian religions because it accepts that they also make specific truth claims, which may be true by Christian standards or untrue, in which case they are respectfully rejected.

There are, however, some fundamental criticisms of exclusivism which include:

- RAE has been the cause of Christian imperialism, religious conflict and suffering. Christians have persecuted other Christians for not believing in their version of the truth. Christians have fought wars against unbelievers; Christianity has been used by states to convert and colonise communities.
- The RAE position presents an unjust and unloving God because of his treatment of those who, through no fault of their own, are not Christian.
- UAE lacks consistency. Vatican II, for example, appears to argue that non-Christian religions may have 'rays of truth' which are sufficient for salvation, but *Dominus Iesus* argues *extra ecclesiam nulla salus* – i.e. that without being a member of the Church the rays of truth are deficient for salvation.
- Barth's emphasis on the ultimate unknowable mystery of God leads to theological agnosticism and incoherency. It is not satisfactory to conclude that we cannot ever know what God intends (that he might save some or all or none) as this undermines all theological attempts to compose a theology of religions.
- Exclusivists wrongly judge universalism as undermining Christian controlling beliefs. Universalism's eschatological emphasis recognises God's love for all his creation and that all humans have the ability to enter the beatific vision.

4 Theological inclusivism

Just as we have seen a range of views within theological exclusivism, the same is also the case in **theological inclusivism**. The main difference is that whereas exclusivists argue for explicit knowledge of God gained through *fides ex auditu*, inclusivists argue that this knowledge may be implicit.

D'Costa distinguishes two forms of inclusivism:
- Structural inclusivism (SI)
- Restrictive inclusivism (RI).

(a) Structural inclusivism: Karl Rahner

The structural inclusivist (SI) position is that any religion whose structures develop an openness to God's grace as revealed in Jesus Christ may receive God's salvation. The most sophisticated and influential version of this form of inclusivism was developed by the German Roman Catholic Jesuit, **Karl Rahner**.

Karl Rahner (1904–84): a German Roman Catholic Jesuit who most famously and influentially argued for an inclusivist view of Christianity, which greatly influenced the Second Vatican Council (1962–65). Rahner is sometimes described as holding a 'transcendental Thomist' theological viewpoint (the theology of Aquinas interpreted in the light of philosophers such as Kant, Heidegger, Ignatius of Loyola and Maréchal). He was a prolific writer; many of his essays are collected in the 23 volumes of *Theological Investigations*.

(i) Existential openness to grace

Rahner's theology is not easy but it helps to know that he was strongly influenced by the existential philosophy of **Martin Heidegger**. From Heidegger's analysis of human experience, Rahner argues that:

- all human experience of knowledge is limited and finite
- because human knowledge is finite, humans have to accept that they can only have an unconditional 'openness' to existence
- this 'openness' suggests that all humans, whether they know it consciously or not, desire grace and salvation.

The final bold assertion is reminiscent of Calvin's claim that all humans have, to a lesser or greater extent, a *sensus divinitatis*. However, what Rahner is arguing is that deep down all humans are aware of their mortality and limitations and this prompts them to think about the nature of their existence or 'being'. When they reflect on 'being', however superficially this is done, they realise that 'being' is something which is deeply mysterious and defies definition. It is at this point, Rahner claims, that humans encounter the unfathomable experience of God's infinite grace, which is the source of 'being'.

It is this claim that at the heart of 'being' we encounter God's grace which separates Rahner from Heidegger. It is not something which Rahner can prove but he claims that many of the great religions implicitly support the truth of his claim when they encourage people to behave selflessly, lovingly and charitably to one another and when the structures of worship create an openness to 'being' (and to grace). The only religion that claims to present grace explicitly and fully is Christianity through the revelation in Jesus Christ.

It is the relationship between implicit and explicit knowledge which characterises Rahner's theology and provides him with a framework to explain the nature of salvation before and after Christ, the relationship of non-Christian religions to Christianity (and more especially the Catholic Church) and the **inculpably ignorant** – those who through no fault of their own have no knowledge of God.

Do all people, deep down, desire salvation?

Martin Heidegger (1889–1976): a German philosopher focusing primarily on phenomenology and existentialism. His most influential book *Being and Time* (1927) explores the nature of being and what it means to exist as a human being.

Inculpably ignorant Those who cannot be blamed for not having heard or understood the Gospel due to age, place, culture, time in history or poor teaching.

Key terms

Anonymous Christianity A term coined by Karl Rahner to refer to any religious institution which through its structures, practices and values is a means of grace.

Votum ecclesia The Latin phrase meaning wanting or desiring to be a member of the Church. Aquinas used the phrase to argue that those wishing to be baptised and become members but who had died before this occurred would still be members of the Church. Rahner uses it to refer to anyone who faithfully follows their non-Christian religion, who is therefore a member of the invisible Church.

Key question

Why might not all non-Christian religions be equally legitimate?

Key term

Anonymous Christian A term coined by Karl Rahner for someone who is open to God's grace but not a Christian.

Key quote

Christianity does not simply confront the member of an extra-Christian religion as a mere non-Christian, but as someone who can and must already be regarded in this or that respect as an anonymous Christian.

Karl Rahner, *Theological Investigations* Volume 5, page 131

(ii) Anonymous Christianity

By **anonymous Christianity**, Rahner means any religious institution which through its structures, practices and values is a means of grace. The model of lawful anonymous Christianity is the religion and history of ancient Israel before Christ as recorded in the Old Testament.

So, although the incarnation occurred at a particular time and place among a particular people, its significance was a universal and timeless expression of God's active place in history and creation. The incarnation doesn't so much divide history in two as mark a new development within it.

Therefore, the absolutism of Christianity has to be questioned or else the conclusion to be drawn is that God doesn't wish humans to be saved. This cannot be compatible with the experience of grace and God's love for all of creation. Rahner argues:

> Somehow all men must be capable of being members of the Church; and this capacity must not be understood merely in the sense of an abstract... possibility, but as a real and historically concrete one.

Karl Rahner, *Theological Investigations* Volume 6, page 391

Based on his argument that humans desire grace, Rahner develops Aquinas' notion of the *votum ecclesia*, that even wanting grace by faithfully following a non-Christian religion is sufficient to receive God's grace.

> For this reason a non-Christian religion can be recognised as a lawful religion (although only in different degrees) without thereby denying the error or depravity contained in it.

Karl Rahner, *Theological Investigations* Volume 5, page 121

However, not all non-Christian religions are equally legitimate. For a religion to be lawful it must be judged by the quality of salvation which it offers. A religion must be more than simply a personal experience; it also needs an organisational authority to regulate truth and falsehood.

Even so, there are some individuals who do live morally and religiously good lives outside the institution – how should they be judged? The Old Testament prophets existed outside Israel's religion and yet are regarded as the main proponents of Israel's doctrine of grace. This suggests that in addition to anonymous Christianity there are also **anonymous Christians**.

(iii) Anonymous Christians

Rahner considers two important Christian notions *a priori*. First, that all humans are ignorant to some extent according to the doctrine of Original Sin. Second, all humans are loved unconditionally by God according to the doctrine of Grace.

This is not what official Catholicism teaches. For the Catholic Church, all religions are soteriologically *invalid* unless they convert and become part of the historical and visible Catholic Church. Rahner disagrees. He cites the famous speech given by St Paul at the Areopagus in Athens, where Paul refers to the altar of 'an unknown god' he has seen in Athens as a basis for his argument that although the Greeks worship what they cannot see, Christians know this unknown God explicitly through their

The Areopagus is a prominent rock in Athens, which in classical times was used as a law court. In part of his speech on the Areopagus St Paul is recorded as saying, 'Athenians, I see how extremely religious you are in every way. For as I went through your city and looked carefully at the objects of your worship, I found among them an altar with the inscription, "To an unknown God." What therefore you worship as unknown, this I proclaim to you.' The Acts of the Apostles, 17:22–23.

Key question

Will all good people be saved?

encounter with Christ. In Rahner's interpretation of the speech, Paul doesn't condemn the Greek religion but sees it as a way for those who have yet to hear the Gospel to know God.

(iv) The invisible and visible Church

The final part of Rahner's argument in *Theological Investigations* 5 considers the Church's role in salvation. For Rahner, the Church cannot be an 'exclusive community' but has an important role to play in bringing the teachings of Christianity into the wider world. In an increasingly secular world, the role of the Church is therefore all the more significant. This may appear presumptuous to non-Christian religions and to non-religious people but a Christian has a duty to make God (who is greater than the Church) known to the world. Rahner concludes by citing St Paul's speech to the Athenians:

'What therefore you do not know and yet worship (and yet worship!) that I proclaim to you' (Acts 17:23). On such a basis one can be tolerant, humble and yet firm towards all non-Christian religions.

Karl Rahner, *Theological Investigations* Volume 5, page 134

It is the role of the visible Church to proclaim the explicit means of grace as expressed in the person of Christ.

So, will all good people be saved and, if so, why would someone wish to become a Christian? The answer is that a moral action is only good if it conforms to the example set by Christ who is the mediator of grace and judged by the visible Church. Even then, although salvation is possible it is only provisional. In order to experience the fullness of God's grace, an anonymous Christian ought to convert to Christianity and become a member of the Church.

(b) Restrictive inclusivism

Restrictive inclusivists (represented by many Catholic, Orthodox and Protestant theologians) argue that although God makes provision for individuals who have not heard the gospel but nevertheless respond positively to natural law, conscience and true elements of their religion, they do not consider that a non-Christian religion can be salvific, as Rahner does. A non-Christian religion at best may only be a good preparation for salvation.

(c) Criticism of inclusivism

The chief criticism of restrictive inclusivism (RI) is that it is really no different from universal access exclusivism (UAE). The problem is that although it uses the term inclusive it is really an exclusivist theology; it is not inclusive of non-Christian religions, only a few exceptional individuals. In this respect Rahner's structural inclusivism is a much more successful attempt to value non-Christian religions for their own sake and to respect their integrity.

However, there are many criticisms of Rahner's structural inclusivism (SI) which include the following:

Key question

How might you respond to these criticisms in Rahner's defence?

- He has made Christianity imperialist and offensive to non-Christians — especially his use of 'anonymous' to describe non-Christians.
- It might be more accurate to say that Christians are anonymous Buddhists or Jews — if so, that suggests that Christianity is not the truth as it is supposed from the traditional Christian point of view.
- He has focused too much on grace independent from Christ. This is because despite his best efforts to maintain the *sola Christus* principle, his idea that all humans have a general experience of God is more important.
- Anonymous Christianity and the invisible Church is unbiblical. The Church grew out of the Israelite religion so it is not in that sense an independent religion. It is therefore a false analogy to compare a non-Christian religion to the Israelite religion of the Old Testament.
- As the *fides ex auditu* principle is clearly not possible for anonymous Christians, then how are they able fully to confess their sins, repent and seek 'amendment of life'? As D'Costa considers this as a fundamental condition of being a Christian, then how can someone implicitly confess their sins in a way which is recognisably Christian?
- He has misused the notion of *votum ecclesia*. The phrase refers to those who consciously wish to become members of the Christian Church; it does not make sense implicitly to wish to become a member of something without knowing what it is.

Finally, are anonymous Christians better off *not* being Christians? If, for example, a devout non-Christian of a lawful religion were to listen to the gospel but reject it, would he be better off not having heard it? If so, then is the structural inclusivist position seriously flawed?

5 Theological pluralism

Key term

Theological pluralism The view that there are many ways to salvation, of which Christianity is one path.

See pages 264–5 on the impact of these events and secularism.

Key question

The offices of the satirical magazine *Charlie Hebdo* were attacked by Islamist terrorists in 2015 after it published a series of cartoons of Muhammad. Twelve members of staff were killed. Why might an event like this illustrate the need for theological pluralism?

Theological pluralism is the most recent development in the theology of religions. Its attractiveness lies in its desire to develop the secular liberal aim that successful societies are ones where people of different beliefs coexist. Since events such as the religiously motivated bombings of the World Trade Center, New York (11 September 2001), the London suicide bombings (7 July 2005) and the *Charlie Hebdo* shootings in Paris (7 January 2015), the theological and ethical desire to remove any imperialist motives from religions claiming to be superior to one other has been a major driving force for theological pluralists.

Many people identified with the victims of the Charlie Hebdo attack by holding placards that read 'Je Suis Charlie'.

Although there are several versions of theological pluralism, they all hold the view that there are many ways to salvation (or liberation), of which Christianity is one path. D'Costa distinguishes three forms or versions of theological pluralism:

- unitary theological pluralism (UTP)
- pluriform theological pluralism (PTP)
- ethical theological pluralism (ETP).

(a) Unitary theological pluralism: John Hick

John Hick (1922–2012): formerly, the H.G. Wood Professor of Theology at Birmingham University (1967–1982), then professor at Princeton Theological Seminary and later at Claremont Graduate University, USA. In his early days, he was an evangelical Christian and an ordained minister in the Presbyterian Church, but by the 1970s his experience of multi-faith Birmingham and his philosophical views of God prompted him to take a more liberal and pluralist interpretation of Christianity. He was editor of and contributor to the controversial *Myth of God Incarnate* (1976) and throughout his life developed his pluralist theology through many books, most notably *God and the Universe of Faiths* (1973). Later he was appointed vice-president of the World Congress of Faiths. Towards the end of his life he ceased to be a minister, attended Quaker meetings and practised Buddhist meditation.

Key terms

Global theology An overarching pluralist philosophical and theological framework to aid greater understanding between the great world religions.

Noumenal and phenomenal knowledge In Kant's philosophy noumenal reality is what a thing is in itself or *ding-an-Sich* (in German). Phenomenal knowledge is the world as we experience it and as it appears to us. We can only postulate a *ding-an-Sich* through reason, we cannot know it directly.

Key question

Is it reasonable to claim that all religions believe in the same underlying reality?

John Hick is a familiar name in the world of the philosophy of religion and the theology of religions. His influence in both spheres has been colossal. His motivation was to develop a **global theology**, which would give a philosophical and theological framework for greater co-operation and understanding between the great world religions.

(i) The philosophical basis

Unlike exclusivists and inclusivists, the starting point of Hick's theological pluralism is philosophical rather than the theology of a particular Christian tradition. His emphasis is on developing a **natural theology**; he places very little emphasis on traditional ideas of revelation.

- **Kant and the an-Sich**. It soon became apparent to Hick that not all religions are theistic (believe in God) or have any belief in God. Hick found a solution in Kant's epistemological distinction between **noumenal and phenomenal knowledge**. Hick uses the distinction to argue that although religions are phenomenally different, noumenally they are all referring to or postulating the same underlying *an-Sich*, or reality (which he also refers to as the Eternal One or the Real).

- **Wittgenstein, religious experience and 'seeing-the-world-as'.** Evidence of the phenomenal-noumenal relationship is demonstrated by the wide range of religious experiences people have. As a natural theologian Hick does not think that *an-Sich* reveals itself to humans

On Natural theology see Year 1, pages 288–91 and 299–300.

Is this a picture of a duck or a rabbit?

For more on Wittgenstein, Hick and religious experience see Year 1, pages 96–7; see also Chapter 6 of this book.

Key term

Reality-centred life John Hick's description of the spiritual or religious life focused on the Real (or *an-Sich*). A Reality-centred life is unselfish and concerned for the welfare of others.

Key term

Myth A word or story which expresses in symbolic terms an idea or experience that cannot easily be put into ordinary language.

but rather it is we who experience it according to the culture and times in which we live. As we would expect using Wittgenstein's analysis of language, expressing the experience of the world is naturally ambiguous. Hick refers to Wittgenstein's famous example of the duck-rabbit picture to illustrate how some might 'see-it-as a duck' while others might see it 'see-it-as a rabbit'. As the Real or *an-Sich* is subject to the same ambiguity then it must be supposed that different religions express it 'as Brahman' (Hinduism) or 'as the Trinity' (Christianity) or 'as Tao' (Taoism) and so on.

■ **Morality and the Reality-centred life**. Hick's test for all authentic religions uses Kant's categorical imperative test for moral behaviour, i.e. what I will for myself is only 'the good' if it is a duty for all – otherwise known as the golden rule. Hick argues that all authentic religions are those which uphold the categorical imperative and treat one's neighbours as one treats oneself. The great contribution all authentic religions make to human existence is that by focusing on the Real they uphold the categorical imperative by turning self-centred behaviour to Reality-centred unselfish concern for others. Even though moral laws may vary from religion to religion and even though religions have often caused terrible suffering, Hick argues that there have been enough moral 'saints' to illustrate the positive contribution religions make to the world.

(ii) The theological task

Having established the epistemological foundations of UTP, Hick's second task is to show where and how Christian theology has to adapt itself for the present age. It is important to note that as a Christian pluralist theologian Hick is not arguing for the superiority of Christianity over other religions but its distinctive contributions to the world.

■ **Theocentric not Christocentric**. The first important step in Hick's plural theology is therefore to argue that revelation emanates from God not Christ (or Scripture on the Church). Hick's suggestion is that Christianity should be theocentric (focused on God – what he calls 'Reality-centred') and not Christocentric (Christ-centred). The task of theologians is to reinterpret the doctrines of the incarnation, atonement and resurrection as myths not facts.

■ **The myth of Jesus' divinity**. The biggest hurdle of Christianity's relationship to other religions, Hick and other pluralists argue, is the belief that Jesus is uniquely the incarnate Son of God. Hick provides a number of reasons why the *sola Christus* should be abandoned. The first is that the incarnation was originally a **myth** or metaphor to explain Jesus' very special consciousness of God – so close that he could talk of God as father. But over time this myth has become falsely objectified and treated as fact that he was ontologically (by nature) God's Son. Hick illustrates how the same process happens in

For example, the Buddha was gradually transformed from the great enlightened teacher Gautama (as maintained by Theravada Buddhism) who taught the dharma to be revered, into the embodiment of the dharma as the eternal Buddha (as believed in Mahayana Buddhism):

Thus Gautama was the Dharma (Truth) made flesh, as Jesus the Word made flesh; indeed the Burmese translation of the New Testament treats Dharma as the equivalent of Logos, so that the opening sentence of St John's Gospel reads (in Burmese) 'In the beginning was the Dharma...'.

John Hick, *The Myth of God Incarnate*, 1993, page 169

■ **Jesus as a gift to the world**. For the pluralist project to work and for Christianity to adapt to the modern world then, Hick argues, it must rid itself of the ancient doctrines laid down at the great councils of Nicaea (325) and Chalcedon (451), which defined the divinity of Christ and established the idea of the Trinity. These notions have never been well understood and should be understood as myths. Once Christianity rids itself of these exclusive doctrines, then Jesus can be appropriated by other religions who see in him a man who can 'enlarge the relationship with God to which they have already come within their own tradition' (*The Myth of God Incarnate*, page 181). Jesus' social teaching and example is therefore a gift to the world just as other great religious leaders contributed to the world.

(b) Pluriform theological pluralism

The main difference between pluriform and unitary theological pluralists (UTP) is that whereas UTPs such as Hick argue that there is one underlying Real, pluriform theological pluralists (PTP) argue that there are many 'reals' as they are *experienced* by each religion. Therefore, as no one religion can have a definite knowledge of the Real (or *an-Sich*) each religion has its own particular authentic version of salvation, liberation or knowledge (whatever term is used to describe a religion's overall aim). **Keith Ward**, who supports this view, argues that sometimes we just have to conclude that beliefs between religions are different and conflicting, but reasons for them can be equally valid. Ward makes the important point that as knowledge is gained through religious experience and not revelation, then there cannot be a competition for exclusive truth; furthermore, as experience changes in any religion so does the presentation of its truth claims over time.

John Hick likens his version of pluralism to the parable of there being many lamps but one light. Keith Ward likens his version of pluralism to the Buddhist story of Indra's net which contains infinite brilliant jewels which all reflect each other in infinitely brilliant ways. What do these two analogies attempt to explain about the relationship of religions to each other?

Key question

Do all religions share a common aim to overcome a world of suffering, injustice and oppression?

Key person

Paul Knitter (1939–): a Roman Catholic theologian and was Professor of Theology at Xavier University, Cincinnati, USA and is presently Professor of World Religions and Culture at Union Theological Seminary, New York City. He has written many books on theological pluralism including *Without Buddha I Could not be a Christian* (2009).

For more on liberation theology, read Chapter 16.

(c) Ethical theological pluralism

Although Hick emphasised the moral advantages of his Reality-centred life over the imperialism of theological exclusivism, other pluralists have considered that the danger of his unitary system is that it suffers from the same kind of imperialism he was aiming to avoid. Consider, for example, how his notion of the Real is imposed on the traditional Christian core teaching about the divinity of Christ, making him an inspirational teacher but not God's Son. In responding to these issues the Catholic pluralist theologian **Paul Knitter** has developed an ethical theological pluralism (ETP) based on the view that all religions share a soteriological aim of liberating humans from suffering, injustice, intolerance and falsehood; all religions he argues are 'soteriocentric' not Reality-centred. His argument is that because each religion understands soteriology in different ways, dialogue between religions can be especially creative and fruitful.

Knitter is inspired by the method of Latin American **liberation theology**, especially its central idea that the primary purpose of a religious community is *praxis* – or action – in dealing with social injustice. Knitter argues that all religions have the same primary aim, which is for justice and concern for others. The purpose of theology is to provide the means whereby the different religions can share and discuss their differing perspectives of justice according to their belief systems. Far from diminishing the special claims of each religion, Knitter considers that dialogue will enhance and develop each religion's distinctive interpretation of reality. All that is required is that the different religions are open to new interpretations and share their common desire for a better world.

(d) Criticism of theological pluralism

The general criticism of all forms of theological pluralism is that it undermines the *sola Christus* principle. In general, Christian pluralism tries to avoid the particular beliefs about Christ and his revelation of God, and so it is questionable whether Christian pluralism is in fact Christian, at least from the 'controlling beliefs' point of view.

Other criticisms of theological pluralism include the following:

- Many consider that Hick's unitary theological pluralism (UTP) is a form of exclusivism. His form of pluralism (UTP) claims a privileged position of knowing what the Real (or *an-Sich*) is and then judges other religions by this.
- Hick builds his UTP on the foundations of Kantian epistemology and moral philosophy. But why should Kantianism be superior to the revelation or truth which religions claim independently of Kant?
- Hick's use of Kant leads to agnosticism. Kant himself argued that we cannot know the noumenal *an-Sich*, yet Hick has tended to avoid this problem and presented the *an-Sich* with a certainty that Kant never gave it.
- UTP presupposes that all religions have a sense of the Real, but many forms of Buddhism reject such a notion; other religions think their deity is the ultimate – there is no real beyond it.
- Many suspect pluralism (and especially ethical theological pluralism) promotes a form of imperialist global power-based ideology just as the Church used exclusivism to do so in the past.
- Although it is right to judge religions by their contribution to moral outcomes, this is a very restricted notion of what different world religions are claiming. This is especially so of Knitter's ethical theological pluralism (ETP), which appears to claim that religions are only interested in *praxis* and social liberation.
- By suggesting that all particular religions' claims are myths and not to be treated objectively, pluralism destroys what religious people actually believe themselves. Global theology has no specific content, according to D'Costa.

■ Both ETP and UTP undermine the traditional Christian idea of salvation. Is it sufficient for people merely to seek 'moral liberation' or simply a better understanding of reality (without the need for controlling beliefs), which is how these forms of pluralism characterise religion?

Summary diagram: Religious pluralism and theology

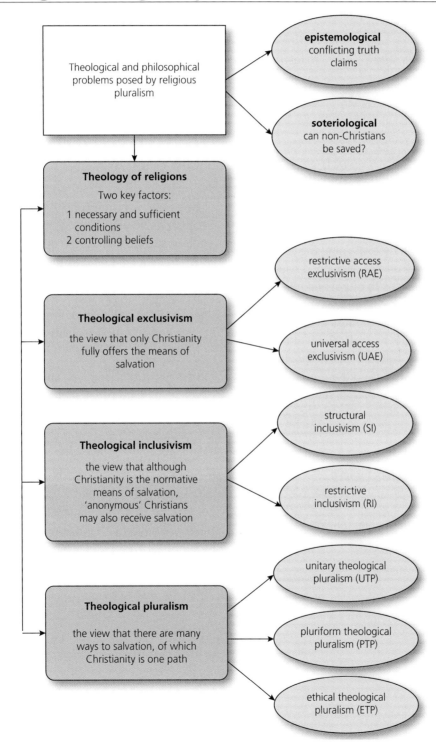

By the end of this chapter you should be able to explain why the theological and social relationship between religions is of increasing significance in plural societies. You should be able to distinguish the various theological approaches to the question of whether Christianity is the only means of salvation and the implications of each response.

Can you give brief definitions of:
- *fides ex auditu*
- middle knowledge
- unicity
- *extra ecclesiam nulla salus*
- inculpably ignorant?

Can you explain:
- restrictive access exclusivism
- universal access exclusivism
- structural inclusivism
- restrictive inclusivism
- unitary theological pluralism
- pluriform theological pluralism?

Can you give arguments for and against:
- the view that only one religion can be true
- anonymous Christianity
- the claim that all good people will be saved
- ethical theological pluralism?

Sample question and guidance

'Theological pluralism does not undermine Christian beliefs.' Discuss.

Your essay might begin by explaining the reasons why theological pluralism has developed over the past 50 years in responses to plural and multi-faith societies and an increasing awareness that different religions share many ideas in common. The essay might set out the main elements of John Hick's global theology, notably his philosophical claims gained through his use of Kant and Wittgenstein and his claim that all religions have a sense of the Real.

The essay might then analyse whether Hick's view is compatible with Christian teaching. You might set out what D'Costa has termed the 'controlling beliefs' such as belief in Christ as the means of grace, hearing the Gospel and belief in the triune God. Your analysis might then consider whether these are necessary or sufficient or both. These conclusions can then be used to evaluate Hick's theocentric not Christocentric version of Christianity.

In essays of this kind, you should always try and avoid running through all the theological positions (i.e. exclusivism, inclusivism, pluralism), as this will not stay focused on the essay question. Being selective is an important A Level skill.

Further essay questions

Critically assess the argument that the most honest view is that only one religion can actually be true.

To what extent is theological inclusivism not persuasive?

'A loving God would not save all people.' Discuss.

Going further

Gavin D'Costa, *Christianity and World Religions* (Wiley-Blackwell, 2009). Read parts I and IV for D'Costa's very clear summary of the present situation and his own thesis.

John Hick, *God and the Universe of Faiths* (reissued edition, Oneworld, 1993). This is Hick's influential and popular book setting out his pluralist theology.

John Hick and Brian Hebblethwaite, eds, *Christianity and Other Religions: Selected Readings* (Oneworld, 2001). Contains a very useful selection of primary sources including Karl Barth, Karl Rahner, Vatican II, Paul Knitter, John Hick and *Dominus Iesus*.

Alister E. McGrath, *Christian Theology* (fifth edition, Wiley-Blackwell, 2011). Chapter 17 'Christianity and the World Religions' provides a full and useful overview.

Keith Ward, *The Case for Religion* (Oneworld, 2004). Read Chapter 12 'Indra's Net' for his analysis of conflicting religious truth claims and his version of pluralism.

Other books discussed in this chapter are:

- Baggini, J. and Fosl, P. *The Philosopher's Toolkit* (second edition, Wiley-Blackwell, 2010).
- Barth, K. *Church Dogmatics* Volume 1 Part 1 (1969, second edition 2003, Bloomsbury T&T Clark).
- *Dominus Iesus* (Congregation for the Doctrine of Truth, 2000).
- Hick, J. ed. *The Myth of God Incarnate* (second edition, SCM Press, 1993).
- Knitter, P. 'Christian Theology of Liberation and Interfaith Dialogue' (*Anaradi Journal of Theological Reflection* Vol VI, 1(Jan–June 1993), reprinted in Hick and Hebblethwaite, *Christianity and Other Religions* (Oneworld, 2001).
- Pope Paul VI, *Nostra Aetate* (1965).
- Rahner, K, *Theological Investigations* Volume 5 (Crossroad Publishing Co, U.S.; new edition, 1970).

Chapter 12

Religious pluralism and society

Chapter checklist

This chapter begins by considering the factors which have led to the development of multi-faith societies such as globalisation and migration. The chapter then explores how Christian communities have responded to the challenges posed by encounters with other faiths (inter-faith dialogue). This leads on to the practical issues about inter-faith dialogue, its purpose, problems and theological justification. The final section sets out the aims and processes of scriptural reasoning and how it might aid inter-faith understanding.

1 Introduction

Southall in west London is one of the most multi-faith parts of the UK.

In Southall, west London, with a population of 70,000 over 55 per cent is Indian or Pakistani. There are ten Sikh gurdwaras, two large Hindu temples, a Buddhist vihara and three mosques, as well as ten Christian churches belonging to many different denominations including Anglican, Roman Catholic, Baptist, Methodist and Pentecostal. Not all of the United Kingdom or Europe is as diverse as Southall, but in microcosm Southall represents the shift in the way western societies have developed, especially over the past 100 years. Here is how one resident of Southall describes his experience:

This is a world unimaginable just a generation ago, a world in which the ancient stereo-types of East and West no longer apply. To walk these streets is to become vividly aware that, for all the grand talk of globalisation, the global only ever exists within the local. Underneath the romantic image conjured by exotic fruit, fragrant aromas and multi-coloured saris, the reality is more intractable. The tensions and rivalries of whole continents are forced to live cheek by jowl within single blocks.

Michael Barnes SJ, *Theology and the Dialogue of Religions*, 2002, page 4

How have contemporary multi-faith societies developed in the west and what practical challenges do these present for Christian communities in particular?

Three reasons for the development of plural, multi-faith societies are: globalisation, post-Enlightenment mindset and migration.

2 The development of contemporary multi-faith societies

(a) Globalisation

One major factor in the rise of multi-faith societies in the western world is the effect of **globalisation**. Globalisation has become a fashionable term since the 1970s to describe the way we think about the world as increasingly interconnected.

Globalisation is used in a variety of ways, both negatively and positively. Economically, it is often used to refer to the ease of cross-border transactions and de-regularisation of trade restrictions between countries. Socially, as Manfred Steger suggests, it describes the way in which human lifestyles, consciousness and fashions can influence each other from one side of the globe to the other:

Key quote

Globalisation refers to the expansion and intensification of social relations and consciousness across world-time and world-space.
Manfred B. Steger, *Globalization: A Very Short Introduction*, 2009, page 15

Key quote

Globalisation is the progressive eroding of the relevance of territorial bases for social, economic and political activities, processes and relations.
Andrew Crane and Derek Matten, *Business Ethics*, 2004, page 16

Consider, for example, how western culture, such as music, media and dress, has been exported and adopted as far afield as China and Japan.

Globalisation has been facilitated by the advancement of technology, including communications technology, for example telephone, email and the internet. It has also been facilitated through politics, for example through the liberalisation of laws which makes travel and free trade comparatively easy. Crane and Matten have therefore defined globalisation as 'deterritorisation'.

The impact of deterritorisation means that religious knowledge and belief systems are not isolated to particular cultures and geographical locations but are encountered locally and often literally next door to each other as the example of Southall illustrates.

Although many regard globalisation positively as a new and exciting phase in human development, others are much more critical. It is seen as a destructive phenomenon, which has relativised faith and moral values and undermined cultural identity. As Michael Barnes suggests, behind the romantic images conjured by multi-faith and plural societies, at a local level people have deep worries about their identity and beliefs. One of the challenges for inter-faith dialogue, as we shall see, is how to preserve distinctive religious beliefs and at the same time acknowledge the reality of a globalised world.

(b) The post-Enlightenment mindset

The second significant reason for the development of multi-faith societies is the **post-Enlightenment** emphasis on tolerance and human rights. Since the eighteenth century western societies have developed values based on human reason and experience and not on religion or revealed knowledge. Post-Enlightenment societies have established what Steven Pinker has called the 'humanitarian principle', the proposal that humans get on better when each person takes into account the interests of others.

211

Key question

Is being a member of a religion just a lifestyle choice?

For more about the humanitarian principle, see Year 1, page 260.

Key term

Migration The act or process of a person or group of persons moving from one region of a country or from one country to another.

Key quote

In the middle of such a chaos of human religiosity, the mainstream Christian churches can be forgiven for feeling overwhelmed.

Michael Barnes SJ, *Theology and the Dialogue of Religions*, 2002, page 4

This works on the assumption that we are rational beings capable of respecting the interests of others.

A key precept of the post-Enlightenment mindset is not to judge a person's particular lifestyle unless it is seen as being harmful in some way to society. Western societies therefore regard the place of religion in society as a personal lifestyle choice, as it is not for society to distinguish the truth of religions if they contribute to the welfare of society as a whole.

The tolerance of many kinds of religions, based on the humanitarian principle, has therefore led to the development of multi-faith societies. But although society may tolerate religions merely as a lifestyle, for the followers of different religions, religious adherence is not just about adopting certain customs and moral practices but living according to basic convictions about truth. Another practical challenge for multi-faith dialogue is how to balance tolerance of diverse religious practices and yet retain integrity of beliefs.

(c) Migration

The diversity of places like Southall illustrate the third factor which has led to multi-faith and plural societies: **migration**. There are a number of different reasons why a person or group of persons might move from one region in a country or from country to country.

These reasons may include economic improvement (economic migration), family reunification (i.e. to places where family members have already migrated) and (in the case of refugees or asylum seekers) safety (i.e. when refugees move to a new country or region 'owing to a well-founded fear of persecution for reasons of race, religion, nationality, membership of a particular social group or political opinions' (Convention Relating to the Status of Refugees, 1951)).

In Southall, as well as in the UK in general, many people, especially from the Indian subcontinent, migrated to Britain in the middle of the twentieth century from former colonies. During the Second World War many Jews fled Nazi Germany and settled in Britain and since then there have been refugees and asylum seekers from parts of Africa and Eastern Europe. During the earlier part of the twentieth century, Southall also experienced an influx of Welsh and Polish people seeking work. The result is not just the proliferation of non-Christian religions, notably Islam and Hinduism, into a nominally Christian Protestant country but different forms of Christian practice – such as the evangelical Pentecostal Christianity from Africa and traditional Roman Catholicism from Poland.

Aside from the political and social effects, migration poses many challenges for the existing mainstream Church denominations. For example, established Christian communities can no longer assume they are the primary provider of religious needs. Until recently religious leadership was by default Christian – and that gave the Churches certain power and status in their communities – but migrants and immigrants now look to faith leaders from their own traditions for guidance and authority. As Michael Barnes says, the situation for some established Christian communities can sometimes feel 'overwhelming'.

3 Inter-faith dialogue

The way in which Christian churches adjust to multi-faith communities not only has an important contribution to social cohesion as a whole but to their own understanding of what it means to be a Christian in the twenty-first century.

Some scholars argue that in some ways the situation echoes the position the early Christians found themselves in after the death of Christ and before Constantine adopted Christianity as the religion of the Roman Empire from 313AD. The period when the books and letters of the New Testament were written and when Christianity was emerging was a time when Christianity was a minority religion and Christians were often persecuted by Romans and Jews and fighting for identity in the religiously plural world of Asia Minor (most of modern Turkey), Rome and Greece. Without any political power the Christian communities had to negotiate with their neighbours of different faiths in their social and spiritual day-to-day existence.

(a) The 'other' and dialogue

It might be argued that without the existence of the 'other' (other religions, other political ideologies, neighbours and strangers), Christianity would not have developed its own distinctiveness and rich range of beliefs. The word 'other' has a wide range of meaning and use but it has a very useful part to play in developing the purpose of contemporary **inter-faith dialogue**.

It is important to note the relationship between the use of 'other' and 'othering'. Although the 'other' is often used negatively (i.e. people who are not like us) it may also be used positively to acknowledge that there exist multiple interpretations of the world. These different interpretations are necessary in challenging oneself to develop a deeper understanding of one's own beliefs. The post-modern philosopher **Jacques Derrida** called this open-ended view of the world *différance*. When the 'other' as *différance* is applied to those of other religious beliefs then the purpose of dialogue becomes a creative process of mutual understanding.

'Othering' represents the negative aspect of treating people as 'other'. It reduces people to objects, and limits their existence by defining and categorising them as outsiders. 'Othering' is a source of racism and sexism. One of the important aims of inter-faith dialogue is to overcome othering and to understand other cultural and religious points of view. At its most optimistic, inter-faith dialogue hopes to overcome the prejudices which are often the causes of racism, sexism, violence and war.

Key terms

Inter-faith dialogue The co-operative and creative process by which people of different religious faiths meet and exchange ideas in order to understand each other's belief system better.

Différance An idea developed by Jacques Derrida and other post-modern philosophers to describe the open-ended nature of the world. It suggests that meaning is never 'closed off'; meaning continues and develops. Meaning is not absolute but deferred.

Key person

Jacques Derrida (1930–2004): a controversial French philosopher most closely associated with post-structuralism, post-modernism and radical hermeneutics.

Key question

What is the most effective form of inter-faith dialogue?

(b) Inter-faith dialogue and theology of religions

Without a theological structure inter-faith dialogue would have very little meaning or purpose. Besides finding out what a person of a non-Christian religion believes the notion of *dialogue* as an open-ended, co-operative and creative process would be very limited. Similarly, if inter-faith dialogue were (as often happens) merely to develop mutual support of faith communities against aggressive secularism, then it would lack any critical appreciation of what makes each religion distinctive and different.

In short, for inter-faith dialogue to have a dynamic purpose it has to be fully integrated within a theology of religion. As we have seen in the previous chapter, as different theologies of religions propose different beliefs about truth, salvation, liberation and mission, then the methods and purpose of dialogue will inevitably differ.

(i) Theological exclusivism and inter-faith dialogue

What is the purpose of inter-faith dialogue for restrictive access exclusivist (RAE) Christians? Besides wishing to be better informed about a non-Christian religion, they would probably see dialogue as an opportunity to introduce others to the Gospel with the hope of conversion (*fides ex auditu*). As it is not possible to know who the elect are and who they are not, then for them it is a Christian duty to use all opportunities to bring people into direct contact with Christianity. If this objective is clearly understood by other non-Christians then dialogue is possible as it is based on honesty and integrity.

However, although universal access exclusivists (UAE) share this desire for honesty and integrity, they consider that for dialogue to be genuine there has to be respect for those we often treat as outsiders or 'others'. This means acknowledging that the truth of God's revelation is not restricted to Christianity, because as Vatican II taught, the Catholic Church accepts that non-Christian religions 'often reflect a ray of that Truth which enlightens everyone' (*Nostra Aetate*). Since Vatican II, Roman Catholicism has seen inter-faith dialogue as a means of increased respect and understanding, which is fundamental to the Church's desire to develop its **pastoral care** of all people including non-Christians.

Nevertheless, as Michael Barnes argues, inter-faith dialogue is taking a more 'risky option' for Christians as it necessarily means that those involved will have to question the teaching of the Church past and present. It requires them to have a 'vision of a Church committed to mediation and building bridges' (*Theology and the Dialogue of Religions*, 2002, page 4). Part of the risk is that in a genuine desire to find the middle ground between Christianity and non-Christian faiths and in seeking to find beliefs and values in common, Christian truth becomes relativised. One of the aims of *Dominus Iesus* was to draw a line between accepting 'rays of truth' outside the Church and maintaining the doctrine that salvation is only possible by being a member of the Roman Catholic Church as the one true Church. The tension in the Roman Catholic Church between pastoral inclusivism (i.e. treating non-Christian people with respect) and soteriological exclusivism (i.e. believing that only Christians can be saved) is not easily resolved.

Key term

Pastoral care Means of providing emotional and spiritual support and welfare.

From a Protestant point of view Karl Barth's theology of religion comes to a similar conclusion as the Roman Catholic Church but for different reasons. Whether Barth is a theological exclusivist or inclusivist his theology reminds Christians and people of other religious faith against human arrogance which claims to have any monopoly of the truth.

In inter-faith terms, Barth's theology calls for Christians to enter dialogue with deep humility and openness. That is because it is not for humans to dictate when and where God reveals himself, but God alone. Dialogue is therefore about developing one's own faith in Christ as the light of the world by also recognising that the world contains 'lesser lights' (as Barth calls them in *Church Dogmatics* IV.3) which reflect the light of Christ. These lesser lights include non-Christian religions.

Many find Barth's theology frustratingly opaque and unclear, especially when it comes to developing a coherent inter-faith theology. Although dialogue only effectively operates in a spirit of openness, humility and non-judgement the question remains whether Barth's theology avoids the charge of Christian imperialism (suggested, for example by his characterisation of non-Christian religions as 'lesser lights', which, if true, would undermine genuine dialogue).

(ii) Theological inclusivism and inter-faith dialogue

The aim of theological inclusivism in inter-faith dialogue is to address the charge of Christian imperialism and therefore to develop open and genuine discussion which is not competitive. This doesn't mean to say that those involved in dialogue may not make critical judgements from their own faith position. If this didn't happen then the integrity of one's particular religion would be reduced but it does mean being, as Karl Rahner taught, 'tolerant, humble and yet firm towards all non-Christian religions' (*Theological Investigations*, V, page 134).

The distinction between the two kinds of theological inclusivism is especially important when it comes to the practicalities of inter-faith dialogue. Whereas structural inclusivists (SI) believe that a non-Christian religion as a *whole* may be the means to salvation, restrictive inclusivists (RI) reserve salvation to *individuals* based on the quality of their personal faith. For structural inclusivists, inter-faith dialogue is aimed at developing institutional changes and understanding (i.e. of a religion as a whole), whereas for restrictive inclusivists, dialogue focuses on *individuals*.

For example, the structural inclusivist **David Ford**, who is an Anglican, scholar and inter-faith pioneer, argues inter-faith dialogue works most effectively once the theological common ground has been established between those in the dialogue, then differences can be discussed in the spirit of **collegiality**. Far from seeing differences as a hindrance, Ford argues that these are a form of blessing. They are a blessing because they force people to think hard about what they themselves believe; they create an environment of study, discussion, debate and friendship. He calls this 'an ecology of blessing', as each person comes from their own religious environment but shares the same world *of* religion (but not the same religion). The model for this ecology of blessing is to be found in the biblical story of the call of Abraham. In the story God says that he will bless those who bless Abraham and curse those who curse him (Genesis 12:1-3). As Abraham is regarded by Judaism, Christianity and Islam as the epitome of faith, all are brought together under the same covenantal blessing.

Read pages 196–7 on Barth's theology of religion.

Key question

What is the difference between being inclusive and theological inclusivism?

Key person

David Ford (1948–): Regius Professor of Divinity at Cambridge University until 2014. He is the founding Director of the Cambridge Inter-Faith Programme and one of the two founding members of the Society for Scriptural Reasoning. He has written extensively on theology, hermeneutics, the theology of religions, inter-faith and Christian education.

Key term

Collegiality The co-operative and supportive relationship achieved between those engaged in a common task.

As a structural inclusivist, Ford believes that as all three religions are united by the biblical covenant then each religion has a great deal to teach the other. Two publications illustrate how much successful work has been achieved in this area – one from Jewish scholars and leaders and the other from Islamic scholars and leaders:

- *Dabru Emet* or 'Speak the Truth' was published in 2000. Its subtitle is 'A Jewish Statement on Christians and Christianity' and it is signed by over 150 rabbis and Jewish scholars from the USA, Canada, UK and Israel. It calls for Jews 'to learn about the efforts of Christians to honour Judaism' and to 'reflect on what Judaism may now say about Christianity'. It is a bold statement, especially given the terrible ways in which Christians have treated Jews for centuries culminating in the holocaust where Christian anti-Semitism played its part. *Dabru Emet* challenges individual Christians but more especially Christianity as an institution to rethink its teachings (or doctrines), how it reads scripture, the nature and language of its worship, its education and church policies.

- *A Common Word Between Us and You* (usually referred to as *A Common Word*) was published in 2007 as a letter from 138 Muslim scholars and leaders to the leaders of Christian churches. The title is based on the Qur'an 3:64, the 'common' word being the love of God and neighbour in the quest for peace and justice. *A Common Word* has generated a great deal of inter-faith discussion, meetings and publications. One of the largest meetings was convened by Dr Rowan Williams, as Archbishop of Canterbury. Fifty church leaders and scholars from around the world met and produced a letter by way of response called *A Common Word for the Good*. The dialogue between the two letters represents how inter-faith work can operate internationally at an institutional level.

In contrast, the focus of restrictive inclusivism (RI) inter-faith work is on individual dialogue, often because it is sceptical of institutions to change and because theologically salvation is the result of personal faith and commitment and not via the Church. Inter-faith work is therefore aimed at local communities and less at the global conversations such as *Dabru Eret* and *A Common Word*.

The great strengths of inclusivist theology of inter-faith dialogue is that it balances finding the common or middle ground between religions while respecting religious differences. However, critics consider that theological inclusivism reduces the creativeness of dialogue. For dialogue to be really effective, Christians cannot presume any privileged position as all truth is open-ended.

Key question

Is the aim of inter-faith dialogue to eventually create a single world religion?

(iii) Theological pluralism and inter-faith dialogue

Pluralists make the notion of *différance* the foundation of inter-faith dialogue. Theological pluralists argue that as religious truth is multi-faceted then dialogue with the 'other' becomes a genuine quest to enlarge one's own spiritual view of the world.

Keith Ward, for example, who broadly supports pluriform theological pluralism (PTP), argues that inter-faith dialogue is a significant aid in developing what he calls a 'global faith'. A global faith is an attitude of openness by anyone of faith who wants to understand another tradition in order to deepen and develop their own. He summarises global faith as follows:

> This explains why we should tolerate and respect views other than our own. For many diverse views seem equally justifiable to their own adherents, in terms of the experiences and interpretations which form their basis. We should not condemn others for conscientiously holding the view they believe to be best justified. And we should not be too certain that we have formulated the truth as adequately as possible. It could be that diverse views flourish precisely because the way we formulate ours is so inadequate, and because it omits aspects of spiritual practice and experience which other traditions may emphasise. In this way different traditions may have much to learn from each other.

Keith Ward, *The Case for Religion*, 2004, page 230

Developing global faith through inter-faith dialogue doesn't mean always looking for the common ground (a weakness of inclusivist dialogue) but actively enjoying disagreement and difference. Disagreement resists the tendency of globalisation to treat all religions as if they are essentially the same without any distinctiveness and that they are all worshipping the same God.

On the other hand, universal theological pluralists (UTP) do think that different religions are aspects of the same underlying reality (the 'Real', as John Hick calls it). They believe that an appreciation of this provides inter-faith dialogue with the very real possibility of establishing world peace. They use inter-faith dialogue to develop and promote a 'global theology'; part of this task is to educate people that the myths of each religion are not concerned with making ultimate claims about Truth, but are instead about overcoming ego and selfishness and living a Reality-centred existence.

But for ethical theological pluralists (ETP) this goal is too abstract. While they agree with the underlying principle that inter-faith dialogue should place emphasis on the importance of living unselfishly, the way to do this and establish a fairer and more just world is by using the diverse insights of the great world religions. Paul Knitter argues that the purpose of inter-faith dialogue is not in the first instance theological, as Hick argues, but practical. According to Knitter, religions must first act to resolve common problems such as working for peace in combating extremism and **radicalisation**; only after that is done must each religion reflect and discuss theologically/philosophically how it understands and applies its teachings.

Key term

Radicalisation A process by which an individual or group comes to adopt increasingly extreme religious ideals which reject or undermine society's accepted values.

Key quote

But the reflection we are talking about here will be done not only in separate religious camps; it will be done inter-religiously, together. In such a context followers of different religious ways can understand not only themselves, but each other anew.
Paul Knitter in John Hick and Brian Hebblethwaite, *Christianity and Other Religions*, 2001, page 148

Key question

Should Christian communities seek to convert people from other faiths?

Proselytising Preaching with the intention of bringing about a religious conversion. The term 'evangelism' is also used and has the same meaning.

For theological pluralism to work effectively in inter-religious dialogue it would require all participants to support the pluralist model of religions. This is especially problematic for universal theological pluralists as it effectively means abandoning their faith as a source of truth and seeking to create a common world religion. This notion of inter-faith dialogue is firmly rejected by all Christians. Ethical and pluriform theological pluralists regard the purpose of dialogue is to celebrate difference and work towards a more harmonious and fairer world.

(iv) Problems

Many fear that if *différance* is the philosophical foundation of inter-faith dialogue then it subtly undermines the faith of each participant as it implies that everyone's beliefs are temporary and that no one may claim that what they believe is actually true.

Others consider that inter-faith can become superficial as people may be unwilling to say why another person's religion is wrong or where differences are irreconcilable.

Finally, inter-faith dialogue can either become too theological, technical and focused too much on faith leaders or teachers and therefore marginalise ordinary members of faith communities or be superficial. Superficial dialogue occurs when dialogue takes place among those without sufficient theological or philosophical knowledge to understand the complexities of their belief system.

(c) Mission and conversion

Is there any difference between having a political view and persuading others to adopt that view and having a religious view and persuading others to believe in it as well? It seems only natural that if we believe something is right or true that we should want others to believe it too. There are many secondary reasons which support why this is desirable: holding values in common binds us together and produces a more co-operative and purposeful society; having the same belief system validates values and gives them creditability; holding beliefs in common gives power and control to a group or leader.

Persuasion in Christian theological terms equates to mission and conversion. Christianity is in essence a **proselytising** religion, as is Islam. The theological motivation for Christian mission is driven by a desire to prepare people for the Kingdom of God either in this world (to establish a world of peace and justice) or in the afterlife (to pave the way for a union with God in heaven). But in the contemporary western world and in multi-faith societies overt proselytising in seeking converts to any religion is regarded as an infringement of liberal principles and as an inappropriate use of power. The underlying assumption is that if religious beliefs are essentially private then it is wrong to 'impose' your views on others.

This poses Christian churches with a dilemma. On the one hand, the New Testament calls the Church to 'make disciples of all nations' (Matthew 28:19), but on the other hand overt mission and conversion is widely considered to be aggressive and dangerous.

The Church of England's position articulates this dilemma in the following statement:

> It is precisely because of this deep seriousness that, in a divided and unequal society, conversion can be perceived to carry with it the implication of betrayal – of extinguishing old identities and loyalties in which there was much that was good. Such sensitivities mean that our language of conversion must be generous and handled with care.

Church of England, *Sharing the Gospel of Salvation*, 2010, Foreword

(i) The problem of the meaning of salvation

The problem is what exactly is meant by salvation. As we have seen, exclusivist, inclusivist and pluralist theologies offer a variety of interpretations. But the issue is essentially the same as the analogy with politics made earlier: if you hold a firmly held belief because it is 'true', then you would want others to hold it as well. Here is how the Church of England summarises its inclusivist position on mission:

> Because this ultimate salvation is found in Christ, mission remains the central task of the Christian Church... hence we naturally pray that God will bring all people, including those of other faiths, to explicit faith in Christ and membership of his Church. This is not because we believe that God revealed in Christ is unable to save them without this, but because Christ is the truest and fullest expression of his love.

Church of England, *The Mystery of Salvation*, 1995, page 184

But when a theological pluralist such as Paul Knitter uses the term conversion, he doesn't mean conversion to accept salvation in Christ but an openness and willingness to work to overcome suffering and injustice. This is because for ethical theological pluralists salvation means liberation and the transformation of this world rather than preparation for life after death which would be the traditional view of salvation.

(ii) Mission and inter-faith dialogue in the Roman Catholic Church

The aims of mission in the Roman Catholic Church are set out in *Redemptoris Missio* (1990). The subtitle of Pope John Paul II's **encyclical** is: 'On the permanent validity of the Church's missionary mandate'. Paragraphs 55–57 in particular deal with the place of mission in inter-faith or inter-religious dialogue, and are summarised as follows:

- 'Inter-religious dialogue is a part of the Church's evangelizing mission' (para. 55) as it is 'one of its expressions' and an opportunity for it to give an explicit account of Christian belief.
- Dialogue is possible with non-Christian religions because all religions provide spiritual riches even when they contain 'gaps, insufficiencies and errors' (para. 55). Dialogue, though, must not be motivated by 'tactical concerns or self-interest' but respect because all lawful religions are led by the Holy Spirit (para. 56).

Key term

Encyclical In the Roman Catholic Church, a formal statement or letter issued by the Pope to bishops and other senior leaders of the Church, often on matters of doctrine.

- Through dialogue, the Church seeks to uncover the rays of truth, 'found in individuals and in the religious traditions of mankind' (para. 56).
- For dialogue to be effective there must be honesty from both sides and desire to overcome prejudice and intolerance.
- Paragraph 57 deals with different types and modes of dialogue such as: exchanges between experts and official representatives; co-operation with all those safeguarding religious values; sharing spiritual experiences; developing a 'dialogue of life' by sharing spiritual values and giving examples of how these should be lived 'to build a more just and fraternal society'.
- *Redemptoris Missio* gives a special role to the laity (the non-ordained members of the Church) in developing mission through dialogue because they are witnesses of how Christianity can be lived in everyday life.
- Even though missionaries and Christian communities are often misunderstood and their motives questioned, *Redemptoris Missio* encourages them to be persistent.

In summary, *Redemptoris Missio* is arguing that all members of the Catholic Church have a duty to be in respectful dialogue with people of other religious faiths. In this way members of the Church can learn more about God's revelation in the world through non-Christian religions. Dialogue for ordinary people also gives them the opportunity to witness by example how the Christian gospel can be lived authentically. Even though dialogue is essential for a better understanding between faiths, nevertheless the Church has a duty to proclaim the truth of the Christian gospel.

(iii) Mission and inter-faith dialogue in the Church of England

The aims and practicalities of mission in the Church of England are set out in its document *Sharing the Gospel of Salvation* (2010). The document begins by outlining the missionary situation in Great Britain and the reasons why members of the Church should be bolder expressing their beliefs in society:

> *The experience of parishes and people working in multi-faith contexts is that, whilst stridency is counterproductive, failure to be open about our beliefs is equally unhelpful. Others want to know why we do things as well as seeing what we do. Because God loves all His people, encounters begin with respect for the other. If we are too cautious of sharing openly the foundations of our beliefs and the nature of our discipleship – if we hold back the most important aspect of our motivation – we put constraints on that respect and deny a little of God's nature.*
>
> Church of England, *Sharing the Gospel of Salvation*, 2010, Foreword

Sharing the Gospel of Salvation goes on to make the following points:
- Mission in the Church is part of the history of Great Britain but in a plural and multi-faith society it has to be done with a great deal more sensitivity than in the past. To immigrants of non-Christian faiths, the Church of England must show 'hospitality ... develop good inter-faith relations ... in the hope that they will come to faith and be baptised' (para. 30).

- The most effective form of mission is when Christian communities live authentically as Christian communities; they are not there merely to 'prop up other social institutions' (para. 73).
- Inter-faith work will only work properly when motivated by a shared sense of the 'common good' for society as a whole and not from self-interest.
- The Church of England has many opportunities for mission such as: teaching, ministry, chaplaincy, university, forums, councils, networks, meetings, schools and churches.

Sharing the Gospel of Salvation also provides many examples of good practice and the ways in which church communities have adapted to living in a multi-faith society, often in places where they have become the minority religion.

If mission means to proclaim a person's beliefs as a Christian then this should be an important reason for engaging in inter-faith dialogue:

> *Proclamation is not the same as selling a product in the market place; it means to tell people what you think is good about what you believe and practise. So this is not incompatible with inter-faith dialogue.*
>
> Church of England, *Sharing the Gospel of Salvation*, 2010, para. 96

Sharing the Gospel of Salvation (para. 97) endorses the fourfold classification of dialogue:

- **the dialogue of daily life** – encounters on the doorstep or at the checkout
- **the dialogue of the common good** – engagement together in tasks beneficial to the community
- **the dialogue of mutual understanding** – often in more formalised structures or conversations such as scriptural reasoning
- **the dialogue of spiritual life** – encountering each other at prayer and worship.

In summary, *Sharing the Gospel of Salvation* encourages Christians to be more confident in expressing their faith openly in society. This has to be done with sensitivity, in the spirit of openness and generosity but ultimately it is hoped non-Christians might come to accept the truth of Christianity. Inter-faith dialogue provides the opportunity for the Church and people of other faiths to work for the good of society.

(iv) Should Christians have a mission to those of no faith?

The answer to this question might seem to be obviously yes. It might be thought that having no faith (i.e. no religious faith) is no different from having a non-Christian faith. The mission to convert is the same in each case. However, there are several reasons why a distinction does need to be made.

First, those who are strongly atheistic may have very good reasons why having a religious faith is unacceptable. Any attempt to persuade them otherwise would be counter-productive and contrary to Christian teaching on the common good.

Second, from a restrictive theological exclusivist (RAE) point of view, those who have rejected the Gospel so firmly are not among the elect.

> **Key quote**
>
> The pursuit of the common good starts from the observation that we inhabit the same world. In terms of practical politics, the interests of one group or faith are not wholly different from those of another.
>
> Church of England, *Sharing the Gospel of Salvation*, 2010, para. 78

On the other hand, having no *religious* faith does not exclude a person from inter-faith dialogue if the purpose of dialogue is to develop a more cohesive society. Increasingly, inter-faith meetings and conferences are being aimed at 'all faiths and none'. It is a debatable point what 'none' means but in many cases it refers to those who belong to new religious movements (NRMs) and alternative spiritualties such as Wicca, Feng Shui and certain forms of humanism (such as spiritual humanism). The challenge for the Christian Church here is to what extent it can adapt its missionary language to those whose notion of faith is very different from the established world religions.

(d) Inter-faith dialogue, social cohesion and impact

Key question

Does inter-faith dialogue aid social cohesion?

It should by now be becoming clear that one of the primary aims of inter-faith dialogue is to promote the common good. The common good refers to all elements of a fair, just, cohesive and functioning society. The question as to whether inter-faith dialogue contributes in any significant way is very hard to measure, but those who consider that it does contribute positively do so for two reasons.

- First, religions have a powerful sense of community through traditions, foundational texts and formulated beliefs. A religious community has a far clearer sense of its own values than a purely secular one and, therefore, when there is co-operative inter-faith work and dialogue, then there are likely to be very great advances in social cohesion.
- Second, even if inter-faith dialogue has little *national* impact compared to other social cohesion initiatives, in some communities where there is a greater density of religious groups the effects are very significant even though they are localised.

It is hard to measure impact. For example, *A Common Word for the Good* has generated over 600 articles on Muslim-Christian relations and has been sufficiently significant that leaders such as Prince Ghazi of Jordan have publicly endorsed it. It has encouraged many Muslims and Christians to delve deeper into their shared beliefs and removed mistrust and built up trust.

On the other hand, inter-faith dialogue is not considered an effective tool when dealing with religiously conservative communities and leaders. Dialogue only occurs because there is already a willingness to participate. For very conservative religious leaders inter-faith work is a sign of weakness and lack of commitment to the truth of one's faith. Extreme conservatism or fundamentalism is especially attractive to those who feel that society has marginalised them or that society is morally corrupt.

However, radicalisation and fundamentalism have provided inter-faith dialogue organisations with even more incentive to reconsider their methods and aims. There are more reasons than ever to be persistent and to adopt multi-faceted approaches through the creative use of social media, sports and media personalities. Most urgent is the need for each religion to provide its followers with better religious education and understanding of its traditions. Inter-faith work can support this by sharing good and effective practice between the different religions.

4 The scriptural reasoning movement

The constant challenge to inter-faith work is how to maintain effective dialogue without it becoming stale or superficial. One particularly fruitful area of development, the third route of the fourfold classification of dialogue, is the dialogue of mutual understanding through the study of scripture.

A significant inter-faith method which has developed since the 1990s to read and study scripture is called **scriptural reasoning** (SR) founded by David Ford and **Peter Ochs**. David Ford calls scriptural reasoning 'first inter-faith theology' because for all religions and especially the three monotheistic religions of Judaism, Christianity and Islam, scriptures are foundational for the development of belief, worship and morality. The term 'reasoning' refers to the close reading and critical explanation of texts, and is extremely important. There are two levels of reasoning:

- **the internal reasoning** of the text itself (such as its structure, use of language, themes, context in scripture and history)
- **the external reasoning** of the reader as interpreter reflecting on their contemporary situation within their religious tradition.

Critical explanation can take place at many different levels from very technical scholarly study to a more personal spiritual response, but in whatever way a text is read there must be a willingness to accept that there is no one definitive interpretation. Just as there are multiple ways of presenting a Shakespeare play, so there are numerous ways of reading scripture. Advocates of scriptural reasoning argue that when scriptures are read collaboratively and in the spirit of collegiality, then everyone learns and is enriched in their own religious traditions.

(a) Aims of scriptural reasoning

Unlike other forms of inter-faith dialogue, scriptural reasoning does not aim to produce public statements such as *Dabru Emet* or conduct conferences but to work in small groups of Jews, Christian and Muslims. Ford presents three aims of scriptural reasoning:

- **Wisdom**: members of a scriptural reasoning group are committed to a common quest for knowledge and wisdom, which will involve discussion and dispute.
- **Collegiality**: reading texts is a shared enterprise; interpretations from the different faith traditions are presented and discussed by a group equally.
- **Hospitality**: texts are read and interpreted without making value judgements. There must be a spirit of openness which allows for difference of views and opinions to be expressed and exchanged.

The 'first theology' of each religion will naturally be of a very different kind but the starting point for textual study will usually be shared problems or theological ideas such as: how to deal with literalists and fundamentalists; effectiveness of prayer; the purpose of worship; dealing with secularism; music; peace and good will; and women and equality. The result is not to create a global theology (as Hick has argued) but, as Ford summarises, for the exchange or ecology of blessings:

Key term

Scriptural reasoning An open-ended practice of reading, reasoning and interpreting texts in dialogue among members of the three Abrahamic traditions – Judaism, Christianity and Islam.

Key person

Peter Ochs (1950–): the Edgar M. Bronfman Professor of Modern Judaic Studies at the University of Virginia, USA. His interests include Jewish philosophy and theology and the nature and meaning of language. He and David Ford were the co-founders of the scriptural reasoning movement.

See page 215 on Ford's idea of ecology of blessings.

The result is not syncretistic theology [a theology proposing the amalgamation of different religions] but one that is Jewish, one that is Christian, and one that is Muslim – yet shaped in many ways by a wisdom-seeking collegiality that might be described as a setting for the exchange of blessings.

David Ford, *The Future of Christian Theology*, 2011, page 143

(b) Methods of scriptural reasoning

There are no set methods for scriptural reasoning but a number of suggested 'gateways' have been developed by different groups and found to be effective. The scriptural reasoning website at the University of Virginia outlines its overall method as follows:

Scriptural Reasoning (SR) is an open-ended practice of reading- and reasoning-in-dialogue among scholars of the three Abrahamic traditions. There are no set doctrines or rules of SR, since the rules are embedded in the texts of scripture and their relation to those who study and reason together. Individual practitioners of SR do find it useful, however, to reflect occasionally on their group practice and identify its leading tendencies.

http://jsrforum.lib.virginia.edu//gateways.html, University of Virginia

Scriptural reasoning does not need necessarily to be a 'dialogue of scholars', however it does need members of each religion to be well informed and passionate about the scriptural texts they are presenting. The Cambridge Inter-Faith Programme (University of Cambridge) suggests one possible process or 'gateway' for scriptural reasoning, which may be summarised by the following diagram:

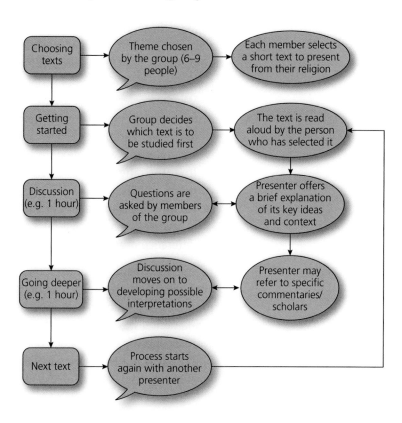

How a scriptural reasoning session might work. (Diagram based on The Cambridge Inter-Faith Programme)

3 Developments in Christian thought

The group might have a facilitator whose job it is to propose questions to be asked and ensure that all members of the group are fully involved. It is important that plenty of time is given for discussion. No one in the group is considered to be an expert and representative of their religion; the views they express are their own. The aim is not to arrive at a group consensus but to have increased in wisdom and understanding of the common good.

(c) Criticism of scriptural reasoning

Although many have found scriptural reasoning very stimulating, some are critical of its methods and effectiveness.

- **Orthodoxy**. As every member of a group represents themselves and is not an official voice of their tradition there is a danger that the views gained of each religion are removed from the orthodox or normative teaching of that religion.
- **Reasonableness**. As there are no right interpretations, who decides if an interpretation is unreasonable or unsupported? This might be especially so in non-academic groups where there are only enthusiastic amateurs.
- **Authority of scripture**. Even within religious traditions there are a variety of different views about what constitutes scriptural authority. This affects the way a person interprets their texts. For example, those who believe that their scripture is exclusively God's revelation might question whether an interpretation by someone outside their belief system has any validity. For scriptural reasoning to work it seems certain underlying theological assumptions are being made about the nature of revelation in different religions' scriptures. In short, can scriptural reasoning really be done by theological exclusivists?
- **Non-Abrahamic faiths**. Scriptural reasoning began because of the common ground between the three monotheistic Abrahamic faiths. Many question whether it can really be extended effectively to non-Abrahamic faiths such as Buddhism and Hinduism, which have very different origins, textual traditions and interpretation.
- **Relativism**. Despite its best efforts to preserve the integrity of each religion, it is argued by some that scriptural reasoning has relativised religious beliefs. In other words, as participants are not allowed to be judgemental or be critical of each other's religious truth claims, then it effectively treats all beliefs as if they are equally valid. The same criticism is often made of theological pluralism.

Key question

What are the weaknesses of scriptural reasoning?

Summary diagram: Religious pluralism and society

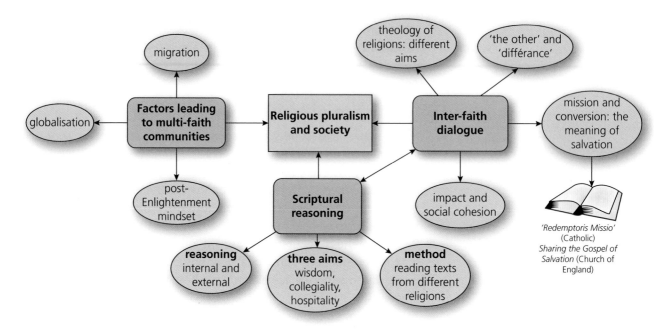

'Redemptoris Missio'
(Catholic)
*Sharing the Gospel of
Salvation* (Church of
England)

Revision advice

By the end of this chapter you should be able to explain the reasons for the increase in multi-faith societies including migration and the aims, strengths and weaknesses of inter-faith dialogue for social cohesion and tackling radicalisation. You should be able to explain the theological challenges of mission and conversion from different Christian perspectives. Finally, you should understand the strengths and weaknesses of scriptural reasoning.

Can you give brief definitions of:
- migration
- pastoral care
- proselytise
- salvation
- radicalisation?

Can you explain:
- the 'other' and 'othering'
- the aims of inter-faith dialogue from a theological inclusivist viewpoint
- what David Ford means by 'ecology of blessing'
- the aims *of Dabru Emet*?

Can you give arguments for and against:
- Christian mission to non-Christians
- scriptural reasoning
- religion as just a lifestyle choice
- theological pluralism as the best means of tackling social cohesion?

Sample question and guidance

Critically compare *Redemptoris Missio* and *Sharing the Gospel of Salvation*.

The essay title does not expect you to quote in detail from the set texts but to show sufficient knowledge of their aims and themes. The aim of *Redemptoris Missio* is to explain the purpose of inter-faith dialogue as an opportunity for mission. You may wish to discuss its aims with reference to Roman Catholic theological universal access exclusivism. The aim of *Sharing the Gospel of*

Salvation from a theological inclusivist position is to encourage members of the Church of England to be more open and explicit in their faith, especially in the workplace.

Your essay should evaluate the different notions of mission as presented in the two documents and whether they are legitimate, aid or detract from inter-faith dialogue and contribute positively or negatively to living in multi-faith societies.

Further essay questions

'Social cohesion is not the aim of inter-faith dialogue.' Discuss.

Analyse the view that Christians should not seek to convert people from other faiths to Christianity.

Evaluate the claim that migration is the primary cause of multi-faith societies.

Going further

Catholic Church, *Redemptoris Missio* (1990). This is one of the prescribed texts on the specification. It can be found here: http://w2.vatican.va/content/john-paul-ii/en/encyclicals/documents/hf_jp-ii_enc_07121990_redemptoris-missio.html

Church of England, *Sharing the Gospel of Salvation* (2010). This is one of the prescribed texts on the specification. It can be found here: https://www.churchofengland.org/media/39745/gsmisc956.pdf

A Common Word Between Us and You. 5-Year Anniversary Edition (MABDA, English Monograph Series, No. 20, 2012). This very influential document may be found on the Oxford Foundation website. The Oxford Foundation is dedicated to improving Muslim education and inter-faith dialogue. www.theoxfordfoundation.com/

David F. Ford, *The Future of Christian Theology* (Wiley-Blackwell, 2011). Chapter 7 is specifically about inter-faith dialogue and scriptural reasoning, but to make more sense of the ideas Ford presents it

is well worthwhile reading the rest of the book.

John Hick and Brian Hebblethwaite, eds, *Christianity and Other Religions* (Oneworld, 2001). This is a very useful source book and includes extracts from Barth, Rahner, and Knitter.

www.scripturalreasoning.org Click on the 'Text Bundles' tab for suggestions of themes and texts for scriptural reasoning.

Other books discussed in this chapter are:
- Barnes, M. *Theology and the Dialogue of Religions* (Cambridge University Press, 2002).
- Crane, A. and Matten, D. *Business Ethics* (Oxford University Press, 2004).
- The Doctrine Commission of the General Synod of the Church of England, *The Mystery of Salvation* (Church House Publishing, 1995).
- Steger, M. *Globalization: A Very Short Introduction* (Oxford University Press, 2009).
- Ward, K. *The Case for Religion* (Oneworld, 2004).

Chapter 13

Gender and society

Chapter checklist

The chapter begins by looking at the changing roles of men and women in society in relation to marriage, cohabitation and other family formations. A key issue is the debate about women's rights and gender. The chapter sets out Christian teaching on gender from the Bible and then from Catholic and protestant traditions. The final part of the chapter reviews various contemporary Christian responses to gender, parenthood and different family formations.

1 Introduction

The family from the popular American TV series (1958–1966) *The Donna Reed Show*. Is there an ideal family?

Was there ever a 'golden period' of the family? There have always been unhappy families; there have always been those who have suffered under oppressive fathers, negligent mothers and cramped living conditions. But as some sociologists argue, a single, universal family ideal has never existed. The picture to the left was never universally true because the notion of the nuclear family is essentially a middle-class, western (Northern European/North American) product of the mid-twentieth century during a time of industrial prosperity. Nevertheless, the nuclear family of mother, father and two or three children living together in love and harmony is also one popularised by traditional Christian teaching.

However, since the 1950s there have been rapid changes in society, which have altered the idea of the family and presented society and the Christian churches with significant challenges. Some consider that the family is in decline and that everything should be done to sure it up while others welcome these so-called challenges as positive and liberating.

Key quote

The case for two-parent biologically related family can be exaggerated. Not all biological fathers and mothers are competent parents. Not all two-parent families are just and life-enhancing...The facts indicate, however, that alternatives are on average worse, especially if they are systematically generalised.

Don Browning, 'World Family Trends' in *The Cambridge Companion to Christian Ethics*, 2001, page 246

Factors that have changed the family social landscape in Britain

- **Ease of divorce**. The average length of marriage before divorce is 11.7 years (2014).
- **Decline in marriage**. In 2014 there were 247,372 opposite sex marriages in the UK (the lowest since 1972).
- **Wedding ceremonies**. There has been a general decline of religious marriages with 28 per cent of marriages being religious ceremonies in 2014, a decrease of 0.8 per cent compared to 2013.
- **Single parents**. There are increasing numbers of single or lone parents. In 2014 there were around 2 million single parents making up a quarter of all families with dependent children.
- **Births outside marriage and civil partnerships**. The number of non-marital births rose to 47.7 per cent of all births in 2015. From 2005–2015 60 per cent of all births were to cohabiting couples.
- **Gay and lesbian relationships**. There were 4,850 same-sex marriages in 2014 (just after the Marriage (Same Sex Couples) Act came into force).
- **Cohabitation**. Cohabiting couple families grew by 29.7 per cent 2004–2014, making it the fastest growing type of family in the UK. There were 3.2 million cohabiting families in 2015.
- **Blended families/step children**. In 2011 there were 544,000 (or 11 per cent of couple families) stepfamilies with dependent children.

Statistics based on various government sources for England and Wales.

2 Feminism and changing views of gender

One of the major drives for change since the 1960s has been the increasing independence of women and shifting understanding of gender roles.

(a) Feminism

Since Mary Wollstonecraft wrote *A Vindication for the Rights of Woman* (1792) there has been a shift, some would say revolution, in the way in which women have been perceived in society. **Feminism** has gone through many stages or waves. These waves mark different historical developments as well as distinctive shifts in aims.

(i) Rights and equality

The 'first wave' of feminism focused on equality of rights. The philosopher **Harriet Taylor** forcefully set out the arguments in *Enfranchisement of Women* (1851) for the right to vote and also for 'equality in all rights, political, civil, and social, with the male citizens of the community'. She argued that true partnership between men and women would also mean equal pay and financial independence. First wave or liberal feminists in recent years have brought about social reform such as state-funded child-care, flexible working hours, and maternity leave for women.

> ### Key term
>
> **Feminism** Refers to the many political, philosophical, economic, psychological and sociological movements which have sought to free women from male dominance and give them independence and dignity. There are many different types of feminisms.

> ### Key person
>
> **Harriet Taylor** (1807–58): philosopher and wife of John Stuart Mill. In her *Enfranchisement of Women* (1851) she argued for the ballot and also for 'equality in all rights, political, civil, and social, with the male citizens of the community'. She was also effectively the co-author of Mill's *On Liberty* (1859) – the landmark in liberal thinking of the nineteenth century.
>
>

(ii) Tackling patriarchy

The 1960s gave rise to 'second wave' feminism. Women of the second wave realised that true equality was only possible once men and women's mindset changed. Without a deep change of attitude, society's institutions would still remain male-dominated, or **patriarchal**. One of the key figures of second wave feminism was **Betty Friedan** and her ground breaking *The Feminine Mystique* (1963). Friedan's research showed how although middle-class women of the late 1950s played the role of the dutiful wife and homemaker, they were far from fulfilled but bored and frustrated. Her book transformed the lives of thousands because once women realised that the ideal housewife role which they felt obliged to play (the 'feminine mystique') was disliked by countless other women it gave them courage to abandon the traditional expectation of becoming a mother and to pursue their own careers and independent lives.

(iii) Women's false-consciousness

Another approach in the secular gender debate focuses on the role women themselves need to play in tackling gender stereotyping. **Simone de Beauvoir's** influence on late twentieth-century feminism has been instrumental in transforming equality feminism (equal rights for women and men) to consider deep-seated prejudices which regard women to be inferior to men. The distinctiveness of de Beauvoir's argument is that it isn't just the mindset of men that needs challenging but more significantly that of women. She argued that even the most independent women still suffer from the **false-consciousness**, which supports society's gender-typical roles of men and women. Until this false-consciousness is dispelled then women can never truly be free.

In her influential book *The Second Sex* de Beauvoir acknowledges that women have allowed themselves for centuries to become the second sex and to act the role of the wife, the lover, and the sex object according to the needs of men. While they continue in this form of false-consciousness they cannot live fully authentic, liberated and fulfilled lives. Women's existence is defined by men for men and women have unconsciously allowed this to happen.

> One is not born, but rather one becomes a woman. No biological, psychological, or economic fate determines the figure that the human female presents in society; it is civilization as a whole that produces this creature, intermediate between male and eunuch, which is described as the feminine.

Simone de Beauvoir, *The Second Sex*, 1997, page 295

So, existentially women and men are born without gender roles; that is what de Beauvoir means when she says 'one becomes a woman'. For modern women, gender is 'intermediate between male and eunuch', because they don't have the freedom to choose their gender identities; they have become defined and trapped by society – that includes the expectations of other women just as much as those of men.

De Beauvoir argued that for too long women have accepted and encouraged themselves to believe in **'the eternal feminine'**, the idea that as the second sex their role is to be an ideal of what men expect of them. Women have allowed themselves to become the passive bystanders in society.

The aim of *The Second Sex* is to expose all the areas where women have traditionally considered that their gender roles and duties are intrinsic to their sex. As there is no eternal feminine, then women are liberated to choose the lifestyles they want. They may choose to conform to society's notion of the feminine, they might opt to become mothers but equally they may wish to do the kinds of jobs traditionally assigned to men.

(iv) Women in society

We can see how much of de Beauvoir's vision has come true today – women are members of front-line armed forces, top judges and managing directors of large companies, scientists, and so on. However, many would say that there is a great deal still to be done. There is a persistent gender divide in many such traditionally 'male' roles, with a minority of women working in such industries, many of whom are paid less for doing the same job as their male counterparts. There is also an apparent **'glass ceiling'** for women in reaching the top jobs in science, politics and the legal profession.

Women hold important roles in society, but a glass ceiling still exists.

(b) Changing secular views of gender and gender roles

It is generally accepted that a person's sex refers to whether they are male or female biologically. Gender, on the other hand, is more complex and is taken to refer to a person's masculine or feminine traits and their way of behaving and thinking.

It might reasonably be assumed that sex determines gender but over the past two hundred years in the west there have been considerable changes in the way men and women understand their gender roles. For example, whereas in the eighteenth century a woman would have understood her role as marriage, children and caring for her husband the modern woman almost certainly does not define herself only in this way. The keenly debated issue is whether gender is only partially related to biological sex or whether it is entirely a social construct and the result of upbringing.

(i) Sex and gender

One of the most controversial debates between feminists and non-feminists alike is the significance of biological sex and gender. The nature-nurture debate is still an issue where the arguments may be summarised by two approaches: the essentialist view and the existential view of biological sex-gender relationship.

Are gender roles entirely socially acquired?

- **The essentialist view** is that there are distinctive feminine and masculine characteristics which are not the product of society but intrinsic to biology or nature. Women's bodies, for example, are 'designed' to bear children and so their gender identity is naturally to be more nurturing and domestic. Men's bodies tend to be more muscular than women's bodies because their gender roles are to be more competitive in the workplace.
- **The existentialist view** is that biological sex is of little significance and that gender characteristics are the product of nurture through culture and upbringing. Male-dominated societies throughout history have tended to objectify and sexualise women's bodies, but existentialists would argue that this objectivity is socially constructed. For example, in certain cultures and periods of history women who have curvy bodies are considered to be more attractive than slim bodies; in some cultures, women's breasts are considered sexually attractive whereas in other cultures it is the shape of the face or eyes or lips which are more sexually erotic. The existentialist position doesn't deny the importance of the body as a source of a person's identity.

(ii) Gender and power

One influential secular (non-religious) approach is to abandon the essentialist/existentialist distinction and to focus on the problem of sexuality from the perspective of power. Scholars who have pursued this line of thought have preferred to use the term sexuality rather than gender as it includes sexual practices as well as gender identity. Their argument is indebted to Marx's notion that human interactions are usually about power and which group dominates the other and controls them.

This analysis of sexuality was developed by the influential French philosopher **Michel Foucault**. Foucault's analysis of human sexual history from the ancient Greeks to the present day demonstrated that human sexuality cannot be defined in simple binary terms as male/female but covers a spectrum of sexual practices such as: straight (heterosexual) men and women; lesbian women; gay men; bisexual women; bisexual men; transvestite women; transvestite men; transgender women; and transgender men. Foucault's point is that sexuality in this case can't easily be defined as heterosexual or homosexual or bisexual. The purpose of sex is for pleasure, companionship and education. Foucault calls this the *ars erotica*.

Controlling sexual practices (Foucault calls this the *scientia sexualis*) is a useful means of maintaining power. A good example of the *scientia sexualis* (the science of sexuality) can be seen in the way the Church's place in Western society was maintained by its control and regularisation of men and women's sexual practices and gender roles through marriage. As the Church's influence has weakened, its role has been replaced by doctors, psychoanalysts and sociologists, each of whom has imposed their particular ideas of 'correct' sexual behaviour.

Key person

Michel Foucault (1926–84): a French philosopher, historian and social theorist. His writings cover a wide range of topics including *The Archaeology of Knowledge* (1969), *Discipline and Punish* (1975) and the three-volume *The History of Sexuality* (1976–84). His central concern was to show how language, values, systems and thought are governed by the control of power.

Key quote

Sexuality must not be thought of as a kind of natural given … It is the name that can be given to a historical construct: not a furtive reality that is difficult to grasp, but a great surface network.

Michel Foucault, *The History of Sexuality: The Will to Knowledge*, 1979, page 105

3 Biblical teaching on the roles of men and women in the family and society

Traditional Christian teaching on the gender roles of men and women in the family and society is explicitly based on two biblical ideas: the order of nature and God's covenant ideal.

(a) Order of nature

According to Genesis 1 men and women are both created in the image of God and their primary roles are to reproduce and maintain the natural order of the world.

There are natural gender distinctions but these become exaggerated after the Fall (Genesis 3) where, as a result, God commands that women will be mothers and they will be ruled over by their husbands (Genesis 3:16) and men will work and provide food for the family (Genesis 3:17–19). The traditional biblical view establishes the important principle that there is a natural order of creation where men operate in the public sphere of work while women are to rule the private, domestic sphere of the home.

However, although the biblical principle of men inhabiting the public sphere of work and women the private generally holds true, there are also many examples where this principle is developed and possibly challenged.

(b) God's covenant ideal

In traditional Christian teaching the effects of the Fall mean that human nature has become so distorted that men and women cannot live according to the natural order alone. God re-establishes human relationships as a covenant ideal given through a series of biblical commands.

In the Old Testament the prophet Jeremiah looks forward to a new covenant which will establish a new social order between humans and with God. Jeremiah's covenant (Jeremiah 31:31–34) is based on the heart and on relationships (external characteristics do not matter). This notion of covenant is central to Jesus' teaching and his message appears to have offered women in particular a liberated sense of their gender roles.

For example, in the story of Mary and Martha (Luke 10:38–42) Mary is allowed to listen to and learn from Jesus' teaching – in effect to prepare for the public role of being a disciple or teacher, traditionally only occupied by men, whereas Martha is criticised because she can only think about her domestic duties. Mary therefore represents the new extended female gender role; Martha represents the older traditional female gender role.

In a famous passage in his letter to the Galatian churches St Paul describes the new covenant's effect on gender and family as follows:

> As many of you as were baptised into Christ have clothed yourselves with Christ. There is no longer Jew or Greek, there is no longer slave or free, there is no longer male and female; for all of you are one in Christ Jesus.
>
> Galatians 3:27–28

Most Christians would not take this passage completely at face value (it is unlikely, for instance, that Paul thought that there were no gender differences). It is more likely that Paul has a vision of a new social order founded on Christian values of co-operation and friendship free from existing, unfair social structures.

This vision of a fairer, more balanced, society can be seen as a challenge to the natural order of the time, yet other New Testament teachings show how this vision was adapted pragmatically by early Christians to accommodate the social order of the time. For example, there are several passages where the writers provide **household rules** or a code of behaviour. Issuing household rules such are these was common practice in the ancient Greek and Roman world and was designed to maintain social stability.

A good example of a household rule list is to be found in St Paul's **Letter to the Ephesians**. The letter covers a wide range of moral issues (e.g. speaking truthfully, sexual purity, honesty and care for the poor), which are necessary for the ordering of Christian church communities. In Ephesians 5: 21–33 the following advice is given on gender roles:

- **Women**. The first rule is: 'Wives be subject to your husbands as you are to the Lord' (Ephesians 5:22). The reason for their obedience is because their husbands are 'the head of the wife just as Christ is the head of the church'.

There has been much discussion as to what Paul means when he says the husband is 'the head of the wife'. Traditionally it is interpreted to mean that the wife is subservient to her husband's will because by analogy Christ (male) is the head or ruler of the Church (female – the Greek word for church is feminine). But 'head' (or *kephale* in Greek) may also mean 'source of life' and refer back to Genesis 2:21–23 where the man is the source of woman's creation. This interpretation puts the emphasis on relationship and not so much on authority. Some scholars remind us that in Ephesians obedience is mutual (5:21 – 'be subject to one another') even if the nature of obedience is different according to gender.

- **Men**. The second rule is: 'Husbands love your wives, just as Christ loved the church and gave himself up for her' (Ephesians 5:25).

Unlike Roman or Greek household rules the Christian version is ordered by the principle of love. St Paul says the husband should love his wife just as much as he loves his own body, for just as he nourishes and cares for his own body (Ephesians 5:29), so he should nourish and care for his wife. 'Body' in this context doesn't just refer to the physical but to the relationships between people, just as Paul uses the term to describe the Church not as a physical entity but as a set of relationships.

There are many other versions of the household rules in the New Testament, all of which reflect the patriarchal times in which they were composed which presuppose the male control of his wife as 'the weaker sex' (1 Peter 3:7), family and society. This is particularly so in Paul's household rules for the Christian community at Corinth. In 1 Corinthians 14:34–36 Paul forbids women to speak in church and stipulates that they should seek to be educated by their husband at home – a view he reiterates in his letter to Timothy:

Key terms

Household rules Developed in ancient Greek and Roman societies and list the duties to be performed by members of the household. Early Christians developed their own versions of them such as Ephesians 5:21–33 and 1 Timothy 2:8–15.

Letter to the Ephesians St Paul's letter to the Christian community in Ephesus (now in modern Turkey). Originally a Greek city, Ephesus came under Roman control and at the time when Paul knew it was a very large city. Many scholars consider that the letter was not written by Paul but one of his disciples. One of its main themes is the idea of the Church as the 'body of Christ'.

Key question

What does Paul mean when he says a husband is 'the head' of his wife?

Let a woman learn in silence with full submission. I permit no woman to teach or to have authority over a man; she is to keep silent. For Adam was formed first, then Eve; and Adam was not deceived, but the woman was deceived and became a transgressor.

1 Timothy 2:11–14

The biblical view of gender and society is ambiguous and not entirely consistent. For more traditional Christians what matters are the explicit commands such as that men should love their wives and wives should be obedient to their husbands. But for other Christians the fundamentally important idea is the development of the covenant ideal in which there would be no gender division and relationships would move beyond traditional conventions.

The issues facing Christians today such as marriage, cohabitation, single parent families, same-sex families, gender roles and motherhood, depend to some extent on how the New Testament is interpreted.

4 Christian responses to secular gender roles, parenthood and the family

Key question

Should Christian teaching on the gender resist current secular views of the family?

As well as contributing to society it has always been the case that Christianity has had also to respond and adjust to the secular changes in society. This poses a fundamental problem about the nature of Christian theology: should it resist change and maintain what it considers to be its timeless values but then become largely irrelevant; or should it adapt to current needs but lose its distinctiveness?

(a) Conservative Protestant Christian responses

Conservative Protestant Christian teaching largely takes the view that biblical theology is timeless and should resist buying into secular changes in society. Not all conservative Protestant theology is biblicist, but the Bible is the foundation for many of its teachings.

(i) Gender roles

Kathy Rudy's summary of conservative Protestant Christian teaching on gender (in the USA, but shared by conservatives in the rest of the world), illustrates the power **the 'Right'** exercises on American politics and society. These teachings are rooted in traditional views from Augustine via Luther to the present day, and their driving force is a mistrust of socially liberal ideologies based on secular sociological, psychological and philosophical knowledge. For example, the Right is especially critical of 'liberal ideologies' such as feminism, which it considers to be a root cause of family break-down, contributing to the destabilising of society and traditional values. The Right has argued that feminism has confused gender roles and set up unrealistic expectations for women, which cause disappointment and dissatisfaction.

Abortion poses many challenges to Christian beliefs.

Key question

Has feminism undermined the spiritual and social foundations of the family?

USA religious gender politics

Those who are ideologically socially liberal (the 'Left') may also favour abortion rights (a woman's right to choose), rights for transgender people, civil and workers' rights. The opposite of social liberalism is social conservatism. Those on the 'Right' who are socially conservative would tend to oppose such ideas.

The Right's views include the belief that social liberalism and feminism in both secular and Christian forms are the principal causes of increased divorce, dysfunctional families and sexual immorality (in particular homosexuality) which 'corrupt' the morals of the young and ultimately undermine the 'American dream' of a happy prosperous nation. Conservative Protestant theology believes that men and women are created **equal but different** by God, each to fulfil their different gender roles. This is because:

- God created men and women differently from the beginning (Genesis 1: 27).
- God ordained that men and women would have different gender roles and that society functions best when these 'orders of creation' are observed. This means recognising that in marriage man is the 'head of woman' (as stated in the New Testament family household rules – see pages 234–5).

Based on these biblical ideas, conservative Protestants reject the existential idea of gender which is not, as Foucault and other secular radicals consider, a product of culture but determined by biological sex as ordered by God in his creation and after the Fall.

(ii) Motherhood and parenthood

Conservative Protestants believe that a women's role is to be wife and mother and create the **domestic haven** where her husband can escape from the external world. But, while others might consider such a submissive role for women outdated, they don't equate it as weakness.

This role of wife and mother is traced back to the biblical figure of Eve, partner of Adam, whose name means 'the mother of all living' (Genesis 3:20). She was the first mother.

In a similar way, a mother's role is to bring life into the world, to nurture and lead it into the knowledge and love of God. Conservative theology is especially critical of those who undermine these roles. A woman who works outside the home not only removes a job from a man, but diminishes a man's role and his responsibilities to his wife. Nevertheless, a woman may work if she also carries out her domestic duties and her job doesn't detract from her role as mother – in the same way as the 'capable wife' in the Bible, balanced motherhood and a job:

She rises while it is still night
and provides food for her household
and tasks for her servant-girls.
She considers a field and buys it;
with the fruit of her hands she plants a vineyard.

Proverbs 31:15–16

A man's role is to be a companion to his wife by providing for the family and assisting in the education and discipline of his children. St Paul writes the following about a husband's duty:

And whoever does not provide for relatives, and especially
for family members, has denied the faith and is worse than an
unbeliever.

1 Timothy 5:8

> ### Key question
>
> What constitutes the ideal family?

> ### Key terms
>
> **Blended family** Where at least one of the partners has divorced/separated from another partner and has remarried/formed a new relationship bringing with him/her the children from his/her former marriage/partnership.
>
> **Eroticisation** The process where people are treated as sexual objects and sex is purely for pleasure.

(iii) Different types of family

■ Conservative Protestants are generally suspicious of any so-called family which is not heterosexual and where parents are not married. The arguments for this are two-fold. First, they argue that the Bible's account of the order of creation requires parents to complement each other in terms of gender – this means that all families with same-sex parents are not truly families in a Christian sense. Second, despite being suspicious of secular sociological research, they endorse evidence – such as the influential report produced in the USA by Sara McLanahan and Gary Sandefur (1994) – which indicates that children do less well educationally and couples are less happy in **blended families**, single-parent families (but not where one of the parents has died), same-sex parented families and where non-married parents cohabit.

Conservative Protestant theology is critical of contemporary secular feminism and the social trends which have permitted the rise of cohabitation and same-sex relationships. This, they argue, is because:

■ they have led to the **eroticisation** of western society. Foucault, for example, is typical of those who have defined love as pleasure rather than love as commitment

■ relationships have become too private and egocentric, whereas Christian teaching on the family is that it should be outward looking, through church attendance and by contributing towards society as a whole

■ couples expect too much from their relationships and with the ease of divorce and social acceptance of cohabitation there is no compulsion to make relationships work, whereas Christianity teaches having clear gender roles and expectation of marriage as a permanent state, with the result that couples have strong reasons to make family life work.

(c) Liberal Protestant Christian responses

Liberal Protestants more readily accept the secular insights of sociologists, psychologists and biologists on questions of gender and family, which conservatives tend to reject. As liberals interpret the Bible as a sourcebook of experiences rather than revelation, many see in the New Testament the struggle and tensions between those Christians who considered that all the old rule-based teaching of gender, family and sexuality had been replaced and those Christians who were anxious that Christian teaching should conform to socially acceptable behaviour. This is why the household lists were introduced.

(i) Gender roles

Liberal Protestants remind us that the point of the biblical covenant ideal which governs gender roles is that gender is not intrinsic in nature because the covenant is a human reflection on what it means to be in a relationship with God. The great insight and contribution of various forms of feminism and critics such as Foucault is to liberate gender from sex and from the controlling power of the Church so as to allow each person to search out his or her own identity and role in society and in the family. Foucault has provided a way of interpreting St Paul's teaching that as there 'is no longer male and female', then the notion of the family may be gay and lesbian.

Nevertheless, many liberal Protestants question Foucault's reduction of sexuality merely to the level of pleasure because for Christians, love is not just *eros* (sexual pleasure) but also *philos* (friendship) and *agape* (generous love as expressed in the God-human covenant).

(ii) Motherhood and parenthood

For traditional Christians motherhood is essential for a woman's identity and purpose but motherhood for liberal Protestants has no particular symbolic or ontological significance. For some women (as it is for some men), being a parent is a means of directing one's creative energies into forming a family and seeing one's children grow up into mature adults. But for liberals there is no *imperative* that parenthood is something adults should aspire to.

Furthermore, liberal Protestants acknowledge that not all adults make very good parents and, where this is the case, then it clearly makes more sense to find a different vocation in life. Liberal Christians take seriously the insights of secular feminists on motherhood and would be more inclined to share some of de Beauvoir's and Friedan's views that the Church's motherhood ideal is sometimes a source of false-consciousness. Liberal Protestants tend to find the emphasis on Mary the Mother of Christ as the symbol of womanhood stereotyped, although they consider that some secular feminists are too quick to dismiss the moral, spiritual and emotional benefits of parenthood.

(iii) Non-traditional families

Jesus' teaching on the Kingdom of God was based on a new covenant idea first suggested by Jeremiah that the old social order would give way to a more inclusive, non-hierarchical and non-judgemental society. Jesus' ministry was aimed at the marginalised, including women and those treated as sexual outsiders. For this reason, liberal Protestants argue that their various churches need to be much more flexible in their understanding of family and to exercise what they call 'justice love'.

Liberal Protestants are generally persuaded by the optimistic evidence provided by sociologists such as **Jessie Bernard**, that where children are loved, feel secure and provided for then a family might equally be a single parent, blended, same-sex, and so on.

Key question

Have secular views of gender equality undermined Christian gender roles?

Read pages 175–6 on the debate in the Church of England about same-sex marriage.

Do the churches need to be more flexible in their understanding of 'family'?

Key question

What is the most important foundation of a family – blood ties or a loving relationship?

Key person

Jessie Bernard (1903–96): an influential sociologist and feminist. In her book *The Future of Marriage* (1972) she argued that marriage was generally advantageous for men but not women.

Liberal Protestants also hold that the Bible itself illustrates that there has never been one kind of family – the families referred to in the New Testament household lists include servants and possibly their children. Furthermore, in the New Testament the Christian family may also refer to all members who are related to each other through love and faith and not blood kinship – a 'community of friends', which suggests a more inclusive model of family than is typically recognised as being desirable by traditional Protestant Christianity.

Finally, no one pretends that family life is easy. Not only are liberal Protestants critical of the very restricted view of the conservative Christian Protestant notion of the family, they are also wary of the conservative ideal as being unrealistic and the cause of tension when that ideal is not achieved.

Key quote

Jesus: 'Here are my mother and my brothers! Whoever does the will of God is my brother and sister and mother.'

Mark 3:34–35

Key quote

Although the liberal theological response should be applauded for its openness, clarity and sense of justice, it was slow in recognising the depth of family disruption and new evidence that mere social acceptance and state supports were inadequate remedies.

Don Browning, 'World Family Trends' in *The Cambridge Companion to Christian Ethics*, 2001, page 248

(c) Roman Catholic responses

Even though there are many Roman Catholic feminist writers, official teaching of the Roman Catholic Church is ambivalent about feminism. On the one hand, it applauds feminism because it raises the dignity and place of women in society; on the other hand, it is suspicious of its secular agenda, which diminishes gender differences between men and women, especially in their distinctive spiritual contributions to the family, society and Church.

The effects of feminist theology (both positive and negative) can be seen in Pope John Paul II's Apostolic Letter, *Mulieris Dignitatem*. The letter acknowledges that the relationship and roles of women and men have not always been understood well – especially in the treatment of women, and the purpose of the letter is to correct this. It does not do this, however, by using the language of women's rights, or by recourse to any modern liberal views of gender, but instead uses the Bible, tradition and natural law as its foundations. At the heart of the letter is the paradigm of Mary, the Mother of God and *theotokos*. Mary's role illustrates the special role of women in the process of salvation, for by giving birth to Christ she illustrates the human virtues of obedience and dignity for both men and women.

Key terms

Mulieris Dignitatem An Apostolic Letter issued by Pope John Paul II in 1988. Its subtitle in English is 'On the Dignity and Vocation of Women'.

Theotokos is the Greek word for 'God-bearer' and refers to Mary's special role as the Mother of God (i.e. Jesus Christ).

239

Key quote

The biblical text provides sufficient basis for recognizing the essential equality of man and woman from the point of view of their humanity.

Mulieris Dignitatem 6

Key question

Should motherhood be a goal for women?

Key term

Annunciation is the occasion when the angel Gabriel announced to Mary that she would give birth to Jesus (see Luke 1:26–38).

(i) Gender roles

Mulieris Dignitatem is concerned to show how the Church responds to feminists who have accused the Church of patriarchy and sexism. The Letter begins by stating that the Christian basic notion of gender is that men and women are made equally in the image and likeness of God. In developing this, the Letter clearly responds to current secular views of gender by rejecting the traditional view that man is the active principle and woman the passive. It states that because both men and women are made in God's image then both are equally creative and active but in *different* ways. The difference is most strikingly observed in the woman's capacity to be a wife and mother.

God's order of creation determines that while gender roles may be affected by environment, the Church does not accept the existential notion that gender is entirely culturally and environmentally determined.

Mulieris Dignitatem makes it clear that although man is the 'head of woman', marriage is a mutual relationship of equals; being the 'head' does not mean that he should have 'dominion' or 'possess' his wife but treat and respect her as an equal. However, this does not permit women to take on male roles, which would confuse the genders.

> *Consequently, even the rightful opposition of women to what is expressed in the biblical words, 'He shall rule over you' (Genesis 3:16) must not under any condition lead to the 'masculinization' of women. In the name of liberation from male 'domination', women must not appropriate to themselves male characteristics contrary to their own feminine 'originality'.*
>
> *Mulieris Dignitatem* 10

In this respect the Church resists what it regards as the dangerous effects of some forms of feminism, which undermine the dignity of the woman as mother, but on the other hand, it endorses secular women's rights, which protect the dignity of women especially those who are abused and marginalised.

(ii) Motherhood and parenthood

> *This mutual gift of the person in marriage opens to the gift of a new life, a new human being, who is also a person in the likeness of his parents. Motherhood implies from the beginning a special openness to the new person: and this is precisely the woman's 'part'.*
>
> *Mulieris Dignitatem* 18

Motherhood and the unique role of women in society is at the heart of *Mulieris Dignitatem*. The letter acknowledges the significant and positive social shift in attitudes to women in recent times but very firmly rejects the kind of feminist criticisms made by writers such as de Beauvoir that motherhood (especially the form of motherhood that is taught by the Church) can be seen as demeaning to women. *Mulieris Dignitatem* sections 18–19 which focus on motherhood may be summarised thematically as follows:

■ **Mary the model of motherhood**. Mary's role as mother of Christ illustrates her unique place in God's salvation of the world. The **annunciation** is a sign of Mary's readiness to be a mother and accept new life. Mary's example illustrates the special value God places on motherhood for all women.

- **Mystery of generation**. The mystery of generation is the idea that men and women are both equally and uniquely created by God. By desiring to be parents (as mother and as father), men and women reflect the mystery of generation inherent in the Holy Trinity.
- **Special gift**. Having a child is a special and 'sincere gift of self' of a mother in marriage and also a visible sign (in their child) that husband and wife have become 'one flesh' (Mark 10:8).
- **Mutuality**. A mother's role as parent is demanding and special but it is not hers alone but an example to the man of what is required of him: 'in their shared parenthood he owes a special debt to the woman'.
- **Active motherhood**. Motherhood changes and challenges the man so he can learn from her how to be a good father because his nature is 'not so psychologically predisposed to parenthood'. Being a mother is therefore far from passive. In its struggles and joys it is also actively part of God's covenant.

Despite its attempts to address contemporary feminist criticisms, the Catholic Church is nevertheless at loggerheads with feminists such as de Beauvoir and Friedan who argue that motherhood is a false-consciousness of the 'eternal feminine' or 'feminine mystique'. While it is true that compared to earlier Church teaching female and male roles are far more egalitarian, and the role of mother as a 'special gift' is shared by many non-Christian feminists, even so many Catholic theologians feel that it has omitted some fundamental Christian teaching which would engage the Church fully with contemporary society. Some of these criticisms by Catholic feminists are set out below.

(iii) Different types of family

The Roman Catholic Church argues that sociological evidence supports the case that children raised in **intact families** where parents are heterosexual and married are psychologically stronger than those where parents are cohabiting or in blended family relationships. The Catechism comments on cohabitation, even when it is a 'trial marriage':

> the fact is that such liaisons can scarcely ensure mutual sincerity and fidelity in a relationship between a man and woman... Human love does not tolerate 'trial marriages'. It demands total and definitive gift of persons to one another.
>
> *Catechism of the Catholic Church*, para. 2391

As marriage is strictly heterosexual, then same-sex relationships however committed can never constitute legitimate forms of family.

(d) Roman Catholic feminist responses

The rise of second wave feminism and its critique of gender and society has given many Catholic women the inspiration to reform the Catholic Church. Contrary to their secular counterparts, they don't think that the Church is essentially flawed but they do think that many of its traditions and teachings have become institutionally patriarchal. They also argue that a reformed Church has a significant part to play in society by

Key term

Intact family A family where both parents are married and have not divorced or separated.

Read pages 172–3 on the Catholic Church's teaching on homosexuality.

Key question

Can feminism reform Roman Catholic teaching on gender and society?

challenging purely secular views of the family and developing a Christian spirituality which enhances gender relationships.

(i) Gender roles

A view shared by many Catholic feminists is that the Church has consciously and unconsciously written women out of Christian history when, in the first Christian communities' very early days, women played an equally significant role as men. The Catholic feminist theologian **Elisabeth Schüssler Fiorenza** argues that there were any number of significant women leaders such as Priscilla (Acts 18:1, 18, 26), Apphia (Philemon 1:2) and Phoebe (Romans 16:1–2). Uncovering the very early history of Christianity therefore reveals a radical challenge to current Church teaching and organisation. Knowing this enables Christian women today to act in sisterly solidarity with those pioneering women in challenging gender stereotypes. As Fiorenza says (quoting Judy Chicago) 'our heritage is our power'.

> I argue that on the contrary, that women were not marginal in the earliest beginnings of Christianity; rather, biblical texts and historical sources produce marginality of women. Hence texts must be interrogated not only as to what they say about women but also how they construct what they say or do not say.

Elisabeth Schüssler Fiorenza, *In Memory of Her*, 1994, page *xx*

Other Catholic feminist theologians argue that structural changes to gender roles need a more radical shift in gender-role consciousness. For example, the Catholic feminist **Catharina Halkes** argues that as Jesus' teaching on the Kingdom of God required social and spiritual transformation, so women must learn to develop their gift of care into the public sphere while men must give up their privileged sense of entitlement and learn the virtue of care in the everyday. Her analysis therefore criticises the 'headship' teaching in *Mulieris Dignitatem* for failing to extend female/male mutuality far enough and for still privileging the male's role in the public sphere.

Key person

Elisabeth Schüssler Fiorenza (1938–): professor of Divinity at the Harvard Divinity School and a Catholic feminist theologian whose interests lie in the historical reconstruction of Christianity through the biblical texts. Her most influential book is *In Memory of Her: A Feminist Theological Reconstruction of Christian Origins* (1984).

Key person

Catharina Halkes (1920–2011): Roman Catholic Dutch feminist theologian and first professor of feminism and Christianity in Holland. She was forbidden to address Pope John Paul II during his visit to the Netherlands in 1985.

Catharina Halkes

(ii) Motherhood and parenthood

In general, Catholic feminists consider that the Church's teaching on motherhood is over-romanticised and while they may not go as far as de Beauvoir in her condemnation of the motherhood, they agree that motherhood should be an option, not a burden. The problem with statements such as *Mulieris Dignitatem* is although it is trying to accommodate current more liberated views of women, it defines women almost entirely in terms of motherhood. There is, therefore, an underlying patriarchal bias, which can guilt a woman into thinking that if she takes on work outside the family she is being a bad mother and wife.

Mary the Mother of Jesus. Why might this picture be criticised by Latin American feminist theologians?

(iii) Non-traditional families

Another concern of Catholic feminists is the way in which the Church presents Mary the Mother of Jesus as the model of human and womanly purity – as seen for example in *Mulieris Dignitatem*. In Latin America, where the figure of Mary is particularly popular, women there don't see her in these idealised terms but as the single working mother, coping with failure – for this is also the everyday reality of many Latin American Catholic women. Feminist Latin American theologians **Ivone Gebara** and **María Clara Bingemer** use this experience to highlight the false-consciousness perpetuated by the Church's emphasis on Mary's virginity as an ideal of sexual purity. Moreover, in the first century a young girl of marriageable age who was still a virgin was not a sign of virtue but failure when society depended on having children. For Latin American Catholic single parent families, Mary is a figure of inspiration, for despite her 'failure' she remains open to God and finds the spiritual strength to create and sustain her family.

Feminist Catholic theologians therefore seek to broaden and extend the Church's narrow view of family to be more inclusive and less judgemental. This doesn't mean it has to let go of the marriage ideal but it does mean broadening it out perhaps to include long-term committed cohabitation and possibly same-sex relationships.

Key persons

Ivone Gebara (1944–): Brazilian Roman Catholic nun and feminist theologian. In 1990 the Vatican forbad her to teach because of her radical views on abortion.

María Clara Bingemer (1949–): Brazilian Roman Catholic feminist theologian and academic.

Summary diagram: Gender and society

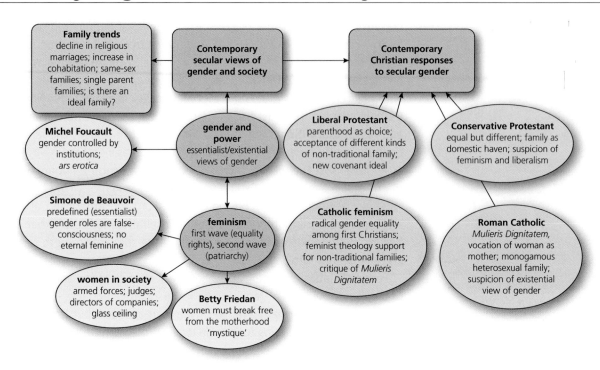

Family trends
decline in religious marriages; increase in cohabitation; same-sex families; single parent families; is there an ideal family?

Contemporary secular views of gender and society

Contemporary Christian responses to secular gender

Michel Foucault
gender controlled by institutions; *ars erotica*

gender and power
essentialist/existential views of gender

Liberal Protestant
parenthood as choice; acceptance of different kinds of non-traditional family; new covenant ideal

Conservative Protestant
equal but different; family as domestic haven; suspicion of feminism and liberalism

Simone de Beauvoir
predefined (essentialist) gender roles are false-consciousness; no eternal feminine

feminism
first wave (equality rights), second wave (patriarchy)

Catholic feminism
radical gender equality among first Christians; feminist theology support for non-traditional families; critique of *Mulieris Dignitatem*

Roman Catholic
Mulieris Dignitatem, vocation of woman as mother; monogamous heterosexual family; suspicion of existential view of gender

women in society
armed forces; judges; directors of companies; glass ceiling

Betty Friedan
women must break free from the motherhood 'mystique'

Revision advice

By the end of this chapter you should be able to outline and explain the contemporary social situation in terms of gender, types and diversity of families and the reasons for them. You should be able to explain different types of feminist analysis of society and the roles of women in particular. You should also be able to explain why the biblical view of the family is ambiguous and the ways in which different Christians have developed this ambiguity when considering the issues raised by gender and society today.

Can you give brief definitions of:
- *scientia sexualis*
- feminism
- intact family
- household rules
- patriarchal
- family as domestic haven?

Can you explain:
- Simone de Beauvoir's feminism
- the essentialist/existential view of gender
- New Testament household rules
- equal but different view of gender
- liberal Protestant inclusive view of family?

Can you give arguments for and against:
- the view that feminism has undermined the family
- whether women should be mothers
- blended families
- whether *Mulieris Dignitatem* presents a liberated view of women?

Sample question and guidance

'There is no such thing as an ideal Christian family.' Discuss.

There are many ways of approaching this question but the key is to focus on a particular idea and follow it through. You might argue that there is an ideal Christian family, which has its roots in the Bible, the order of creation and tradition. This view is supported by both Roman Catholicism and conservative Protestants. Your biblical examples might indicate that families should be heterosexual (the need for children), monogamous and in accordance to the parental duties of obligation as set out in household rules (refer to Ephesians – a prescribed text). Church tradition emphasises the 'equal but different' notion of gender difference (refer to *Mulieris Dignitatem* – a prescribed text) as this dignifies men and women. This view of the

family finds support in the evidence that without intact families society cannot function properly.

Your analysis should focus on the word 'ideal'. You might argue that the liberal Protestant notion of the family based on covenantal 'justice love' is much more realistic and closer to the ideal as established by Jesus in his radical approach to society of his own day. You might consider the 'order of nature' approach of conservative Protestants and Roman Catholics unjustly condemns many new social developments such as single parent, same-sex and blended families, which liberals are happy to accommodate in their broader notion of family. Your analysis should conclude with a reflection on the adequacies and inadequacies of the liberal Protestant position.

Further essay questions

Critically assess the view that man is 'the head of the wife' (Ephesians 5:22).

To what extent should Christians resist secular views of gender?

'Men and women are equal but different.' Discuss.

Going further

Simone de Beauvoir, *The Second Sex* (Vintage Classics, 1997). This is a classic text to be dipped into.

Betty Friedan, *The Feminine Mystique* (Penguin Classics, 2010). Read Chapter 5 for her critique of Freud and gender.

Robin Gill, ed., *The Cambridge Companion to Christian Ethics* (Cambridge University Press, 2001). There are two very helpful chapters on gender and the family which are well worth reading: Chapter 8 'Gender and Christian Ethics' by Lisa Sowle Cahill and Chapter 17 'World Family Trends' by Don Browning.

Neil Messer, *SCM Study Guide to Christian Ethics* (SCM Press, 2000). A very useful guide to Christian ethics. Read Chapter 8 on feminism and Christian ethics.

Rosemary Tong, *Feminist Thought* (Routledge, 2013). A very helpful introduction to many different types of feminisms. Read Chapter 1.

Other books discussed in this chapter are:

- *The Catechism of the Catholic Church* (Geoffrey Chapman, 1994).
- Schüssler Fiorenza, E. *In Memory of Her: A Feminist Reconstruction of Christian Origins* (second edition) (SCM Press, 1994).
- Foucault, M. *The History of Sexuality: The Will to Knowledge,* translation R. Hurley (Penguin, 1979).
- Rudy, K. *Sex and the Church: Gender, Homosexuality and the Transformation of Christian Ethics* (Beacon Press, 1998).

Chapter 14

Gender and theology

Chapter checklist

This chapter begins by considering why many feminists think that Christianity is the cause of sexism because of the Bible and its view of God. The views of two significant feminist theologians, Rosemary Radford Ruether and Mary Daly, are then presented to examine whether Christianity is sexist. Their views are then compared, contrasted and critiqued.

1 Introduction

Key question

Is Christianity essentially sexist?

Key term

Patriarchy Refers to a system of male-centred rule and describes societies and cultures where men and male values are given priority.

Religion in general (and Christianity in particular) is generally not well received by many feminists. For many feminists, Christianity is a cause of female oppression and even though elements of it may be seen to aid women, in essence Christianity is felt to reinforce traditional gender roles and the subservience of women to men.

There are two main reasons for this from a secular feminist perspective.
- **The Bible**. If taken as a whole, the Bible regards women as the weaker sex and the cause of social problems. The Bible reinforces **patriarchy**.
- **God**. The God-human relationship creates a master-slave morality, which in turn justifies a male-female patriarchal hierarchy that diminishes the value of women by making women subservient to men. The role of the institutionalised Church has been to reinforce the master-slave, male-female relationship.

Christian feminist theologians, however, disagree. Far from seeing Christianity as diminishing women (and men) they consider that it is a source of spiritual and social liberation. Their task is to offer convincing solutions to the two challenges.

Key question

Can God and the Bible be reinterpreted in ways that meet the needs of contemporary feminism?

2 God, the Bible and feminism

Background

Key person

Margaret Atwood (1939–): a Canadian novelist and poet. *The Handmaid's Tale* (1985) is set in a totalitarian post-feminist state and has been made into a film (1990) and opera (2000). Her other novels include *Cat's Eye* (1988) and most recently *Hag-Seed* (2016).

In **Margaret Atwood**'s powerful novel *The Handmaid's Tale* (1985) she describes a dystopia where, sometime in the near future, after a nuclear war between two superpowers, the new society which emerges has been taken over by an ultra-conservative religious regime keen to cleanse society of all its old liberal values. It blames the collapse of family values on feminism and a failure to maintain biblical values: women and men are defined in accordance within fixed hierarchical gender roles as they correspond to certain figures the Bible.

For example, there are handmaids like Bilah (see Genesis 30:3) whose sole role it is to provide children for childless couples; there are wives who just run the households for their husbands (see Ephesians 5:22); Marthas are servants whose only purpose is to do housework (see Luke 10:40); Jezebels are prostitutes (see 2 Kings 9:30).

This is a fundamentally patriarchal dystopia, which values hierarchy and order – even men are defined and ordered according to their function. The notion of God is used by the state to keep the people under control as the all-seeing eye that watches everyone and ensures they keep to their pre-designated roles.

Key term

Dystopia A future frightening and nightmarish society (in contrast to a utopia which is a future perfect society). Dystopias are used by writers as warnings about where a present society might be heading.

Atwood's well-known novel *The Handmaid's Tale* (see background box) describes a rigidly patriarchal society reinforced by state religion – a warning about what happens when a fundamentalist religious ideology is allowed to develop unchecked. For those who are critical of Christianity, Atwood's **dystopia** is more than mere fiction; as a major cause of sexism it justifies why Christianity should be excluded in gender reforms.

The radical post-Christian feminist Mary Daly neatly summarises the view of many feminists when she says:

> *It might be interesting to speculate upon the probable length of a 'depatriarchalised Bible'. Perhaps there would be enough salvageable material to comprise an interesting pamphlet.*

Mary Daly, *Beyond God the Father*, 1986, page 205

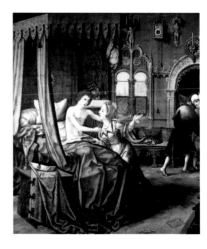

Read 2 Samuel 13:1–22, the story of the rape of Tamar by her brother Amnon. What purpose does this biblical story serve?

(a) The problem with God

Some secular feminists consider that belief in a God who is totally different from the world is a major cause of sexism. This is because a belief in a transcendent creator God creates a master-slave relationship, which in turn reinforces the patriarchal mindset of a male (master)-female (slave) hierarchy.

(b) Feminist theologies

There are many different feminist theologies just as there are different forms of non-religious feminisms. Feminist theologians share many of the same concerns as secular feminists but on the whole they do not reject the Bible as a source of inspiration or the existence of God as a necessary aspect of human spiritual existence.

Feminist theologians consider that it is not Christianity which is at fault but secular feminism which is deficient; for without material and spiritual liberation neither women nor men can live full human lives. The two major secular feminist objections to Christianity outlined above are constant challenges to feminist theologians but as difficult as they are they are they not necessarily insuperable; many feminist theologians think they can offer coherent responses.

The two theologians, Mary Daly and Rosemary Radford Ruether, who we are now going to consider, present two very different responses to these secular feminist challenges.

Both Ruether and Daly share the view that society and its relationship to nature urgently require the rejection of patriarchy with a transformed spirituality; but in all other respects they are very different.

Key question

Is a belief in God a major cause of sexism?

Read pages 229–31 on the different types of secular feminisms.

3 Rosemary Radford Ruether

Praxis means ideas as action. See pages 287 and 290.

Rosemary Radford Ruether is a Roman Catholic feminist liberation theologian. She argues that the insights of feminism provide the necessary means for reinvigorating Christian spirituality and praxis.

Key term

Episcopalian Church The name of the Anglican Church (which includes the Church of England) in the USA.

Key person

Rosemary Radford Ruether (1936–): born in 1936 in St Paul, Minnesota, USA. She was brought up as a Roman Catholic, although her father was a member of the **Episcopalian Church**. Ruether says her mother offered her critical but positive views of Roman Catholicism. In 1954 she attended Scripps College, Claremont, California where she studied classics before moving on to study the history of religions. Her interest in historical and sociological development of religions was to be a foundation of her later feminist theology and her belief that religions cannot claim exclusive truths about the spiritual life.

→

Women-Church Founded in 1983 after a conference in Chicago. It has no permanent leadership or central organisation but is composed of local churches or 'base communities' in affiliation with one another. These communities complement the main Protestant and Catholic Churches which women may belong to while giving them the moral and spiritual support to transform them.

After graduating she become involved in the civil rights movement in the 1960s and in 1965 joined the Delta Ministry in Mississippi. The two encounters helped form her view that theology must emerge from the historical experiences of oppression and from the 'underside of history'. As a white middle-class woman, Ruether realised that a theology which begins with the historical and material conditions of millions of marginalised people challenged her own preconceptions of God and what she calls the 'redemptive transformation of creation'. Her theological aim is to transform all human relationships with each other and with nature. In 1983 she helped to found the **Women-Church** and she has long been an advocate of women's ordained ministry in the Catholic Church.

From 1966–76 Ruether taught at Howard University, Washington DC, School of Religion where she developed her theology against the background of the African-American struggle. Subsequently she taught at the Pacific School of Religion, the Graduate Theological Union and Garrett-Evangelical Theological Seminary. She has written many influential books including *Sexism and God-Talk: Towards a Feminist Theology* (1983), *Goddesses and the Divine Feminine: A Western Religious History* (2005) and an autobiography *My Quests for Hope and Meaning* (2013).

Key question

Why might monotheist religions tend to reinforce patriarchy?

(a) Monotheism and Goddess theology

Ruether argues that in order to understand how Christian theology has developed its oppressive patriarchy, it is first necessary to go back to earlier times when this was not the case. She is particularly struck by how polytheistic religions are far less sexist and patriarchal than monotheist religions. Strict monotheism:

- tends to reinforce a patriarchal hierarchy where the single (male) God exerts authority over nature and the world
- justifies male superiority over women as men consider this to be part of the God-given hierarchy of nature.

(i) The Goddess

Ruether's argument is that the roots of Judaism from which Christianity developed were not strictly monotheistic and God was far less male orientated. Although Judaism is a monotheistic religion it retained its respect for nature by maintaining the idea of the Goddess as the source of life into its worship and relationship with God.

For example, in a passage from the Prophet Isaiah God is depicted as the mother Goddess going through the pain of childbirth. Isaiah uses the mother analogy as a means of expressing God's suffering love for Israelite people because of their faithlessness.

Key quote

For a long time I have held my peace,
I have kept still and restrained myself;
now I will cry out like a woman in labour,
I will gasp and pant.

Isaiah 42:14

(ii) God as the female wisdom principle

Another strand in monotheism where the femaleness of God is retained is in what is known as wisdom. In the ancient world wisdom was universally understood to be the divine source of knowledge and life. She is always presented in female terms; the Hebrew word for wisdom is *hokhmah* and in Greek it is *sophia* – both feminine words. So, we can see again why ancient Judaism did not support a strict monotheism.

Although wisdom plays an important role in many books of the Old Testament, it is the late book of **The Wisdom of Solomon** where God's wisdom is particularly well developed. Here she is described as 'a breath of the power of God' and a 'reflection of his eternal light' (Wisdom 7:25). She is the knowable and relational aspect of God; she is also described as King Solomon's bride (Wisdom 8:2) because when God asked King Solomon what he most desired, the king asked for wisdom.

> ### Key quote
>
> For wisdom is more mobile than any motion;
> because of her pureness she pervades and penetrates all things.
> For she is a breath of the power of God,
> and a pure emanation of the glory of the Almighty;
> therefore nothing defiled gains entrance into her.
> For she is a reflection of eternal light,
> a spotless mirror of the working of God.
>
> The Wisdom of Solomon 7:24–26

Having established that Judaism does not have a strict monotheism, Ruether goes on to show that Christianity preserves the feminine aspect of God in the **incarnation** and the Trinity.

Many of the early Christians immediately saw the connection between the female *sophia* as expressed in The Wisdom of Solomon and Jesus Christ. Presenting Jesus as divine wisdom explained his relationship to God, his identity on earth and the source of his teaching. St Paul, for example, says, 'we proclaim Christ crucified ... to those who are called, both Jews and Greeks, Christ the power of God and the wisdom of God' (1 Corinthians 1:23–24) and the author of John's Gospel presents Christ as 'eternal wisdom' using a masculine Greek equivalent word to *sophia*, *logos* (meaning 'word') because Jesus was male. As *logos*, God created the universe (John 1:1–3) and then was incarnated in the form of Jesus (John 1:14).

In addition, the Holy Spirit is also depicted in *sophia* terms as the immanent, relational aspect of God. Therefore, in the Christian notion of God as Trinity, there is no strict male/female division: the Son is wisdom/*logos* and the Holy Spirit is wisdom/*sophia*. Ruether's claim is that the Trinity is a relational and gender-inclusive spiritual experience.

Yet, despite all this Biblical evidence, Christianity has ignored the female/Goddess aspect of God and promoted its strict (male) monotheism. Ruether's argument is that there is ample evidence to tackle sexism in the Church not only by reshaping the way Christians think of God but also in rethinking its organisation.

> ### Key term
>
> **The Wisdom of Solomon**
> Written in the late second century BC. It is found in the Greek version of the Old Testament/Hebrew Bible called the Septuagint and in the deuterocanon (Catholic) or apocrypha (Protestant) of the Christian Bible.

> ### Key question
>
> Is Ruether right to claim that Jesus was the incarnation of the feminine wisdom principle?

> ### Key term
>
> **Incarnation** Literally means 'to become flesh'. The Christian doctrine of the incarnation is that God as *logos* took on human form in the person of Jesus.

(iii) New antipatriarchal communities

One of Ruether's major concerns is that many Churches have lost their radical egalitarian roots. Her argument is that there is plenty of historical evidence to give the Churches the authority they need to change.

Her argument is that Jesus' relationship to God was based on trust and respect. He called God, *Abba*, the Hebrew for father or daddy and not sir or lord. Early Christians used this as a model for their relationships. In the new Christian communities traditional family ties are challenged and all its members are brothers and sisters living as friends; there are no masters and servants. Jesus' words in John's Gospel are foundational for this radically new way of life:

> *You are my friends if you do what I command you. I do not call you servants any longer, because the servant does not know what the master is doing; but I have called you friends, because I have made known to you everything that I have heard from my Father.*
>
> John 15:14–15

But despite this, the language of God the Father has often become a justification for patriarchy rather than a challenge to it, especially once Christianity ceased to represent an alternative way of life and became mainstream. Throughout Christian history there have always been small radical groups who have protested against the patriarchal mainstream. The basic Christian command should be, 'obey God, not men!'; Ruether's involvement in the Women's Church movement is one way of addressing the present situation.

(b) The apophatic path and inclusive language

One criticism that is often made of feminist theology is that using feminine language to address God is as sexist and alienating as patriarchal language. It also assumes that there is a distinct or essentialist female-gendered experience. But as we have seen in the previous chapter, essentialist ideas of gender are highly controversial. Second, the tendency by theologians is to use gendered male language to emphasise God's **transcendence** and female-gendered language to focus on God's **immanence** but it limits what God is to purely gendered terms.

However, as God is infinite and as human language can only refer to finite things, then all theological language referring to God must be based on the **apophatic** assumption that God is beyond language and in that sense beyond gender.

Nevertheless, gendered language may act as analogies and symbols of how humans experience God. Ruether concludes that it is true to say that God/ess is by analogy as much he/she as he is *not* he/she. Feminist theology is not claiming exclusive female-gendered language about God/ess but rather warning against retaining only male and patriarchal language:

> *Most of all, images of God/ess must be transformative, pointing us back to our authentic potential and forward to new redeemed possibilities... Adding an image of God/ess as loving nurturing mother, mediating the power of the strong, sovereign father, is insufficient.*

Rosemary Radford Ruether, *Sexism and God-Talk*, 1983, page 59

Key quotes

Because God is our king, we need obey no human kings. Because God is our parent, we are liberated from dependence on patriarchal authority.
Rosemary Radford Ruether, *Sexism and God-Talk*, 1983, page 55

The radical meaning of *Abba* for God is lost in translation and interpretation.
Rosemary Radford Ruether, *Sexism and God-Talk*, 1983, page 56

Key question

Should the Christian God be presented in female terms?

Key terms

Transcendence and **immanence**
When applied to God these terms refer to his existence apart and beyond the material world (transcendence) and yet also existing and participating in the material universe (immanence).

Apophatic: the method of referring to God by what he is not, because he is beyond all human language. Read pages 44–8 for an explanation in more detail.

Key question

Can a male saviour save women?

Key question

How and why has sexism and patriarchy developed in mainstream Christianity?

(c) Can a male saviour save women?

The question, 'can a male saviour save women?' is posed by Ruether as the heading to Chapter 5 of *Sexism and God-Talk*. This chapter builds on many of the ideas we have looked at already and broadens out her thesis that while Christianity offers a distinctive understanding of God, it is by no means exclusive. In fact, it is one of Christianity's strengths that many of its ideas are to be found in other non-Christian religious, philosophical traditions and experiences. Yet, the presentation of traditional Christianity as developed in the established Churches has often been to exclude these 'non-Christian' elements and to control what is and what is not considered to be truth. It is these church traditions that support a male-centred and patriarchal version of Christianity.

(i) No, a male saviour cannot save women

The reasons why Ruether argues that Jesus Christ or Christianity cannot save women are two-fold:

- First, Jesus Christ is not only historically male but as the Word or *Logos* of God he is also the perfect example of what it means to be human, which means being male. For a woman to be saved would mean denying the kind of person she is and adapting herself to a male mindset.
- Second, when Christianity was adopted as the official religion of the Roman Empire in 380AD it actively promoted Jesus the triumphal 'king' who would return to bring in his new kingdom. This very male presentation of Jesus has serious implications for women. The Church justified only having male Church officials who could represent Christ in its organisation; women could only achieve salvation through the control of men.

Is it right that the Roman Catholic Church only allows men to be ordained as priests?

Even today the Catholic Church is still reluctant to ordain women to the ministry. For centuries Aquinas' teaching that women are 'misbegotten' or distorted men was used by the Church to explain why God as '*Logos*' couldn't have been incarnated as a 'defective' woman but only as a perfect man. This in turn justifies the argument against women's ordination. For example, in the Declaration *Inter Insigniores* (1976) the Pope stated that as 'there must be a "natural resemblance" which exists between Christ and his minister', then women cannot become members of the ordained ministry.

> The same natural resemblance is required for persons as for things: when Christ's role in the Eucharist is to be expressed sacramentally, there would not be this 'natural resemblance' which must exist between Christ and his minister if the role of Christ were not taken by a man: in such a case it would be difficult to see in the minister the image of Christ. For Christ himself was and remains a man.
>
> *Inter Insigniores*, 'On the Question of Admission of Women to Ministerial Priesthood' section 5

Ruether's conclusion is that traditional Christianity is sexist and cannot be a means of salvation or liberation for women.

(ii) Yes, a male saviour can save women

There is a counter argument, also made by Ruether, that Christian salvation or liberation for women is possible once its ancient and more radical tradition is rediscovered.

First, the death and resurrection of Christ is especially significant in this respect as it touches on a very basic human experience of nature in the annual cycle of the death of the old year and birth of the new. In the ancient world this was often represented as the death of the kingly god of vegetation who was raised to new life by the Goddess. Far from undermining Christianity, Ruether argues that because this idea is so deeply ingrained into the human psyche, it gives the Christian story particular power and validity.

Second, Jesus' role as messiah deliberately challenged the warrior-king expectation of his day. His teaching on the Kingdom of God was not about having worldly power but gaining justice and dignity for the marginalised. The Kingdom is not only a reward after death but healing and restoring all human relationships now.

Third, the Holy Spirit continues the work begun in Jesus' lifetime by healing relationships and challenging human institutions which are more concerned with their own power. Ruether gives many examples of Christian communities and teachers who resisted the tendency to make their Christologies conform to mainstream patriarchal society and its practices. For example:

- The story of Pentecost (Acts 2:1–41) describes how after Jesus' ascension, the Spirit was poured out on to men and women as a sign of a new period of history. Pentecost has inspired some subsequent Christian groups to consider the historical Jesus as less important than the Spirit, which represents God's spiritual presence and works to transform the world spiritually and materially.
- The **Shakers**, for example, believe that women are particularly receptive to the Holy Spirit and therefore should play essential roles in Christian leadership in the preparation for Christ's Second Coming.

Ruether argues that these Christian movements (such as the Shakers) and their Christologies have done more than merely feminise God. Their notions of salvation tackle the weaknesses of all humans, so that is why a male saviour in a Spirit-filled sense can save women.

(d) Christ the liberator

In conclusion, Ruether acknowledges that there is no clear 'yes' as to whether a male saviour can save women. The problem is that the New Testament offers various Christologies and differing views as to what salvation is. It may be that for some women the fact that Jesus is male may always be a problem. But Ruether argues that once we understand how Christianity developed then the patriarchal elements of the New Testament and later Christianity can be removed.

When this done, what is revealed is Jesus the liberator who challenged the social, religious and spiritual assumptions of his own day for both women and men. That is why Jesus' maleness is ultimately not relevant. Ruether concludes:

Key quote

I will pour out my Spirit upon all flesh,

and your sons and your daughters shall prophesy...

Even upon my slaves, both men and women.

Acts of the Apostles 2:17–18

Key persons

Shakers: a Christian group founded in the eighteenth century in England, though many moved to the USA; there are Shaker communities today. They believe that the Holy Spirit continues to develop Jesus' teaching and provides new revelations. They believe women are particularly receptive to the Holy Spirit and therefore should play essential roles in Christian leadership in the preparation for Christ's Second Coming.

Jesus as liberator calls for a renunciation, a dissolution, of the web of status relationships by which societies have defined privilege and deprivation... Theologically speaking, then, we might say that the maleness of Jesus has no ultimate significance.

Rosemary Radford Ruether, *Sexism and God-Talk*, 1983, page 115

4 Mary Daly

Mary Daly was originally a Roman Catholic theologian, but as a radical feminist she argued that women must abandon Christianity for a **post-Christian** spirituality.

Key person

Mary Daly (1928–2010): Daly grew up in an Irish Catholic family in Schenectady, New York. She attended the College of St Rose in Albany, New York where she attempted to study Catholic philosophy but was unable to do so as this was thought unsuitable for a woman. After obtaining an MA in English in 1952 she  attended St Mary's College, Notre Dame, Indiana, where she completed a PhD in Thomist theology only to find it was regarded as a second rate 'women's degree' by the Catholic universities. Unable to study for another doctorate at Catholic universities in the USA, she travelled to Switzerland in 1959 and completed two PhDs, the first in theology and the second in philosophy at the University of Fribourg. On her return to the USA she took a teaching position at the Jesuit-run Boston College, where she was to remain all her academic career.

For more on **Simone de Beauvoir**, see page 230.

The first sign of Daly's critical view of the Church was marked by the publication of *The Church and the Second Sex* in 1968 – a book which owed much to Simone de Beauvoir.

Her aim here was to draw attention to the marginalisation of women in the Church in the hope that the Church authorities would reform their organisation and theology. The result was that the university tried to terminate her contract but the students protested and Daly was given promotion and a permanent teaching position.

From that moment on, Daly become more convinced that the Catholic Church in particular and Christianity in general could not be reformed because of its inherent sexism and patriarchy. The decisive moment was in 1971 in the Harvard Memorial Chapel when in her sermon she encouraged men and women to leave the Church and Christianity. Her new philosophical and theological position was stated in her landmark book *Beyond God the Father* (1973) where she attacked the Church as being the chief source of women's abuse.

Daly subsequently developed the view that in earlier times women had achieved a spiritual relationship with nature which patriarchal cultures had destroyed using God as a justification. Although critical of Nietzsche (see below), she shared his love of reusing and rediscovering lost or 'archaic' meanings of words as a means of uncovering this hidden relationship with the elemental power of nature. Daly used archaic language to shift consciousness and give women the tools to stand outside the current culture as outsiders. In her book *Gyn/Ecology: The Metaethics of Radical Feminism* (1978) she showed how women as 'hags' are to 'exorcise' the spirit of patriarchy and seek instead the spiritual forces of nature. She describes herself as 'a traveller' seeking out new forms of living beyond patriarchy.

The extent of her new vocabulary necessitated her own dictionary, which she published in 1987 called *Websters' First New Intergalactic Wickedary of the English Language*. Her new language also established a new code of language, chants and incantations designed to free radical feminists from patriarchy and to aid in their communication with 'be-ing', the on-going processes of nature.

The end of her academic career in 1999 was caused when she apparently refused to allow male students to attend her lectures. She was dismissed from her lectureship and spent the rest of her life in her home. She published her intellectual autobiography, *Outercourse: the Be-Dazzling Voyage* in 1992, which charts the various stages (or 'galaxies') and future development of radical feminism from the present patriarchal age to a new 'Amazon' age.

Although Daly is often presented merely as radical feminist and anti-religion, her own life-story indicates that what she really rejected was the formal nature of religion as an institution, along with its doctrines and forms of control. According to Daly, central to the Church's means of power is the belief in and doctrines about God. As these doctrines have been developed by men to favour men, then Daly argues that it is not sufficient to present God in female terms because a female version of God would still be male in essence. Daly is famous for saying, 'if God is male then the male is God'. For Daly, what is required is a **transvaluation** of the whole of Christianity.

(a) Transvaluation

> **Key person**
>
> **Frederich Nietzsche** (1844–1900): a German philosopher, poet and classical scholar. He was appointed professor at Basel at the very young age of 24 but suffered a mental breakdown aged 44 from which he never fully recovered. His philosophy challenges all absolute cultures and objective systems of thought in favour of what he called perspectivism. He published many influential books including *Thus Spoke Zarathustra* (1883).

Daly's aim in *Beyond God the Father* has something in common with the nineteenth-century philosopher **Frederich Nietzsche**'s concern that to deliver humans from their self-imposed cultural imprisonment requires

> **Key question**
>
> What are the implications for Christianity 'if God is male then the male is God'? (Mary Daly)

> **Key term**
>
> **Transvaluation** The process of re-evaluating and transforming something by a new standard or set of values.

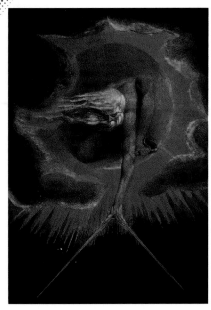

How is God to be transvaluated?

transvaluation – a complete re-evaluation of all existing values. Daly not only borrows from Nietzsche some of his language but also his notion that to enter into this new era of human consciousness then everything which ensures the existence of the present culture must be overturned. Both Nietzsche and Daly envisage that this new era will not be possible without the death of God and Christianity.

Daly uses the following ideas of Nietzsche:

- **Two aspects of human nature**. The two conflicting sides of human nature are the Apollonian or passive self and the Dionysian or the energetic and creative self. Daly thinks only women can be Dionysian.
- **The Apollonian veil**. The Apollonian veil is created when humans falsely create ideas that they then believe are true which alienate them from their naturally creative and imaginative selves. Daly argues that only women have the ability to remove these false ideas.
- **Becoming and be-ing**. Being human is a creative on-going process, there is no perfect end point at which one can say this is what it means to be human because there is no objective creator God. Daly argues that only women understand the creative process of 'be-ing'. 'Be-ing' as the spiritual process of living completely replaces any idea of an objective God in Daly's philosophy.

(b) Beyond God the Father

Although Daly shares many of Nietzsche's ideas of transvaluation she disagrees on one fundamental point: Nietzsche's transvaluation of God merely substituted God the Father with man the god, Nietzsche's Dionysian *Übermensch* or overman (or superman). This indicates, Daly argues, how deeply engrained patriarchy is, so much so that even the great Nietzsche remained blind to the Apollonian veil which he thought he was removing. Ironically as Nietzsche often termed Apollonian values 'feminine', he is himself unwittingly supporting a patriarchal view of society. Therefore, as men have failed to transvaluate the 'feminine' patriarchy, Daly's vision is that it is only women who will be able to complete the task.

> *Nietzsche, the prophet whose prophecy was short circuited by his own misogynism wanted to transvaluate Judeo-Christian morality, but in fact it is women who will confront patriarchal morality as patriarchal. It is radical feminism that can unveil the 'feminine' ethic.*

Mary Daly, *Beyond God the Father*, 1986, page 102

The transvaluation of all phallic values (Daly's equivalent term for patriarchal values) begins therefore with a complete annihilation or 'castration' of God. This means the abolition of the word God and all associated ideas. As she says, this is not the same as rationally arguing for the non-existence of God, but something deeper in which the old God is replaced with authentic human existence.

> *If God is male then the male is God. The divine patriarch castrates women as long as he is allowed to live on in the human imagination. The process of cutting away the supreme phallus can hardly be a merely 'rational' affair.*

Mary Daly, *Beyond God the Father*, 1986, page 19

Daly does not consider herself an atheist as atheists still retain an idea of God, nor does she consider herself an agnostic as the agnostic lacks convincing knowledge of God. For Daly 'be-ing' replaces God; be-ing is a spiritual process of the continual discovery of the richness of nature.

(c) New language and be-ing

> ... women will have to assume the burden of castrating the phallic ethic (which 'appears' as a feminine ethic or a passive ethic) by calling forth out of our experience a new naming in the realm of morality. To this it will be necessary to understand the dynamics of the false naming in the realm of ethics that has been encased in patriarchy's definitions of good and evil.
>
> Mary Daly, *Beyond God the Father*, 1986, page 106

The process of transvaluation is the conscious and radical re-invention of language. Daly's often provocative use of old vocabulary used in new ways is to give women the means to articulate their vision of a new world entirely free from all forms of patriarchy. The patriarchal world is characterised by two forms, the Foreground and Background.

- **Foreground** is the world dominated by patriarchial Apollonian values. It is a false world, which is sucking the life-force out of women and nature. She calls its male leaders 'snools'; female snools are 'hench-women' who gain their power from snools.
- **Background** existence is the world of women and true be-ing. Women have become used to living in the shadow of men but the Background is older, more energetic and is closer to the reality of be-ing itself.

Archaic or old-fashioned language is a means of re-connecting women with their ancient relationship with nature or be-ing. Some of the old-fashioned words transvaluated by Daly were patriarchal Foreground 'false naming' words designed to disempower women, such as **hag**, **crone**, **nag** and witch but as Background words they have become empowering terms with the power to exorcise (the role of the witch) and lead to ecstasy (spiritual freedom).

As be-ing is not static, women are also **spinsters** 'spinning' new meanings/history; they are 'courageous explorers' of new non-patriarchal ways of living.

(d) The Most Unholy Trinity: abuse and the failure of Christianity

Daly is outspoken in her claim that a root cause of western society's abuse of women is Christianity. We have seen earlier that God of Christianity justifies patriarchal values and ways of thinking for 'if God is male then the male is God'. But she goes further. In *Gyn/Ecology* (1979) she argues that all Christianity stands for is its desire to destroy women and elevate male values. She considers Christianity as a root cause of women's abuse over the centuries.

For example, she sees the symbol of Jesus' death on the cross as an expression of male enjoyment of pain, torture and sexual dominance over women. Another failure of Christianity is the way in which the

---

Key question

Is it only women who can develop a genuine spirituality?

Key quote

The liberation of language is rooted in the liberation of ourselves.
Mary Daly, *Beyond God the Father*, 1986, page 6

Key terms

Hag An ugly old woman, a witch or sorceress.
Crone Also means hag as well as an ugly old wise woman.
Nag A constantly nagging old woman.
Spinster A term which originally referred to an unmarried girl or woman who worked by spinning wool. It has now taken on a negative connotation to refer to a woman who is unmarriageable. In Daly's usage it is the unique power women have to be part of the spiritual process of be-ing.

Key question

Is Christianity a significant reason for the abuse of women?

Key quote

If God is male then the male is God.
Mary Daly, *Beyond God the Father*, 1986, page 19

Catholic Church in particular has presented the Virgin Mary, as a symbol of purity and womanhood. But the reality, Daly argues, is that she is a passive 'hollow eggshell', the 'Total Rape Victim' who has been forcefully impregnated by God (*Gyn/Ecology*, page 84) to bear the Son of God. The image of the Virgin Mary has legitimised the abuse of women by the Church and society for centuries.

(i) The Most Unholy Trinity

In developing her claim that the Christian God and the Church is the chief cause of women's abuse, Daly parodies the central notion of God as the Trinity by substituting its three Persons, Father, Son and Holy Spirit, with three male symbols of power which she considers that the Church has promoted. 'The Most Unholy Trinity of Rape, Genocide and War is a logical expression of phallocentric power' (*Beyond God the Father*, page 122). The Most Unholy Trinity is the cause of:

- **Rape**. A phallocentric 'rape culture' is one based on power and not on true community. Rape is both literal and metaphorical. In its metaphorical sense, Christianity has been a major reason why women have been abused and treated as passive objects.
- **Genocide**. A rape culture represents an alienated society where one group destroys another, just as one race murders and destroys another. Daly argues that the Catholic Church also commits genocide when it forces women to have unwanted children as a result of rape because of its anti-abortion teaching. It also promotes genocide in its support of war and the slaughter of innocent citizens.
- **War**. War symbolises the very worst of Apollonian values, which have been praised by the Church. The process of 'un-veiling' shows just how inconsistent moral theologians (and politicians) are when they defend war to ensure justice yet condemn other compassionate forms of killing such as abortion and euthanasia.

(ii) Friendship and lesbianism

On the issue of sexuality, Daly argues that true friendship can only be lesbian. She is deeply critical of forms of lesbianism which imitate male characteristics (e.g. 'butch' lesbianism). In *Beyond God the Father,* the issue of whether radical feminists are lesbians or not is a 'pseudo problem' (page 126). For Daly, the notion of homosexuality is another example of patriarchal idea, which the Church has developed because it has a clear idea of male and female difference.

However, Daly believes that biological difference is not destiny; all relationships are valid if they work within the Holy Whole Trinity of radical feminist values.

(iii) Neither male nor female

Often Christians have claimed that despite Daly's accusation that as God is male then the male is God, Jesus' teaching opened up a vision of a new transformed society in which gender distinction would disappear. St Paul, for example, taught that, 'there is neither male or female; for all of you are one in Christ Jesus' (Galatians 3:28). But Daly considers that this is a feeble attempt to make Christianity palatable. St Paul never imagined that

Key quote

The circle of destruction generated by the Most Unholy Trinity and reflected in the Unwhole Trinitarian symbol of Christianity will be broken when women, who are by patriarchal definition objects of rape, externalize and internalize a new self-definition whose compelling power is rooted in the power of being. The casting out of the demonic Trinities is be-coming.
Mary Daly, *Beyond God the Father*, 1986, page 122

gender would become irrelevant because as Christ was male, then women would have to become like men. As we have seen, for Daly the Church is a living example of how true this is.

(e) Spinning: a new spirituality

Key question

Is it only women who can develop a genuine spirituality?

Daly is certain that radical feminism will triumph and overcome all the last vestiges of post-Christianity society and create what she calls the 'cosmic tapestry' comprising the Most Holy Whole Trinity of power, justice and love. Unlike other radical feminists, Daly's vision is a deeply spiritual one, which unites women with the elemental forces of nature. It will not be easy, for just as nature can suffer from the ravages of human exploitation, women also experience the same 'earthquake' moments of patriarchy. She describes women's spiritual journey using the traditional tasks performed by women as spinners or spinsters. But whereas today 'spinster' has a negative meaning of a lonely single woman, for Daly spinster describes women working together (as they would have done in the past as spinners), creating from nature cloth. The way of life which women are now spinning is transformed spirituality which is free from Christian patriarchy and which she hopes will also eventually transvaluate all of society.

5 A comparison of Ruether's and Daly's feminist theologies

Key question

Can Christianity be changed to meet the challenges of feminism or should it be abandoned?

(a) Common ground

Ruether and Daly share the view that traditional Christianity is a source of sexism but that there is a spirituality which feminism draws attention to. This may be summarised as follows:

- **Goddess**. Both agree that calling God 'she' is not enough because adding a female pronoun doesn't fundamentally alter the patriarchal perception of the divine.
- **Ecology**. Both agree that only feminism adequately deals with human relationship and the environment. Patriarchy assumes a hierarchical dominance over nature which feminism challenges.
- **Praxis**. Both argue that the purpose of feminist theology should be to transform society and its relationship with nature. Both consider women have a unique role to play in the transformation.

(b) Differences

Ruether and Daly disagree over whether Christianity can be reformed. Some of their main differences include:

- **God**. Whereas Ruether retains the existence of God who can be known as Spirit and Wisdom, Daly rejects the existence of God and replaces him with nature.
- **Separatism/co-operation of men and women**. Whereas Ruether agrees with Daly's radical feminism that there is sometimes a good reason for women to operate separately from men, ultimately she considers there is no advantage to lesbian separatism. Daly disagrees; only women have the sensitivity to transform the world.
- **Goddess/God**. Daly completely rejects the notion that God is female/male and that being 'in Christ' (i.e. being a Christian) there is 'neither male nor female' because patriarchy is too strong ever to do this

justice. Ruether, on the other hand, considers the experience of God in female/male terms is ancient and preserved in Christianity.

- **Church**. Daly rejects the Catholic Church because it is fundamentally sexist and patriarchal. Ruether, though, argues that although the Church is sexist, it can be reformed – the Bible, tradition and reason provide sufficient evidence to do so.

(c) Criticism

There are many feminist theologians who take less radical approaches to the challenges of secular feminisms than Ruether and Daly but between them Ruether and Daly cover many of the key issues which continue to be debated today.

(i) Critique of Ruether

One of the greatest strengths of Ruether's feminist theology is that her theology is inclusive. She does not see herself in competition with other religions, with secular feminists or with men: her aim is to integrate and respect them all. As we have seen, the Spirit/Wisdom is not unique to Christianity – although she considers it to be expressed clearly in the life of Christ, her vision is that the Spirit is the means by which society and nature can live in harmony.

Many argue that Ruether's theology is flawed:

- **Church tradition**. Although Ruether is a Catholic and wishes to reform the Church, many consider that she goes too far. She does this in various ways. First, she makes Jesus too political and revolutionary. Second, she is very selective about which passages she chooses from the Bible and often refers to very minor and discredited movements (such as the Shakers) outside mainstream Christianity.
- **God's sovereignty**. By including 'Goddess' language and experience from religions outside Christianity, Ruether has compromised the unity and sovereignty of God.
- **Male/female difference**. Catholic teaching is that men and women are equal but different. The New Testament teaches that the natural and God-ordered relationship of men and women is different – women's vocation is to be mothers in imitation of Mary the Mother of Jesus. Ruether's theology confuses and disregards this natural order.

(ii) Critique of Daly

Although many Christians and non-Christians find Daly's ideas obscure and alienating – particularly her separatist approach to men and her bizarre use of language – there are others who find that by treating her prophetic language symbolically they gain particular insight into the nature of human relationships and society's deep-seated flaws. Far from rejecting Christianity, Daly helps renew the Christian vision of humanity's relationship with the world and God. For these reasons Ruether is able to say about Daly:

> By reconnecting Daly's call for exorcism and ecstasy with an all-embracing love and concern for women and men across many races, classes, and cultures, **Cassandra's** speech might be deciphered and heard as good news for a growing society.

Rosemary Radford Ruether, *Women and Redemption*, 1998, page 221

Rosemary Radford Ruether, *Women and Redemption*, 1998, page 221

Key quote

...we seek an ecological society in which human and nonhuman ecological systems have been integrated into harmonious and mutually supportive, rather than antagonistic, relations.

Rosemary Radford Ruether, *Sexism and God-Talk*, 1983, page 195

Key term

Cassandra The daughter of King Priam in ancient Greek mythology. She was given the gift of prophecy but was cursed by not being believed when she prophesised. She is often used by feminist scholars as a metaphor of women who speak the truth but are not taken seriously.

3 Developments in Christian thought

Many feminists consider Daly's feminist thought is deeply flawed because it is too:

■ **Exclusive**. She has fallen into her own trap by alienating many women who do not conform to her views. Her vision of the new elect is implicitly aimed at white, lesbian, professional and western women. She has not included women of different ethnicities, poor women, those of different classes and different sexualities (including heterosexual women).

■ **Narrow**. Despite her call for a wider understanding of spirituality she is very dismissive of those who find spiritual liberation in Buddhism, Hinduism, Christianity and Judaism – she places these in the foreground (as snools) and labels them 'totally demonic'.

■ **Irrational**. Despite her brilliant and imaginative insights, her demonisation of men as the cause of 'rape culture' is not the view that many feminists have of men. Furthermore, in demonising men she alienates many men (and women) who might share her views of human relationships, spirituality and nature.

Revision advice

By the end of this chapter you should be able to explain why many secular feminists often find Christianity problematic in achieving women's liberation because of the inherent patriarchy of the Bible. You should be able to explain the two different ways in which Ruether and Daly have responded to the challenges of secular feminism, i.e. Radford's female/male inclusive feminist theology and Daly's radical transvaluated post-Christian theology. You should be able to compare and contrast their theologies.

Can you give brief definitions of:
● patriarchy
● Women-Church
● incarnation
● dystopia
● God's immanence/transcendence?

Can you explain:
● why many feminists consider the Bible and feminism are incompatible
● the role of wisdom in the Old Testament
● why the Catholic Church argues that only men can be priests
● transvaluation
● Daly's most Unholy Trinity?

Can you give arguments for and against:
● monotheism as a cause of patriarchy
● the view that Mary Daly's theology is sexist
● the claim that Ruether's feminist theology is not Christian
● presenting God as Goddess?

Sample question and guidance

Assess the view that a male saviour cannot save women.

Although this question can be approached from any theological position, the specification refers explicitly to Ruether so your essay will probably wish to focus on her ideas in the first instance.

You will probably want to set out why as Jesus was historically a man there is a problem. The problem, as set out by Ruether, is that the fact that Jesus was male has justified Christian patriarchy and in so doing alienated women in their relationship with God. You could discuss the Catholic Church's teaching that only a male priest can fully represent Christ in the sacraments and the official running of the Church.

Your essay might then consider Ruether's argument that the Old Testament wisdom tradition preserves the female dimension of God, which is then applied to the person of Jesus in the New Testament. You might explain how Jesus' rejection of the warrior kingly messiah role and the radically egalitarian communities, which the early Christians established after his death, illustrate that women are not excluded from salvation or liberation (you will need to explore different ideas of what 'save' means).

You might then consider the essay title from Daly's point of view and her critique of God and her fundamental rejection of salvation through a person and institution (i.e. the Church).

Your essay should have assessed the validity of each of these views at each stage but the second half of your argument might then go on to consider the place of the Church as the institution which represents Christ and whether it is really true that women feel alienated from a male saviour.

Further essay questions

'Daly's radical feminist theology is inspirational but wrong.' Discuss.

To what extent does it matter whether God is presented in male or female terms?

Critically compare Daly's and Ruether's teaching on God.

Going further

Mary Daly, *Beyond God the Father* (The Women's Press, 1986). Read Chapters 1 and 4 on the death of God, transvaluation, the Most Unholy Trinity, the Most Holy Whole Trinity and discussion of homosexuality.

Rosemary Radford Ruether, *Sexism and God-Talk* (SCM Press, 1983). This is now a classic text on feminist theology. Read Chapter 5 on Christology and whether a male saviour can save women and Chapter 9 for her analysis of three different forms of feminism.

Rosemary Radford Ruether, *Women and Redemption* (SCM Press, 1998). Very useful short introductions on significant women throughout Christian history.

Phyllis Trible, *Texts of Terror* (Fortress Press, 1984).

Read the Introduction and Chapter 2 on her feminist interpretation of the rape of Tamar.

Michael Wilcockson, *Social Ethics* (Hodder Education, 2010). Read Chapter 2 on different types of secular and theological feminisms.

Other books discussed in this chapter are:

- Atwood, M. *The Handmaid's Tale* (1985) (Vintage, 1996).
- Daly, M. *Gyn/Ecology: The Metaethics of Radical Feminism* (The Women's Press, 1978, 1991 with new introduction).
- *Inter Insigniores* or 'On the Question of Admission of Women to the Ministerial Priesthood' (Catholic Church, 1976).

Summary diagram: Gender and theology

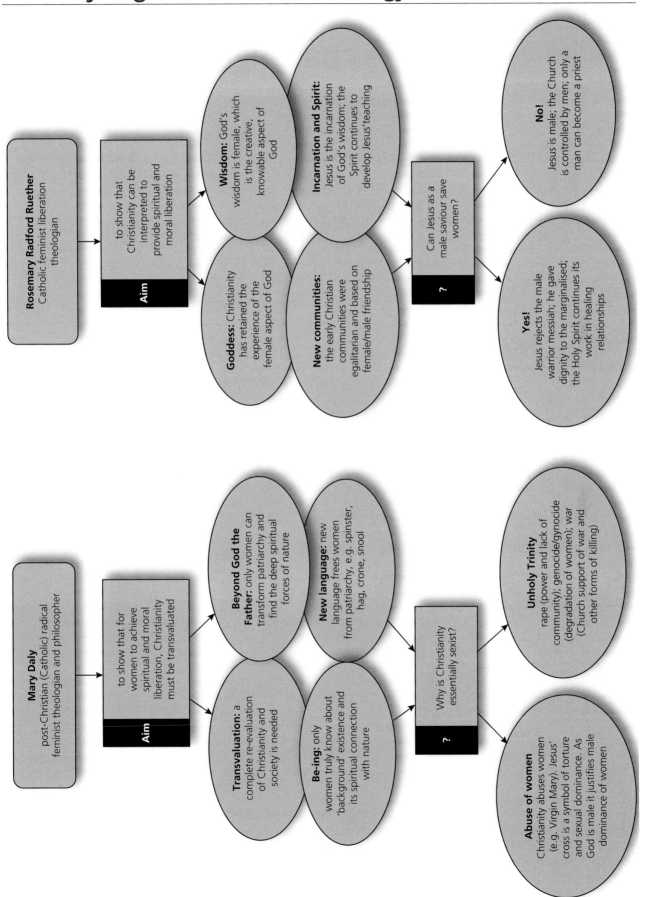

Rosemary Radford Ruether
Catholic feminist liberation theologian

Aim
to show that Christianity can be interpreted to provide spiritual and moral liberation

Wisdom: God's wisdom is female, which is the creative, knowable aspect of God

Goddess: Christianity has retained the experience of the female aspect of God

Incarnation and Spirit: Jesus is the incarnation of God's wisdom; the Spirit continues to develop Jesus' teaching

New communities: the early Christian communities were egalitarian and based on female/male friendship

? Can Jesus as a male saviour save women?

No! Jesus is male; the Church is controlled by men; only a man can become a priest

Yes! Jesus rejects the male warrior messiah; he gave dignity to the marginalised; the Holy Spirit continues its work in healing relationships

Mary Daly
post-Christian (Catholic) radical feminist theologian and philosopher

Aim
to show that for women to achieve spiritual and moral liberation, Christianity must be transvaluated

Beyond God the Father: only women can transform patriarchy and find the deep spiritual forces of nature

Transvaluation: a complete re-evaluation of Christianity and society is needed

New language: new language frees women from patriarchy, e.g. spinster, hag, crone, snool

Be-ing: only women truly know about 'background' existence and its spiritual connection with nature

? Why is Christianity essentially sexist?

Unholy Trinity rape (power and lack of community); genocide/gynocide (degradation of women); war (Church support of war and other forms of killing)

Abuse of women Christianity abuses women (e.g. Virgin Mary). Jesus' cross is a symbol of torture and sexual dominance. As God is male it justifies male dominance of women

Chapter 15

The challenge of secularism

Chapter checklist

The chapter begins by outlining what is meant by secularism and exploring secular arguments about the extent to which religion should play a part in public life. It then reviews the secularisation thesis and considers whether Christianity will eventually die out in the West under the influence of science and changing lifestyles. The chapter then considers the atheist analysis of religion by two scientists: Sigmund Freud and Richard Dawkins. The chapter concludes by reviewing the place of Christianity in public life today especially in education and in the state.

1 Introduction

Did the destruction of the Twin Towers on 11 September 2001 by al-Qaeda change everything?

It is probably an exaggeration to claim that the destruction of the Twin Towers of the World Trade Center, New York on 11 September 2001 by the terrorist Islamic group, al-Qaeda, changed everything, but it certainly altered many European and North American values. For example:

■ It challenged the capitalist, liberal and western globalisation mindset which considers religion to be a matter of private belief.
■ It indicated that for non-westerners, religion is inextricably bound up with politics.

Key terms

Endism The belief that history has 'ended' with capitalism and liberal democracy as there is no better system that can follow it.

Secular Derived from the Latin word *saecularis* meaning worldly or non-religious.

- It has reinforced the view held by many that religion is irrational and, left to its own devices, dangerous.
- It challenged the optimistic **endist** western view that liberal capitalist democracy is the peak of human history.

Since the 9/11 attacks it has been hard to ignore the fact that religion continues to play a major role in world affairs. In other words, the western **secular** ideal that religion and worldly affairs should be separate has been challenged by the rise of religious fundamentalism. The ripple effect of militant Islamism on western consciousness has been to reconsider whether more strenuous efforts should be made to exclude all religions from all public life or conversely to acknowledge that far from excluding religion from public life, properly understood religion is a fundamentally important aspect of human existence and can bring enormous benefits to civilisation.

2 Secularism

Key terms

Secularism The belief that religion should play no role in the running of the state, the affairs of government and in public life.

Procedural secularism The belief that the role of the state should be to take into account the interests of all its citizens and their institutions, meaning that it should not give preference to religion but treat it equally along with all other institutions.

Programmatic secularism The belief that the role of the state should be purely secular. Proponents of this view believe that all religious views or practices should be excluded from public institutions.

Secularism is not an easy idea to pin down but broadly it is the belief that religion should play no role in the running of the state, the affairs of government and in public life. Secularists are not claiming that religious beliefs are right or wrong but that in all public matters and in matters of state governance religious beliefs should remain private. The secularist position is summed up well in the following well-known episode from the New Labour era:

> Tony Blair's most senior advisers have intervened to prevent him discussing his faith in public, according to two new profiles of the Prime Minister.
>
> The bar on the topic is so rigid that Alastair Campbell, Mr Blair's director of strategy and communications, intervened in a recent interview to prevent the Prime Minister from answering a question about his Christianity. 'We don't do God,' Mr Campbell interrupted.

Colin Brown, 4 May 2003, *The Telegraph*

There are generally held to be two forms of secularism: **procedural secularism** and **programmatic secularism**.

- **Procedural secularism:** the role of the state is to take into account the interests of all its citizens and their institutions. This means that it should not give priority or preference to religion but treat it equally along with all other institutions.
- **Programmatic secularism:** the role of the state in a plural society is to be purely secular. All religious views or practices should be excluded from public institutions such as government, public events (such as holidays), schools and universities.

But it will be noticed that in fact the two versions of secularism are implying different value-judgements about religion. Procedural secularism is not discounting religion from the 'public square' whereas programmatic secularism is. This suggests that there is more to secularism than merely balancing the interests of the community. The picture is often confusing and contradictory in practice.

Key question

Is a secular state entitled to ban the wearing of religious symbols in public even though this may infringe the right to freedom of expression?

Key terms

La laïcité The principle enshrined in French law (1905 Separation of the Churches and the State) which separates the state and religions.

Secularisation The active secularising of society by removing religion and other ideologies from all public institutions; can also mean the erosion of religion's social and cultural significance over time.

One problem is when is procedural secularism in fact a form of programmatic secularism. For example, consider the following statement from former US President Barack Obama and quoted by the UK's National Secular Society on their website as an example of their secularist aims:

> *Democracy demands that the religiously motivated must translate their concerns into universal, rather than religion-specific values. Their proposals must be subject to argument and reason, and should not be accorded any undue automatic respect.*

President Barack Obama (quoted on the National Secular Society website www.secularism/org.uk/)

This poses a problem. If religions (or any other non-religious belief group) are to 'translate their concerns' into non-religious and 'universal' values, do they remain the same values? Is Obama's secularist view procedural or programmatic? This poses a further question as to which form of secularism is preferable. The former Archbishop of Canterbury, Rowan Williams, favours procedural secularism as this views the state's role as being a 'community of communities' (*Faith in the Public Square*, 2012, page 3) and allows people to acknowledge the authority of their own religious beliefs as well as the authority of the state. Williams argues procedural secularism has always been a Christian idea from the start: the role of the Church was to proclaim the gospel to society not to govern. For Williams, secularism is a welcome challenge to the Church. He encourages people not to 'privatise' their Christian beliefs but instead to engage as Christians with all aspects of society and so to challenge the dangerous assumptions of programmatic secularism.

On the other hand, the view taken in France according to their principle of **la laïcité** is that only through programmatic secularism can the state maintain the values and democratic beliefs of the nation. The principle has been much debated. For example, at what stage the state may prohibit religious practice in public in the wearing of religious clothing or artefacts. There is also the question of human rights and the liberty to express one's beliefs. The issue has been much debated in France and the rest of Europe after the French government passed a law in 2004 that banned the wearing of any conspicuous religious symbols in state schools.

(a) Secularisation

Very closely associated with programmatic secularism is **secularisation**, the active secularising of society by removing religion and other ideologies from all public institutions. It can also refer to the erosion of religion's social and cultural significance over time. There are broadly two reasons for secularisation:

- **Sociological evidence** has been used to justify the removal of religion from the public sphere, because as religion is practised by fewer and fewer people it has ceased to have a privileged place in society.
- **Religious harm**. Some have argued that the active secularisation of society is beneficial because of the harm religion causes, especially its opposition to human rights and civilised behaviour.

The **secularisation thesis** is a controversial sociological term describing the process of secularisation. The 'classical' meaning of secularisation is the growing number of people who profess to have no religious affiliation, or where religion has lost its influence on society. The thesis is that over the past hundred years there has been a decline in church attendance in most industrial societies and this indicates that it is true that people are rejecting religion in favour of non-religious beliefs and ways of life. In western European industrial societies and North America secularisation is also referred to by the shorthand 'de-churching' because the culture is predominantly Christian.

Secularisation is a highly controversial issue because of the difficulty in pinning down what secularisation actually is. Some of the difficulties are outlined as follows:

- **Measuring and defining terms**. It is not clear how the process of secularisation is to be measured and defined. For example, between 1900–2000 the number of people in the USA who indicated that they had 'no religious preference' has doubled. But of these many said they still continued to pray, and many believe in God or higher power. This suggests that although lack of attendance at church, synagogue or temple is an indication of being less committed to traditional forms of religion, many still have spiritual beliefs.
- **Influence and authority**. Another debate is how much influence and prestige religions have in society. For example, how much influence does the Church of England have on social policy in Britain, or the Catholic Church in Italy? Some argue that as the traditional Churches decline in influence and status they are being replaced by new and popular religious movements which are rapidly gaining social acceptance in local communities. In other words, society isn't becoming more secular – it's simply that mainstream religions and formal religious institutions have declined.
- **Religious commitment and evidence of the past**. Those who support the secularisation thesis argue that in the past more people were religiously committed than today, so it is true that society is becoming more secular. But others argue that in the past although church attendance was socially expected that doesn't mean people were necessarily more religiously committed. Today, people who attend church or religious institutions do so because they want to and not because it is expected of them.

As contentious as the secularisation thesis is, it is true that the influence of Christianity itself has declined in the industrial west. Secularism does indeed pose a challenge to traditional forms of Christianity, but does that necessarily mean that Christianity will eventually die out in western societies? Even in the USA, where Christianity continues to flourish, some argue that secularisation is also taking place but at a slower pace than in Europe.

Reactions to the secularisation thesis are often forceful. For those living in societies where Christianity is associated with traditional ways of life and national values, the secularisation thesis is seen as an invention of liberals to justify diminishing the influence of church organisations on state matters.

Key term

Secularisation thesis A term used by sociologists to describe the process of secularisation. It is defined as the growing number of people who profess to have no religious affiliation. It can also be defined as a situation where religion has lost its influence on society.

On the other hand, the secularisation thesis is embraced by those who are ideologically opposed to religion and favour programmatic secularism.

The reasons in favour of secularism are explored in the following section.

3 God as illusion, wish fulfilment and source of harm

Key term

Secular positivism The idea developed by Augustus Comte that scientific reasoning will take over from religion.

Programmatic secularism developed from the late eighteenth century onwards. European intellectuals developed many powerful arguments for the abolition of religion and the active secularisation of society. **Auguste Comte** held the view that civilised society develops from the theological (religious view of the world) to the metaphysical (abstract view of the world) and finally the positive (scientific/rational view of the world). He believed that religion would give way to **secular positivism** and that the power of scientific reasoning would rid society of all its false views of the world.

Key person

Sigmund Freud (1856–1939): trained as a medical doctor but became increasingly more interested in psychoanalysis. He claimed as a scientist to be able to explain all the functions and malfunctions of the mind in physical terms. Even though he was an atheist he was fascinated by the development of religion, which he analysed in three major works: *Totem and Taboo* (1913), *The Future of an Illusion* (1927) and *Moses and Monotheism* (1939).

Key person

Auguste Comte (1798–1857): a French philosopher who founded sociology as an academic discipline. He greatly influenced John Stuart Mill, Karl Marx and George Eliot with his idea of 'positivism', which aimed to define the empirical (physical) goals of science. He believed that religion would give way to secular positivism.

The view of Comte supports the arguments of liberalism that we live happier, more just lives without the superstition of religion. But more than this, religion is regarded as harmful and even dangerous for the individual and the development of civilised society.

Two scientists who have followed in Comte's footsteps are **Sigmund Freud** and **Richard Dawkins**. Both have argued that the scientific method is the only means to discern truth from falsehood; and that by extension, religion in general and Christianity in particular is an indicator of a less civilised society. Similarly, both have forcefully argued for the secularisation of society on the grounds that Christianity is infantile, repressive and a major cause of mental and physical conflict.

(a) Sigmund Freud

Key term

Neuroses Functional mental disorders such as a severe anxiety attack and irrational fears.

Like Marx and Nietzsche before him, Freud also considered more developed forms of society and civilisation as major causes of oppression. He believed that **neuroses** were the result of natural human instinctual fulfilments being systematically repressed by tradition and conformity. In this way, Freud considered that religion, notably Judaism and Christianity, was a primary cause of psychological illness.

Although Freud was a Jew and supported many Jewish groups that worked for social reforms and for the poor, he did not practise his religion nor did he believe in God. However, he was fascinated by religion in all cultures and wrote extensively about them, especially focusing on Judaism and Christianity. His central claim was that religion belongs to the **infantile** or early stage of human social development before a person has developed powers of reason and is therefore in need of external support and comfort. The philosopher and atheist **David Hume** had earlier come

Read 'A Religious Experience' in Sigmund Freud, *The Future of an Illusion, Civilization and its Discontents and other Works*, 1928, pages 168–72.

Key terms

Infantile Means childish but Freud uses the term to refer to the first few years in a child's development in which the ego (self) is formed.

Psychoanalysis A system of analysis which claims that the conscious life is deeply affected by the unconscious self. The formation and development of the unconscious and conscious is particularly significant in infancy and childhood.

Key quote

Examine the religious principles which have, in fact, prevailed in the world. You will scarcely be persuaded that they are other than sick men's dreams.
David Hume, *The Natural History of Religion*, section XV

Key person

David Hume (1711–76): one of the most important philosophers of the eighteenth century. He was born in Edinburgh and was educated at a time when Isaac Newton's natural science was influential in Scottish universities. He was sceptical of religion as seen notably in his book *Dialogues Concerning Natural Religion* (1779).

to a similar conclusion that religion is childish and mainly practised by the many uneducated people of the world; but those who are mentally grown up have no need for religious beliefs.

It seems certain that, according to the natural progress of human thought, the ignorant multitude must first entertain some grovelling and familiar notion of superior powers.

David Hume, *The Natural History of Religion*, 1757, section I

However, whereas Hume had no particular evidence to support his view that religion is 'sick men's dreams', Freud considered that his use of **psychoanalysis** would show that religion is a sickness, which can badly infect individuals and societies.

As a scientist, Freud, like Hume, argues that only by employing reason and questioning superstitious beliefs can humans and human societies live happy lives. These ideas are explored in his essay, *The Future of an Illusion* (1927). In this essay Freud invents a debate with an imaginary opponent (much like one of Plato's dialogues). To every objection his imaginary opponent raises, Freud's response is that in the future reason (and science) will prevail; religion will end and the instinctual life will win. Only then will humans be able to live truly content lives.

(i) Religion as the result of wish fulfilment

An interesting insight into Freud's understanding and analysis of religion can be seen in a very short article he wrote in 1928.

In the previous year, an American doctor had written to Freud describing how as a young medical student he had seen a dead 'sweet-faced dear old woman' in a dissecting room which had caused him to lose his Christian faith only to rediscover it shortly afterwards through a powerful conversion experience. The purpose of the doctor's letter was to persuade Freud to rethink his atheism and embrace Christianity. Freud's gentle reply was two-fold. First, that as God had not revealed himself to Freud nor had he answered any of his prayers, then he had no good reason to believe in his existence. Second and more significantly, Freud's analysis of the man's experience offered a rational explanation for the doctor's renewed faith in God and Christ as a classic example of an Oedipus Complex moment.

Freud questioned why seeing this old woman was different from the many other dead bodies the medical student must have come across in his training. The answer he gave was that the 'sweet-faced' woman must have reminded him of his mother. The experience 'roused in him a longing for his mother which sprang from his **Oedipus Complex**, and this was immediately completed by a feeling of indignation against his father'. His infantile anger manifested itself as his anger against God the Father, whom he blamed for the mistreatment of his mother – in this case the old woman. The voices he heard were a 'hallucinatory psychosis' warning him to be obedient to his father, just as he had learnt as a child. The original guilt he had felt as a child of wanting to rebel against his father, which he had repressed, was for a moment revealed in his adult life triggered by the experience in the dissecting

269

Key terms

Oedipus Complex The last stage in an infant's psychological development where the child's ego learns emotional independence and at the same time obedience to its parents. The Oedipus Complex results from an initial conflict where each child sexually desires to possess the parent of the opposite sex but learns that this is not possible.

Wish fulfilment The process by which unconscious desires are projected into conscious experience such as dreams, daydreams and hallucinations.

Key quote

The gods retain their threefold task: they must exorcise the terrors of nature, they must reconcile men to the cruelty of Fate, particularly as it is shown in death, and they must compensate them for their sufferings and privations which a civilized life in common has imposed on them.

Sigmund Freud, *The Future of an Illusion*, 2001, page 18

Key term

Obsessional A persistent idea, feeling or desire. It may also refer to compulsive repetitive behaviour.

room. The religious conversion was therefore no more than a **wish fulfilment** to restore his childhood sense of security and can therefore be explained in psychoanalytical rational terms.

(ii) Religion as an infantile illusion

In his book, *The Future of an Illusion*, Freud argues that religion has been one of the most powerful and effective means of overcoming human fears of death and suffering caused by human civilisations. *The Future of an Illusion* is particularly interested in the way in which religion has continued to provide comfort and meaning against the experience of the 'terrors of nature', helplessness against the fate of death, and sufferings caused by society.

According to Freud, religion provides comfort through its ritual and worship. For just as little children find comfort in living a disciplined and ordered life imposed by their parents through rituals such as washing hands and control of bladder and bowels, religious rituals continue the process through the 'suppression, the renunciation of certain instinctual impulses'. This is especially noticeable in the repetition of religious ceremonies in worship and prayers, which acknowledge the worshipper's guilt and ask for forgiveness. Repetition of this kind is **obsessional** because it keeps the ego from being controlled by sexual and irrational urges.

Hence, as Freud concludes, religion is 'a universal obsessional neurosis'. The repression of basic (e.g. sexual) urges are replaced by the promises of after-life and rewards (or punishments). But these are illusory and merely devices to ward off fear and compensate for pleasures forfeited in this life.

So, Freud's conclusion is that although religion may do some good, for society to grow up and develop rationally religion should be abolished. Therefore, just as a neurotic patient has to be treated for his irrational fears, so society must rid itself of religion so that people can be freed to live happy and contented lives. Freud is optimistic that this will happen; his essay ends with the claim that 'our science is no illusion', the illusion is to think that religion is the source of true happiness.

(iii) Critique of Freud

Freud was a reductionist, he wanted to explain everything in material and mechanical terms. Yet, as the philosopher and theologian Keith Ward remarks, reductionism is hardly an adequate explanation for the overwhelming religious and spiritual experiences millions of people have of existence: 'the reduction of all this to blind purposeless blunderings of bits of matter seems desperately inadequate and superficial' (*The Case for Religion*, 2004, page 73). Mystical experiences are to be found in almost every religious tradition. They are characterised by the merging of the self and sense of the 'other' (nature, God, spirit, the holy, the absolute) and the imparting of deep spiritual knowledge of existence. In fact, Freud himself is not nearly as much a scientific reductionist as he purports to be. Despite Freud's deep suspicion of religion and culture, which fails to let humans develop, there is some evidence to indicate that he wasn't wholly critical of mystical experiences. In 1927 a friend of Freud, Romain Rolland, wrote to him about one such experience, which he called the **oceanic experience** – a mystical sense of being at one with nature.

> *I would have nevertheless liked to see you analyze the spontaneous religious feeling or, more exactly, that of the religious sensation which is (...) the simple and direct fact of the feeling of the eternal (which can very well not be eternal, but simply without perceptible boundaries, and as if oceanic).*

Romain Rolland, Letter to Sigmund Freud (1927)

Freud does not reject the validity of the experience even though he has not experienced the 'oceanic' feeling, for as he says, 'it is not easy to deal scientifically with feelings'. Despite his deeply sceptical analysis of institutionalised religion, he concludes:

> *From my own experience I could not convince myself of the primary nature of such a feeling. But this gives me no right to deny that it does in fact occur in other people. The only question is whether it is being correctly interpreted and whether it ought to be regarded as the* **fons et origo** *of the whole need for religion.*

Sigmund Freud, *Civilization and its Discontents*, 2001, page 65

Other responses to Freud include the following:

- **Truth claims**. Although Freud may be right that some aspects of religion are the result of neurotic and obsessional behaviour, these are emotional and psychological states of mind, they do not in themselves disprove the truth claims made by religion.
- **Religion is enabling**. Freud argues that religion is an obsessional, infantile illusion, which is disabling and cuts a person off from the real world. This might be so for some, but for others it is enabling and gives one a spiritually deeper and richer appreciation of life and the world. Rather than being the cause of social discontent it helps form communities with shared values and a sense of purpose.
- **Guilt**. Freud is right to illustrate how religion can be a cause and perpetuation of guilt and we should use his analysis to warn against religious traditions which are deeply controlling. But that does not mean that all religion is controlling. There are many religious traditions that are not hierarchical and dogmatic which provide a source of meaning and spiritual fulfilment that is lacking from a purely material existence.
- **Wish fulfilment**. Although some wish fulfilment is a source of illusion this is not always the case. Wish fulfilment can be a source of creativeness and fuels the imagination.

(b) Richard Dawkins

Key persons

Richard Dawkins (1941–): an academic biologist and formerly the professor for the public understanding of science at Oxford University. His book *The Selfish Gene* (1976) developed Darwin's notion of species evolution and quickly became a bestseller. As a committed atheist many of his other books such as *The Blind Watchmaker* (1986) and *The God Delusion* (2006) have attacked religious beliefs, especially beliefs that deny evolution. He has produced many television programmes including the Channel 4 series, *The Root of all Evil?* (2006) and More4's *Faith School Menace* (2010). Sometimes he has been included in a group nicknamed the 'new atheists' along with Daniel Dennett, Christopher Hitchens and Sam Harris.

Key question

Is Christianity a major cause of personal and social problems?

Richard Dawkins supported this advertisement placed on London buses in January 2009. Does it follow that being an atheist means one is happier?

As a scientist and champion for secularism Dawkins' argument is that religion is presently given a disproportionate place in society and appears immune from criticism because society still respects religious beliefs even when these beliefs are dangerous and are themselves intolerant.

Despite some inoffensive elements of religion and indeed some religions (such as Buddhism which Dawkins argues is not a religion but more a philosophy of life), overall Dawkins argues that supernaturalist monotheistic religions such as Judaism, Christianity and Islam are the particular cause of mental and physical harm. This is not just because belief in God is unfounded but the very notion of a creator God justifies irrational and dehumanising behaviour. As a programmatic secularist his aim is to persuade all right-thinking people that God is a delusion and atheistic secularism is the only plausible alternative.

Although his arguments are rehearsed in many of his books they are most clearly and trenchantly set out in *The God Delusion*. The book's aim 'is intended to raise consciousness – raise consciousness to the fact that to be an atheist is a realistic aspiration, and a brave and splendid one' (*The God Delusion*, 2006, page 1). Specifically, *The God Delusion* urges us to:

- imagine a world without religion
- accept that the God hypothesis is weak
- realise that religion is a form of child abuse
- accept atheism with pride.

(i) Science and reason, religion and delusion

Dawkins begins his attack on monotheistic religion by first questioning why anyone would want to believe in something for which there is no evidence. For Dawkins, the clearest explanation of the processes of nature has been provided by Darwin and his theory of evolution. The theory of evolution does not need a God hypothesis to make sense of it and as nature is not developing towards some grand goal it doesn't need a supernatural mind or 'God' to lead it to perfection. Unlike God, the theory of evolution is supported by a significant and widely accepted body of evidence. Dawkins argues that such a weight of evidence means it makes more sense to believe in an evolutionary process from which minds, beauty and morality emerge without the need for another kind of supernatural stuff that controls it in some way. As a result, Dawkins argues that belief in a divine creator is unnecessary, and deluded.

Delusion, Dawkins claims, is the persistent false belief contrary to the vast body of evidence which now lends weight to the theory of evolution; therefore, those who continue to believe in God are deluded. Those who try and reconcile the material and the spiritual by claiming that religion and science belong to different categories are well meaning but intellectually naive. For example, **Stephen Jay Gould's** notion of 'non-overlapping magisteria' (or NOMA) attempts to distinguish the factual world (described by science) from the supernatural world experienced and described by religion. NOMA advocates argue that as the supernatural world is of a totally different kind from the material world then it cannot be subject to scientific rational enquiry.

But Dawkins will have none of this. He argues that all things must be subject to rational enquiry otherwise one could believe equally that there is a celestial tea-pot circulating out of sight round the earth or that the world was created by a Flying Spaghetti Monster. When reason is applied to religion, all rational arguments for God's existence can do is demonstrate that at the very best his existence is inconclusive. This could leave one an agnostic waiting for more conclusive evidence. But, for Dawkins, as the advancement of science makes the 'God hypothesis' more and more implausible then the only rational and honest position to hold is atheism.

(ii) Religion as indoctrination and abuse

If the debate were merely about God's existence then Dawkins might have concluded that there are many sad, deluded and harmless people in the world and we should let them believe what they want. But Dawkins argues that deluded religious beliefs are not harmless because they create conflict (especially monotheistic religions) and, worse still, when they are taught to children they are a form of child abuse. Chapter 9 of *The God Delusion* focuses on this issue – it is the third of Dawkins' consciousness-raising aims.

> ### Key quote
>
> Our society, including the non-religious sector, has accepted the preposterous idea that it is normal and right to indoctrinate tiny children in the religion of their parents, and to slap religious labels on them – 'Catholic child', 'Protestant child'...
>
> Richard Dawkins, *The God Delusion*, 2006, page 339

Religion is abuse because so many of its deluded beliefs damage people and especially children psychologically. Dawkins gives a wide range of examples such as the Hell Houses in the USA where children are taught

---

Key quote

... any creative intelligence, of sufficient complexity to design anything, comes into existence only as the end product of an extended process of gradual evolution.

Richard Dawkins, *The God Delusion*, 2006, page 31

Key person

Stephen Jay Gould (1941–2002): evolutionary biologist, palaeontologist and historian of science who taught and researched largely at Harvard and Yale universities. In addition to his academic work he published many popular works on science and argued that science and religion are distinctive and have completely separate magisteria or areas of interest (what he called non-overlapping magisteria). He himself was an agnostic.

Key quote

The presence or absence of a creative super-intelligence is unequivocally a scientific question.

Richard Dawkins, *The God Delusion*, 2006, page 59

about the terrors of hell and how to avoid it. He is particularly critical of the ways in which religions initiate their children into their religious mindset and label them a Jewish child or Muslim child or Christian child before that child has any opportunity to understand what this means. He argues that it is a form of abduction or kidnapping:

> Even without physical abduction, isn't it always a form of child abuse to label children as possessors of beliefs that they are too young to have thought about?
>
> Richard Dawkins, *The God Delusion*, 2006, page 315

Some of his examples are hard to reconcile with the moral principles advocated by the religion. Time and again, the Christian notions of love and compassion are contradicted by religious leaders who practise opposite principles.

A recent example (not given by Dawkins but which illustrates his point), which has been produced as a film, is the real life story of Philomena Lee who become pregnant as a teenager and was sent by her Catholic parents to a convent home for single mothers to have her child. In exchange for her food and lodging her child was taken from her and sold by the nuns; the child was subsequently told that his mother had died in childhood. Later, when as an adult she enquired about the whereabouts of her child, the nuns told her the records had been lost when in fact they had burnt them.

Finally, Dawkins reserves some of his most outspoken criticisms for schools that explicitly reject the teaching of evolution in favour of creationism or intelligent design. It is a complete scandal to teach children that the world is only 6,000 years old because the Bible appears to say so, when the overwhelming scientific evidence suggests the universe is at least 14 billion years old.

(iii) Critique of Dawkins

Reactions to Dawkins' secular atheism have been expressed in extreme measures by those he has attacked most, namely conservative, fundamentalist Christians who completely reject his evolution model of life. But is it reasonable to reject all Christian beliefs simply because of a few extreme believers, many of whom live in the USA? Dawkins' response to this is that these views may seem extreme from a European perspective; however, they are far more the norm in the USA and other non-European countries.

Dawkins' challenges (along with those of the new atheists) are persuasive but there are many (scientists, theologians and philosophers) who consider that his arguments for secularism are not in the end convincing. One such proponent is the Oxford theologian and scientist **Alister McGrath**. In his book (written together with his wife, Joanna Collicutt McGrath) *The Dawkins Delusion?* (2007) he presents many arguments pointing out the weakness of Dawkins' views. Some of these are:

■ **Reason and faith**. Unlike Dawkins, many Christians don't think that faith is irrational and independent from reason. Reason is necessary in order to test true and false beliefs but ultimately faith makes a leap to the transcendent. It is also the case that however rational one is, there are some things we believe without being able to prove them categorically.

The film *Philomena* (2013) is based on a book *The Lost Child of Philomena Lee* by the journalist Martin Sixsmith, which tells the real life story of Philomena Lee – how she went in search of her child sold by Catholic nuns after she had given birth as a teenage single mother.

Key person

Alister McGrath (1953–): professor of science and religion at Oxford University. He is a scientist (biochemist and biophysicist), theologian and Anglican priest. He is the author of many books, his most recent being, *The Big Question: Why We Can't Stop Talking About Science, Faith, and God* (2015).

- **Complexity**. Dawkins is right to criticise the 'God of the gaps' argument; that is the view that as the universe is so complex and cannot be explained by science then the answer is that it was created by God. But the alternative to the God of the gaps argument isn't necessarily atheism. The fact that the universe is intelligible and can be described scientifically may point to a greater intelligence, God. Science and religion are not in conflict.

- **Metaphysics**. Dawkins argues as a positivist that answers to the big metaphysical questions such as why is there a universe, what is the meaning of life, etc. are meaningless as they are outside scientific investigation. But many scientists reject this limited positivist view and consider that science as well as theology and philosophy provide useful insights into these important questions.

- **Science and religion's complementary relationship**. Dawkins' biased analysis of NOMA forgets that many scientists and theologians argue that there is a complementary relationship between science and religion as they reflect different aspects of human experience, the material and the spiritual.

- **Violence as a necessary condition of religion**. Although Dawkins gives many examples of physical and mental harm caused by religion, it is not a condition of religion – Jesus specifically taught against the use of violence. The same charge might be aimed at atheism, which has also caused terrible human suffering (for example in communist regimes), but Dawkins doesn't accept that violence is a necessary condition of atheism.

(c) Objections to the secularisation thesis

(i) Charles Taylor

The philosopher **Charles Taylor** questions why we find it easy in modern Western society not to believe in God, while this has been the norm throughout history. He claims that the answer is what he calls 'subtraction stories'. These are the dominant stories we now use to demonstrate the truth of secularisation by removing religion as if that is the obvious thing to do. Taylor summarises subtraction stories as follows:

> Concisely put, I mean by this stories of modernity in general, and secularity in particular, which explain them by human beings having lost, or sloughed off, or liberated themselves from certain earlier confining horizons, or illusions, or limitations of knowledge. What emerges from this process – modernity or secularity – is to be understood in terms of underlying features of human nature which were there all along, but had been impeded by what is now set aside.

Charles Taylor, *A Secular Age*, 2007, page 22

In other words, we have outgrown religion, and the 'stories' or explanations we now use to explain the world are designed to show that we can live full and complete lives without the need for God or a dimension which is greater than nature itself. These subtraction stories (such as those developed by Comte, Freud and Dawkins) lead to what

Charles Taylor

See page 285 on liberation theology's similar critique of secularism.

Taylor calls 'self-sufficing humanism' – but all these stories are deeply unsatisfactory.

- First, Taylor argues that a failure of secular humanism is that it gives too much importance to the individual and his or her private experiences but this is undesirable as it breaks down the communal aspect of society.
- Second, it is not that we have suddenly discovered that God doesn't exist but rather that this is a phase of Western history which is out of kilter with the dominant historical world narrative. For the majority of world history humans have experienced and spoken of the divine as an essential aspect of life.

Taylor's argument is that until we steer ourselves out of this secular phase of history we won't experience the fullness of life which means having a sense of the divine as expressed in Christianity and other religions.

(ii) Terry Eagleton

Terry Eagleton's suspicion of secularism is derived unusually from his Marxist and Christian beliefs. Although Marxism is traditionally anti-religious, Eagleton considers that Marx was wrong to eliminate the religious imagination and what it contributes to human existence. His use of Marxism makes him suspicious of secular capitalism and the impact it has had on culture.

First, although it is true that religion has been harmful, this has to be weighed against the extraordinary contribution the religious imagination has made to human culture through art, architecture, literature, poetry, drama and so on. Secularists think that all these things can occur without religion, but only religion can capture the highest spiritual aspect of human experience. Secularism is 'largely doomed', he argues, because it cannot replace what religion captures of human experience:

> I say 'largely doomed' because religion is an exceedingly hard act to follow. It has, in fact, proved to be far the most tenacious, enduring, widespread, deep-seated symbolic system humanity has ever known, not least because it is able to connect the everyday customs and practices of billions upon billions of ordinary people with the most august, transcendent, imperishable truths.

Terry Eagleton, *The Death of God and the War on Terror*, https://oxfordleftreview.com/

Ultimately, the significance of religion is that it touches on deep truths about existence which people have been prepared to die for. No one is prepared to die for aesthetic values alone, even the great music of Beethoven or the novels of Dickens. Not even sport, the secular religion replacement, is so important that people are prepared to make the kinds of sacrifice which religious belief often demands.

Second, in Eagleton's view the root cause of secularism is not Dawkins' positivism but the way in which Western secular capitalism has valued free competition by privatising everything. This has a negative knock-on effect where morality and especially religion are also considered to be private and irrelevant in the public sphere.

Finally, Eagleton argues that the events of 9/11 indicated that the positivist dream of a world without religion is not only wrong but without a proper understanding as to its true nature it can appear in a highly toxic form of fundamentalist extremism. Although Eagleton is not condoning violence, his analysis is that 'fundamentalism has its source in anxiety rather than hatred' – that anxiety is caused by the perception that Western secularists are spreading their anti-religious message throughout the world.

9/11 highlights two extremes of anxiety: faithless Western secular atheism and its fear of religion (and hence its reaction as the 'war on terror') and faithful religious fundamentalism and its fear of positivism, capitalism and secularisation. Both secularism and religious fundamentalism, Eagleton argues, are equally flawed.

4 Christianity and public life

Key question

Should Christianity continue to be a significant contributor to society's values?

Key question

Are spiritual and ethical values just human values?

Key term

The Amsterdam Declaration
A set of seven statements agreed on at the 50th anniversary World Humanist Congress in 2002 and adopted by the International Humanist and Ethical Union (IHEU) General Assembly.

The answer as to whether Christianity should continue to be a significant contributor to society's culture and values will depend on whether you consider Christianity offers special insight into the challenges facing society or whether Christianity should be removed from public discourse and replaced with secular humanist values.

(a) Secular humanism

Secular humanism is a very broad term, which describes all those who believe that humans can live good and noble lives according to reason and without the need for religion. Freud and Dawkins are examples of secular humanists. Beyond these basics there are many variations of humanist beliefs, especially over the issue of religion and whether society should actively remove religion from all public organisations (programmatic secularism) or allow it to have its place in society but without giving it any special privileges (procedural secularism).

The **Amsterdam Declaration** (1952, updated in 2002) sets out the main aims of modern humanism through seven statements. In summary, these are:

1 **Humanism is ethical**: all humans have dignity, worth and autonomy.
2 **Humanism is rational**: science should be used creatively and as a basis for solving human problems.
3 **Humanism supports democracy and human rights**: democracy and human rights are the best way in which humans can develop their potential.
4 **Humanism insists that personal liberty must be combined with social responsibility**: the free person is responsible to society and the natural world; humanism has no dogmatic beliefs.
5 **Humanism is a response to the widespread demand for an alternative to dogmatic religion**: reliable knowledge of the world and ourselves arises through a continuing process of observation, evaluation and revision.
6 **Humanism values artistic creativity and imagination**: the arts transform and enhance human existence.

7 **Humanism is a lifestance aiming at the maximum possible fulfilment**: the challenges of the present can be achieved through creative and ethical living.

Source: based on The Humanist and Ethical Union, iheu.org/humanism/the-amsterdam-declaration

Humanists are clear that ethical and spiritual values are not derived from any higher spiritual power but express human values and aspirations.

(i) Education and schools

Richard Dawkins is a vocal and outspoken critic of the provision of faith schools in a secular society. Some argue that having many types of faith schools contributes positively to social diversity and social cohesion. But Dawkins considers this argument to be outmoded and confused. 'Diversity' he says 'may be a virtue, but this is diversity gone mad' (*The God Delusion*, page 334). Is it the case that the inclusion of faith schools is 'diversity gone mad'?

The arguments against faith schools may include:

- faith schools create isolated communities and fail to integrate pupils into the wider secular society
- many faith schools fail to teach science properly especially those which have conservative and fundamentalist beliefs
- faith schools (especially Muslim and Sikh) leave pupils open to radicalisation
- the state has no responsibility to teach faith. Faith is a private matter and should be carried out by local faith communities
- religious education should be part of the school curriculum along with other subjects, as long as this includes teaching of all major world religions and non-religious belief systems. Children should be taught that there are diverse faith claims, that the Bible is one of many books of sacred literature and that some religious truth claims (such as treat your neighbour with respect) are no different from non-religious truth claims.

The arguments in favour of faith schools may include:

- there are no value-neutral schools. Faith schools and non-faith schools operate according to their religious or secular values, which together reflect the diversity of the British culture
- faith schools offer a distinctive education based on moral and spiritual values. These values enhance and do not detract from the wider curriculum
- faith schools aid social cohesion because they support and value the culture of local religious communities
- they are popular with parents
- many faith schools do not make religious faith a requirement for entry but are better able to foster religious and non-religious beliefs because they have a better understanding of faith than secular schools which can sometimes be suspicious of faith of any kind.

Key fact

There are around 6,400 primary and 600 secondary faith schools in Britain today – that is about one-third of the national total. Most are Christian (Church of England or Roman Catholic); 36 are Jewish; six are Muslim; two are Sikh; one is Greek Orthodox; one is Seventh Day Adventist.

(ii) Government and state

Since the eighteenth century and the Enlightenment era, the generally accepted view in Western society is that 'Church and State' (i.e. religion and the governance of society) should be separate. The secular assumption is that faith is a private matter and should not interfere with public matters of state, which are decided by reason and law.

The creation of the United States of America in 1776 after its secession and independence from Great Britain is a good example of how the creators of its constitution (1789), founded on the rights of life, liberty and the pursuit of happiness, came to separate Church and State. The Establishment Clause in the First Amendment (1791) allowed freedom of religion but prohibited Congress from establishing a state religion. At the time, reasons for the separation of church and state were to avoid the problem of conflicting political claims between different Christian denominations but with the influx of migrants of many different religious persuasions to the USA there is an even greater reason to separate state from religion. However, this has not been to the detriment of religious practice. If anything, the freedom to practise one's religion has made the USA one of the most religiously observant countries in the western world.

The alternative to the separation of church and state would be some form of **theocracy**. Theocracy is the belief that religion should play a role in public life and in the governance of society. Programmatic separatists generally consider theocracies to be undemocratic and intrusive but there are some Americans today who argue for theocracy. For example:

■ **Dominionists** argue that America should be governed according to biblical laws. Dominionists are mostly protestant, evangelical and conservative. Dominion theology is based on Genesis 1:28 where God commands humans to have dominion over the earth. Dominionists believe God's command applies also to the stewardship of matters of state as well as the world as whole.

■ **Reconstructionists** are Calvinists. They share the Dominionist notion of society but also justify theocracy by pointing to the law in the Old Testament where Israel's life was ordered and governed according to the laws God gave to Moses.

In Britain the situation is different from the majority of European countries. In England the Church of England is the national church and the Queen is 'Supreme Governor'. Twenty-six bishops of the Church of England automatically sit in the House of Lords as 'Lords Spiritual' and at significant state events the Church presides. Citizens, regardless of their faith, may make use of their Church of England parish church for baptisms, marriage and funerals. While some regard this as outdated, others consider this to be the way in which the state provides a spiritual service to all, much like the National Health Service (NHS).

Britain, though, is not a theocracy. However, some programmatic secularists argue that the last vestiges of its theocratic past should be abolished if the country is to be a fully democratic modern society. The National Secularist Society, for example, states:

> If Britain were truly a secular democracy, political structures would reflect the reality of changing times by separating religion from the state.

www.secularism.org.uk/what-is-secularism.html

Key quote

Faith is the root of freedom and programmatic secularism cannot deliver anything comparable.
Rowan Williams, *Faith in the Public Square*, 2012, page 32

But the view of many Christians is that programmatic secularism is anti-democratic as it actively removes the historic place of Christianity from all public institutions. Procedural secularism, on the other hand, is not anti-democratic as it offers the Church the opportunity to be fully engaged in society and contribute to making secularism a success by offering the widest set of opportunities for all its citizens, religious and non-religious. The Church, Rowan Williams argues, has a key role to play in resisting the anti-democratic fundamentalist elements of religions which regard secularism as a threat.

The challenge of secularism is therefore not necessarily a threat to Christianity. It is right that it should give a reasonable account of itself and justify its place in society where there are many different belief systems, which in a democracy seek to live harmoniously together.

Summary diagram: The challenge of secularism

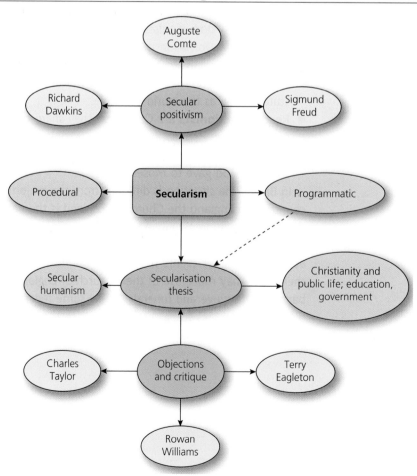

By the end of this chapter you should be able to explain why there are different ideas of secularism and how these are related to secularisation and especially its impact on Christianity in the West. You should understand why the secularisation thesis is controversial but why it is supported by secular positivists such as Freud and Dawkins who consider religion incompatible with modern society. You should be able to critique Freud and Dawkins and consider to what extent science is equipped to deal with all aspects of life. You should be able to use scholars' views (Eagleton, Taylor, Williams) in your analysis of secularism and the role of Christianity in society.

Can you give brief definitions of:
- endism
- procedural secularism
- programmatic secularism
- psychoanalysis
- non-overlapping magisteria
- theocracy?

Can you explain:
- the difference between secularism and secularisation
- the secularisation thesis
- secular positivism
- Freud's view that religion is infantile
- aims of secular humanism?

Can you give arguments for and against:
- religion as a major cause of abuse and harm
- Charles Taylor's claim that secularism is not the natural state of society
- the desirability of faith schools
- having an established Church or state religion?

Sample question and guidance

Assess the view that Christianity should be a significant contributor to society's culture and values.

You might begin by reviewing those who think that Christianity does have a contribution to society's culture such as Terry Eagleton's claim that Christianity's development of art, music and literature has had a profound impact on our civilisation and culture. You might consider Rowan Williams' argument that Christian social values and concern for the marginalised are distinctive contributions to the 'public square'. You might illustrate this by reviewing the contribution of the Church and its provision of schools and education.

Your analysis might consider the view of secular humanists and their claim that humans are naturally imaginative and that religion isn't the only source of values, culture and means of living a good life. The argument might go on to be more critical than this and suggest, using Freud's analysis, that Christianity actually diminishes culture and society by perpetuating guilt and illusion.

Finally, the argument must analyse what 'should be' from the essay title means. This might be done by reviewing procedural and programmatic secularism and your view of Christianity's contribution in society at present.

Further essay questions

'Freud's analysis of religion as wish fulfilment was right.' Discuss.

To what extent are spiritual values just human values?

'Secularism does more harm than good.' Discuss.

Going further

Owen Chadwick, *The Secularization of the European Mind in the 19th Century* (Cambridge University Press, 1975). Chapter 9 on Comte, Darwin, Henry Sidgwick and others on the relationship of religion and morality.

Richard Dawkins, *The God Delusion* (Bantam Press, 2006). Chapters 1–2 and 9 set out his views of the rationality of science and the unreasonableness of a belief in God and the damage religious belief can have on society.

Sigmund Freud, *The Future of an Illusion, Civilization and its Discontents and Other Works*. General editor James Strachey (Vintage Books, 2001). Both these essays set out Freud's claim that the human spirit is crushed by many aspects of civilisation, notably religion.

Alister McGrath and Joanna Collicutt McGrath, *The Dawkins Delusion?* (InterVarsity Press, 2007). An easy-to-read analysis of Richard Dawkins' *The God Delusion*.

Keith Ward, *The Case for Religion* (Oneworld, 2004). Part 1 is especially helpful in analysing the sociological and psychological arguments for and against religion.

Rowan Williams, *Faith in the Public Square* (Bloomsbury, 2012). Read Part 1, especially Chapters 1 and 2 on different types of secularism and how Christianity still has a role to play in the public square.

Other books, articles and websites discussed in this chapter are:

- The Amsterdam Declaration: http://iheu.org/ humanism the-amsterdam-declaration/
- Brown, C. 4 May 2003, *The Telegraph*: www. telegraph.co.uk/news/uknews/1429109/ Campbell-interrupted-Blair-as-he-spoke-of-his-faith-We-dont-do-God.html
- Eagleton, T. *The Death of God and the War on Terror*: https://oxfordleftreview.com/olr-issue-14/terry-eagleton-the-death-of-god-and-the-war-on-terror/
- Hume, D. *Dialogues Concerning Natural Religion, and The Natural History of Religion,* ed. G.C.A. Gaskin (Oxford University Press, 2008).
- National Secular Society: www.secularism.org.uk
- Taylor, C. *A Secular Age* (The Belknap Press of Harvard University Press, 2007).

Chapter 16

Liberation theology and Marx

Chapter checklist

This chapter begins by considering the social and political context of Latin America in the 1970s when Oscar Romero was assassinated and liberation theology was emerging. It then considers why some theologians used Marx in the development of their ideas, especially his teaching on historical materialism. The chapter explores liberation theology's teaching on praxis and the meaning of the term a 'preferential option for the poor'.

1 Introduction

Key person

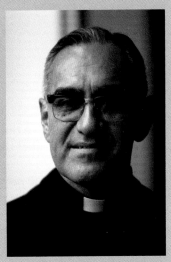

Oscar Romero (1917–80): born in El Salvador, South America, the son of a carpenter. He was ordained priest in 1942 and completed his doctorate in 1943. He worked for over 20 years as a parish priest before being appointed auxiliary bishop of San Salvador (the capital of El Salvador) and then Archbishop in 1977. In 1979 the Revolutionary Government Junta came to power. Their human rights abuses caused the Salvadoran Civil War. Romero criticised the USA for giving military aid to the government. He was assassinated on 21 March 1980 while celebrating mass. His funeral was attended by 250,000 people. He was beatified by Pope Francis in 2015.

Key term

Liberation theology A contextual theology which considers that the heart of the Christian message is to bring spiritual and material justice and freedom to those who are oppressed.

On 21 March 1980 the Archbishop of San Salvador, **Oscar Romero**, was in the act of celebrating mass in a city chapel when he was shot and killed. The day before he had given one of his influential radio sermons in which he had pleaded with the army's soldiers as Christians not to continue to murder and exploit the poor. This was sufficient for him to be branded a communist and murdered as a rebel. Romero had said previously, 'As a Christian, I do not believe in death without resurrection. If they kill me, I will rise again in the Salvadorian people.' His martyrdom has continued to inspire many to fight against injustice and exploitation in Latin America and throughout the world.

Although Romero was not a liberation theologian, what he stood for and the reasons why he died stand at the heart of **liberation theology**.

What makes liberation controversial is its active engagement with a sociological and political analysis of society and its often outspoken critique of secular culture as well as of the Church itself.

Favela and luxury apartments illustrate the rich-poor divide in Latin America.

Key term

Favela A shanty town or slum area.

Latin America economic key facts

- On average, half of each nation's income goes to the wealthiest 15 per cent of the population.
- In Brazil, the richest 10 per cent of the population accounts for 46 per cent of the wealth, while the poorest 50 per cent accounts for just 14 per cent.

Liberation theology grew out of the political, social and pastoral situation in Latin America during the 1960s and 1970s. At that time the contrast between the rich landowners and the poor was even greater than it is today. Then, as today, the poor often lived in **favelas** or shanty towns of houses made of corrugated iron and other scraps of materials overlooked by luxury apartments of the rich. There was no proper sewerage system, infant mortality was high and gangs of children often roamed city streets in search of food and shelter. El Salvador, where the liberation theology movement gained its momentum, is still one of the most violent countries in the world with an average of one murder taking place every hour.

By nature Romero was conservative and cautious about the politicisation of theology. But he changed his mind after the murder in 1977 of his close friend and fellow priest Rutilio Grande, who had stood up for the rights of the poor. Romero's conscience dictated that to be true to Christ's example he had no option but to abandon political neutrality and act in solidarity with the poor. Standing up for justice against the government cost him his life. He was not the only one to lose his life. In 1989 the Salvadoran army also murdered six Jesuit priests, their housekeeper and her daughter at the Universidad Centroamericana in San Salvador. Because of their teachings on liberation theology they were regarded as anti-government terrorists.

2 Marx and liberation theology

Key term

Contextual theology A type of theology by which theologians reflect on a specific situation in the light of experience and within the Christian tradition.

(a) Contextual theology

Contextual theology is a type of theology by which theologians reflect on a specific situation in the light of experience and within the Christian tradition. In responding in particular to the plight of the poor politically and spiritually, liberation theology is self-consciously a contextual theology. For example, in liberation theology, the 'first step' is to deal with the situation of oppression and injustice, the 'second step' is to reflect theologically. However, by placing the needs of the poor and oppressed before the official teaching of the Roman Catholic Church, liberation theology has often been regarded as radical, subversive and dangerous by church and state authorities.

(b) Challenge to Western secularism

Criticism of traditional theology has also led liberation theologians to a critique of northern European and North American culture and, in particular, its secular tendency to 'privatise' religion and give priority to materialism over spiritual matters.

But liberation theologians consider that it is quite right and proper for the Church to be involved with the material conditions of society. They consider that as God created the material world, matter and spirit are not separate but different aspects of the same reality. Therefore, it would be quite wrong to treat politics and religion as being independent from each other. Liberation theology has therefore been called a 'bottom-up theology' as it begins first with the material conditions of the poor, the marginalised and exploited, rather than beginning with and imposing official Church teaching on the poor. These are the same conditions that **Karl Marx** also found to be unacceptable, inhumane and unjust. Although an atheist, his economic and sociological analysis of the conditions which have led to alienation and exploitation of the poor has been of great use to many liberation theologians. Following in his footsteps, many liberation theologians have also been critical of institutions such as the Church (along with schools, universities and governments), which impose laws rather than work for those who don't have the power to tackle injustice.

3 Marx's teaching on alienation and exploitation

Key person

Karl Marx (1818–83): born in Trier then part of German Rhineland. Although his father converted to Christianity from Judaism for social reasons, his grandfather was a much-respected rabbi. At university he came under the influence of a radical group of Hegelians, the 'young Hegelians', and through them developed his atheism and later his analysis of economics. He was aided financially and academically by Friedrich Engels (1820–95) and they collaborated on many works. Marx fled Paris in 1849 and settled in London where he wrote and worked as a journalist. His influential writings include *The Communist Manifesto* (1848) – written with Engels – and *Capital* (1867–83).

At the heart of Marx's philosophy is the idea that all processes of the world are governed by physical material forces. Humans contribute to the material conditions of the world and in turn are affected by them. When

On Jean-Jacques Rousseau
(1712–78), see Year 1, page 249.

3 Developments in Christian thought

Key terms

Historical materialism In
Marxism, describes the material
or physical conditions of all
processes in the world, including
history, which develop through
a process of conflict, then
harmony, only to fall into
conflict again.

Alienation Occurs when a person
is treated as a thing or object,
rather than being valued as an
individual.

Key terms

Capitalism The belief that human
societies flourish best when
operating in a free competitive
market motivated by profit.

Communism The belief that
human societies flourish best
when everyone shares equally
the means of production and are
not motivated by profit but the
desire for social harmony.

humans and the material forces are in harmony with each other, then
people feel useful, productive and purposeful. But, according to Marx,
history indicates that societies rarely manage long periods of stability.
Every moment of history is a material or physical process working
towards harmony, which then collapses and has to be rebuilt. This
historical process is often referred to as historical materialism, which is an
aspect of Marx's more general view of the world referred to as **historical
materialism**.

Marx's aim was to investigate the causes of social instability. He shared
some of **Rousseau's** assumptions that there was a stage in a 'state of
nature' when families all shared the means of production without anyone
being exploited. The initial cause of disharmony is not clear but was
probably the result of disputes with other families over land ownership.
Since that time many factors have led to competition and **alienation** –
the degrading of the human person into a thing or object, rather than as
a valued and purposeful individual subject.

(a) God and religion

> The abolition of religion as the illusory happiness of the people
> is the demand for their real happiness. The demand to give up
> the illusions about their condition is the demand to give up a
> condition that requires illusion.

Karl Marx, *Deutsch-französische Jahrbücher* in David McLellan,
Karl Marx Selected Writings, 2000, page 71

Marx argued that a major cause of alienation is belief in God. The reason
is two-fold:

■ First, he rejected that God is the driving force of history. The material
forces of history are blind; belief that God controls history is false-
consciousness and leads to false hopes and illusions.

■ Second, the place of religion gives power to the state or ruling group
to control the population by stating that God's natural order is that
some humans are born to be rulers and others servants. If this seems
unfair then it will all be sorted out in the afterlife when those who
have suffered in this life will be recompensed in heaven.

This is why Marx argued that the abolition of religion should be the
first move in over-coming exploitation and alienation.

But next to religion Marx argued that **capitalism** was a major source of
alienation and exploitation. In his vision of a harmonious society Marx
imagined that everyone would willingly share their material and intellectual
goods, but that capitalism's competitive nature makes this harmonious life
impossible, therefore the only viable economic alternative is **communism**.

(b) Means of production

One of the primary causes of exploitation and alienation is ownership of
the means of production. As Marx argues in *The Communist Manifesto*
(1848), in a capitalist society when what matters is production of goods,
everyone becomes alienated and dehumanised. This is particularly so for the
worker because he has no power to control production and is merely 'an
appendage of the machine'. Working in the factory he has no creative input

into what he makes; he is alienated from the product and hates his work. Finally, even when he receives his wages, the bourgeoisie (owners, ruling class) still manage to exploit him because they own the shops where he spends his money on goods and his lodgings where they charge him rent.

(c) Bourgeoisie and proletariat

Finally, in his analysis of history Marx observed that at various times the exploited have come to realise that their position is not ordained by God or nature and have attempted to free themselves. Such moments had often been met with violent oppression by their masters who feared that their power and easy way of life would be lost. For Marx, the polarisation of master and slave was particularly stark in the nineteenth century with the rise of industrialisation. He named two classes: the **bourgeoisie** (the owners of production) and **proletariat** (the workers).

> The history of all hitherto existing society is the history of class struggles... Society as a whole is more and more splitting up into two great hostile camps, into two great classes directly facing each other: Bourgeoisie and Proletariat.

Karl Marx and Fredrick Engels, *The Communist Manifesto* in David McLellan, *Karl Marx: Selected Writings*, 2000, page 246

(d) Praxis

Praxis is one of the most important ideas derived from historical materialism. Praxis is the belief that as history is constantly changing, then humans have the ability to understand the material conditions of any situation and change them. Praxis begins by analysing a situation where there is oppression or injustice, working out what has caused it, and then changing it. The problem with philosophy, Marx said, is that it may analyse the world but it does nothing to change it. He famously said:

> Philosophers have only interpreted the world in various ways; the point is to change it.

Karl Marx, *Theses on Feuerbach* XI in David McLellan, *Karl Marx: Selected Writings*, 2000, page 173

Liberation theologians agree: theology like philosophy has become too abstract, the point is for it to change the world not merely to think about it theoretically.

4 Liberation theology's use of Marx

Key question

Should Christian theology engage with atheist secular ideologies?

Liberation theologians and Marxists agree that even though human life is intrinsically good, it is also human nature which has been the source of human misery. Marxism explains this tension in terms of material and historical conditions. Liberation theologians find Marx's analysis useful as it refocuses theology on the world whereas traditionally theology has used more abstract terms such as 'sin' and 'original sin'. This illustrates why Marx has been a useful device for many liberation theologians – even if, as Gutiérrez says, confrontation with Marxism has helped develop his theology.

Key terms

Bourgeoisie and **proletariat** The terms Marx used to describe those who own the means of production (bourgeoisie) and workers or those who have no ownership and are alienated from production (proletariat).

Key term

Praxis The belief that as history is constantly changing, then humans have the ability to understand the material conditions of any situation and change them.

But, at the same time, almost no liberation theologian would argue that Marx is essential for Christianity, for if that were the case then it would suggest that Christianity has been defective until Marx. However, theologians have varied enormously in the way they have used Marx. There are those who make explicit use of Marx and those who use him only to analyse an economic situation. More radically, there are those who find his language and general concepts useful for a re-thinking of many basic Christian ideas. In other words, Marx is a useful tool or instrument for doing theology; as Leonardo and Clodovis Boff comment, Marx is a useful 'companion on the way', but there is only one teacher, Jesus Christ.

(a) Historical materialism and reversal

It is Marx's central idea of historical materialism that establishes liberation theology as a contextual theology by reversing traditional 'top-down' with a 'bottom-up' theology. As Marx argued, once we see how history has developed the material and economic basis for society then we can understand on what basis other human institutions are formed. Once these structures are understood we are then in a position to reform these structures from the bottom up.

Many liberation theologians find Marx's analysis of historical materialism very useful. For example, the idea of reversal can be seen in the argument that theology should begin with the condition of the poor as the underside of history rather than 'top down' abstract doctrines such as the nature of God. A bottom-up theology begins with actual human experience of suffering, alienation and hope. Seen in this way, Christian historical materialists argue that the Kingdom of God isn't heaven, but a transformation or reversal of material society based on Christian values; the meek not the powerful will inherit the earth. Thought about in this way Jesus' teachings about the Kingdom of God take on new meaning:

Blessed are the meek, for they shall inherit the earth.

Matthew 5:5

The kingdom of God is not coming with things that can be observed; nor will they say, 'Look, here it is!' or 'There it is!' For, in fact, the kingdom of God is among you.

Luke 17:20–21

(b) Critique of capitalism

Marxist analysis is most useful when in a particular situation of injustice and exploitation a church leader needs to reflect on what the causes are: who the oppressors are, who owns the means of production, and the ideologies which have reinforced the situation of exploitation. In essence, all injustices can be traced to the inherent unfairness of capitalism, which always creates an exploited underclass (or proletariat).

Liberation theologians share the basic Marxist idea that as humans are designed to work and be productive (Genesis 1:28), then failing to share in the means of production is a major cause of alienation and exploitation. For this reason, liberation theologians often present Marx in the same prophetic tradition (stretching from the 8th century BC prophets to Jesus), which attacked the social and economic conditions that exploited the poor.

José Porfirio Miranda used Marx's suspicion of private ownership of property as the basis for his liberation theology. For Marx, private ownership of land is the root cause of injustice because it creates in the mind of the owner the idea that as an owner he can treat people who live on his land as objects. This illustrates Marx's fundamental principle set out in his first *Theses on Feuerbach* that alienation and oppression are caused when humans objectify the world and treat it as their own possession.

This important Marxist insight, Miranda argues, brings our attention to a similar idea which is also at the very heart of the Bible. Thanks to Marx, this idea, which has become lost through centuries of western theology, can now be recovered. However, Miranda argues that once recovered, it will be seen that the biblical view is in fact more radical than Marx for two reasons:

- **Human nature**. According to Miranda, Marxism has underestimated the insight of the biblical writers that capitalism since the start of human civilisation is due to human sin – not just external material economic causes. In describing the fallen aspect of human nature the Bible gives a much fuller reason than Marx as to why humans oppress and exploit others.
- **Idolatry**. Marx fails to give an adequate explanation for the causes of private ownership because of his rejection of God. The answer is provided in the second of the Ten Commandments, the command against idolatry, which warns against treating God as a thing or object. The abandonment of this commandment in the west has been the fundamental reason why the world has not been treated with respect as God's creation and why capitalism (as exemplified in private ownership) has been worshipped instead.

(c) The Church and the People's Church

The meeting of Latin American Catholic bishops at **Puebla** in 1979 marked a significant moment in the development of liberation theology. One of the terms they often used in conjunction with liberation was **integral liberation**, to indicate how liberation is not an additional idea but fundamental to all aspects of Church life. Puebla constantly reinforced the view that it is the essential duty of the whole Church to deal with the external economic conditions which have created the social structures of sin and injustice and not just personal sin.

Even more revolutionary was Puebla's call that for integral liberation to be truly effective it must involve ordinary people as part of the Church decision-making process. Puebla developed the controversial notion of the People's Church or *iglesia popular*. It was controversial because it recognised that for many of the poor the official Church was no more than an extension of the state, an institution that was the source of their alienation and exploitation. Puebla shared the Marxist suspicion that all institutions tend to give power to the few over the many. Puebla's call for an *iglesia popular* challenged the very essence of the Church's authority on moral and spiritual teaching; the Church should not be an institution but a community founded on love and solidarity.

(d) Praxis, social sin and alienation

Liberation theologians share Marx's notion that it is we who can change society. This may sound obvious but often people forget this or feel that it is God's will that things are the way they are. As Marx says:

> *The materialist doctrine concerning the changing of circumstances and upbringing forgets that circumstances are changed by men and that it is essential to educate the educator himself.*

Karl Marx, *Theses on Feuerbach* III in David McLellan,
Karl Marx: Selected Writings, 2000, page 172

(i) Praxis

As we have seen in the life of Romero and elsewhere, theology cannot be a purely personal and theoretical subject because the Gospel and the example of Jesus indicate that the Christian life must involve action to tackle injustice and deal with those who live on the 'underside of history'. Liberation theologians quote with approval Marx's maxim that the purpose of philosophy (or theology in their case) is not merely to interpret the world but change it.

But for praxis to be effective some analysis is needed of the social, economic and political conditions that have caused injustice. Christian theology doesn't have the tools to do this analysis and that is why many liberation theologians turn to Marx as a sociological system which does offer the means for explaining the causes of exploitation.

See Year 1, pages 310–13 for more on the idea of Jesus the liberator.

(ii) Social sin and alienation

Marxism therefore provides a useful way of re-thinking traditional Christian notions of sin in material terms. Whereas sin, in traditional terms, refers to personal disobedience of God's will, liberation theologians consider sin in the social and economic structures of society.

Liberation theologians refer to this kind of social sin as **structural sin**; it is one of the great contributions of liberation theology to contemporary theology. Structural sin is dialectical:

> *When humans sin, they create structures of sin, which in their turn, make human beings sin.*

José Ignacio González Faus, 'Sin' in Sobrino and Ellacuría,
Systematic Theology, 1996, page 198

Key term

Structural sin Refers to the social and economic organisation of society, which causes its members to be alienated from each other and perpetuate injustices.

Structural sin means that humans are alienated from each other because, at a deep level, there is no recognition of each other as humans. Structural sin is therefore a deeply ingrained form of social alienation in which every member of society is dehumanised. For example, Faus illustrates how structural sin in Latin America based on the false truth of capitalism that a 'human being is not worth anything' and the false truth of communism that 'a human being is always an enemy', led to the situation where during a great earthquake in Mexico City the owners of some firms saved their machinery out of the ruins before rescuing many of the buried but alive women workers.

For a fuller explanation of false-consciousness, see page 230.

For more on **original sin**, see Year 1, pages 256–7.

Key term

Hermeneutic of suspicion
The process of interpretation of a text or situation in which one questions the official or commonly accepted explanation. A Marxist hermeneutic of suspicion considers the underlying economic motivations of the accepted views.

Key question

Has liberation theology engaged with Marxism too much or too little?

Key person

Gustavo Gutiérrez (1928–): a Peruvian Catholic priest and theologian who lives and works with the poor in Lima. His book *A Theology of Liberation* (1971) was foundational in the development of liberation theology.

Key quote

At no time either explicitly or implicitly have I suggested a dialogue with Marxism with a view to a possible 'synthesis' or to accepting one aspect while leaving others aside.

Gustavo Gutiérrez, *The Truth Shall Make You Free*, 1990, page 63

Liberation theologians argue that this collective sense of alienation is already contained in the Christian doctrine of **original sin**. Sin cannot exist in isolation; sin exists because humans are fallen and corrupt and this state is continually perpetuated through false-consciousness.

Understanding structural sin helps liberation theologians apply what is known as a **hermeneutic of suspicion**. In the example of Jesus' encounter with the rich ruler (Luke 18:18–25) the usual interpretation is that the man is a good man (he has kept the commandments not to steal, not to lie and to honour his parents) but is unable to give his money to the poor because of his personal sin. Traditional Church teaching is that he was not wrong to have wealth; the test is how he should have used it.

But liberation theologians question this interpretation as it favours capitalism, the Church's institutional teaching, and reduces sin to one individual rather than seeing him as part of a wider social system of injustice. The hermeneutic of suspicion asks:

- How has this man gained his riches?
- If he belongs to the ruling class then he will certainly own lands, so doesn't he control the means of production of the poor?
- If he has control of production then hasn't he in effect stolen and lied to the poor because he has perpetuated a structural system of sin?
- Can he really have honoured his parents when he doesn't honour God's covenant to honour and protect the poor by showing them justice and mercy (Hosea 6:6)?

Although using Marx is not necessary to apply a hermeneutic of suspicion, using him as a 'companion along the way' (L. and C. Boff) reveals new and fresh challenges in texts where the meaning has lost its force.

(e) Should theology engage with Marxism?

To what extent have liberation theologians used Marx (or Marxism) as a means of analysing poverty and oppression? While some, such as Leonardo Boff, Clodovis Boff, José Miguez Bonino, Juan Luis Segunda and José Miranda have all explicitly used Marx as a tool for analysis, others, such as **Gustavo Gutiérrez** and Jon Sobrino, are far more guarded. Over time, Gutiérrez made it clear that Marx and Christianity could not be combined, even if they share some common ground.

Gutiérrez's hesitancy might be due to the criticisms which the Vatican raised against liberation theology because of its engagement with Marxism as an overtly atheistic political system. Others, though, consider that in fact Marxism and Christianity share a lot in common and their relationship should be encouraged and developed.

(i) Too much engagement with Marxism

In 1984 the Congregation of the Doctrine of the Faith issued its *Instruction on Certain Aspects of the 'Theology of Liberation'* (or *Libertatis Nuntius*) chaired by Cardinal **Joseph Ratzinger**. The core of the *Instruction* was an outspoken critique of Marxism, and by extension, liberation theology. At first, the *Instruction* is less hostile and speaks of 'theologies of liberation'. It is sympathetic to those theologies that use the term 'liberation' to mean that justice should prevail in defence of the weak but it is extremely critical of other radical liberation theologies which have been 'insufficiently critical' of Marxism.

Key person

Joseph Ratzinger (1927–): professor of theology at various German universities. In 1981 he was appointed Prefect of the Congregation for the Doctrine of Faith (whose role is to protect the Catholic faith against errors in teaching and doctrine). In 2005 he was elected Pope and took the name Benedict XVI. He retired as Pope in 2013.

Key quote

Taken by itself, the desire for liberation finds a strong and fraternal echo in the heart and spirit of Christians.

Instruction on Certain Aspects of the 'Theology of Liberation' III.1, 1984

Key term

Reductionism The idea that everything can be explained simply in basic, often physical, terms. Reductionist arguments are often in the form 'x is nothing but y'.

Key person

Alistair Kee (1937–2011): was Professor of Religious Studies at Edinburgh University. His many publications include *Marx and the Failure of Liberation Theology* (1990) and *The Rise and Demise of Black Theology* (2006).

As stated in its introduction, the aim of the letter was:

> … *to draw the attention of pastors, theologians, and all the faithful to the deviations, and risks of deviation, damaging to the faith and to Christian living, that are brought about by certain forms of liberation theology which use, in an insufficiently critical manner, concepts borrowed from various currents of Marxist thought.*
>
> Congregation of the Doctrine of the Faith, Introduction,
> *Instruction on Certain Aspects of the 'Theology of Liberation'*, 1984

Although positive about the place of liberation in Christian theology, the *Instruction* is critical of the way the liberation theologians have limited theology in the following ways:

- Liberation is at the heart of Christian theology, but it is the liberation from 'the radical slavery of sin' not economic conditions.
- There are many kinds of freedom; liberation theologians tend to stress only the political kind.
- Liberation theology has placed too much emphasis on temporal or political liberation – it fails to look sufficiently at human sin.
- Liberation theology is **reductionist**. By interpreting sin in terms of social structures it equates salvation with praxis and revolution, not God's grace.
- Liberation theology makes truth exclusive only to those who practise a certain kind of praxis.
- Establishing the Kingdom of God is mistakenly interpreted to mean human struggle, whereas it is only possible through God's grace.

It is for many of these reasons that Oscar Romero was also critical of liberation theology. For him, liberation must first be spiritual and then practical; too much emphasis on Marxist materialism undermines the distinctiveness of Christianity.

(ii) Too little engagement with Marxism

> *My criticism has been that it is not Marxist enough. Or rather liberation theology, far from using Marx's philosophy 'in an insufficiently critical manner', has not cared deeply enough or dared to apply it in a sufficiently careful and comprehensive manner… in fact resistance to Marx is the cause of its failure.*
>
> Alistair Kee, *Marx and the Failure of Liberation Theology*, 1990, pages 211 and 257

Alistair Kee's thesis is that the Vatican's criticism that liberation theologians have used Marx too much and in an insufficiently critical manner is almost entirely wrong. In his view, the problem is that even those theologians who have used Marx critically, have done so without ever really tackling Marx's fundamental premise that the criticism of religion is equally a criticism of all other ideologies. Kee's point is that liberation theologians cannot just select the bits of Marx they find helpful and avoid the basic premise on which they are built.

At first, Kee's argument appears contradictory. Why would liberation theologians embrace Marx's atheism which states that religion is the primary source of alienation and false-consciousness? Kee argues that despite his atheism, Marx's historical materialism relies on a strongly spiritual sense in which each historical stage gives way to the next driven by an idea of a better world. Marx may have tried to justify this in purely physical or material terms, but science does not support his claim; this is because his historical materialism is in fact an ideology. So, in fact Marx and Christianity are not so very different; the difference for Kee is that Christianity accepts that it is an ideology: history is determined by material forces but also by God or Spirit.

However, the value of Marx's historical materialism, which Christian theology should take much more seriously, is that every new historical stage requires a radical re-assessment of its beliefs and ideas. If Christianity is to survive as a radical force in the next stage, its task now is to consider how it is to tackle the mindset of the present age of secular capitalism. Sadly, Kee argues, liberation theology is far too conservative and traditional to meet this challenge; that is why it has failed.

So, Kee concludes, liberation theology has lost the opportunity to tackle the greatest challenge to human existence in this capitalist and liberal age: secularism. Although Marx personally professed to be an atheist, this does not mean to say that the next dialectical stage of historical materialism should be secular. A more radical progression, even in Marxist terms, would be to suggest that in the dialectic historical process the next stage after secular capitalism could be spiritual socialism.

5 Liberation theology's teaching on the 'preferential option for the poor'

In addition to the theme of integral liberation the meeting at Puebla also developed an idea which has now become absorbed into standard Catholic social teaching, the **'preferential option for the poor'**. The first thing to notice about the phrase is that it is not aimed at the poor but those who are in a privileged position to act in solidarity with the poor in the battle against exploitation. The use of 'preference' is aimed at all Christians (especially Church leaders and teachers) who are not poor and therefore have the power and means to place the poor first. 'Option' means that solidarity is a free act where the privileged learn to be poor themselves by discarding any feelings of arrogance and superiority. In this way the Church becomes what it was always intended to be – radically egalitarian.

We affirm the need for conversion on the part of the whole church to a preferential option for the poor, an option aimed at their integral liberation.

Puebla *Final Document* number 1134

(a) Theological motivations for a preferential option

The Boff brothers (*Introducing Liberation Theology*, 1987, pages 44–6) outline five theological motivations that justify the preferential option for the poor:

- **Theological motivation**. This motivation focuses on the God of the Bible as a living God who is immanent in the world and involved in human history. God hears 'the cry' of his people (Exodus 3: 7) and

See Year 1, pages 272–3 for a detailed discussion of the parable of the Sheep and the Goats.

Key question

Is it right for Christians to prioritise one group, such as the poor, over another?

Key term

Utopia Can mean 'no place' (an imaginary perfect world) or a 'good place'. Because of its ambiguity Leonardo Boff prefers the term 'topia' to refer to this world transformed.

Camilo Torres Restrepo (1929–66): see Year 1, pages 310–11.

seeks justice. When the Church imitates God it must hear the cry of the poor and seek justice.

- **Christological motivation**. Jesus sided with the poor and acted in solidarity with those who were marginalised by society.
- **Eschatological motivation**. The moment when God judges the world will be based on whether a person has sided with the poor according to Jesus' parable of the Sheep and the Goats (Matthew 25:31–46).
- **Apostolic motivation**. After Jesus' death the first apostles organised a general levy on all Christian groups to raise money for the poor. They did not distinguish between Christian and non-Christian poor.
- **Ecclesiological motivation**. All Christian members of the Church should, as a matter of faith and commitment, seek the transformation of society.

(b) Revolution and solidarity with the poor

In the Marxist material view of history, circumstances evolve to provide moments; those who can read the signs of the time, recognise the moment and force history to move on to the next stage. Revolution is necessary because there will always be those reactionary forces who resist and therefore impede change. In Marxism, revolution does not begin with the oppressed but those philosophers who can interpret the world, and, by acting in solidarity with the oppressed, organise change. Marx's view was that the only way of changing the deep-seated situation of exploitation was through 'despotic inroads' (powerful, violent means) – but only if other methods failed.

The 'preferential option for the poor' is indebted to Marx as it awakens the conscience of those in power to force the Church into a 'class struggle' against injustice. Taking inspiration from Jesus the liberator, theologians point to his example of siding with the marginalised as a response to his call to prepare for the kingdom of God. For liberation theologians the Kingdom of God is not an abstract **utopia** because as Marx pointed out, the promise of utopia or heaven to the poor is the ultimate false-consciousness; Boff prefers to call the Kingdom of God a 'topia' or place, where the present existing social conditions have been transformed.

Liberation theologians have certainly been persuaded that the capitalist status quo will not change merely by tinkering with the system, but most are reluctant to use the revolutionary 'despotic inroads' to bring about change. The exception is the iconic figure of **Camilo Torres Restrepo**, who argued that words without action are empty and if this meant revolution, even violence, then it was a sign of faith to be involved. As a priest, his decision to join the guerrillas was instantly shocking, daring and inspirational.

If the Marxist problem is closely analysed, I believe that an affirmative answer is possible. Dialectical and historical materialism in the mental process of Marxists appears to be so useful for revolutionary methods that it can be considered quite objective... with firm decision and without timidity, we should enter into this collaboration...

Camilo Torres Restrepo, speech in 1964

So, for liberation theologians it is right for Christians to prioritise one group, such as the poor, over another.

6 Orthodoxy and orthopraxis

Fundamental to liberation theology is the distinction between right action (orthopraxis) and the official or 'right' teaching of the Church (orthodoxy). Some summarise the relationship of **orthopraxis** and **orthodoxy** as 'bread before theology' – the idea that feeding the poor should come before urging them to be obedient to Church teaching. The point being made here is that being a good Christian in terms of church attendance and church loyalty is meaningless without endeavouring to be a good human being. In other words, a preferential option for the poor is in the first instance not a *theological* endeavour but a *human* project. As we shall see, in practice it is not as simple as this as praxis is not merely action but the (dialectical) relationship of beliefs and practice.

Orthopraxis as it has been developed by church workers operates in two acts or steps: first act praxis and second act praxis.

(a) First act praxis

First act praxis is **pre-theological**, it does not begin with doctrine or the official teaching of the Church but with the simple realisation that injustice and human exploitation are wrong. First act praxis begins when Christians act in solidarity with the poor, live alongside them as humans and learn what the conditions are which have led to this situation. So, as Leonardo and Clodovis Boff describe in their book *Introducing Liberation Theology* (1987), a preferential option begins with a 'preliminary stage' where church workers and theologians might act through:

- **visits** to the base communities/pastoral work
- **alternating** scholarly work and pastoral visits
- **living permanently** alongside the poor.

Although this is not a theological stage, it would be wrong to say that this lacks theological *motivation*. Those who opt to side with the poor do so because they already have a theological view of the world which recognises that God in Christ chose to be part of the human condition and to bring joy out of suffering. As Leonardo and Clodovis Boff put it:

First act praxis is closely related to the much quoted passage from the New Testament, Jesus' parable of the Sheep and the Goats (Matthew 25:31–46), when Jesus praises those who have acted spontaneously from faith by feeding the hungry, giving water to the thirsty and visiting those in prison.

(b) Second act praxis: the three mediations

Although second act praxis is the most theoretical aspect of liberation theology, its origins are practical and pastoral. Gutiérrez says that theology 'rises at sundown', meaning that it is essential after the day's social and pastoral activities to sit quietly and reflect. As he says, 'theology does not produce pastoral activity; rather it reflects on it' (Gustavo Gutiérrez, *A Theology of Liberation* (1974), 2001, page 55).

In the 1950s, parish priests were already developing their own strategies to provide practical care for the poor; gradually a well-known process evolved of 'seeing, judging and acting'. These form the foundation of the three mediations. A **mediation** is a distinctive phase of theological praxis; the mediations form the heart of liberation theology.

(i) Socio-analytical mediation: seeing

Socio-analytical mediation, the first mediation, is about analysing and understanding the socio-economic reasons for oppression in a particular situation. At the time when the liberation theologians of Latin America were developing their theology, a scepticism of capitalism and development naturally led to a suspicion of any economic system which supported the free markets of northern Europe and the USA. These systems were seen to be the fundamental causes of poverty and injustice. The first mediation, therefore, favours a socialist or even Marxist critique of the economic situation. Some theologians have explicitly used Marx, while others have used his language but not necessarily all his thinking. Again, Marxism has provided a useful 'companion on the way' for analysing the causes of poverty and injustice.

For example, using Marx highlights different ways in which people think about the causes of poverty and its solution. The Boff brothers suggest three:

- **Empirical poverty** is the view that poverty is the result of vice, laziness and ignorance. This analysis of poverty is weak because the solution is usually through the giving of aid or charity, which simply treats the poor as objects of pity not as persons.
- **Functional poverty** is the view that poverty is the result of backwardness. This view is typical of liberal capitalists who tackle poverty through loans and development aid. Even though this view recognises collective responsibility to solve the problem, in a capitalist world it can make the situation worse by creating a situation of dependency where the poor rely on the rich rather than dealing with the structural problems that have caused poverty.
- **Dialectical poverty** is the view that poverty is the result of oppression. Marxist or socialist analysts consider that poverty is the result of exploitation, exclusion from the process of production and priority of capital over labour. Tackling poverty requires revolutionary and radical confrontation with oppressive social conditions and structures.

The socio-analytic mediation also broadens the notion of the poor to refer to all those who are oppressed and marginalised because of deep-seated social prejudices and discrimination such as racism, ageism and sexism.

Key term

Mediation A distinctive phase of theological action or praxis.

Key term

Socio-analytical mediation
The first of the three mediations; a phase of praxis whereby the socio-economic reasons for oppression in a particular situation are analysed and discerned.

Key question

Why is the hermeneutical mediation necessary if a person is already motivated by being a Christian?

Key term

Hermeneutical mediation The second of the three mediations. This mediation involves reflecting on a situation of oppression or exploitation from a specifically Christian perspective through the study of the Bible.

Key quote

Liberative hermeneutics reads the Bible as a book of life, not as a book of strange stories... Liberative hermeneutics seeks to discover and activate the transforming energy of the biblical texts... rereading of the Bible stresses its historical context in order to construct an appropriate – not literal – translation into our own historical context.

Leonardo Boff and Clodovis Boff, *Introducing Liberation Theology*, 1987, page 34

(ii) Hermeneutical mediation: judging

Once they have understood the real situation of the oppressed, the theologians have to ask: What has the word of God to say about this? This is the second stage in the theological construction – a specific stage, in which discourse is formally theological.

Leonardo Boff and Clodovis Boff, *Introducing Liberation Theology*, 1987, page 32

The hermeneutical stage is the most explicitly theological moment in the process. Having analysed the socio-economic reasons for oppression in a particular situation, the task of **hermeneutical mediation** is then to reflect on it from a specifically Christian perspective. As the Boff brothers put it, 'what has the word of God to say about this?' Liberation theologians are not fundamentalists but nor are they sceptics; for them, the primary source for the word of God is the Bible. The Bible offers insights from many moments in history, which can be reinterpreted according to the present historical situation.

Reading the Bible from the experience of the poor produces new interpretations of the biblical texts. Providing opportunities for the poor to interpret the Bible directly also helps them to become aware of its challenges and to become more aware of their own spiritual and political situation. As the Boff brothers say, the primary aim of liberation theologians is to favour *application* rather than *explanation* of texts; the role of professional theologians is therefore to provide scholarly information but not ready-made answers.

For example, as we have seen (page 291) in the story of the Rich Ruler (Luke 18:18–25), the poor recognise the ruler as typical of the rich landlords they experience who perpetuate injustices even if superficially they might appear to have kept the commandments. The theologian may offer some historical background about landowners in Galilee at the time of Jesus. Reflection might note how Jesus did not ask the ruler to give some of his wealth away but for a complete transformation of his lifestyle. This in turn might inspire the poor to see that God sides with them and not the rich and that they should be persistent in their quest for justice.

(iii) Practical mediation: acting

Liberation theology is far from being an inconclusive theology. It starts from action and leads to action... And so, yes: liberation theology leads to action: action for justice, the work of love, conversion, renewal of the church, transformation of society.

Leonardo Boff and Clodovis Boff, *Introducing Liberation Theology*, 1987, page 39

Key term

Practical mediation The third of the three mediations. This mediation leads to action by empowering the poor to bring about economic, social and spiritual change.

The first moment of action comes when siding with the poor in solidarity. Having analysed the situation socio-economically and through theological reflection, then those involved are obliged to act – this is the **practical mediation**. Action requires a change of mind and material conditions not just reform.

(iv) Critique

Many critics point out that the first mediation is the only really important one. If action is required to change a situation in the local community, which is unjust or causing harm, economic analysis is more appropriate than reading the Bible. However, if the second mediation is removed then the process is not really Christian and the spiritual values which the Bible offers become powerless and irrelevant. If this is the case, then the whole liberation theology project appears to be crumbling away. Perhaps theology cannot change the world.

Summary diagram: Liberation theology and Marx

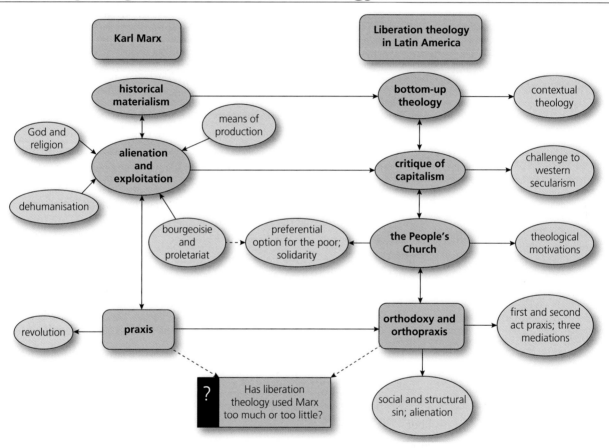

By the end of this chapter you should be able to explain the aims of liberation theology as a contextual theology. You should be able to explain the main ideas of Marx and how his ideas of historical materialism were used by liberation theologians to develop their orthopraxis. Finally, you should be able to explain whether liberation theologians have used Marx too much or too little.

Can you give brief definitions of:
- historical materialism
- alienation
- capitalism
- praxis
- integral liberation?

Can you explain:
- liberation theology's challenge to secularism
- what the Boff brothers mean by saying Marx is a 'companion on the way'
- Miranda's claim that the Bible is more radical than Marx
- structural sin
- preferential option for the poor?

Can you give arguments for and against:
- whether Marx and Christian theology are incompatible
- the view that liberation theology is too focused on the poor
- the view that theology should begin 'from below' with humans not 'from above' with God
- the claim that religion is the cause of alienation?

Sample question and guidance

'The sole concern of theology should be the preferential option for the poor.' Discuss.

The essay might begin by explaining how the phrase 'preferential option for the poor' emerged from the situation of extreme poverty and exploitation in Latin America from the 1970s. You may wish to explain that it is aimed at Christians who have the means to deal with the condition of the poor and not, in the first instance, the poor themselves.

You might then consider the theological justification of a preferential option. You might refer to the example of Jesus as liberator and his teaching and treatment of the marginalised (you should use the examples from the topic on Jesus Christ from Year 1) and discuss that one possible

meaning of the Kingdom of God is the reversal and transformation of the world today.

Your essay might then focus on the claim that it is the 'sole concern' of theology to focus on the poor. You might agree that given Jesus' teaching on judgement in the parable of the Sheep and the Goats and the message of the prophets before him, that acting justly as expressed in siding with the poor does support the claim.

On the other hand, you might consider that theology is also concerned with human nature, personal sin, the nature and knowledge of God and many other important ideas other than the poor. The essay title invites you to select what you have studied from other parts of the course and not just ideas in this chapter.

Further essay questions

To what extent should theology be about changing the world not interpreting it?

Assess the view that in theology orthodoxy is more important than orthopraxis.

'Marx does not offer a satisfactory solution to the problem of the exploitation of the poor.' Discuss.

Going further

Leonardo Boff and Clodovis Boff, *Introducing Liberation Theology* (Burns and Oates, 1987). A short and very readable introduction written when liberation theology was at its height.

David McLellan, ed. *Karl Marx Selected Writings* (Oxford University Press, 2000). Comprehensive selection of all Marx's key texts with very useful introductions by the editor.

Christopher Rowland, ed. *The Cambridge Companion to Liberation Theology* (Cambridge University Press, 1999). A wide range of articles on different aspects of liberation theology. Chapter 9, by Denys Turner, is on Marxism and liberation theology.

Michael Wilcockson, *Christian Theology* (Hodder Education, 2012). Chapters 6–10 focus on liberation theology, its origins, relationship with Marx and present development.

Other books and other resources discussed in this chapter are:

- Congregation of the Doctrine of the Faith *Libertatis Nuntius* or *Instruction on Certain*

Aspects of the 'Theology of Liberation' www.vatican.va/roman_curia/congregations/ cfaith/documents/rc_con_cfaith_ doc_19840806_theology-liberation_en.html

- Gutiérrez, G. *A Theology of Liberation* (SCM Press, 1974, 2001).
- Gutiérrez, G. *The Truth Shall Make You Free* (Orbis Books, 1990).
- Kee, A. *Marx and the Failure of Liberation Theology* (SCM Press, 1990).
- Nickoloff, J. *Gustavo Gutiérrez: Essential Writings* (SCM Press, 1996).
- Puebla *Final Document* libguides.marquette. edu/c.php?g=36663&p=232900.
- Sobrino, J. and Ellacuría, I. eds *Systematic Theology: Perspectives from Liberation Theology* (SCM Press, 1996).
- Wilkinson, M. and Wilcockson, M. *Religious Studies for A Level Year 1 and AS* (Hodder Education, 2016).

Index

Page numbers in **bold** indicate definitions.